ROUTLEDGE LIBRARY EDITIONS: POLITICAL GEOGRAPHY

Volume 2

ESSAYS IN POLITICAL GEOGRAPHY

ESSAYS IN POLITICAL GEOGRAPHY

Edited by
CHARLES A. FISHER

LONDON AND NEW YORK

First published in 1968

This edition first published in 2015
by Routledge
2 Park Square, Milton Park, Abingdon, Oxon, OX14 4RN

and by Routledge
711 Third Avenue, New York, NY 10017

Routledge is an imprint of the Taylor & Francis Group, an informa business

© 1968 Charles A. Fisher

All rights reserved. No part of this book may be reprinted or reproduced or utilised in any form or by any electronic, mechanical, or other means, now known or hereafter invented, including photocopying and recording, or in any information storage or retrieval system, without permission in writing from the publishers.

Trademark notice: Product or corporate names may be trademarks or registered trademarks, and are used only for identification and explanation without intent to infringe.

British Library Cataloguing in Publication Data
A catalogue record for this book is available from the British Library

ISBN: 978-1-138-80830-0 (Set)
eISBN: 978-1-315-74725-5 (Set)
ISBN: 978-1-138-81324-3 (Volume 2)
eISBN: 978-1-315-74827-6 (Volume 2)
Pb ISBN: 978-1-138-81325-0 (Volume 2)

Publisher's Note
The publisher has gone to great lengths to ensure the quality of this reprint but points out that some imperfections in the original copies may be apparent.

Disclaimer
The publisher has made every effort to trace copyright holders and would welcome correspondence from those they have been unable to trace.

 Printed and bound by CPI Group (UK) Ltd, Croydon, CR0 4YY

Essays in
Political Geography

EDITED BY CHARLES A. FISHER

METHUEN & CO LTD
11 NEW FETTER LANE LONDON EC4

First published 1968
© *Charles A. Fisher 1968*
Printed in Great Britain by
Butler & Tanner Ltd
Frome and London

Distributed in the U.S.A.
by Barnes and Noble Inc.

Contents

Preface   *page* ix

1 Introduction   1
   [*Charles A. Fisher · Professor of Geography with
   reference to Asia in the University of London,
   School of Oriental and African Studies*]

PART I · GEOGRAPHICAL ASPECTS OF THE
         STRUCTURE AND INTER-RELATIONSHIPS
         OF STATES

2 Political Geography and Administrative Areas:
   *A method of Assessing the Effectiveness of Local
   Government Areas*   13
   [*J. N. H. Douglas · Lecturer in Geography, The
   Queen's University, Belfast*]

3 Morphology of the State Area: *Significance for the
   State*   27
   [*Richard Hartshorne · Professor of Geography,
   University of Wisconsin*]

4 Some Fundamental Elements in the Analysis of the
   Viability of States   33
   [*Preston E. James · Professor of Geography, Syracuse
   University*]

5 Political Organizations at Higher Ranks   39
   [*W. Gordon East · Professor of Geography,
   University of London, Birkbeck College*]

6 The Contemporary Geopolitical Setting:
   A Proposal for Global Geopolitical Equilibrium   61
   [*Saul B. Cohen · Director, Graduate School of
   Geography, Clark University*]

PART II · CASE STUDIES IN DECOLONIZATION

7 Malaysia: *A Study in the Political Geography of
   Decolonization*   75
   [*Charles A. Fisher*]

8 Ceylon: *Some Problems of a Plural Society* 147
[*B. H. Farmer · Director of the Centre of South Asian Studies, University of Cambridge*]

9 The Problem of Nagaland 161
[*Ulrich Schweinfurth · Professor of Geography South Asia Institute, University of Heidelberg*]

10 Minority Unrest and Sino–Soviet Rivalry in Sinkiang, China's North-western Frontier Bastion, 1949–1965 177
[*Michael Freeberne · Lecturer in Geography, University of London, School of Oriental and African Studies*]

11 The Evolution of the Boundary between Iraq and Iran 211
[*Vahé J. Sevian · Consulting Engineer formerly Inspector General of Irrigation, Ministry of Agriculture Iraq*]

12 The Geographical Background of the Jordan Water Dispute 225
[*Moshe Brawer · Head, Department of Geography, University of Tel Aviv*]

13 The Case of an Indeterminate Boundary: *Algeria–Morocco* 243
[*Anthony S. Reyner · Professor and Head of Department of Geology and Geography, Howard University*]

14 Politics and Transportation: *the Problems of West Africa's Land-locked States* 253
[*David Hilling · Lecturer in Geography, University of London, Bedford College*]

15 The Ewe Problem: *A Re-assessment* 271
[*B. W. Hodder · Reader in Geography, University of London, Queen Mary College*]

16 Nationalism, Regionalism and Federalism: *The Geographical Basis of Some Political Concepts in East Africa* 285
[*B. W. Langlands · Senior Lecturer in Geography, Makerere University College*]

17 The Further Partition of the Northwest Territories of Canada: *An Aspect of Decolonization in Northernmost North America* 311
[*N. L. Nicholson · Professor of Geography, University of Western Ontario*]

PART III · ASPECTS OF POLITICO-GEOGRAPHICAL
CHANGE IN THE OLD WORLD

18 A Local Perspective on Boundaries and the Frontier
Zone: *Two examples in the European Economic
Community*   327

   [*J. W. House · Professor of Geography, University
   of Newcastle-upon-Tyne*]

19 The Russian Image of Russia: *An Applied Study
in Geopolitical Methodology*   345

   [*Ladis K. D. Kristof · Research Associate, Studies of
   the Communist System, Institute of Political Studies,
   Stanford University*]

To STEPHEN B. JONES whose contribution to political geography we acknowledge, and whose presence at our symposium we appreciated, this book is dedicated by all who have contributed to it.

Preface

With the exception of the brief editorial introduction, all the essays in this volume are directly based upon papers prepared for the Twentieth International Geographical Congress held in the United Kingdom in 1964, and all but two of them were personally presented by their respective authors at the Symposium on Political Geography, held at Sheffield under the editor's Chairmanship as part of the proceedings of that Congress. Nevertheless this volume is not an official publication of the Congress or of its sponsoring organization, the International Geographical Union, but is the outcome of a joint initiative by participants in the symposium and Messrs Methuen and Co. Ltd.

The original proposals for the symposium stated that, while papers on any aspect of political geography would be welcomed, it was hoped to devote special attention to the problems of the newly independent states and the wider methodological implications of work in this field. In the event the greater part of the contributions submitted dealt with some aspect of what may be called the political geography of decolonization, but although several of these – and of others – had significant methodological implications, explicit emphasis on methodology received rather less attention than had been expected. Moreover, although studies in the political geography of ex-colonial territories in both Asia and Africa were well represented, most of them were by Western scholars, and it was a source of regret that no nationals of such major ex-colonial lands as India, Pakistan, Indonesia or Nigeria were present to read papers or to participate in discussions.

In spite of this, however, the discussions contributed significantly to the present collection of papers, for most of the latter have in varying degree been re-written at least partly on the basis of comments made by other participants in the symposium, to whom our collective thanks are due. All the authors who contributed papers to the symposium were invited to submit them – with or without modification as they chose – for inclusion in this collection, and all but three did so.

Inevitably in the circumstances the resultant collection has the character more of a random scatter than of a co-ordinated coverage of the field with which the symposium was concerned. Furthermore, while in common with other students of political phenomena, political geographers attempt to apply scholarly principles in their work, they also have varied viewpoints both methodological, political, and national, and in contributing to this collection each author assumes sole responsibility for what appears under his name.

Equally inevitably, however, the preparation of such a collection of papers, from contributors in many different parts of the world, involves some delays, and in the rapidly changing circumstances, particularly of the ex-colonial lands, statements of fact and expressions of opinion may quickly and sometimes drastically be overtaken by events. Wherever possible an attempt has been made to deal with such cases by late revision or the addition of postscripts. But no such arrangements can ever seem wholly satisfactory to an author, and for the shortcomings which remain on this score the editor accepts full responsibility.

School of Oriental and African Studies   CHARLES A. FISHER
October 1967

Note: In view of the diversity in scale and character of the essays included in this collection it has been decided to treat each as an entity in itself. For this reason Figures and Tables are numbered separately for each essay, and not serially throughout the book, and the method of showing references has in certain cases been varied to fit the individual needs of particular essays.

I

Introduction   CHARLES A. FISHER

The symposium upon which this collection of essays is based[1] was held almost exactly twenty-five years after the outbreak of the Second World War, and directly or indirectly all the essays it contains bear witness to the great changes which have taken place in both the methodology and the subject matter of political geography during this fateful quarter century.

In its modern form political geography originated under the primary inspiration of Friedrich Ratzel (1844–1904) in the rapidly advancing Germany of the late nineteenth and early twentieth centuries. At a time when the new industrial technology was revolutionizing age-old relationships between man and the earth, and when the shrinkage of effective distance brought about by the railway and steamship was dramatically expanding the range of territory over which effective political control could be maintained – whether by land as in the United States and Russia or by sea as in the great colonial empires of Britain, France and other European powers – Ratzel, a biologist by training and deeply influenced by the new Darwinian ethos, viewed the resultant transformation of the political map of the world in ecological terms as the product of the struggle between rival state organisms for space in which to live. It was in this context that he attempted in 1896 to formulate laws of the spatial growth of states[2] and later in 1901 elaborated his concept of *Lebensraum* (living space).[3]

Notwithstanding the overtones which the second of these acquired in more recent times and the alarm which the first produced among a generation of Frenchman still suffering from the trauma of the Franco-Prussian War, both of these works, and above all Ratzel's great *Politische Geographie*,[4] were serious and scholarly contributions towards an understanding of the change that was coming about in one of the most

---

[1] For further details see Preface, pp. ix–x.

[2] F. Ratzel, 'Die Gesetze des räumlichen Wachstums der Staaten. Ein Beitrag zur wissenschaftlichen politischen Geographie', *Petermanns Mitteilungen*, 42, 1896, pp. 97–107.

[3] F. Ratzel, 'Der Lebensraum. Ein biogeographische Studie', *Festschrift für Albert Schaffle*, Tubingen, 1901, pp. 103–89.

[4] F. Ratzel, *Politische Geographie*, Munich and Leipzig, 1897.

2 Essays in Political Geography

fundamental aspects of human experience, namely the relationship of man with his natural environment. However, whereas in his own country Ratzel inspired a distinguished band of followers, the effect of his thinking outside Germany, and more particularly in France, Britain and the United States, was rather to provoke a reaction against the excessively deterministic arguments which too often followed from his acceptance of the organic concept of the state. Nevertheless, although much of the work by political geographers which followed in these countries – from *Le sol et l'état* by Camille Vallaux[1] in France to Derwent Whittlesey's *The Earth and the State*[2] in the United States – presented different interpretations from those of Ratzel, most of the leading Western political geographers prior to the Second World War did not dispute that the study of the relationship referred to in these two titles represented the central theme of their study.

From a purely academic point of view it is permissible to regard the thirty years or so which followed the publication of Ratzel's *Politische Geographie* as constituting the golden age of political geography. Nevertheless, throughout that period Germany remained the primary centre of activity in this field, and elsewhere only two works by political geographers, namely Halford Mackinder's *Democratic Ideals and Reality*[3] and Isaiah Bowman's *The New World*,[4] ever aroused any significant interest among the thinking public at large.

Both of these books appeared in the aftermath of the First World War, Mackinder's in 1919 as a warning – which went largely unheeded – to the Versailles treaty-makers, and Bowman's initially in 1921, as a country-by-country stocktaking of the world's politico-geographical problems which remained unresolved, and in varying degree potentially explosive, notwithstanding the peace settlement which had been reached in Europe. In the event, however, the impact which both books made – at least in their respective countries of origin – proved to be short-lived. Thus although *The New World* ran into several editions and increased in bulk as it strove to keep pace with the growing number and complexity of the problems with which it was concerned, its appearance coincided with the reversion of the United States to its traditional isolationism, in which political geography was of interest only to a handful of specialists. And while the facts of geography permitted

---

[1] Camille Vallaux, *Le sol et l'état*, Paris, 1911.
[2] Derwent Whittlesey, *The Earth and the State*, New York, 1939.
[3] Halford J. Mackinder, *Democratic Ideals and Reality*, London, 1919.
[4] Isaiah Bowman, *The New World*, New York, 1921.

Introduction 3

Britain to indulge only in the lesser luxury of insularity, British habits of mind were far more receptive to discussion of the political nature of communism and later of fascism than to the consideration of the geographical basis of a possible Russo-German alignment which Mackinder had feared. Thus *Democratic Ideals and Reality* was quickly forgotten, and twenty years later the Czechoslovakian bastion, the centre-piece of Mackinder's proposed 'Third Tier', was allowed by a British Prime Minister who knew little geography to be eliminated by a Germany which was saturated in it.

The significance of the profound difference between the British and the German appraisal of the relevance of geography to statecraft had been repeatedly commented upon by Mackinder for over forty years, but it had become even more menacing with the development of a specifically German *Geopolitik* (geopolitics) after the First World War. The term geopolitics had in fact been first employed by the Swedish political scientist, Rudolf Kjellén in his book *Staten som lifsform* ('The state as a way of life') which appeared in Swedish in 1916 and in German translation a year later.[1] As this title implied, Kjellén's work owed much to Ratzel, but the subsequent development of geopolitics, which was almost exclusively a German phenomenon during the inter-war years, owed far more to Karl Haushofer (1869–1946) and his followers. In this process *Geopolitik* became increasingly divorced from the scholarly tradition of the older German (and other) political geographers, many of whose concepts it simultaneously plagiarized and distorted to produce a kind of admass political geography designed to promote the cause of German territorial expansion.

It was one of the lesser tragedies of the Nazi period, under which *Geopolitik* enjoyed its short-lived heyday and in so doing inevitably attracted the alarmed attention of the non-German press, that many intelligent people in other countries, who had little or no knowledge of political geography, came to confuse the two, and all too often as a result chose to throw away a thoroughly promising baby with some exceptionally dirty bathwater.

Notwithstanding the enunciation in their declining years by both Mackinder (1861–1947)[2] and Bowman (1878–1950),[3] two giants of a

[1] Rudolf Kjellén, *Staten som lifsform*, Stockholm, 1916; *Der Staat als Lebensform*, Leipzig, 1917.
[2] Halford J. Mackinder, 'The round world and the winning of the peace', *Foreign Affairs*, 21, 1943, pp. 596–605.
[3] Isaiah Bowman, 'The geographical situation of the United States in relation to world policies', *Geographical Journal*, 112, 1948, pp. 129–45.

4 *Essays in Political Geography*

previous generation, of extremely perceptive politico-geographical appraisals of the factors which would shape events in the new 'new world' that would emerge after the Second World War, and the posthumous publication of the masterly study *The Geography of the Peace* by Nicholas Spykman,[1] the American political scientist who but for his premature death might have inherited the spiritual mantle of Mackinder, the harm had been done.

In Germany itself it seemed that political geography – as well as Karl Haushofer – had committed suicide, and in virtually all other Western countries except the United States, where its relevance to the new American role in world affairs was at least partially recognized, it remained under a cloud of suspicion which has by no means wholly dispersed even today.

The effect of this setback has been the more regrettable in that the period since the Second World War has witnessed an even more fundamental redrawing of the world political map than that which followed the Treaty of Versailles. Indeed, in the quarter-century from 1939 to 1964 the world has undergone a politico-geographical change comparable in scale – though in certain vital respects opposite in direction – to that which occupied the entire century which followed the Congress of Vienna and hitherto represented the most revolutionary geopolitical transformation in the whole of recorded history.

With the decolonization of the greater part of Asia and Africa, the world political map has become immensely more complicated. In place of a few great maritime empires controlled from Western Europe there have arisen well over fifty independent successor states, ranging in scale from sub-continental giants such as India to insular fragments like Singapore, and by at least a partially complementary process the significance of Europe in the power pattern of the world has been dramatically reduced relative to that of the two extra-European super-powers, the United States and the Soviet Union.

To what extent these momentous changes are explicable in terms of the analyses of Ratzel, Mackinder and Spykman is a subject which, in the contemporary obsession with economic growth and the accelerating deracination of increasingly urbanized societies from their physical environment, is a question which has hitherto received but scant attention,[2] though to the writer it seems clear that the relevance of

---

[1] Nicholas J. Spykman, *The Geography of the Peace*, New York, 1944.
[2] Note, however, the important article by W. G. East, 'How strong is the Heartland?', *Foreign Affairs*, 29, 1950, pp. 78–93.

Introduction 5

geography to international relations is not one whit less today than it was twenty-five, fifty or a hundred years ago.

No less serious has been the almost complete neglect[1] during the critical post-war decade of the politico-geographical problems in innumerable parts of Asia and Africa which were meanwhile being summarily solved, ignored or created by the hectic demolition of most of the remaining colonial empires. And while it would be naïve to pretend that any amount of such research would have significantly modified the more deeply-rooted passions which in so many places have exploded into violence as the tidal wave of decolonization has swept across Asia and Africa, it remains a disturbing fact that, in the absence of impartial academic analyses of the problems concerned, both the statesman and the educated public in outside countries, who might otherwise have been able to make more constructive suggestions, have too often had to base their judgments on a far from adequate appreciation of the relevant facts.

Nevertheless, particularly during the past decade, a small but growing number of political geographers has been working on studies of this kind, and it was in the belief that a comparative consideration of a series of such case studies might simultaneously contribute to a rethinking of our methodology and indirectly help to draw the attention of a wider public to what the political geographer has to offer in this connexion, that the decision was taken to make the political geography of decolonization the central theme of the Sheffield symposium, and hence also of this book.

The sequence of essays presented here follows closely though not exactly that in which the papers were given in the symposium. Thus the first part, which deals systematically with various geographical aspects of the internal structure and the external relationships of states, introduces several of the concepts which are examined in specific regional contexts in the second and much the longest part, on decolonization, while the two essays in the brief final section serve to remind us that many of the problems which have been seen to proliferate in the newly independent lands also have their analogues in the changes which are taking place in the old world as well.

[1] Two articles by O. H. K. Spate on the partition of India constitute significant exceptions to this trend, namely 'The partition of the Punjab and Bengal', *Geographical Journal*, 110, 1948, pp. 201–22, and 'The partition of India and the prospects of Pakistan', *Geographical Review*, 38, 1948, pp. 5–29.

6 Essays in Political Geography

Notwithstanding their generally more theoretical character, the three papers in Part I concerned with the internal structure of states have considerable direct or indirect relevance to the political geography of decolonization. Thus, while the study of political geography and administrative areas by Mr J. N. H. Douglas is based specifically upon conditions in the British Isles, the problems with which it deals, namely those caused by the retention of local administrative units long after the circumstances in which they originated have ceased to exist, are found in many other parts of the world. And indeed a particularly intractable variant occurs in virtually all ex-colonial lands, through the survival, at least for a time after independence, of internal administrative patterns originally designed to serve the convenience of the colonial regimes rather than the quite different ends of an independent state.

Likewise Professor Richard Hartshorne, in considering the morphology of the state area, illustrates his arguments primarily by reference to a particular case, namely that of the United States in 1787, immediately prior to the Constitutional Convention. And in thus examining four basic factors with which the founding fathers of the first and greatest ex-colonial state of modern times had to contend, he provides an invaluable basis for the comparative study of the problems of newly independent states in our own times.

From this it is a logical step to examine some fundamental elements in the analysis of the viability of states, and in doing so Professor Preston James *inter alia* points to the great problem facing most of the states of sub-Saharan Africa, namely that of finding positive state-ideas (or *raisons d'être*) to replace the purely negative aim of escaping from colonial domination.

Part I of this collection is completed by two studies, respectively by Professors W. G. East and Saul Cohen, of the contemporary trend towards closer association between states. While some interesting differences of emphasis and interpretation are evident between these two studies – the first by a British and the second by an American scholar – both are to a considerable extent concerned with the need to establish new patterns of alignment to give greater coherence to the present fragmented political geography of what many economists, but significantly few geographers, are nowadays disposed to bracket together as the 'Third World'.

Part II, which forms the core of the book, contains eleven case studies of the political geography of decolonization, all but one of which deal with the Afro-Asian world.

Introduction 7

Beginning in Asia, where the recent phase of decolonization was initiated with the granting of independence to the Philippines in 1946 and to the Indian sub-continent in 1947, attention is focused first upon two ex-British dependencies, namely Malaysia and Ceylon, which are considered in Chapters 7 and 8, respectively by Professor C. A. Fisher and Mr B. H. Farmer. With populations of approximately 10 million each, these countries are both relatively small by Asian standards (though nevertheless significantly larger than all but a handful of the new African states) and further similarities exist in respect of their strategic locations *vis à vis* the British sea route to the East and above all in that their internal politics since independence have been complicated by serious minority problems which, though not caused by British rule, were certainly intensified under it. Moreover in both cases the critical minority community – Indian in Ceylon and Chinese in Malaysia – is geographically speaking an outlier of a vastly more populous and more powerful neighbour. Given this degree of similarity between Malaysia and Ceylon, comparative study of their attempts to solve their communal problems might well prove to be of more than local relevance, though clearly in both cases the attitudes of the respective ancestral homelands of the minorities concerned, namely India and China, may well represent a significant factor in the equation.

Some indication of the great difference of attitude towards minority peoples which exists between these same two Asian giants may be obtained by a comparison between the next two chapters, on the problem of Nagaland, by Professor Ulrich Schweinfurth, and on minority unrest and Sino-Soviet Rivalry in Sinkiang, by Mr Michael Freeberne. In both of these cases the boot is, so to speak, on the other foot, for here the two greatest Asian powers are faced with discontented minority peoples within strategically sensitive sectors of their immensely extended land frontiers. And here, however much the Nagas may criticize the policies of the Indian Government, the latter, in its willingness to permit genuine autonomy to the minority community, appears to be altogether more enlightened than its Chinese counterpart, which is attempting in effect to smother Uighur nationalism by massive Han colonization.

Between what one Asian writer has called Asiatic Asia[1] (the monsoon lands focusing on the twin centres of India and China) and what may equally justifiably be called African Africa (the lands lying to the south of the Sahara) the Near and/or Middle East, represented in this book

[1] S. K. Datta, *Asiatic Asia*, London, 1932.

8 *Essays in Political Geography*

by three essays respectively from Messrs. Vahé J. Sevian and Moshe Brawer and Professor Anthony S. Reyner, provides an obvious bridge·

Mr Sevian's study of the evolution of the boundary between Iraq and Iran traces the story over some four centuries of history, through the rivalries of two ancient and declining empires, the Ottoman and the Persian, to the present day. In so doing it illustrates two phenomena which have many parallels elsewhere. Like the great majority of traditional frontiers in the Orient, that between the Ottoman and the Persian empires deliberately avoided the precision of the linear boundaries which were the norm in Europe. Thus when Western rivalries – in this case between Great Britain and Tsarist Russia – were projected into Asia, the older style frontiers had to be reduced to definable and mappable boundary lines. And although this process helped at last to stabilize the situation geopolitically, the new boundary here paid scant attention to the interests of the ethnic and religious minorities through whose territory in part it ran. Moreover, the stabilization of the boundary took place before the significance of the local oil resources was properly appreciated, and the resultant problems are typical of those which continue to arise wherever and whenever hitherto unsuspected resources are discovered in frontier zones with such a chequered history as this.

Indeed at the opposite extremity of the Middle East, Professor Reyner's essay on the boundary between Algeria and Morocco is concerned with fundamentally similar problems to those described by Mr Sevian, though in this case they derived from the intrusion (and more recent withdrawal) of French imperialism into what had originally been the western outposts of crumbling Ottoman power.

In between these two, Mr Brawer's paper on the geographical background to the Jordan water dispute takes us to the geographical centre of the Middle East and to one facet of the conflict of interests between Israel and the Arab world. While, as the paper implies, the material aspects of this conflict should be capable of rational solution, the emotional attitudes to which it has given rise have served in recent years to make Israel not merely the flash point of the Middle East but also, in view of that region's geopolitical situation relative to the two great power blocs, and the widening gulf between the richer and the poorer countries of the world, one of the three most serious danger points on the globe.

Written as it originally was three years before the Arab-Israeli War of 1967, Mr Brawer's essay is not directly concerned with these wider

Introduction 9

issues. But it would seem that only through a willingness on both sides to attempt serious discussion of such practical problems as the one with which his study deals is there any real hope of averting either the local or the wider dangers to which this tragic conflict threatens to give rise.

Taken together the three papers on sub-Saharan Africa illustrate several of what may be called the classic problems of political geography. Thus, as Mr David Hilling's account of politics and transportation in the land-locked states of West Africa shows, the age-old politico-geographical problem of access to the sea has appeared in a new form as a result of the cleavages which have accompanied the ill-co-ordinated decolonization of Africa. Moreover, this unscrambling process has done little to re-unite the peoples artificially sundered by the arbitrary divisions resulting from the late nineteenth century scramble for Africa, a problem whose complexity is illustrated by Dr B. W. Hodder's case study of the Ewe question. But although one may accept Dr Hodder's view that such cases constitute one of the bases for closer co-operation between neighbouring African states, the paper by Mr B. W. Langlands on nationalism, regionalism and federalism in East Africa shows only too clearly the difficulties of maintaining such co-operation, even where some tradition of it has already been established between areas formerly under the rule of a single imperial power, and where its economic advantages have already been clearly demonstrated.

In its reference to the communal problems created by the presence of Indians in East Africa Mr Langlands' paper also recalls the discussion earlier in the book of the similar problems in Ceylon and Malaysia. And indeed, notwithstanding the very real differences between the Asian countries, most of which possessed an elaborate indigenous state structure prior to the imposition of Western rule, and those of Africa which was predominantly tribal at the corresponding stage in its experience, many other useful comparisons can be drawn between the Asian and African examples considered in Part II of this book. Among the most important of the topics which call for fuller consideration in such comparative studies is that of the viability of the smaller ex-colonial states, and in this context the often wide discrepancy between political sentiment and economic potential may be of crucial importance, as for example in the cases of both the Ewe and the Nagas.

The last of the papers in Part II, by Professor N. L. Nicholson on the further partition of the Northwest Territories of Canada, suggests other but no less interesting comparisons. For besides reminding us

10 *Essays in Political Geography*

once again that the modern era of decolonization began in North America, it shows that even in an area uncomplicated by most of the problems which have been seen to bedevil it elsewhere, the working out of the decolonizing process continues to the very end to provoke rivalries not wholly different in kind – though here less serious in consequence – from those which have been considered in the ten preceding chapters. Even in the vast northern expanses of Northwestern Canada, surely as remote as it is possible to be from the classic cases of land hunger, the attachment of man to land remains a factor to be taken into account.

More obvious evidence of this attachment, which in the last analysis still provides the *raison d'être* for the study of political geography, is found as might be expected in the two essays which make up Part III of this book though, as Professor J. W. House shows in the first of these, the nature of the man/land relationship is changing at least as much in the old world as it is in the new.

While Professor House is concerned to illustrate changing attitudes to boundaries and the frontier zone, within the context of the developing European Economic Community, the final essay, by Dr Ladis Kristof, looks at the great power whose rise to geopolitical pre-eminence in the old world as a consequence of the Second World War indirectly played a major part in bringing the nations of Western Europe to join together in that Community. Indeed, given the immense size, population and power of the U.S.S.R. the trend of its internal evolution is bound henceforward to exert a profound effect upon the pattern of political alignments in the world outside, and for this reason it is fitting that the final chapter in this collection should be devoted to a consideration of four conflicting views which Russians have held or still hold of their country and its place in the world.

But the inclusion of Dr Kristof's essay is significant also in another respect, for it provides an unmistakable link between political geography as that subject has developed in the English-speaking lands since 1945 and the kind of scholarly and forward-looking geopolitics which some of us still associate with the names of Mackinder and Spykman. To the writer it is therefore a source of particular satisfaction that so eminent a political scientist as Dr Kristof should have demonstrated his appreciation of the significance of both these branches of our subject by contributing so elegant and stimulating a paper to our symposium.

PART I

Geographical Aspects of the Structure and Inter-Relationships of States

2

Political Geography and Administrative Areas: *A Method of Assessing the Effectiveness of Local Government Areas*   J. N. H. DOUGLAS

Conscious of the need for orderly rule, efficient organization and planning, every state develops an administration through which the diverse physical and cultural regions making up the state area can be integrated into a single coherent unit. With this aim in view, all states, with the exception of the smallest, are divided into provincial and/or local political areas. Because of the vital part played by the administration in moulding the nature of the state, the political geographer must always give attention to its basis and structure and must attempt, while so doing, to ascertain its effectiveness. By definition, the effectiveness of administration means the degree to which the national government has successfully adopted the administrative pattern to take account of different cultural regions which exist within the state boundaries.[1]

The Acts which gave birth to the present local government structure in Great Britain were passed by Parliament in 1888 and 1894.

LOCAL GOVERNMENT STRUCTURE IN BRITAIN

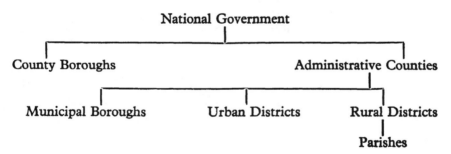

At the time these two local government Acts were welcomed as a major triumph, bringing to the country for the first time a uniform and nation-wide system of administration and replacing the old system of *ad hoc* functional and service areas such as Poor Law Boards, Health and

---

[1] R. Hartshorne, 'The functional approach in political geography', *Annals of the Association of American Geographers*, 40, 1950, p. 105.

14 *Essays in Political Geography*

Sanitary Boards, and Educational Boards. Yet, even as the new structure was being set up, the effectiveness of many of the areas, particularly the smaller urban districts, was reduced because they were delimited by boundaries which followed old agrarian and parish divisions, often dating back to the eleventh century and before. Trends in settlement growth and population change – products of the Industrial Revolution – were not given due consideration. During the twentieth century, population growth has continued and its distribution has changed. Settlements which formerly were separate have gradually merged, and the scope and complexity of administration has enlarged. Despite these changes in economic, social and political life, the original local government pattern still remains largely unaltered. The growth of an attitude of sacred inviolability, on the basis of which many local councils staunchly guard their own vested interests, has created a barrier of inflexibility which even the national government cannot easily disregard.

This resistance to change has had profound effects on the nature of British administration. Successive national governments, unwilling to challenge the weight of vested interest by radically reconstructing the local government pattern, have by-passed the problem by setting up a series of new administrative bodies each with its own structure and regional pattern. The smaller local government units, particularly urban districts and parishes, because they are so small and unsuitable, have the function removed from their jurisdiction and given to the new board. The control of gas, electricity, hospital and, very often, water services has been given to new bodies, and control of police, education and health services has been moved up to county level. As a result, the lower units in the administrative hierarchy have been left as mere rumps with fewer services to perform. Also, as each of these new *ad hoc* bodies is very largely independent of any local government control and is run by a main office administration, centralization has increased. Today, therefore, there exists not one body with multi-functional powers and the ability to co-ordinate and plan as a whole, but rather numerous bodies, independent and isolated, each with its own separate function. The administrative complexity and lack of integration which result can easily be imagined and, with this process continuing steadily, the situation is becoming similar to that which existed before 1888.

The lack of effective government at sub-national and local level and the need for reappraisal became particularly apparent during the Second

Political Geography and Administrative Areas 15

World War and in 1947 the first Local Government Boundary Commission was set up. Since then, successive Commissions have studied the problem but, because of governmental caution and their own lack of power, there has been no master plan for change. Alterations which have taken place seem to be piecemeal and no more than stop-gap solutions.

Each administrative unit, no matter how few its functions, is a politically organized area with a focus, well-defined boundaries and a particular set of spatial relations. As such, it is especially susceptible to geographical treatment. Despite its obvious importance, this field, fertile for geographical research, has been largely untouched and, at least in Great Britain, it lacks constructive literature.

THE SEARCH FOR A METHOD

Does any accepted body of principles exist, according to which effective boundaries might be determined by investigation? We may begin by noting some recent comments by N. J. G. Pounds: 'The study of politically organized areas can be approached from two points of view. The first and more geographical is that of the shape and size of these administrative units and the ways in which those of the lower levels of responsibility are fitted within the boundaries of those higher in the scale. The second is the division of responsibility between the several levels of local government and the state itself. These two aspects are inseparable . . .'[1]

Study of shape, size and function of the politically organized area is necessary but does such a study go far enough? It becomes useful only when the administrative area is related to the basic physical and human conditions on which its boundary has been set and the question remains as to which specific geographical factors are most important in influencing the effectiveness of the administrative unit.

E. W. Gilbert had no doubt where the emphasis should be when he wrote 'Whatever is done or is not done, it is vital that the administrative map of England and Wales should be drawn so that it accords with the social geography of the country'.[2]

Social factors were also considered to be important by the 1947 Local Government Boundaries Commission when it put forward nine criteria

[1] N. J. G. Pounds, *Political Geography*, New York, 1962, p. 193.
[2] E. W. Gilbert, 'The boundaries of local government areas', *Geographical Journal*, 111, 1948, p. 198.

16 Essays in Political Geography

which were to be taken as the basis for the reappraisal of the local government structure and pattern. These were:

(a) community of interest;
(b) development or anticipated development;
(c) economic and industrial characteristics;
(d) financial resources;
(e) physical features, including in particular, but not exclusively, suitable boundaries, means of communication and accessibility to administrative centres and centres of business and social life;
(f) population – size, distribution and characteristics;
(g) record of adminstration by local authorities concerned;
(h) size and shape of area;
(i) wishes of the inhabitants.

From this detailed set of criteria a research method, which will give the necessary meaningful comparison, can be developed. Two main requirements are inherent in the criteria:

1. They demand a thorough analysis of the physical and human geography of the administrative areas being considered, an analysis which shows the nature of the physical features and their relation to the boundary lines, which considers the economic and social facets of the landscape, which portrays the population characteristics and considers the factors of transport and accessibility. Further the criteria point to the need for historical perspective, and in effect demand a close and comprehensive regional study of the area concerned.

2. The inclusion of the 'community of interest' and the 'wishes of the inhabitants' as criteria, adds another dimension to the study. These two inter-related factors are important because they help to create and reflect local unity and *raison d'être*. The administrative area with a strongly developed community of interest is an effective social unit; the absence of such a characteristic usually implies disinterest and apathy.

The community of interest is developed almost entirely by spatial contacts which develop among people.[1] Spatial contact implies movement and movement creates a field of circulation. It is, therefore, the

---

[1] 'Discussion on the geographical aspects of regional planning', *Geographical Journal*, 99, 1942, pp. 61–80.

See also K. W. Deutsch, *Nationalism and Social Communication*, New York, 1953. The theory that national growth is controlled by the nature and degree of social communication can also be applied to the development of community of interest and *raison d'être* at local level.

Political Geography and Administrative Areas 17

circulation fields which do most to create the community of interest which must be studied.

What are the most important circulation fields ? The field created by the journey to work is most significant. It has economic importance but, above all, it conditions the social ties of the working population. The field set up by the journey to shop reflects contacts made by the house-wife, while the field resulting from the journey to school represents contacts made among young people, which often last and have signi-ficance right through life. The field created by movement to afterwork recreation is the other obvious conditioning factor.

Thus, on the basis of this discussion, the method will have two stages:

1. A detailed regional study of the area under review, necessary to give a deeper insight into the background geographical conditions.

2. A study of the important attitude-forming circulation fields. The delimitation of these fields and their representation on maps will allow a visual comparison to be made between the patterns they produce and the pattern of the administrative areas. A close correlation between the two patterns will be likely to indicate effective local government, while a lack of correlation will tend to indicate ineffectiveness and the consequent need for change. These maps will also provide an informative basis for the administrator in charge of directing change.

APPLICATION OF THE METHOD

The lower Dearne valley area of South Yorkshire, located between Doncaster to the south-east, Rotherham to the south and Barnsley to the north, was chosen as the specimen area in the attempt to apply this research method.

This area is underlain by interbedded sandstones and shales of the middle coal measures. The dominant physical feature is the wide, east/west orientated valley of the river Dearne which has cut into the softer shales, while the more resistant sandstones which dip to the north-east stand out as cuestas above the shale valleys. These features give an undulating topography, with relative relief of 150 to 200 feet, and with the steeper slopes facing south-west.

The present settlement pattern is made up of a number of large min-ing villages. These expanding settlements, which are now beginning to merge with one another, owe their industrial character almost entirely to twentieth-century development. Before 1888 when the delimitation of local government boundaries was begun, the settlements were very

18 Essays in Political Geography

different in size and in function. At that time they were predominantly agricultural in character, small in extent, separate and independent, each located on a dry-point site above the ill-drained Dearne valley. Between 1870 and 1890 the basis for modern large-scale coalmining was laid, as deep mine shafts were sunk in the area (Fig. 2.1*a*) but growth in population and the expansion of the settlements was just beginning by 1888. As a result, the local government boundaries were based on the old parish divisions, and each settlement was effectively separated and given local independence. The lower Dearne valley area was divided among nine small administrative units. By 1900, however, population had increased rapidly and settlement had begun to mushroom, and the twentieth century has witnessed continued growth in population and

TABLE 2.1: POPULATION INCREASE IN LOWER DEARNE VALLEY 1871–1961

Settlement	1871	1901	1961	Percentage increase 1871–1901	Percentage increase 1901–1961
Conisbrough	2,119	8,549	17,596	303·4	105·8
Mexborough	4,316	10,430	17,053	141·6	63·5
Swinton	5,150	12,217	13,420	137·1	9·8
Wath-upon-Dearne	2,023	8,515	15,183	320·9	78·3
Bolton-upon-Dearne	596	3,828		542·2	
Goldthorpe			26,493		329·8
Thurnscoe	204	2,336		1,045·0	

Source: *Census Reports of England and Wales*, 1871, 1901, 1961

settlement (Table 2.1). Coalmining has changed the economic character of the area and has given it a uniform basis, yet despite this continuous change the local government pattern laid down in the late nineteenth century and pre-dating modern growth remains only slightly altered by the reallocation of small areas and partial consolidation (Fig. 2.1*b*). Local government in the area remains divided between seven different units (five urban districts and two parishes) (Fig. 2.2*a*) and as these urban districts were too small to be taken as the basis for the administrative and service functions which have developed in the twentieth century, a set of new boundaries has now been superimposed on the old pattern. Administrative functions such as those of the National Assistance Boards and Local Employment Exchanges, and service functions

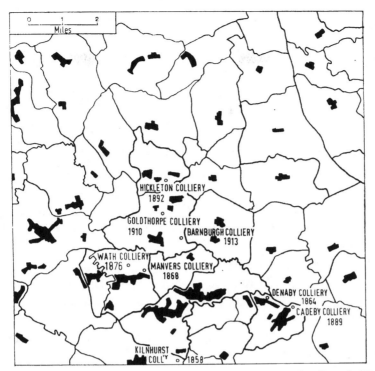

Fig. 2.1a. Settlement and Administrative Areas in South Yorkshire 1908

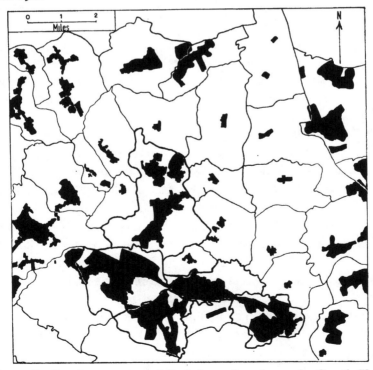

Fig. 2.1b. Settlement and Administrative Areas in South Yorkshire 1963

20 *Essays in Political Geography*

such as gas and electricity supply have their own separate areas and boundaries. A functional reorientation has also taken place within the local government hierarchy: services such as education, health and police control, cramped by smallness of the urban districts, have been removed from them and are now operated by the West Riding County Council. As is evident from Fig. 2.2b, the number and pattern of local political areas resulting from this process is bewildering and chaotic.

Coalmining, which came to dominate the economy after 1890, is still of overwhelming importance; 40 per cent of the total male working population of the area was engaged in the industry in 1961. Other industries, such as glass bottle making and clothing, provide few alternative opportunities for work. Employment for female labour in particular is limited, and women travel daily to find work in towns as far away as Bradford and York. This continued imbalance in economic structure has resulted in part from the extreme fragmentation of local government. The urban districts have little power to attract new industries and they lack the resources to give guarantees against mining subsidence, a widespread problem in an area riddled with coal galleries below ground.

As daily population movements and the resulting circulation fields do not take place in a vacuum but are related to the unequal distribution of opportunities within the area, the pattern of industry is also significant. The wide valley of the river Dearne, formerly ill-drained and avoided, has now become the focus of industry. Modern drainage techniques have made it the concentration point for coal and raw materials, and hence for manpower, which travels from all the urban districts to work in the area.

With the settlements expanding and merging, and public transport providing easy means of access, a reorganization of retail and social characteristics has taken place. The former all-purpose general shop found in each village, which created a degree of self-sufficiency, has been replaced by a modern and more varied retail and social pattern. A retail centre with surprisingly varied facilities has developed at Mexborough. These facilities, much too large for the population of Mexborough alone, have far outstripped those found in the other urban district centres, and the town appears to have become the retail focus for the Dearne valley area. Social and recreational facilities also tend to be concentrated at Mexborough, though the presence of active working men's clubs in all the settlements of this strongly socialist area make this aspect of Mexborough less significant. Therefore, on the basis of

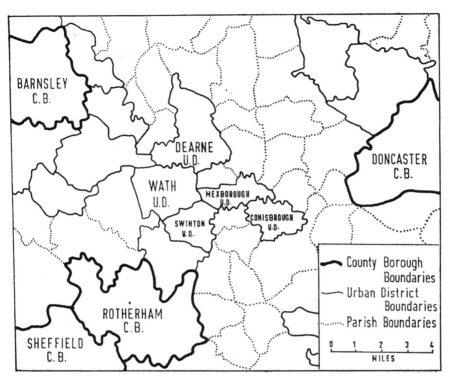

Fig. 2.2a. Local Government Areas South Yorkshire

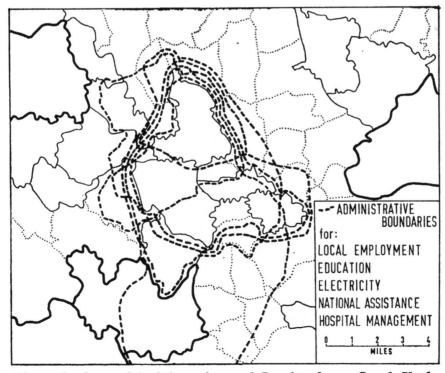

Fig. 2.2b. Some Administrative and Service Areas South Yorkshire

22 Essays in Political Geography

function and facilities, Mexborough has become different from the other settlements of the area. While these others have retained their industrial village character based on point production of coal, Mexborough has become a town with facilities used by all the people of the area.

The extent to which this reorganization of economic and social life has taken place can be shown by the patterns of movement and the circulation fields which exist within the area.

PATTERNS OF MOVEMENT

The Journey to Work. This analysis is based on a survey of the work centres within the five urban districts in the area. The survey was carried out by compiling residence place statistics at each major work centre, and has given a 60 per cent sample of the total working population of the area. The patterns of movement derived from the survey show that there is considerable movement between the urban districts but very little either into or out of the area to find work. Fig. 2.3 shows that Swinton and Wath are primarily work places with a concentration of working population from the other urban districts. Bolton-on-Dearne and Conisbrough show more characteristics of self-containment, but movement which does take place across local government boundaries remains predominantly within the lower Dearne area. Mexborough is predominantly a residence place supplying workers to the other four urban districts. The absence of industrial work centres reflects Mexborough's greater provision of retail and social facilities.

The Journey to Shop. This analysis is based on a questionnaire survey undertaken throughout the settlements of the five urban districts. Fig. 2.4a has been drawn on the basis of most important shopping centres. It shows that, despite the presence of Rotherham, Barnsley and Doncaster within shopping distance, Mexborough has become a significant focus for the lower Dearne area and is surprisingly independent of the three larger towns. Mexborough's superiority is shown in the fact that it has a total of 22·6 shops per thousand people, a total including 10·7 'luxury' and 'speciality goods' shops, whereas the other urban districts, with shopping centres which are considered inadequate except for daily necessities, have an average of 13·2 shops per thousand, including only 5·5 'luxury' and 'speciality goods' shops. The superiority of Mexborough is not complete, however, because those parts of

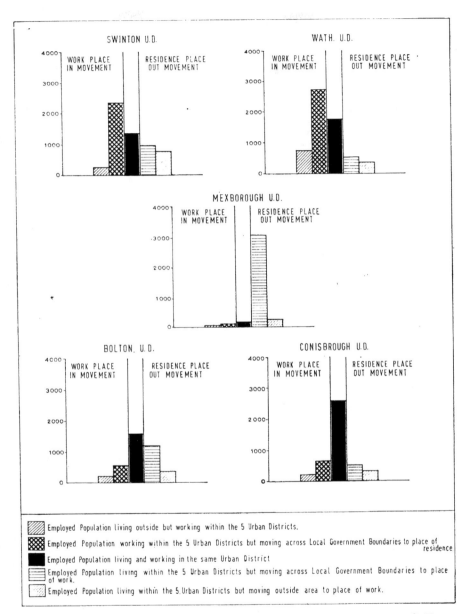

Fig. 2.3. Dearne Valley – Urban Districts – Movement of Employed Population

24 *Essays in Political Geography*

the lower Dearne valley furthest from it and nearest to the greater facilities of the larger towns show, not surprisingly, a more varied shopping pattern, with Doncaster, Barnsley and Rotherham becoming more significant.

Journey to Afterwork Recreation. This analysis, again based on a questionnaire, shows a rather more diffuse pattern of movement. There is a difference between the movements of the older and the younger age groups. The older age groups rely more on the working men's clubs for entertainment and so movement is localized, while the younger people journey more regularly to the larger towns. However, despite the diffuse pattern, Mexborough shows signs of emerging as a social centre able to challenge the pull of the large towns and help to integrate still further the settlements of the lower Dearne valley. (Fig. 2.4*b*)

Journey to School. Movement to primary school is obviously very localized, but journey to grammar school again shows that the urban districts of the lower Dearne valley are effectively integrated yet self-contained with very little movement into or out of the area. (Fig. 2.4*c*)

The interdependence of these settlements in the Dearne valley, shown by the patterns of circulation, has grown with the development of a system of public transport, and at present three bus companies, centred at Rotherham, Swinton and Barnsley, provide the area with excellent facilities. Figure 2.4*d* shows that this transport network favours Mexborough as the most easily reached centre from the rest of the Dearne valley area.

The slow process of growth and rationalization which has taken place in the twentieth century has resulted in these settlements taking on a similar economic character, and developing a well-defined industrial, retail and social focus. Today there exists an integrated economic and social unit of over 90,000 people. The separation and independence of the late nineteenth century has been replaced by a strong interdependence which is characteristic of a continuous urban settlement. Yet this change has found no administrative recognition and the area remains divided among seven distinct local government units.

CONCLUSION

The method demonstrates the lack of effectiveness in the present local government pattern and points clearly to the nature and degree of change that is necessary. The grouping together of the urban districts

Political Geography and Administrative Areas 25

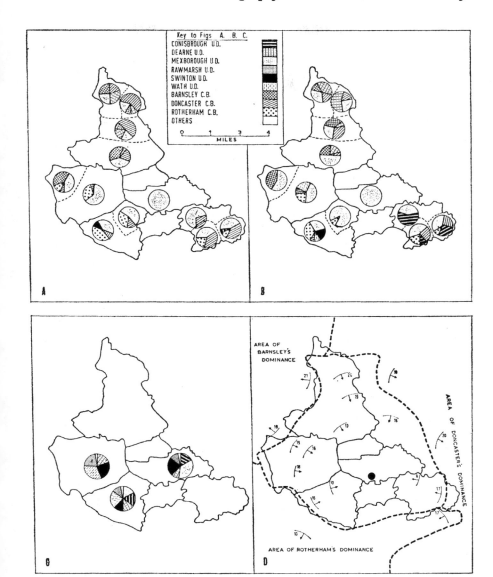

Fig. 2.4. Dearne Valley – Urban Districts – Population Movement and Accessibility

26 Essays in Political Geography

within the lower Dearne area would provide a much more viable economic unit and a more realistic social one. This area of common characteristics could then more effectively tackle its common problems of subsidence and economic diversification. The official recognition of Mexborough as an existing centre of real significance would prepare the way for more rational land use and transport planning. The problem of the multiplicity of administrative areas and centres, and the lack of co-ordination which results, could be overcome by taking the new unit as the basis for a multi-functional region with one administrative centre.

The position in the lower Dearne valley area is but one small example of the ineffectiveness inherent in the British local government structure and the problems facing those who would plan anew. Similar situations and problems exist in most of the country's industrial or industrializing areas.[1] Although much attention has recently been paid to the possibilities and problems of giving more power to the regions, the more fundamental problem of rationalizing local government must be answered before regional devolution can take place.[2] A new pattern reflecting local reality must be laid down; only then can it be certain that the new regional structure will not be just one more superimposed pattern helping to hide the problems and ineffectiveness which lie beneath. To achieve this rationalization, much basic research must be carried out, and although the concept of the circulation field is certainly not new, it could with advantage be used more effectively by all those concerned with the problems of administrative areas. Besides its ability to show up attitude conditioning movements, the circulation field also delimits dynamic units of population. It includes residence place, work, retail and social centres, and so has much greater significance than the static population units, based on totals alone, which are so widely used in determining the size, boundary and rank of administrative divisions. The greater use of the circulation field would be a step forward and would, at the very least, help to overcome the extreme fragmentation of social, economic and political life caused by the pattern of local government within Great Britain at present.

[1] See *Local Government Commission for England. Reports Nos. 1–8*, H.M.S.O., London, 1961–4; L. P. Green, *Provincial Metropolis: The Future of Local Government in South-East Lancashire*, London, 1959.

[2] For consideration of similar problems in France, see *The French Administrative Reform*, Ambassade de France, Service de Presse et d'Information, London, 1964.

3

Morphology of the State Area:
Significance for the State   RICHARD HARTSHORNE

The state is a geographic feature which we visualize on the political map; the most common map in educational and general daily use. No doubt in many cases we identify a state in our minds primarily in its external morphology, notably its size and shape. If these characteristics are cartographically obvious, what is their significance in politicogeographic analysis? In previous discussions of varied approaches in political geography I gave but scanty attention to this topic;[1] experience in teaching the subject has convinced me that it forms an essential part of the geographical analysis of any political unit, but that the analysis of the morphology of the political area must be related to the function of the area, and to the purpose of its organization as a political unit.

Considered geographically the purpose of the political organization of a state is to establish coherent unity and a certain degree of homogeneity over areas which without the state organization are more or less separate and heterogeneous. In other words, the state seeks to create a *region* of high degree of functional unity and in certain respects of high degree of uniformity. Only human political agencies can create such regions; they are not given in nature. 'Manifest destiny' and 'natural boundaries' for political areas are myths which we need not discuss here.

On the other hand it is clear that there are conditions in the morphology of any state area which make easier or more difficult the geographic purpose of the state organization. Comparative study of many different states has led me to conclude that among such factors, several or all of the following are likely to be most significant:

1. contiguity of settled population;
2. homogeneity versus heterogeneity of the population;
3. historical continuity of the political area;
4. coherent unity of the area.

[1] Richard Hartshorne, 'The functional approach in political geography', *Annals of the Association of American Geographers*, 40, 1950, pp. 95–130; likewise in 'Political geography', in Preston E. James and Clarence F. Jones (eds.), *American Geography: Inventory and Prospect*, Syracuse, 1954, pp. 162–225; and 'Political geography in the modern world', *Conflict Resolution*, 4, 1960, pp. 52–66.

28   *Essays in Political Geography*

In each case the condition is to be examined as it exists inside the area, in contrast to relations with areas outside. Further, the analysis can be pointed either primarily to past development, as a study in genesis and development of the particular state as a geographic feature, or primarily to the present or possibly the future, as an analysis of the current problems faced by the state seeking to establish its united and uniform area. It may be helpful to consider these features in relation to a situation which is not hotly controversial and for which much of the factual material is well known,[1] namely the situation of the United States as a political area in 1787, immediately prior to the Constitutional Convention.

CONTIGUITY OF POPULATION

There seems little doubt that a basic reason for the political separation of the United States from Great Britain was the great stretch of ocean essentially empty of any connecting links. In contrast, the settlements from southern Maine to northern Georgia, though established largely by separate movements from across the Atlantic, had grown together so that peripheral settlers in each unit were contiguous with those in the next. In contrast, the settlements in Nova Scotia and in Quebec were separated from the 'American' settlements, and from each other, by great stretches of forested wilderness. Newer settlements beyond the Appalachians were also widely separated by unsettled zones, and in fact developed at least incipient threats of secession, though subsequent developments proved that in itself the Appalachian barrier was but a minor break soon to be overcome.

The importance of discontiguity of population in the history of state development is most readily seen in Latin America, as Robert Platt and Preston James have each demonstrated.[2] In marked contrast is the situation in tropical Africa, notably in Congo, where comparison of the political map with that of population suggests problems in the organization of the new states of that area.

In assessing the importance of discontiguity of populations, one must consider more than the difficulties of physical movements in handicapping close trade relations or transport of officials or of troops.

---

[1] The historical judgments of the situation largely follow those of Merill Jensen, *The New Nation: A History of the United States during the Confederation, 1781–89*, New York, 1950.

[2] Robert S. Platt, *Latin America: Countrysides and United Regions*, New York, 1942; Preston E. James, *Latin America*, New York, 1950.

Morphology of the State Area 29

Absence of intervening population has an effect in social psychology, preventing or destroying the feeling of togetherness, which is the essence of social coherence.

HOMOGENEITY

In the organization of diverse areas into a unit, regional differences in climate, landforms, water resources or minerals no doubt raise complications for central governments, but rarely are these more than minor difficulties in themselves. Much the same is true of regional diversity in economic production; indeed this may well stimulate interchange and so encourage inter-regional coherence. Marked differences in regional economic levels may lead to more serious difficulties, not as economic problems but rather as social problems – *i.e.*, results of differences in human attitudes.

The same is true in respect of physical differences in regional populations. Differences of race – in the proper biological sense – in a state create political problems only if there are conflicts in attitudes toward race. In short, regional heterogeneity creating difficulty for political organization of area is solely that of cultural heterogeneity.

The importance of language is well known and need not be further analysed here. Less commonly recognized is the importance of a common ideology, whether or not this is expressed in a common language, and whether it is formalized as accepted doctrine or more or less unconsciously accepted in a vague body of political attitudes, objectives, and accustomed ways of operating together politically. Switzerland, though divided sharply into several language areas, has long had a high degree of homogeneity in political ideology, markedly different from that of most if not all its neighbours. This, of course, is the essential homogeneity that was never attained, and perhaps never attempted, in the Austro-Hungarian Empire.

In the United States of 1787 there was a high degree of linguistic-cultural homogeneity and perhaps an even greater degree of homogeneity of political attitudes. These were the common heritage from Great Britain, but had been strengthened by common experience in eliminating feudal residues and in operating local democratic governments. In contrast, the situation in Nova Scotia and Quebec was notably different.

There was one major respect in which the United States of 1787 was markedly heterogeneous: one part of the country was entrenched in a

30 *Essays in Political Geography*

caste system which was almost absent in the other. The caste system was essentially cultural in its historic basis of slavery, but it was commonly observed in physical—i.e., racial characteristics which were obvious and unalterable. Although the contrast in regional attitudes on this subject created difficult problems, it appeared that these could be compromised for the present and would decrease in importance in the future. As it turned out, the contrast became even greater in subsequent decades, and the resultant problems were to lead to the one great threat to the maintenance of the territorial unity of the country.

HISTORICAL CONTINUITY OF THE POLITICAL AREA

Once an area has been authoritatively established as a political unit, the processes of political organization tend to develop forces of inertia to maintain the territorial organization even in spite of drastic revolutions in form of government. This is being illustrated most strikingly today in the territorial stability of most of the new states in Africa; although the colonial division, as Whittlesey among others had shown,[1] was markedly discordant in respect of distribution of population, or ethnic groupings, the pattern is retained almost without change by the new independent states. Even when the territorial unit has little organization in fact, existing only as a legal structure, as a tradition of legitimacy it remains a potential power that can be used; consider for example the importance during the period of feudal disorganization in France of the continuance of the legal and traditional concept of the kingdom of the West Franks.

The United States in 1787 represented the heritage of two conflicting concepts of territorial organization. All parts had from the beginnings of their continuous history been parts of a single realm, the British Empire, and in separating from that realm had done so as a unit, through a single army, a single Congress, and its diplomatic representatives. But there was also a strong history of separate units, as colonies completely independent of each other in which there had developed the concept of greater respect for local state government than for national. This paradox was to continue as one of the distinctive characteristics, and persistent problems, of the national state.

[1] Derwent S. Whittlesey, *The Earth and the State*, New York, 1939, pp. 331–4, and 367–8.

COHERENT UNITY OF THE AREA

It is difficult to discuss this condition without appearing to argue in a circle. In part, I suppose, one is saying that 'nothing succeeds like success'. More usefully perhaps, we may say that in the man-environment relationship at any time, what man has established in the past is a part of man's environment today. Applied to our problem in political geography, we may say that the analysis of a current problem in the organization of any particular area into a state must assess the degree to which economic, social or political organization of area have hitherto been established. Or, if as yet there is little such organization, one may attempt to measure the degree to which the society, the economy, and the underlying conditions for communication would make easy or difficult the development of a coherent organization.

What is clear from the history of long-established states is that once an area has been organized into a coherent unity, it has marked strength, whether of influence or direct power, over adjacent regions less effectively integrated; it has the capacity to grow, to expand geographically not merely as a political realm, but as an area of coherent political integration.

The significance of this condition is seen in its simplest in the well-known cases of states like France, or Russia, which developed as nodal units from an historic, dominating core area, as described in numerous cases in Europe in the recent study by Pounds and Ball.[1]

The United States of 1787 was certainly not a case of that type. Its thirteen units had originated independently of each other and no one had been joined to another until all joined together. Throughout the period of formation of political union, no unit or group of units attained a dominant position, whether economically, socially or politically. Nevertheless a considerable degree of coherence had been developed throughout the populated area of the seaboard. Migration among the settlements had promoted some degree of social coherence, particularly in church organization. Communication and trade had been facilitated by coastwise sea routes and by post road – *i.e.*, first externally and therefore subject to external interference, but then internally and thereby more securely. Steps toward political coherence were well under way even before the proclamation of independence, beginning in the

---

[1] Norman J. G. Pounds and Sue Simonds Ball, 'Core areas and the development of the European states system', *Annals of the Association of American Geographers*, 54, 1964, pp. 24–40.

32 Essays in Political Geography

Continental Congress of 1774. In sum, whether in the process of formation or in ultimate operation as a political unit, coherent organization does not necessarily require integration from and dominant control by a single nodal core. But undoubtedly a structure composed of many more or less equal cores presents problems of organization which may require different forms of political solution from those successful in organizing from a core area.

The world today contains a larger number of newly independent states than was ever the case in the past. In some of these the territorial areas have been determined by indigenous political forces prior to colonial rule; in others the territories are the resultant of decisions among outside colonial powers. In either case, the task of establishing the necessary conditions of uniformity and a high degree of functional coherence will be facilitated or made more difficult by the form and structure of the area as it now exists. Judging from the record of past state development, it seems likely that the four conditions here outlined will prove significant in the new states.

4

Some Fundamental Elements in the Analysis
of the Viability of States · PRESTON E. JAMES

The analysis of the viability of states is one of the concerns of political geography. A state may be regarded as a politically organized segment of the earth's surface, and viability is a measure of the effectiveness with which a state can be administered to fulfil the purposes for which it was created. Each state must formulate a set of purposes to which the citizens of the state can subscribe, which has the necessary appeal to command widespread support, and which is sufficiently distinct from the purposes formulated by other states. Such a statement of purposes, with which the citizens of a state can identify themselves, constitutes the *state-idea*.[1]

The state-idea is a complex of traditions, experiences, and objectives. It is made up of written history, folklore, stories of national heroes, religious beliefs, and the language and art forms in which these things are communicated. It is the body of literature, the painting, the architecture, the music which are distinctively national. And it is the characteristic economic, social and political institutions. The state is created to defend and develop the state-idea.

The state-idea is not always easy to identify. Political scientists and social anthropologists sometimes provide insights into the elements of a state-idea, but usually do not identify these elements as such. Although the identification of the state-idea requires considerable study of the literature, it also requires direct contacts and close observation within the state itself. It is not easily quantified; yet these attitudes and objectives can be measured, and certainly they can be mapped.[2] Only beginnings have been made to provide anything like a systematic study of the state-ideas of specific countries.[3]

[1] Richard Hartshorne, 'The functional Approach to political geography', *Annals of the Association of American Geographers*, 40, 1950, pp. 95–139; and *idem*, 'Political geography', in P. E. James and C. F. Jones (eds.), *American Geography, Inventory and Prospect*, Syracuse, 1954, pp. 167–225.

[2] Edmund R. Thompson, 'Malaya's state-idea: an application of the unified theory of political geography', unpublished M.A. thesis, Department of Geography, Syracuse University, Syracuse, 1958.

[3] Preston E. James, *Latin America*, 3rd edition, New York, 1959; *idem, An Introduction to Latin America*, New York, 1964; and *idem, One World Divided*, New York, 1964.

34 *Essays in Political Geography*

FORCES FOR INTEGRATION AND DISINTEGRATION

The effectiveness with which a government can fulfil the purposes of a state is a result of the balance between two opposed sets of forces: those of integration and those of disintegration. These forces may be internal or external. In any state, however, there are certain forces leading to unity and coherence, and others that lead toward division and may even threaten the break-up of the state. An analysis of viability involves a discussion of the balance between these forces.

Of course a state with a positive state-idea to which the great majority of the citizens adhere with enthusiasm is a relatively viable state. A positive state-idea, strongly held, can overcome the disintegrative effect of differences of language and religion. In a few states the forces for disintegration are very weak: but in most of the world's states it is necessary to strive not only to defend but also to enlarge the state-idea in the struggle to develop and maintain unity and coherence. The forces for disintegration include competing state-ideas, differences in economic development or differences in political status – as when dependent territories are included within a state.

In the analysis of viability the political geographer focuses attention on the geographic arrangement of the forces for integration and dis-integration. The national territory is first divided into two parts: the part from which the citizens of the state derive a living – namely the *effective national territory;* and the part which remains essentially un-productive and unoccupied. If there is to be a state-idea associated with a segment of the national territory there must be people, for state-ideas exist only in the minds of men. It becomes a matter of importance, therefore, to note whether the effective national territory is arranged in a concentrated area, or is isolated and scattered. Within the effective national territory there may be different and competitive state-ideas. If two competing sets of purposes are intermingled throughout the state area, the disintegrating effect is not great. But if each of two competing sets of purposes each occupies distinct and separate parts of the state area, the disintegrative effect is more difficult to overcome. The most dangerous situation exists when a distinctive state-idea is strongly held by people who occupy only a peripheral part of the national territory. If the state is divided into three or more sections, each with a different state-idea, the situation may be less dangerous than when the state is divided simply into two parts.

Every individual state has its own unique pattern of arrangement of

Analysis of the Viability of States   35

the forces for integration and disintegration, and the analysis of the meaning of these areal differences involves the use of intuitive judgment, which the more scientific members of the geographic profession prefer to avoid. Yet the need for such analysis is clear. To foresee the problems of viability is a matter of great practical importance, and one which would become much less subjective if a body of theory could be formulated.

SOME ILLUSTRATIVE CASES

A few specific examples of the analysis of viability are offered to illustrate the interaction of the forces for integration and disintegration. The great majority of the new states created since the Second World War, like the states into which Latin America was divided during the early part of the nineteenth century, began their independence with purely negative state-ideas. The one purpose to which all citizens subscribed was the demand for freedom from colonial rule. In Latin America, this negative demand for freedom from outside interference in domestic affairs is still a dominant purpose. In Haiti, the people will support their state only if it provides the greatest possible freedom even from interference by the government in the lives of individual citizens. A major problem in Latin America, as in many other of the world's cultural regions, will be to transform negative state-ideas into positive ones. It was the lack of a state-idea that caused the failure of the Federation of the West Indies, for in this case no set of purposes was formulated that was powerful enough to overcome the state-ideas of Jamaica and Trinidad.

There are numerous countries where strong state-ideas provide coherence, and a high degree of viability. Examples that come to mind of strongly integrated states, in which the forces of disintegration are weak, are Uruguay and Sweden. In each of these states there is a concentrated area of settlement, and a unity of language and religion. Yet Sweden is an old state, with a long historical tradition, whereas Uruguay has become a strongly integrated state only in the present century. In Switzerland a powerful state-idea compensates for marked differences of language, religion and economy, yet this kind of state-idea would perhaps have been less effective in the creation of coherence had it not been for the position of the Swiss territory astride the pass routes between segments of the middle part of Charlemagne's empire. Similarly in Belgium the state-idea compensates for differences of language and religion in a particular kind of geographic position.

Three examples may be offered to illustrate the effect of divergent

36 *Essays in Political Geography*

state-ideas in different geographic patterns. In the case of Spain, the north-eastern territories which comprise Catalonia not only use a different language, but have a notably different historical tradition. Catalonia was a part of Charlemagne's empire, and remained mostly free from Muslim rule. In modern times Barcelona has become an industrial city, having felt the full impact of the ideas of the Industrial Revolution, while most of the rest of Spain remained untouched by these events. The result was a strongly divergent state-idea in a peripheral part of the national territory. The forces of disintegration were overcome by civil war and the state was held together by force.

In Brazil, on the other hand, the pattern of divergent state-ideas has not led to civil war. Divergence in Brazil is a result of the rapid economic development of São Paulo in comparison with the rest of the country. If São Paulo were located on the periphery of the national territory it is not impossible that the forces for disintegration would have resulted in a break-up of the state: but there has never been an example of the centre of a state breaking away from the periphery.

The third example can be taken from the historical political geography of the United States. Before 1840, the national territory was divided into three distinct political areas. There was the industrialized north-east, which was in favour of tariff protection for new industries, and opposed to slavery. There was the north-west – a frontier region of pioneer settlement, seeking a market for lumber and hogs down-river to New Orleans, and interested in expansion westward. And there was the south – with its plantations of cotton and tobacco worked by negro slaves, which favoured free trade. But between 1840 and 1860 the north-east and the north-west were linked by railroads and highways, and the products of each section found a market in the other. The national territory was divided sharply into the north and the south, each with a notably divergent state-idea. The result was civil war. Since that time a large number of new sections have appeared, and the south itself is no longer a unit. The result is an increase in the degree of viability.

In some cases the integration of diverse elements is brought about as a result of conditions outside the national territory. Israel, populated by Jewish settlers from some seventy different countries, includes the greatest variety of ingredients. To be sure, there is the common purpose of defending the Jewish religion.[1] But the development of a coherent

---

[1] Editor's note: Nevertheless Israel is a secular state, and its Ministry of Religious Affairs has departments for the Christian, Muslim and Druze minority communities, as well as for the Jewish faith.

Analysis of the Viability of States 37

Jewish state is at least in part the result of pressures from a hostile Arab world in which Israel is embedded. In the case of Tsarist Russia, on the other hand, not only was there a notably weak state-idea, but also the power of the central authority was weak. The inclusion of so large a segment of the earth's surface in one state can be interpreted in part as the result of isolation from outside pressures. Even today there are very few routes of communication crossing the Soviet borders all the way from the Caspian Sea to the Pacific. In isolation from the rest of the world, the Soviet state with its powerful state-idea of developing a communist society, has overcome the disintegrated effect of diverse nationalities located in peripheral positions.

In no other culture region is the need for the formulation of positive state-ideas more critical than in Africa south of the Sahara. A large number of new states of small size have been created, mostly with only the negative state-idea of escaping from colonial status. Furthermore, most of the new states are superimposed on a pattern of tribal areas, including numerous separate tribes in each new state, and often leaving certain tribes to form parts of neighbouring states. Yet in much of Africa the basic loyalties are still to the tribe. Each new state, if it is to become viable, must formulate a state-idea powerful enough to over-come the disintegrative effect of tribal loyalties, and distinct enough from the state-ideas of neighbouring states to command the support of the citizens. The task, with some notable exceptions, would seem almost impossible to carry out. We may expect, therefore, to see the political map of Africa change considerably in the years ahead, with new com-binations of territory, perhaps with new federations to which several of the smaller states can adhere.

5

Political Organizations at Higher Ranks

W. GORDON EAST

'The theory of nationality, therefore, is a retrograde step in history.' LORD ACTON

'En fait, l'union politique de l'Europe est déjà commencée.' *La Communauté Européenne en Marche 1950–63*

The present international world witnesses on the one hand the hey-day of the independent state and on the other a no less marked trend towards the forging of international organizations at a higher level. These two trends might appear to be diametrically opposed, the one being politically disintegrative, the other integrative. Are they to be conceived of as independent and parallel movements, or is the second merely a reaction to the first? In either case, both processes have been and continue to be vigorous: even though the pressures towards independent statehood have much relaxed since they have largely achieved their objects, they have not yet wholly spent their force. While the apparently counterpoise movement towards the closer association of groups of states has already made effective progress, it may well be still at an early stage of its activity. How will the world political map reshape itself in the decades ahead under the effects of these revolutionary movements? There are complex problems here, to the understanding of which political geography may seek to contribute.

THE PROLIFERATION OF NEWLY INDEPENDENT STATES

'Decolonization' is a novel term imported from France, yet the process to which it relates is old enough and well attested by the events – for the most part violent – which produced the independent states of North and South America by stages after 1776. The new term may be justified by the relatively pacific character of the twentieth-century process, yet it compares closely with, and is no less revolutionary than, that designated as 'national self-determination' after the First World War.[1] Behind these movements has lurked continually the political force of

[1] C. E. Carrington, 'Decolonization: the last stages', *International Affairs*, 38, 1962, pp. 219–40.

40 Essays in Political Geography

'nationalism', although this has not always been evidently present. While 'nationality' has been a recognizable fact of the more developed societies throughout history – a Roman citizen might well have been, for example, a Briton, a Gaul or a Greek – the 'nation', as the focus of political sentiment and ambition, is a relatively new development, and 'nationalism', the political expression of a national group, was long held in check as a dangerous and politically fissiparous force. Vigorous and vociferous nationalism no doubt goes far to explain the emergence of many new states, the peoples of which were formerly contained within multi-national empires, in every continent. However, the principle 'one

TABLE 5.1: THE NUMBER OF INDEPENDENT STATES BY CONTINENTS

	Europe*	North America†	South America	Middle America‡	Asia	Africa	Austral-asia	World
1914	26	1	10	9	6	2	0	54
1937	33	3	10	10	11	4	2	73
1964	34	3	10	12	26	36	3§	124

* Including the U.S.S.R., Turkey and four microstates sovereign in status; the additions by 1964 were Iceland, Cyprus, Malta and the German Democratic Republic; the subtractions were Estonia, Latvia and Lithuania.
† Including Cuba.
‡ Including Mexico.
§ The addition here is Western Samoa, formerly held by New Zealand, but independent since 1964.

nation one state' has not been the only principle applied. Many of the new states are markedly multi-national (for example Yugoslavia, Czechoslovakia, India and Malaysia), and in Africa it has seldom been clear that nationalism applies, given the existence of tribally organized groups and of nationalities not yet transmuted into self-conscious nations.

The disintegrative effect of decolonization leaps to the eye and can be shown by arithmetic, simple and yet not without the difficulty of deciding what precisely to add. During the last fifty years the number of sovereign states has more than doubled: the increase was striking after the First World War, much greater after the Second World War, and most rapid in and after 1960. At its inception in 1945 the membership of the United Nations Organization was only 45; and in 1964 it

Political Organizations at Higher Ranks 41

had risen to 113 – and for various reasons this figure falls short of the world total of so-called sovereign states. In 1914 politically dependent states characterized the political maps of Africa, Asia, Australasia and indeed much of the Americas. Even in Europe, the birthplace of the sovereign state, the Irish and the Poles especially were then acutely aware of their dependency. By 1937, although Europe had generated new national states and although, in North America and Australasia, Cuba and the British Dominions had attained full sovereignity, little such change had been effected in Africa but rather more in Asia. Table 5.1 measures the advances made in the several continents during the last fifty years.

Only two brief comments need be made here on this Table. First, South America stands out as being among the earliest to shed the disadvantages – and advantages – of dependency, secondly, the remarkable change in Africa (Fig. 5.1) and Asia relate primarily to the transfers of power made by the United Kingdom and France, although the advent of the independent Philippines (in 1946) and the emergence of Indonesia (in 1949) should also be noted.

Although the two great wars of this century inevitably required at their conclusion some reshaping of the political map of the world, this process of change was achieved, on the one hand, by internal pressures, nationalistic or pseudo-nationalistic in character, and, on the other, was stimulated (for divergent reasons) after the Second World War by the two greatest powers, both victors in that war. This last aspect has special interest here in that it points out the new role of continentally based states. Both the United States and the U.S.S.R. control sub-continental territories; both carried out their imperialism very largely in areas contiguous to their original political core-areas. In each case territorial expansion was effected in modern times and towards the Pacific and Arctic coasts, involving both the occupation and settlement of relatively empty areas and successful confrontation with politically organized occupants already there. In each case too a federal solution was established to bring order and unity to societies remarkably multi-national in character, largely produced in the one case by a policy of immigration but in the other inherited from the historical past. Whereas most of the many empires that have disintegrated in this century – those of the British, French, German, Dutch, Spanish, Belgian and Italian – controlled discontinuous territories, being in varying degrees 'sea states', the 'empires' of the United States and the Soviet Union which have survived lie compactly in one piece within sub- or inter-continental

42 *Essays in Political Geography*

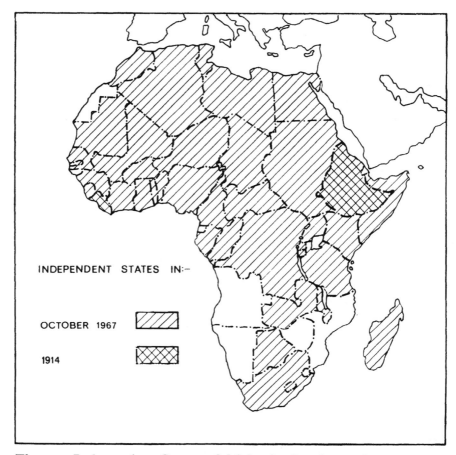

Fig. 5.1. Independent States of Africa in October 1967
Among the African areas left white are the two problem areas of Southwest Africa and Rhodesia: the former is de facto part of the South Africa Republic and the latter has illegally proclaimed its independence as a republic.

frames. However, two empires with continuous territories – the long-lived Ottoman and the Austro-Hungarian – also collapsed and broke up, since in these cases centrifugal tendencies had been accelerated through their defeat in the First World War.

Admittedly, the usual political connotation of 'imperialism' does not easily apply to the United States of the 1960s except perhaps for murmurs in the south, where individual states may at times descry federal erosion of state powers. As to the Soviet Union, writers deserving of attention are not lacking who, forgetful of Portugal, see there the last surviving empire. But while noting the evident contrasts between the

Political Organizations at Higher Ranks 43

U.S.A. and the U.S.S.R. in political ideas, attitudes and organization – which may be summed up in the contrasting senses of 'democratic' on the two sides of the Iron Curtain – it is a matter of importance, and one worth further enquiry, that the two political giants of today present in their territorial posture so much in common. It is enough here to note that in each case a viable system has been applied to associate in working unity citizens diverse in national origin[1] and indeed in ethnic type: a political solution which has never been achieved in Europe west of the U.S.S.R. despite its millennial history of occupation and settlement.

The United States and the U.S.S.R. are not of course the only cases, though certainly the most outstanding ones, of states which have successfully organized many distinct national groups. Other examples leap to the mind, notably that of Czechoslovakia. About a third of mankind is so organized and, in addition, there are many more who live in states where a single dominant national group exists in relative harmony with other minority groups: such are, for example, the United Kingdom, Spain, Rumania, Turkey, Pakistan and Iraq. 'Relative harmony' is not always in evidence, and the cohesion and strength of such states may be challenged from time to time, as when French Canadians, Kurds in Iraq, or Turks in Cyprus see threats to their national identity. The bulk of the 124 independent states of 1964, including therein over 50 states newly emerged since 1945, represent only approaches to the concept of the homogeneous national state, freed of the difficulties and the advantages of more nationally heterogeneous societies. They range in numerical scale from the territorial vastness of India, Algeria, Sudan and Libya to the smallness of Gambia, Trinidad and Tobago, Malta and Western Samoa. Similarly, and sometimes in inverse ratio to their areas, their populations descend from the 470 millions of the Indian Union to the mere hundreds of thousands of Cyprus, Malta, Gambia and Iceland. And they chart their independent courses at a time when political and military power is concentrated above all in the hands of the two dominant multi-national states.

While having achieved their immediate end, independent statehood, the new states, together with those of older vintage, take pride in having control of their own cultural development under political systems and leaders of their choice, and see promise in their membership of the

[1] It should also be noted, however, that whereas in the U.S.S.R. the diversity of nationality originated from the past extension of Russian control over peoples of non-Russian nationality, the diverse peoples who came to settle in the United States, with the exception of the indigenous Indians and the forcibly imported negroes, did so of their own free will.

44 *Essays in Political Geography*

United Nations Organization where the stronger states vie for their support, it is no less clear that they face numerous difficulties incidental to their relative weakness. These result from the basic reality of modern life that resources, skills, manpower and productivity are so unevenly spread and also from the factor of geographical position which can exert a powerful effect. While imperialism in its former cast has largely gone, there remains the power which once sustained it – financial and commercial strength – and this still accrues to certain states. There remain too, in increased number, the backward states, however much we may try by euphemisms to conceal them as 'underdeveloped' or 'developing'. To some states, formally independent, the terms 'satellite' or 'buffer' clearly apply, bearing the implication that their political independence is far from absolute. The inefficiency, indeed absurdity, of the small state as an economic unit, hedged around by tariff walls against its neighbours and others, was exposed by European experience between the wars. The interdependence of the countries of the world, through trade and other exchanges, calls for ever-strengthening relationships between them, while the swings of the market inject continuing risks to the budgets of states with one major export commodity, be it rubber, cocoa, cotton or coffee. And although in their weakness states are not in fact today threatened with extinction by the more powerful, in their search for security they have to make difficult decisions – as between walking the tight-rope of neutralism, falling victim to 'neo-colonialism' so-called, and joining the bandwaggon of one or other of the leading communist powers.[1] In short, most of the states of today, being independent units, are singularly unprepared for the modern world at a time when accelerated means of communication and transport and advances in science and technology and in the provision of sources of mechanical energy all put a premium on the highly developed and extensive state which alone can maximize the material benefits now within grasp.

THE TREND TOWARDS INTERNATIONAL ASSOCIATION

National sovereignty, achieved in fine frenzy, confronts a world not a little disenchanted by its effects on international relations, such as those shown in Europe during the last fifty years. The many states, the territories of which make so curious a pattern on the world map, are parts

[1] Thus Mongolia faces a choice between the U.S.S.R. and the Chinese People's Republic.

Political Organizations at Higher Ranks 45

of a world community where living invites and involves interdependence at many points of common interest. At the least, co-operation between states is a requirement; at best, and offering greater promise, close association seems called for. Already 11 per cent of all independent states are federally organized and testify that this principle can conform to a valid state-idea. These federal states comprise more than a third of mankind and include the two strongest and many of the largest states. But federations offer no easy short cut to wider and wiser state units: so easily conceived in the mind or as blue prints, they survive and flourish only where they rest on a solid base of common interest and desires. The disassembled pieces of the jigsaw patterns of empire may seek to rearrange themselves into new larger coherent wholes. But it is not yet wholly clear that all the pieces themselves are units: will Sudan, for example, succeed in holding together its Semitic and Muslim majority and its minority of negroid Christians in the south? Will Nigeria, notwithstanding the care taken before the transfer of power, effectively maintain its federal structure? It may be recalled how Simon Bolivar's forward-looking attempt to maintain the Colombian Union failed to survive his lifetime. Some of the more recent efforts to create unions or federations of new states have miscarried, while others now suffer threatening pressures. Thus the United Arab Republic exists only in name; the Central African Federation, despite its apparent economic rationality, collapsed through the conflict of political ideas and aspirations; the Arab Federation of Iraq and Jordan and the Federation of Mali and Senegal were short-lived, and the West Indies Federation also did not win enough local support long to survive its take-off.[1] Malaysia's interesting attempt to combine its many racial groups faced challenges from outside and failed owing to the secession of Singapore, and the South Arabian Federation also faces both internal and external pressures. Dubiously, on the credit side of the ledger, one lists Tanzania and the Union of Ghana, Guinea and Mali.

Such developments represent growth from grass roots and may be expected to continue. More ambitious structures have however appeared which have fittingly been called 'political organizations at higher ranks'. The shorthand for this phrase is 'blocs', or more precisely 'international blocs'. In this context 'bloc' is aptly defined in Webster's *New International Dictionary*, 1937, as 'a combination of persons, or interests, usually inharmonious, but temporarily drawn together by a common

[1] See E. H. Dale, 'The state-idea: missing prop of the West Indies Federation', *The Scottish Geographical Magazine*, 78, 1962, pp. 166–76.

46 Essays in Political Geography

cause'. Even though this word is relatively new, it signifies a phenomenon which has been variously visible at many points of historical time. There have been the many defensive alliances between states, under the leadership of 'great powers', designed to secure a 'balance of power'. There have been the imperial structures built up on a dynastic principle such as the Austro-Hungarian empire, or others where military power created and maintained an uneasy association of many national groups. There were others also of varying scale, the permanence of which must have seemed at times doubtful, which have nevertheless proved their durability: witness the Swiss Confederation and the United States of America. The blocs of today reveal points of comparison with those of the past: in that some are primarily either military or economic, some are freely entered into, while in others an element of coercion is no less evident. Although the blocs of today show wide variety and although each is doubtless unique, they tend to express the desire to create variously functional units, usually on a regional basis, and for purposes not only of defence but also for those clearly cultural, economic, and political. The use of the terms 'community' and 'integration' illustrates this higher ambition towards really close association; yet there remain elements of uncertainty as to agreed goals and a mixture of idealism tempered by pragmatism. In so far as, with the European Economic Community, the political goal of integration is clearly envisaged, a new and revolutionary note is struck in that a challenge is thrown down to the outworn concept of national sovereignty. Should such goals become widely conceivable, through the effective functioning of political blocs, mankind would be attempting again to pursue the ultimate ideal of the unification of one fraternal world such as Buddhism, Christianity and Islam tried but failed to create.[1]

BLOCS OF MANY KINDS

An attempt to review existing blocs should seek to establish the reasons for their origin, their composition, their purpose and degree of cohesion, and lastly their achievements and prospects.

The United Nations Organization is clearly the most comprehensive and the most ambitious of the present blocs. Its successful launching owed much to good timing: it was created under the aegis of the victorious belligerents of the Second World War before the actual fighting was over. Its purpose was to establish a peaceful international society

[1] Cf. Max Sorre, *L'Homme sur la Terre*, Paris, 1961, p. 239.

Political Organizations at Higher Ranks 47

by providing means to settle international disputes and to prevent outbreaks of war. Certainly it approaches universality by representing almost all sovereign states: its membership fails to include Switzerland, which does not wish to join, those states too small to share its major responsibilities, several others where political difficulties still obtrude – the two Germanies, the two Koreas and the two Vietnams, and the Chinese People's Republic – and for a while one other, Indonesia, which was the first to withdraw but has subsequently returned. While the composition of the Security Council was designed to respect the realities of political power, the absence of Mainland China necessarily weakens its representative and world stature. The Assembly combines representatives of states remarkably different in every respect – population numbers, stage of material culture, political organization, ideology and military strength. The United Nations has registered successes in checking military aggression in Korea and has intervened – in the Belgian Congo and in Cyprus – to hold the ring until durable settlements can be reached. It has carried out very much quietly effective work of a technical kind through its many Agencies. Yet the common denominator of political agreement is low, even though it provides the vent for considerable expression of divergent views on international affairs. Rather it exposes the many political differences which divide the world. Moreover, it tends to resolve into many blocs of varying scale and strength. Since the states of Africa and Asia make up rather more than half the total membership, the Afro-Asian bloc, for example, can appear at least numerically strong. After twenty years of useful, if uneasy activity, the United Nations bids fair to endure although it abundantly demonstrates the impracticability of world unity and the need for regional organizations at higher ranks.

Next in scale of membership stands the Commonwealth which may be dated from 1931 when the Statute of Westminster established the complete independence of the former 'Dominions' of Canada, Australia, New Zealand and South Africa. Its growth has been remarkable, keeping pace with successive stages in the liquidation of the British Empire, so that its membership in 1965 is put at 22. Former exposure to, and experience of, British rule contributed one common factor, as do also the wide use of the English language and (in varying degrees) of English law and political institutions, and membership (except for Canada) of the sterling bloc. Some[1] have regretted that the Commonwealth did not

[1] See C. E. Carrington, *The Liquidation of the British Empire*, London, 1961, pp. 28–30. This idea is attributed to T. E. Lawrence.

48 *Essays in Political Geography*

try to achieve a yet wider membership by including certain Middle Eastern countries formerly mandated to Britain.

The Commonwealth contains an inner core of countries bound together with some closeness by community of kith and ideas – the United Kingdom, Canada, Australia and New Zealand. However, the bulk of its population is now neither British nor Christian. Its areal extent and demographic weight are striking enough: the latter accounts for between 20 and 25 per cent of world population, being distributed in every continent. For some observers[1] the Commonwealth is a myth or an idea rather than a political reality. What strength it has derives from the fact that its members have freely chosen to stay together. It rests on a substratum of many personal, business, professional and educational relationships which offer convenience and advantage to its membership. The use of sterling for financial and commercial operations has proved useful though not without imposing strain on the United Kingdom. There are day-to-day exchanges of information from London on matters of common interest, and periodically formal discussions are organized which test the highest skills in chairmanship. It is not without importance that membership of the Commonwealth implies friendly relations between members and some measure of mutual support: these are not however invariably forthcoming – witness the protracted Kashmir dispute which led to war in 1965 and still divides India and Pakistan. Clearly also the problem posed by Rhodesia threatened the unity and survival of the Commonwealth as it is now constituted. In so far as it subscribes to a common programme on international relations, this might seem to lie – though again not invariably – in the pursuit of peace, individual liberty and the rule of law.

The Commonwealth constitutes neither a political nor a military bloc. Nor can it be reckoned a 'great power' since it lacks both the community of policy and the degree of political organization which would be necessary to sustain it. There is no common defensive organization for the Commonwealth as a whole, although non-neutralist members confer on defence and certain alliances seek security for parts: thus Canada and the United Kingdom are linked in NATO, while the United Kingdom has treaty obligations to defend Malayia. Indeed the security and functioning of the Commonwealth owe much to the United States; this is clear when note is taken of American obligations under NATO, SEATO and the ANZUS Pact. Certainly the Commonwealth faces many

[1] See H. Seton-Watson, *Nationalism and Communism: Essays 1946–63*, London, 1964, p. 242.

Political Organizations at Higher Ranks 49

threatening problems, notably those of racialism and neutralism. But it has shown the ability, despite the many continuing difficulties which it has faced or faces, to turn difficult corners and yet survive: thus it had sufficient strength and statesmanship to require South Africa's withdrawal in 1961, and it weathered the earlier shock of Britain's Suez war of 1956. Here, then, is one of the widest yet loosest of blocs and one that has grown freely and naturally. It has a certain interest too in that it brings together a medley of nations and creeds, the rich and the poor, the highly developed and the materially backward nations in need of material aid. And it commands a collective wisdom which may be used when serious political problems arise.

The Organization of American States resembles the Commonwealth in that it has one obvious leader and senior partner superior to each of the others in economic, political and military stature; in this respect it contrasts with the Union of African States led by Ethiopia. It is a vast inter-continental confederation of twenty-one states with a population exceeding 400 million. It is very much the outcome of United States' policy and, although it emerged only in 1948, the seeds were planted long ago with the Monroe Doctrine that the Americas should hold themselves aloof from the political intrusion of European powers. Indeed the rejection of European imperialism and the adoption of republican forms of government provide one common ideological basis to O.A.S. Its purposes are, through closer association, the better to maintain independence and security, to settle disputes between members, and to promote peaceful collaboration and economic development. The inter-continental unity of the pattern of O.A.S. is broken only by the gaps left by Canada, Cuba and a few small politically dependent territories. Canadian statesmen have tended to take the view that, as a 'middle power', which shoulders its own difficult yet important responsibilities, Canada can be more useful in international affairs outside the confederation.[1] Unlike most of the American republics, Canada (a kingdom) regards itself as an extension of Europe which it did not reject. Taking a more pragmatic and less ideological view of world affairs, and while linked closely with the United States by financial, commercial and defence arrangements, it retains links with the world through its membership of the Commonwealth, O.E.C.D. and NATO, and is able to retain more independence of policy than would be possible if it joined O.A.S. Cuba was excluded from O.A.S. by a majority vote of the Council, after

[1] John W. Holmes, 'The diplomacy of a middle power', *The Atlantic* (Special Supplement on Canada), 214, November 1964, pp. 100–64.

50 Essays in Political Geography

the confrontation of the United States and Cuba in 1962. O.A.S. functions effectively with the aid of an inter-American Conference, a Council, and a Secretariat – the Pan-American Union – with headquarters at Washington. That it has a certain solidarity and strength is shown by the way in which its members backed the United States during the Cuba crisis when, with dubious regard to its NATO commitments, Canada is reported to have refused the use of Canadian territory to United States forces armed with nuclear weapons.[1] The sheer dominance, in respect of both financial and military power, of the leading member, with which lies the principal responsibility for defence, together with the sharp cultural differences between Anglo and Latin America, combine to impose a break on any movement towards complete political integration. The recent creation by treaty of a Central American Common Market and a Latin American Free Trade Association augurs well for some reduction of state sovereignty in the interests of wider regional association. Doubtless the major difficulties and dangers which lie ahead relate to the internal social and economic problems of the Latin American States[2] which, though early freed from colonial status, were unprepared for self-government and remain politically immature. At least O.A.S. presents a framework within which they may wrestle with their attempts to achieve economic development and social and political stability.

In contrast to the Commonwealth and O.A.S., the Arab League would appear to rest firmly on a common cultural basis, namely that of 'Arabism'. The member countries share a common history and language, and for the great majority of their peoples Islam prescribes a common pattern of social behaviour as well as a religion. Membership of the Arab League, which was founded in 1945, now includes thirteen countries in Africa and the Near East, constituting a continuous area of nearly 4 million square miles (Fig. 5.2) but containing a population of only around 100 millions, and only a modest fraction of all Muslims. Clearly its objective is the collective security and economic and cultural advancement of its peoples. In contrast to both the Commonwealth and O.A.S., the League lacks any one dominant industrial state. However Egypt, the most industrialized of the members, provides the leadership, personified in President Nasser. The intrusion into these countries of Western territorial concepts of nationalism has been deplored as a

---

[1] *The Times*, 2 February 1963.

[2] See Sir George Bolton, 'Problems of economic development in Latin America', *International Affairs*, 39, 1963, pp. 184–97.

Political Organizations at Higher Ranks 51

disruptive and irrelevant force in countries linked by Arabism and chequered by minorities. Former political attachment to either Britain or France introduced some differentiation in attitudes and relationships, as does also the presence or absence of oilfields, although these provide the opportunity to finance development plans.

Pan-Arabism, which the League was created to promote, has been called 'a tragic and spectacular failure'.[1] Certainly the League has proved to be neither strong nor effective in pursuit of its common interests, chief of which is its enmity of Israel. It has shown some success in maintaining a neutralist position as between the U.S.S.R. and the Western countries with which, because of its oil interests, it is closely related. The union of Egypt with Syria and Yemen, with which other Arab countries might have been expected to federate, proved shortlived. The birth of the Arab Common Market early in 1964, linking Egypt with Iraq, Jordan, Syria and Kuwait, is an interesting development, though it does not envisage free inter-migration, and links countries of competitive rather than complementary production. The Arab boycott of Israel is negative and unsuccessful, while the Arab attitude towards Israel over the use of the Jordan waters appears largely obstructive. The lack of unity in the League was also exposed by the divergent attitudes of the Arab countries in 1965 towards the formal recognition of the German Democratic Republic and the related proposal to break off diplomatic relations with the German Federal Republic. For Algeria there was the difficulty that it is an associate member of E.E.C. More promising aspects of recent League activities are the creation of the Kuwait Fund for Arab economic development and the setting up of a committee to study Beduin problems. Even though the Arab League lacks cohesion and firmness of purpose, except *vis à vis* Israel, geographical difficulties both physical and social, clearly militate against political integration – sheer area, desert expanses, territorial distension (Fig. 5.2), and the variant levels of material culture of city and country populations separately clustered and distant from one another. Geographically the extension of the League's territories along the Mediterranean–Red Sea route and at the head of the Persian Gulf is broken only by those of Israel, Aden and certain British-protected sheikhdoms.

[1] See John Major, 'The search for Arab unity', *International Affairs*, 39, 1963, pp. 551–63. Major emphasizes the inner rivalries within the League and notes the weakening effect of the power of veto held by members of the Council. There have been withdrawals from, and returns to, the League by Iraq and Tunisia.

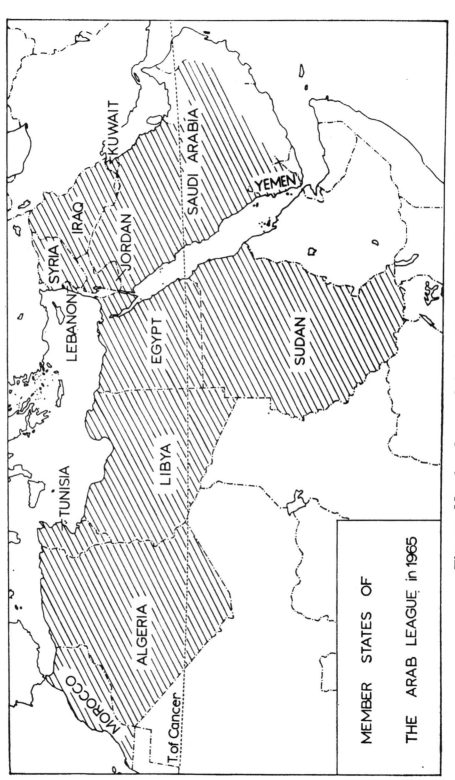

Fig. 5.2. Member States of the Arab League in 1965

Political Organizations at Higher Ranks 53

Another group of blocs can be classified as major alliances based on the principle of collective defence against communist pressures. A feature common to these is the membership of the United States as protagonist of what is variously (and loosely) called the 'Western', 'Free', or 'Democratic' world; the United Kingdom and France also play their part in them. These blocs which are consistent with the United Nations charter, are regionally located and of wider coverage than those of the past. Thus NATO combines the two states of North America and ten of Western Europe, but, conceiving the Mediterranean Sea as an extension of the Atlantic, includes also Italy, Greece and Turkey, which is now accepted as a European country.[1] NATO is of interest on several counts. It exposes the need of the United States to search for security at long range; it exposes no less the political division of Europe along the line of the Iron Curtain and the dependence of Western Europe on American military power to help balance that of the U.S.S.R. (Fig. 5.3).

While NATO would appear to have succeeded in its main purpose – the maintenance of peace in Europe – less headway has been made with its deeper aspiration towards the formation of an Atlantic Community. CENTO, in contrast, attempts to bring a measure of stability to the Middle East, with which the U.S.S.R. makes contact along its frontiers with Turkey and Iran, by organizing for collective defence Turkey, Iran and Pakistan with the United States, Britain and France. This regional system is weakened somewhat by the withdrawal of Iraq, although it is clearly linked with that of NATO by the presence of the American Sixth Fleet in the Mediterranean. SEATO seeks, in effect, to check the direct or indirect expansion of Communist China, while ANZUS provides an outer defence system which includes Australia as a major base.

The Warsaw Treaty Organization was created in 1955 in reaction to NATO and is a similar defensive bloc comprising the U.S.S.R. and its European communist neighbours, namely Eastern Germany, Czechoslovakia, Hungary, Rumania, Bulgaria and Albania. Its cohesion and strength depend primarily on the Red Army, although it has forged close commercial relationships, notably by trade, with the U.S.S.R. The twice-yearly meetings between the members, however, were suspended between June 1963 and January 1965 when Albania did not

[1] In 1949 Turkey was admitted to membership of the Council of Europe and in 1963 to associate membership of the European Economic Community. Since 'Europe' owes its identity primarily to cultural facts and since many European nations derive from Asiatic intruders, the admittance of Turkey to Europe challenges only geographic convention.

54 *Essays in Political Geography*

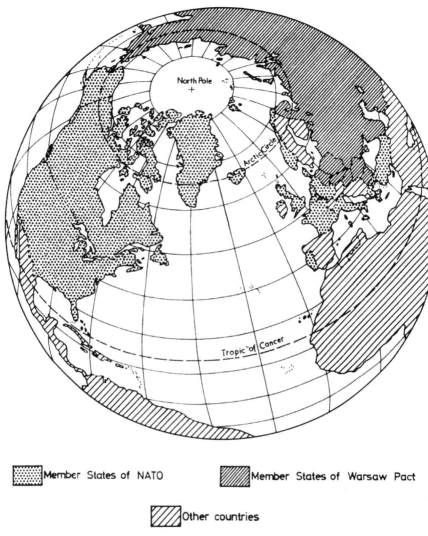

Fig. 5.3. **Member States of NATO and the Warsaw Pact**

attend the Warsaw meeting. The completion of the 'Friendship' oil pipeline in September 1964, which brings Volga–Ural oil to Hungary, Czechoslovakia, Poland and Eastern Germany, is a positive contribution to the economies of member countries, though it indicates no less the U.S.S.R.'s efforts to associate them more closely to itself. There is also an economic backing to this alliance in COMECON or C.M.E.A. (The Council for Mutual Economic Aid), membership of which also includes the Mongolian People's Republic but not Albania which re-

Political Organizations at Higher Ranks 55

signed in December 1962. COMECON has sought to promote trade between communist countries and to apply a policy of economic rationalization to the development plans of the constituent states, within which industrial revolutions are taking place, but faces difficulties, chiefly that of nationalism. COMECON weathered the storms induced by national feeling in 1956 in Hungary, Poland and Eastern Germany, and this now encourages Rumania to pursue its own alternative plans. Thus nationalism, which was thought by Bolshevik leaders to be an outmoded and dying creed, has proved and remains an assertive and divisive force in the Eastern as well as the Western World. The longer-term prospect of a more closely bound political organization at higher rank in Eastern Europe, of which the Soviet Union would be the dominant unit and the begetter, should be envisaged. It would not be in any sense a novel structure since it would be likely to accord with similar empires of the past. That is not to say that it might not offer substantial advantages, as also doubtless drawbacks, to the nations thus brought together.

Lastly, in Europe west of the Iron Curtain also, much energy has been expended on bloc-building, and it is here that one – the European Economic Community – bids fair to become a new super-state. As in the 1920s, so in 1945, Europe appeared 'an outstandingly manifold, outstandingly riven structure' but some dividing lines were then (as they remain) particularly sharp, notably that between Western and Eastern Europe which involves also the political division of Germany. Mitteleuropa, for a time the political centre of gravity, has disappeared as a political force and Europe as a whole has been overshadowed by the growing power of the U.S.A. to the west and the U.S.S.R. to the east. The devastation of the war, coupled with the loss of overseas dependencies, seemed to indicate the absolute fall of Western Europe no less inescapably than its relative decline *vis à vis* the U.S.A. and the U.S.S.R. Yet in and after the 1950s Western Europe made remarkable economic progress, thanks not only to its own energies, but also to the enlightened Marshall Aid Plan. Doubtless the fear of further Soviet westward expansion, and the encouragement and indispensable security provided by the United States through NATO have contributed to the trend towards the closer association of West European states which are no longer appropriate units, either for defence or for large-scale production. As for defence and diplomacy, so also for modern industry, science and technology, the best frameworks within which to operate are much larger than those of West European states. Western Europe fostered its economic recovery by means of the Organization for European Economic

56 *Essays in Political Geography*

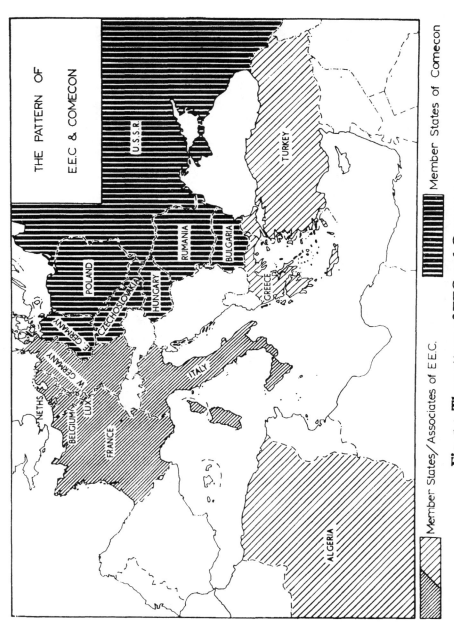

Fig. 5.4. The pattern of EEC and Comecon

Political Organizations at Higher Ranks 57

Co-operation, in which eighteen nations joined. With the addition of three new members – the United States, Canada and Japan – this has become since 1961, the Organization for European Co-operation and Development which aims to promote world trade and economic growth, to raise living standards in member and non-member countries, and thus to narrow the gap between the industrialized and less developed nations. But O.E.E.C. and O.E.C.D. have sought specific objectives and can do no more than prepare the ground for closer political association.

The Council of Europe, which was set up in Strasbourg in 1949 as an attempt to promote the idea of European unity, has an Assembly representing eighteen countries of Western and Southern Europe and a Council of Foreign Ministers. Although it boasts a flag and sponsors much broadly cultural work, it has proved wholly unequal to its political task, mainly because its Council requires unamimity of decisions. Similarly, EFTA exists primarily to stimulate trade exchanges between its members and does not aim at political integration. In contrast, the organizations which have related activities of the six West European countries[1] – the European Coal and Steel Community, EURATOM and the European Economic Community (the Common Market) – have proved politically strong as well as successful: certain aspects of their organization, achievement and objectives deserve attention here since they have political and even geopolitical implications.

E.E.C. appears to mark a turning point in history away from the narrow and mutually opposed nationalisms which for so long and so restrictively flourished in Europe. It rests on a close collaboration between France and Germany which dramatically replaces their historic enmity. Its conception combines appreciation of the material interests of participants with an imaginative belief in the promise of international collaboration. While it is first and foremost a well organized economic bloc, which is creating by stages a common market, it is potentially, too (as its members visualize), a new multi-national state of the future. In this respect E.E.C. recalls, as it may come to illustrate, Lord Acton's view[2] a century ago that 'Those States are substantially the most perfect which include distinct nationalities without oppressing them' and that 'The combination of different nationalities in one State is as necessary a condition of civilized life as the combination of man in Society'.

---

[1] *I.e.* France, the German Federal Republic, Italy and the three Benelux countries (Belgium, the Netherlands, Luxemburg).

[2] Lord Acton, 'Essay on nationality', 1862, *The History of Freedom and other Essays*, London, 1919, pp. 290 and 298.

58 Essays in Political Geography

The Treaty of Rome in 1957 notably subscribed to wide objectives but also outlines a clear and phased programme, prescribing the institutions necessary to effect it. The wider objectives included a new and important role for a united Europe in world affairs, the admittance of more full members and associate members; associate membership was to be offered to – among others – newly independent states formerly dependencies of France, Belgium, the Netherlands and Italy. The more specific aim to be achieved during the 12-15 year transitional period was to create a common market within a common external tariff system. The Assembly, High Authority (with independent powers) and Court of Justice, which had been established already for the European Coal and Steel Community, were available for E.E.C., but a new executive – the Common Market Commission – was so conceived that, though subject to a Council of Ministers of the six countries, it could become strong and efficient. The Commission is made up of nine members who are chosen, independently of their governments, on the grounds of their personal competence as administrators; not more than two of these may be nationals of any one of the six countries.

It must be admitted that the Treaty of Rome set its sights high: to devise and to apply common policies on industry, transport, energy and agriculture, to establish a common monetary system and to facilitate labour mobility within a community of six countries variously differentiated, in each of which marked regional contrasts of social and economic life exist, clearly impose a gigantic task. Even so, much has been accomplished during the ensuing years and many hurdles have been successfully passed. E.E.C. has more than kept to its set programme and it should have created its common market by 1968. Clearly, too, it has justified itself economically by becoming the greatest trading unit in the world, by considerable increase in industrial production (37 per cent during the first five years of 1958–62), and even by reaching agreement on the thorny problem of agricultural policy. It has not, however, grown at all in membership although it has acquired associates in Greece and Turkey and in no less than 20 countries (18 in Africa) formerly dependent on one or other of its member countries. To these it can offer trade advantages and investment funds. Further, it has already become in some degree a supra-national entity: by 1962 the diplomatic representatives of 34 countries were accredited to it at Brussels, its headquarters.

Doubtless the political implication of E.E.C. raises many doubts and problems, even though much is clear about its present status and immediate prospects. By its efforts to integrate the economic and social

Political Organizations at Higher Ranks 59

policies of the Six, the Commission has come to work expertly in the political field, and its activities are preparing a solid groundwork of interlocking interests on which a political structure and external political policy can be built. By some delegation of their sovereign powers to E.E.C. institutions, the six countries have already given the Common Market legal and political personality. The Treaty of Rome appears to have looked towards 'federal' rather than 'confederal' organization – towards a United States of Europe rather than a loose confederation, weak at the centre. Substantial attention has already been given by the Six to their ultimate political unification; differences of view have not yet been reconciled: indeed it would seem over-ambitious to expect that more is attainable at the first stage than a loose *'union des patries'*. Before the major crisis in its affairs in 1965 many qualified observers had come to believe that E.E.C. had passed the point of no return. Discussion over the Commission's proposals for the financial regulation of agriculture within the Community then exposed a major stumbling-block – nationalism, personified by President de Gaulle, who stated clearly that France would not delegate to the Commission the supra-national powers which its agricultural policy implied. Moreover, he was unwilling to envisage that, as from January 1966, decisions of the Council of Ministers would be made by a majority vote. Thus, although the Community overcame successfully these difficulties, it may have to slow down the pace which it originally set itself by the Treaty of Rome. However, it should be noted that the creation of the Common Market has changed the geographical distribution of world power by challenging its dangerous bi-polarity.

Certain doubts about the character and aspirations of E.E.C. turn on its alleged exclusiveness and the challenge it might appear to throw down to United States' leadership in Europe. The communist taunt that it is a Western conspiracy to thwart the legitimate aspirations of the newly emergent nations need not be taken seriously since it is not shared by the associated countries of the E.E.C. It should however be recognized that four countries – the United Kingdom, Ireland, Denmark and Norway – have sought full membership – without success, and that six other states, including three neutral ones – Israel, Cyprus, Spain, Switzerland, Sweden and Austria – have sought to explore, but have not yet achieved, some form of association. Thus the creation of 'Little Europe' of the Six might appear to expose and perhaps even to harden the political divisions of the continent. Yet, in reply to these comments, it might well be argued that E.E.C. has first to establish its own unity before it

60 *Essays in Political Geography*

can absorb new members who will bring new ideas and difficulties to the conference table. And the United Kingdom at least had, but missed, the chance of being one of the founding fathers of the Market. Lastly, regret may persist that the fine concept of a North Atlantic Community has been jeopardized by narrowly European suspicion of the so-called Anglo-Saxon nations.

SUMMARY AND CONCLUSIONS

In summary and conclusion, little more need be said. It is clear that no great virtue and much real weakness is attached to the sovereign state, whether old or new. The nation state, in particular, is too often small alike in territory and spirit, and smallness is at a discount in a world of integrated relationships where advantages for living tend to increase within the larger units. Certainly some small states are outstanding for their cultural and economic achievement, but even Switzerland and Sweden feel the need for closer association with larger communities. As Max Sorre[1] put it, we live 'in the continental era' when diplomatic and military power, if backed by economic and technological strength, are increasingly concentrated in states or blocs with large territories and multi-national societies. The process of bloc formation has been notably successful in the so-called 'capitalist world', even though blocs there remain subject to constant inner strain. E.E.C., freely devised, appears more vigorous than COMECON: and the divisive and weakening force exerted by nationalism might appear rather more evident in the communist than in the 'free world', even when it is admitted that the U.S.S.R. has established effective unity within its own boundaries. In the creation of political organizations at higher ranks nations may yet redeem themselves and disprove Lord Acton's stricture which heads this chapter. Their variety of form is reflected in the variety of terms used to name them: organization, association, league, commonwealth and community. These testify also to the vigour of political thinking and activity, in reaction to a world of continuing change and to the degrees of achievement presently possible – the inevitable limitation which politics impose.

[1] Max Sorre, *op. cit.*, p. 239.

6

The Contemporary Geopolitical Setting:
A Proposal for Global Geopolitical Equilibrium

SAUL B. COHEN

INTRODUCTION

Political Geography, sometimes described as the science of political area differentiation, is concerned with the spatial distribution and space relations of political processes. For the purpose of this discussion such processes may be defined as a series of action of operations which man conducts to establish or maintain a political system, mostly through political institutions. Similarly area may be regarded as the framework within which geographers study these processes, and as such it can be studied either as a morphological phenomenon or as a functionally organized phenomenon, the former dealing with the static and the latter with the kinetic consequences of process.

Nowadays the national state system can no longer be maintained by exclusive concern with the 'closed political space' contained within the national boundary. Just as the individual living within the national state also lives within one or more sub-systems, so also is he affected by political sub-systems which embrace, or at least affect, the national state system. For political forces which knit the man–earth system together are not isolated: they operate in continuous interaction with the global ecosystem and with its major cultural systems. The clash between 'closed national political space' and economic, social and technological forces which overlap political boundaries remains a major problem of our time, but its resolution is no longer in serious doubt. Supra-national political forces, emanating from national, group and individual sources, have become the decisive factors. A new iconography, based upon wider concepts of regionality and internationalism, is in many ways as strong as national iconography and tends to neutralize the barriers which the latter produces.

THE GEOGRAPHER'S RESPONSIBILITY

Two over-riding problems face mankind today, threatening to destroy the delicately balanced system that is comprised of man and the natural

62 *Essays in Political Geography*

environment. These are first, the need to avoid thermo-nuclear warfare, and secondly the task of sustaining a world population, which will be doubled by A.D. 2000, at a living standard several times greater than that of the current global mean. These problems are intertwined and the acquisition of nuclear capabilities by 'have-not' powers might prove decisive in bringing about fundamental changes in global economic patterns.

No science, either physical or social, has a monopoly of concern over these two problems, but all sciences, including geography, have a moral obligation to aid our understanding of them and to contribute to their resolution. In the past geographers have not shirked the responsibility of trying to understand the political aspects of the earth–man system which is the product of the four inter-related processes of population growth, changing utilization of natural resources, technological advance and social and political evolution. Nor should the geographer shy away from such geopolitical hypotheses today, for in viewing these processes spatially he can continue to make his contribution to the well-being of society.

How to maintain a balanced international political system is not exclusively a political problem. It is also inter-related with the economic, social and technological fabric of the man-earth system and for this reason we speak here not of political but of geopolitical equilibrium, which is composed of competing regions of two ranks or orders.

Geographers have long disputed whether the region is a fact of nature or the creation of man, but so far as the political region at least is concerned, it is clearly derived from the decision of men to interact with their fellow men within a circumscribed area. However, the parameters of this area and the degree to which political processes can be effectively applied, both within and outside it, are influenced by the nature of the land and by the available facilities for movement. As man's views change, so he changes the political processes by which he organizes his political community. The result is disconformity between political processes and political area, unless or until the area itself is also changed. Empires, geared to economic specialization and exchange over vast areas, have today given way to a plethora of small independent states. Such states do not appear to be content to develop as self-contained, non-specialist economic units, but this is likely to be their lot so long as they refuse to readjust their aims and processes within new supra-national political forms.

The concern of this paper is with those supra-national systems which

The Contemporary Geopolitical Setting 63

have already evolved, or are likely to evolve, in response to the inadequacy of the existing state system. Supra-national systems are not new, nor are they static. What is unique about them today is that they must be related to strategic realities which have now become global in scale, while at the same time they are able to take advantage of improved means of communication in order to organize large areas of territory more effectively than has ever been done before.

Any geographer who attempts to outline a supra-national system exposes himself to the charge of perpetrating geopolitics or, more properly, *Geopolitik*. But in attempting now to do precisely this, the author may legitimately counter by asking who is better equipped than the geographer to appraise, define, describe and finally to analyse the problems posed by the world-wide interaction of political processes and terrestrial space ?

PAST HYPOTHESES

The concern of modern geography with geopolitical equilibrium goes back to Ritter and Guyot. Nineteenth- and early twentieth-century inquiry into the relationship between national political power and the earth–man system, as undertaken by these two scholars and also by Ratzel and Mackinder, was regarded by political scientists as providing a new and realistic basis for analysing relationships between states. This inquiry has been viewed as the modern basis of international relations.

It was in the studies of Ritter and Guyot that the concept was first propounded of the organization of the earth into united and complementary three-fold north–south divisions which were in effect the forerunners of *Pan-Regions* proposed by the twentieth-century German geopoliticians. Ratzel introduced *Lage* and *Raum* as the evolving framework within which to analyse national states comparatively. Mackinder, viewing the world in terms of different *arenas of movement*, outlined a system of geopolitical equilibrium within which the political earth operated and interacted. German *Geopolitik* attempted to portray geopolitical equilibrium within a changing, dynamic setting, and offered a synthesis of the Ratzelian concept of the large state, the doctrine of Pan-Regionalism, and Mackinder's view of the relationship between the Heartland and the World Island. However, its aim was not the achievement of a global order based upon a balance of contending forces, but instead the imposition of a 'New World Order' dominated by a single state. Other

64   *Essays in Political Geography*

formulae for geopolitical equilibrium have included Spykman's Continental Island–Heartland alignment against the Rimland, de Seversky's Old World–New World division, and Mackinder's last thesis, namely that of a four-fold partitioning of the earth based upon regional clusterings of people and natural resources, united by primary lines of movement. Most of these formulae have been found lacking, because they tended to rely too heavily upon single elements. This can be seen, for example, in Mackinder's early dependence upon movement and historical analogy, and his later emphasis upon uniformity of economies and climates; and again in the Pan-Regional view of unity through complementary climates and agricultural bases, which represents a naïve demand–supply formula based upon the assumption that non-industrial areas would remain content with the *status quo*.

An example of a recent thesis of geopolitical equilibrium has been propounded by Toynbee. Strongly influenced by population projections, this thesis foresees a world divided into two parts, namely China and all others. Geopolitical analysis does not support this division, nor does it support a four-fold regionalization based upon the great population nodes of eastern North America, Europe west of the Urals, East Asia and South Asia.

DYNAMIC GEOPOLITICAL EQUILIBRIUM

As used in this paper, the term 'geopolitical equilibrium' applies to what may be called a form of international geopolitical isostasy, and not to a simple political balance of power system. In speaking of political equilibrium, political scientists may mean one of at least four different things, namely equal distribution of power maintained between two forces; equal distribution of power maintained by a third balancing force; maintenance or freezing of the *status quo*, regardless of the weight of distribution of power; or a distribution of power which makes it impossible for one state to achieve world dominance. In most cases, these are essentially single-faceted views of political relations between states, though they recognize the role of internal political relations in affecting external political policies.

Geopolitical equilibrium in the isostatic sense, however, can be likened to the earth's state of physical equilibrium, based upon the irregularity of the continental shell and involving a zone within this outer shell where contrasted masses are distributed, not vertically in columns but horizontally in layers. The movement that takes place, while still as-

The Contemporary Geopolitical Setting 65

suming the fundamental law of flotation, finds levels of compensation by also moving horizontally.

In a geopolitical sense, the earth and its resources can be taken as the level of compensation, with equilibrium being maintained through the continuous action of political processes upon the man–earth relationship. We need not speak of equilibrium in either a purely horizontal sense of national state to national state, or of a purely vertical sense of national state to resources, but rather in both of these senses together. Geopolitical equilibrium can be maintained even when horizontal shifts in political alignments occur, so long as internal or vertical adjustments take place. In these vertical adjustments, not only technology but also the will, efforts and myths of the human groups concerned play crucial roles. Thus geopolitical equilibrium was dynamically maintained when the Middle East was lost to the West and instead became a Shatterbelt, partly because this loss occurred at a time when Maritime European economic and military strength rose in compensation, and partly because of the discovery and exploitation of North African petroleum.

In other instances changes in horizontal alignment take place to maintain geopolitical equilibrium without involving basic vertical changes by way of compensation. The loss of Cuba to the Western fold found its compensation level in the strengthened ties between the United States and such O.A.S. partners as Venezuela and Brazil.

Similar examples can be drawn from the Communist world. In the international power sense, the weakening of the Soviet Union's ties with China has been compensated for by the success of the former's space effort, and horizontal shifts in alignment between the Soviet Union and Albania have found their compensation in a renewal of more positive relations between the Soviet Union and Yugoslavia.

Geopolitical equilibrium, then, is a dynamic, not a static condition. Equilibrium is maintained by flexible lines of influence radiating outwards from power nodes, reflecting the changing conditions within those nodes as well as within peripheral areas of power application. Forces contributing to this dynamism include population growth; rising economic needs; the increasingly widespread distribution of raw materials and the greater ease of their transfer and use; the emergence of new areas of closed national political space in some parts of the world simultaneously with the breakdown of national barriers in other parts; and the spread of nuclear weapon capabilities.

Desires to achieve genuine economic complementarity, national drives for political and psychological equality, and alternative means of

66 *Essays in Political Geography*

improved movement all modify many established geopolitical facts, such as distributional patterns and space relations of people and materials which have grown up within unique physical, ideological and historical settings and oriented to one dominating arena of movement.

Certain forces which may seriously affect geopolitical unity also merit particular attention. Thus, for example, urbanization is breaking down domestic barriers and permitting states to act more cohesively on the supra-national plane. For this reason we may, in the near future, find regional organizations operating as 'leagues' of great cities, a curious repetition of the past. Again, the greater availability of raw materials (such as oil and iron ore) and of finished goods (such as machinery and buses) enables nations to exchange products more freely, in purely political terms, though it also makes distance differential a more important factor economically, and accordingly may be expected in the long run to foster regional unity. Proximity likewise remains geopolitically significant, partly because people *think* it is significant, but also because it is still a crucial factor both economically and, except in conditions of nuclear war, strategically.

Finally, complementarity of natural resources and of economies is a strong force making for geopolitical unity. However, complementarity is not a simple relationship of supply and demand, but rather a matter of mutual exchange. Producers of extractive commodities for the advanced economies regard such exchange not as complementarity but as exploitation. True complementarity occurs by means of specialized exchanges between equally advanced economies when both peoples derive benefits from value added by manufacturing. Japan and Australia can arrive at such complementarity, as have the United States and Maritime Europe. In the absence of technological and social equality, exploitation will mark such exchange unless the higher economic order is willing to share its profits by direct aid, investments, loans, and other human efforts to redress the balance.

Political processes operating supra-nationally are incapable of creating uniform regions as, to a limited extent, national states do within their own borders. Instead, these processes create centralized regions, within which there are varying degrees of influence between the political-economic core area and the periphery. Such core areas possess the size, population, transport facilities and ideological dynamism to lead if not to dominate their regions. Contiguity, whether overland or by sea in the absence of intervening competitors or more powerful 'nearest neighbours', helps to bind such regions together.

The Contemporary Geopolitical Setting 67

GEOSTRATEGIC REGIONS AND THEIR SUBDIVISIONS

The system outlined in the following pages is based on the concept of a global hierarchy or nesting which comprises three orders, namely geostrategic regions, geopolitical regions, and other units. Whereas only a decade ago one spoke of single-power cores, namely the United States and the Soviet Union, today one may speak of multiple-power cores around which the world is becoming reorganized geostrategically.

The *geostrategic region* must be large enough to exert world-wide influence, because today's strategy can only be expressed in global terms. Essentially, such a region is the expression of the inter-relationship of a large part of the world in terms of location, movement, trade orientation and cultural or ideological bonds. While it is a single-feature region in the sense that it embraces areas over which power can be strategically applied, it is a multi-feature region in its composition, because today's strategy has political-economic as well as military characteristics.

The *geopolitical region* is a subdivision, or subsystem of the geostrategic region, in that while the former may be regarded in strategic terms the basis of the latter is tactical. Geopolitical regions are directly derived from geographical regions and thus can provide a framework for more closely organized economic – and often also political – activities. Contiguity, complementarity of resources, historic association, and dominance of single-core areas are generally distinguishing marks of the geopolitical region. Geopolitical regions provide the basis for the emergence of multiple power nodes within a geostrategic region, a process which leads to complications owing to the overlap of interfaces. Thus a core area's dominance over a peripheral member of a geopolitical region can be weakened if that peripheral member strengthens its geostrategic ties with the core area of another geopolitical unit, as shown by the changing relationship of Albania with the Soviet Union and China.

A *Shatterbelt* is defined as a large, strategically-located region which is occupied by a number of conflicting states, and is caught between the conflicting interests of great powers which adjoin or have access to it. Conflict of interests between its regional partners intensifies the complex nature of such shatterbelts.

Using the above categories we can recognize a major division of the contemporary world into two great geostrategic regions, which we call respectively the Trade-Dependent Maritime and the Continental Eurasian, each of which comprises two or more geopolitical regions or

68 *Essays in Political Geography*

subsystems; as well as shatterbelts and other areas which lie outside both of the two great geostrategic systems (Fig. 6.1).

The Trade Dependent Maritime Geostrategic Region is formed bi-nodally, around the Maritime Ring of the United States and urbanized Western Europe. The *Continental Eurasian Geostrategic Region* also has two nodes, the Soviet Industrial Triangle and North China. Thus in each case a new core of power, the one in Maritime Europe and the other in East Asia, has emerged to complement and to challenge its respective 'senior partner'. Successive instances of friction between the United States and Maritime Europe, over Suez, NATO, the Common Market, South-east Asia and Mainland China, represent evolutionary stages in the development of Maritime Europe as a genuinely equal power core. Symptomatic of a similar evolutionary stage of Sino–Soviet relations have been the ideological conflict between these two states, the withdrawal of Soviet aid from China, the Chinese attack upon India, and Sino–Soviet competition throughout much of Asia and Africa. Despite the bitterness of current disputes, the interdependence and mutual vulnerability of the two sets of cores appear likely to override internal differences during the foreseeable future. The existence of multiple cores is more apt, in the long run, to knit together each geostrategic region. For none of the peripheral parts of a geostrategic region desires to be totally dependent upon one core area, and the option of turning alternately to each of the two core areas offers greater security against dominance by one of them. South America's interests in striking a more balanced stage of dependence with Maritime Europe as well as with the United States, and Africa's interests in the reverse direction, are examples as in the other great geostrategic system, is Rumania's balancing act between the Soviet Union and China.

The two great geostrategic regions are differently subdivided, the Maritime one into five, the Continental into two geopolitical regions. The Maritime World includes: (*a*) Anglo-America and the Caribbean, (*b*) Maritime Europe and the Maghreb, (*c*) Offshore Asia and Oceania, (*d*) South America, and (*e*) Africa south of the Sahara. Of these, the first three have a high order of internal unity, the last two have not. The Eurasian Continental World contains: (i) the Asian Heartland and Eastern Europe, and (ii) East Asia.

In addition to the above are the two Shatterbelts, of the Middle East and South-east Asia respectively, which have replaced Maritime Europe as the major zone of Great Power conflict. Finally, South Asia maintains

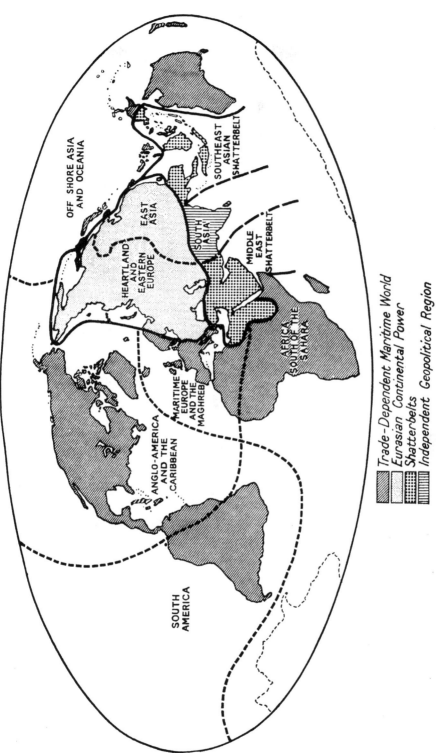

Fig. 6.1. The World's Geostrategic Regions and Their Geopolitical Subdivisions

70 *Essays in Political Geography*

a separate geopolitical identity and is potentially the core of what might become a third but lesser geostrategic region comprising the Indian Ocean basin. Between West and East Europe and East and Offshore Asia, unprecedentedly sharp boundaries have emerged to separate the two geostrategic regions. Among the morphological and functional features of these geopolitical regions are contiguity; economic and social complementarity; effective facilities for movement; moderately settled areas (effective national territories) capable of absorbing additional people; and empty areas which are important strategically, economically and psychologically. These points may be illustrated by a more detailed examination of the structure of the Trade-Dependent Maritime Region.

A unique role within the Trade-Dependent Maritime Region is played by the Maritime Ring of the United States which is making the latter a truly Gulf- and Pacific-facing nation as well as one looking out upon the Atlantic. Thus this urbanized and industrialized ring has strengthened the interdependence between the United States and the rest of the Maritime world.

To consider Maritime Europe and the Maghreb as one geopolitical region is to recognize the breadth and depth of trans-Mediterranean ties, rather than to be diverted by the veneer of current political tides. Ease of communications, complementarity of peoples and products, strategic interdependence and historic association provide strong forces of geopolitical attraction. The presence of over half a million Algerians in France, the role of the French language, culture and economic aid in North Africa, the linking effect of Saharan petroleum, and Maritime Europe's real and imagined needs to secure its southern approaches are all major long-range ties. These helped to explain the ironically intimate, if at the same time bitter and mistrustful, alliance between De Gaulle and Ben Bella. They also help to explain the limits beyond which Morocco, Tunisia and Libya appear unwilling to proceed in making common cause with their Arab neighbours to the east against Maritime Europe as, for example, in the issue of diplomatic relations between West Germany and Israel.

Perhaps an explanation of the concept of an Offshore Asian geopolitical region is also warranted, this unit being somewhat less mature than the others. While Offshore Asia may appear to exhibit considerable uniqueness as a geopolitical region, its morphological character and functional organization have much in common with other geopolitical regions. Notwithstanding the more recent entry of Offshore Asia into

The Contemporary Geopolitical Setting 71

the lists of modern industrial nations, geographical circumstances here have encouraged a seaward orientation and a sea-mindedness that can be likened to that of Maritime Europe. Overseas trade is a prerequisite for all the states of Offshore Asia, either because their economies have specialized to compensate for lack of a broad domestic resource base or, in the case of Australia, because national youthfulness, limited population, and former Imperial and more recent Commonwealth ties have encouraged such specialization. Relative political stability and national cultural unity, certainly related to insular positions, are other characteristics.

Japan's role as the core of the region has not yet clearly emerged. Immaturity of intra-regional trade links and the political–military restraints upon Japan's activities stemming from the Second World War are responsible for this. But, by weight of population (60 per cent of the total), economic strength and strategic–economic ties to the United States, Japan's position of leadership in Offshore Asia is being consolidated. It may also be noted that Offshore Asia is too limited a region to satisfy Japan's needs for international trade, a characteristic which presents an obvious parallel with that of the industrial core area of Maritime Europe.

Within Offshore Asia, Australia offers the only extensive empty areas and major tracts of effective national territory capable of absorbing major increases of population. Such areas are likely to be used as bases for economic development and intra-regional economic complementarity. In one aspect of movement, namely migration, there is a marked contrast between Offshore Asia and Maritime Europe. Within the latter, population mobility enhances social complementarity; within the former, absence of mobility is the characteristic feature. Granted that Australia's traditional 'white only' immigration policy is not likely to be altered substantially, the fact remains that this policy does tend to neutralize some of the unifying effects of regional economic and strategic complementarity, and one might venture to ask whether some compromise cannot be found between exclusion and unlimited immigration.

Without attempting here to consider also the nature of the other Regions shown in Fig. 6.1, the foregoing analyses of the Trade-Dependent Maritime Geostrategic Region and the Offshore Asia Geopolitical Region show that the spatial variability of international geopolitical processes provides a flexible framework for a current geopolitical system. Recognizing that geopolitical equilibrium can exist only where man and

72 Essays in Political Geography

political institutions are conscious of the need for it, geographers nevertheless have a continuing responsibility for inquiring into the nature of such systems.

SELECT BIBLIOGRAPHY

CARR, E. H., *Nationalism and After*, New York, 1945.

COHEN, S. B., *Geography and Politics in a World Divided*, New York, 1963; London, 1964.

DEUTSCH, K., *Nationalism and Social Communication*, Cambridge, Mass., 1953.

GUYOT, A., *The Earth and Man*, New York, 1889.

HARTSHORNE, R., 'The role of the state in economic growth', in H. Aitkin (ed.) *Economic Growth*, New York, 1959.

JONES, S. B., 'A unified field theory of political geography', *Annals of the Association of American Geographers*, 44, 1954, pp. 111–23.

MACKINDER, H. J., 'The geographical pivot of history', *Geographical Journal*, 23, 1904, pp. 421–33.

MACKINDER, H. J., 'The round world and the winning of the peace', *Foreign Affairs*, 21, 1943, pp. 595–609.

SPROUT, H. and M., *Man-Milieu Relationship Hypothesis in the Context of International Politics*, Princeton, 1956.

WHITTLESEY, D., *The Earth and the State*, New York, 1938.

PART II

Case Studies in Decolonization

7

Malaysia: A Study in the Political Geography of Decolonization
CHARLES A. FISHER*

INTRODUCTION: THE REGIONAL SETTING

Every state, according to Ratzel, is a piece of land and a piece of humanity.[1] But precisely how and why particular pieces of each interact to produce stable and viable states while others do not is a matter which cannot be understood in purely internal terms. For the process of state-building is also in large measure the product of external forces which, moreover, may operate within very different geographical contexts at different times. Thus, in attempting to study the formation of new and independent states to replace those of a former colonial era, which in their turn were built not in a vacuum but, with widely varying degrees of continuity, upon the remains of others which had preceded them, it is essential to give appropriate recognition to the operative geographical context at each of the relevant stages.

The force of this argument is well illustrated by consideration of the Federation of Malaysia as the successor state to the former British dependencies in Malaya and the northern third of Borneo. For although most contemporary Western observers are conscious of the critical position which Malaysia occupies at the cross-roads of South-east Asia, the geographical horizons of its indigenous peoples have generally been more narrowly restricted, and even the British themselves, whose activities during the nineteenth century played a decisive part in linking South-east Asia together, seem never to have thought of the latter as a distinctive region until they, along with the French, Dutch and Americans, were forcibly evicted from it by the Japanese occupation of 1942–5. Nevertheless South-east Asia had possessed at least some elements of unity since very early times, and without an appreciation of this fact it is impossible to understand the true significance of the most fundamental problems with which Malaysia is faced today.

---

* In preparing this essay I have drawn extensively on my earlier writings, particularly those listed in the Select Bibliography, pp. 141–5. The latter contains full particulars of all sources referred to in the footnotes.

[1] F. Ratzel, *Politische Geographie*, p. 2.

76 *Essays in Political Geography*

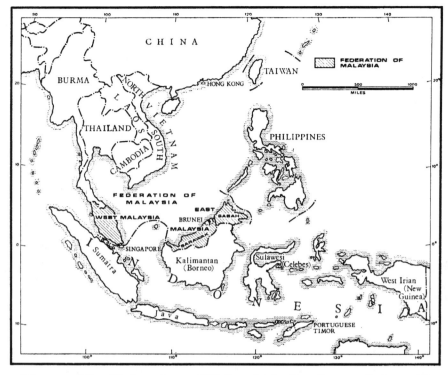

Fig. 7.1. The Federation of Malaysia in South-east Asia, 1966

THE REGIONAL SETTING

The common failure to recognize the measure of unity which exists within South-east Asia arises primarily from the way in which the region has so often been overshadowed by the neighbouring and far more densely populated sub-continents of India and China, in contrast to whose land-based unity, moreover, that of the fragmented insular and peninsular lands which together comprise South-east Asia is essentially pelagic in pattern.

The first significant expression of such unity may be seen in the Austro-Asiatic culture which flourished in the lowlands bordering the South China Sea and its maritime annexes during the last few centuries before Christ. But this was given a new dimension by the thousand years of Indianization which, coinciding roughly with the first millennium of the Christian era, arose from the dissemination, along the sea routes between India and China, of the Hindu and Buddhist religions, and of such related features of Indian civilization as the arts of writing, improved agricultural skills, and the rudiments of urban-centred political organization.

Yet although this process gave a wider measure of unity to the lands on both sides of the seaways,[1] it did not prevent the emergence of new diversities within the region, deriving from the migration of new peoples from the north and the evolution of contrasting patterns of state formation in the different geographical circumstances of the mainland and

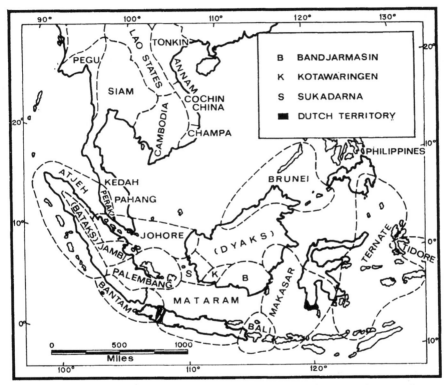

Fig. 7.2. **Main States of South-east Asia in the Seventeenth Century** (after Vlekke, Herrmann and Westermann)

the archipelagoes. Thus whereas relatively large and linguistically distinctive kingdoms emerged in the discrete basins of the principal mainland rivers, the Malayo-Indonesian world,[2] thanks to the ease of maritime communications and a more scattered distribution of population, was characterized by less profound linguistic differences and by a larger

[1] Except the Vietnamese lands where Chinese cultural influence predominated.
[2] The term Malayo-Indonesian world is used to cover what used to be called the Malaysian cultural region, which includes most of Indonesia as well as the Federation of Malaysia.

78 *Essays in Political Geography*

number of relatively small sea-states, whose territories straddled the various inner seas of the archipelago.

Nevertheless within this maritime half of South-east Asia two areas repeatedly stood out as being of far more than local importance. The first of these comprised the fertile and well peopled interior valleys of east-central Java, a region which between the seventh and sixteenth centuries developed the most advanced civilization in the archipelago and made its influence felt over much of central and eastern Indonesia.

By contrast, the second main centre comprised the lands bordering the great maritime cross-roads where the through sea route round the shore of continental Asia is forced south by the Malay peninsula and so meets the local routes frequented since time immemorial by the indigenous seafarers of the archipelago. Between the seventh and thirteenth centuries the commercial potentialities of this unique situation were brilliantly exploited by the empire of Sri Vijaya which, from its headquarters in the vicinity of the modern Palambang, extended its authority over all eastern Sumatra, western Malaya, and the western tips of Java and Borneo, and through its naval mastery of the intervening seas dominated the commerce of this entire region.

Yet, despite its focal position, Sri Vijaya, in common with the rest of equatorial South-east Asia, remained much less densely populated than the tropical lands of east-central Java and the larger river basins of the mainland, a fact which goes far to explain why South-east Asia was never politically united in a single great sea state. Thus while Sri Vijaya provided a geopolitical bridge across the narrow Straits of Malacca, no indigenous state ever emerged which was powerful enough to unite both sides of the much wider South China Sea, though each of the respective halves of South-east Asia was sometimes dominated for long periods by a single great power.

Such a duality occurred after the late fourteenth century when Madjapahit, the last and greatest Hindu-Javanese kingdom, sought to extend its suzerainty also over the erstwhile domains of Sri Vijaya in the western parts of the archipelago, and in so doing came into rivalry with the new Siamese kingdom of Ayuthia, which was reaching down into the Malay peninsula in order to control the trade of the Malacca Straits. It was in these circumstances that the small port kingdom of Malacca grew up in western Malaya, and for a short time and on a much smaller scale resumed something of the commercial and geopolitical role of the former Sri Vijaya.

In this it was aided by two new developments each of which was

Malaysia 79

subsequently to exert profound changes upon South-east Asia. The first of these arose from the spread of Islam in the wake of Gujarati and Bengali traders frequenting the sea routes from India to the spice-producing Moluccas.[1] Having first reached northern Sumatra in the late thirteenth century, Islam was in 1414 accepted as the official religion of Malacca, which thereafter became the primary centre for the further diffusion of the faith in the Malayo-Indonesian world, a process which indirectly led to the downfall of Madjapahit in 1518.

The second new development concerned the growth of Chinese interest in South-east Asia. Although China was much later than India in taking to the sea, its maritime commerce with South-east Asia had become very important by the twelfth century A.D. and was already accompanied by the founding of small settlements of Chinese traders in various parts of the Philippines and Indonesia. Moreover, beginning in 1403, a series of major naval expeditions was despatched to demonstrate Chinese interest in South-east Asia which significantly they called the Nanyang or southern seas.

Thus it was that, recognizing the potential importance of Malacca and the designs which the Siamese in particular entertained upon it, the Chinese brought that kingdom under their protection in 1405. And, strengthened in this way *vis à vis* its local rivals, Malacca thereupon succeeded in developing as the main entrepot of the Muslim spice trade and also in extending its rule over both the rest of the Malay peninsula and, in true sea-state fashion, over various parts of Sumatra on the opposite side of the Straits.

Nevertheless, although Malacca outlasted the short burst of Chinese naval activity in South-east Asia which ended in 1431, its small population and limited food-producing capacity severely restricted its power, and in 1511 it succumbed to the Portuguese who made it their regional headquarters in their take-over of the Muslim spice trade. Thereafter Malacca remained in European hands for over four hundred years, and this alien control of the key point put an end to the developing political unity of the Malay peninsula which gradually disintegrated into a series of small riverine principalities. And meanwhile, with the replacement in 1641 of the Portuguese by the Dutch, whose activities led to the re-emergence of Java as the primary focus of the Malayo-Indonesian

[1] Like the earlier process of Indian acculturation, the dissemination of Islam took place from west to east and from coast to interior. But whereas Indianization spread primarily along the route from India to China, Islam followed the route from India to the Moluccas.

80 *Essays in Political Geography*

world, the Malay peninsula declined to the level of a minor peripheral region. Moreover, since for the first three centuries of the colonial era European control was restricted to scattered parts of the maritime fringe of South-east Asia, from which Western navies could nevertheless dominate the South China Sea, it served to reinforce the new division between the mainland and the maritime halves of South-east Asia which was already becoming apparent with the spread of Islam into the latter.

Whether, if the Europeans had not arrived when they did, the Chinese would ever have followed up their naval activities of the early fifteenth century, one can only speculate. But, despite the introvert political tendencies which early European contact with China served to strengthen, and the ban which the Manchu dynasty imposed upon emigration overseas, the flow of individual Chinese to the Nanyang slowly increased during the seventeenth and eighteenth centuries before bursting into a flood tide in the nineteenth.

During the final phase of Western imperialism, from the early nineteenth century to the Japanese conquests of 1942, the political pattern of South-east Asia was transformed by the extension of Western rule over every part of the region, with the solitary exception of Thailand. In this process the decisive role was played by Britain, whose initiative originated in the remarkable conjuncture of opportunities which had been provided by a head-start in the industrial revolution, the defeat of France in India, and the setbacks to both French and Dutch power by the French Revolutionary and Napoleonic Wars. Nevertheless, until well into the nineteenth century Britain was concerned far more with strengthening the security of India and opening up a further great trading sphere in China than it was with South-east Asia itself. Thus, following their annexation in 1786 of the small Malayan island of Penang, which could serve as a naval outpost for the defence of India and a base from which to command the northern entrance to the Malacca Straits hitherto monopolized by the Dutch, the British successively took possession of still more insular footholds, namely Singapore (1819), Hong Kong (1841) and Labuan (1846), thereby establishing a line of British stations from the Indian Ocean to the China coast.

Meanwhile, further north on the mainland, British concern for the defence of India had also led, under local provocation, to intervention in Burma, and during the course of the next half century, the chain reaction induced by these extensions of British power into both maritime and mainland South-east Asia spread throughout the entire region.

Malaysia 81

Within twenty years of the opening of the British route to China via Penang, Singapore and Hong Kong, the French, bent on short-circuiting it, had begun work on the Suez canal whose opening in fact gave a new stimulus to the British in Asia. For an immense increase of shipping, large and small, now began to provide feeder services linking the three British ports with the local harbours of the whole surrounding region, and the revolutionary reduction in the sailing distance between Europe and South-east Asia made it commercially feasible to develop the latter to become the greatest supplier of tropical produce for the markets of the industrialized West. And while it would be absurd to ignore the rivalries which accompanied this activity and the related extension of British, French, Dutch, and American political influence over more and more of South-east Asia, it remains true that the latter, in being thus drawn ineluctably into the stream of world commerce, became geographically refocused upon the arterial seaways, the key points of which were now in British hands.

But if in this sense one may detect a certain parallel with the developing unity of South-east Asia during the era of Indianization, and even recognize a measure of geographical continuity, notably in Burma, Siam and the Netherlands Indies, between the political units at the end of the Western period and those of pre-colonial times, such similarities must not be exaggerated. And indeed, in so far as South-east Asia was moving towards a new measure of unity under the common experience of Western colonialism, it is arguable that in the long run the most significant aspect of this process will be seen to have derived from the peculiar opportunities which the final century of Western rule provided for Chinese migration into every country in the region.

THE EMERGENCE OF THE BRITISH MALAYSIAN SPHERE

In more senses than one the acquisition of Singapore by the Malayophile Raffles, as a last attempt to force Britain to extend its influence in the archipelago, marked the turning point in the creation of what may be called the Penang-Singapore-Hong Kong axis. And the success which this new foundation soon achieved abundantly vindicated his forecast of what might follow from the establishment of a free port at this natural focus of the eastern seaways which, since time immemorial, had been dominated by the monopolistic tradition. Nevertheless, the British government, anxious to maintain friendly relations with the newly

82 *Essays in Political Geography*

restored Netherlands, was quick to reassure the latter that it contemplated no further colonial expansion in the Malayo-Indonesian archipelago. Thus, under the Anglo-Dutch Treaty of 1824, the British formally limited their sphere of influence there by giving up Benkulen (in southern Sumatra) in exchange for Malacca, and undertaking to found no further settlements to the south of Singapore. And two years later, negotiations with Siam led to a complementary definition of spheres to the north, whereby the Siamese agreed to limit their suzerainty in the peninsula to the Malay States north of Perak and Pahang. With the independence of the peninsula thus secured, the East India Company in 1826 amalgamated the four coastal footholds of Penang and Province Wellesley,[1] the Dindings,[2] Malacca and Singapore, into the single Presidency of the Straits Settlements, whose name aptly defined its geopolitical *raison d'être*, and in 1832 Singapore replaced Georgetown (Penang) as its administrative capital.

However, the 1824 treaty left the way open for British activity along the northern shores of Borneo and, shortly after their annexation of Hong Kong, the British acquired Labuan in 1846, ostensibly for use as a base for anti-piracy patrols and as an intermediate port of call on the South China Sea run. In this way, just as Penang and Singapore had helped to stake out the limits of what later became the area of British interest in the Malay peninsula, so Labuan in effect helped to extend that area to take in also the Bornean hinterland of the South China Sea. Thus by 1846 we can see the outlines emerging within the Malayo-Indonesian archipelago of a British sphere of influence focused on the through sea route, in rivalry to the expanding Dutch sphere centred upon Java (Fig. 7.4).

In view of the comments already made on pages 78–80, it will be apparent that significant historical precedent existed for some such division of spheres, though the British Malaysian sphere which eventually grew out of these beginnings presented only a partial parallel to either Sri Vijaya or medieval Malacca, for while it straddled the through sea route it did so by linking the Malay peninsula not with eastern Sumatra but with northern Borneo. Moreover this positioning athwart the South China sea was essentially a function of nineteenth

---

[1] Province Wellesley, a small strip of the mainland coast opposite Penang island, was acquired from Kedah in 1800, partly for the defence of, and partly to grow food for Penang.

[2] The Dindings, another small strip of coast and some even smaller offshore islands, were acquired from Perak in 1826, ostensibly for use as a base for anti-piracy patrols in the Straits. The territory was retroceded to Perak in 1935.

Malaysia 83

century shipping communications rather than of the age-old indigenous sailing routes, and as such it cut completely across the already established patterns of both linguistic and political geography.

Thus the western Sultanates of Malaya were isolated from their traditional association with Sumatra, the Johore-Riouw kingdom was bisected, and an unprecedented connexion established between the Malay peninsula and the territories hitherto belonging to the Sultanate of Brunei, in which a minority of Muslim Malays occupying the coastal fringe ruled over a large hinterland sparsely inhabited by animist indigenes. And although the Malay language was common both to the peninsula and the coastal zone of northern Borneo, and was also understood by indigenous headmen in the interior, the fact remained that this whole area was merely an arbitrary segment of the total area of Malay speech – which also included the other coastlands of Borneo, eastern Sumatra, and the Batavia region of Java (Fig. 7.3).

Furthermore, owing to their peripheral position within the Malayo-Indonesian world, both northern Borneo and even the peninsula itself at this time were relatively backward and under-populated regions and, partly for this reason and partly because of related British encouragement, these territories offered exceptionally tempting opportunities to Chinese immigrants. This indeed had begun before Western initiative forced the Chinese government to remove its ban on emigration in the 1860s,[1] but thereafter, just as the piercing of the Suez isthmus had opened the commercial floodgates from the West, so the opening of China breached the dam behind which population pressure had been building up, and during the next seventy years millions streamed south to the lands of opportunity in South-east Asia. Wherever opportunity beckoned they followed, regardless alike of the swiftly changing colonial frontiers and the older indigenous differences between one country and another. But above all they followed the new arterial route to Singapore and Penang, and although many eventually returned home with their savings, others stayed to form the largest community in these Straits Settlements ports,[2] and still others went further afield into neighbouring parts of South-east Asia.

[1] The Chinese were brought to recognize the right of their nationals to emigrate from the 1860s onwards, though the first treaty reference to this was in the Burlingame Treaty with the U.S.A. in 1870. V. Purcell, *The Chinese in Southeast Asia*, p. 29.

[2] The two islands of Penang and Singapore had been very sparsely peopled when the British acquired them, as also was Hong Kong at the corresponding stage.

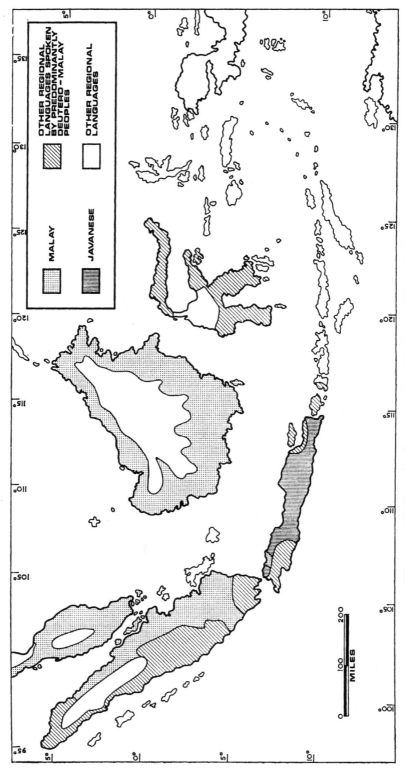

Fig. 7.3. Malayo-Indonesian Archipelago: Linguistic, c. 1940

Malaysia 85

Of these last the largest group consisted of those who, originally on their own initiative, moved into the Malay peninsula itself, either to plant spices and sugar or, more important, to seek out the sources of alluvial tin, already an established item of small-scale local trade, in the foothills of the western Malay states. Since the mining of these relatively accessible and easily worked deposits called only for rudimentary equipment, the Chinese quickly expanded production and, beginning in the 1840s, tin mining spread rapidly through the three western states of Perak, Selangor and Negri Sembilan. From these early mining areas the tin was transported by river and coastal craft to Penang or Singapore for export, and by the 1860s constituted a growing item in their commerce.

However, the tensions created both between rival groups of Chinese, and also between them and the Malays into whose territories they had intruded, proved too much for the indigenous administrative structures to contain, and the resultant chaos threatened to imperil the very basis on which the tin trade rested. It was against this background that, at a time when the wider implications of the cutting of the Suez canal were beginning to be appreciated, the British reversed their declared policy of non-intervention in the Malay states, and between 1874 and 1889 established protection over the western tin-mining states of Perak, Selangor and Nagri Sembilan and also over the large eastern state of Pahang which contained little tin but was reputed to be rich in gold.

In the event this reputation proved to be unfounded, and the remoteness of Pahang constituted a further obstacle to its development. But in the western states even the simple and inexpensive form of protection, under which the Malay Rulers agreed to follow the advice of a British Resident in all matters except those relating to indigenous custom and religion, provided a sufficient degree of law and order to permit the Malays to continue, as they apparently wished to do, in their traditional pursuits of subsistence farming and fishing, and simultaneously to induce a rapid expansion of mining and related Chinese immigration. In these circumstances, and at a time when developing road and railway communications also called for closer co-ordination, the four states in question were joined together in 1896 in the new Federated Malay States, which in effect superimposed a much more elaborate administrative structure, centred in the new federal capital of Kuala Lumpur, on those of the existing states.

Further changes were soon to follow. Although some small-scale commercial agricultural production, notably of coffee, had developed

86 *Essays in Political Geography*

in the Federated Malay States, the latter's exports had hitherto been completely dominated by tin. But with the phenomenal expansion in rubber production which occurred during the decade preceding the First World War, not only was Malaya's economic geography transformed but new trends were set in motion which speedily transformed its social and political geography as well.

In contrast to tin mining, which had so far been essentially the concern of the Chinese,[1] rubber planting was from the start primarily organized by Europeans. Nevertheless the mining industry had set the precedent of relying on immigrant labour for export production while leaving the Malay population to its own devices. And since the Malays still seemed unresponsive to economic stimuli – though in fact the better living conditions in the peninsula were already attracting a growing influx of immigrants from across the Straits who, being both Muslims and Malay speakers, were readily accepted as Malays – the European rubber planters likewise inclined to the use of immigrant labour. But, although many Chinese were thus employed in the early days, the planting community soon came to prefer southern Indians whom they regarded as more amenable to the regimented routine of rubber tapping,[2] and accordingly between 1901 and 1911 the number of Indians in the Federated Malay States rose from 58,211 to 172,465.[3]

In a geographical sense also the patterns established by tin helped to condition those of rubber, for the latter, which seemed to thrive on most of Malaya's predominantly lateritic soils, was quick to take advantage of the road and railway facilities already developed for the former. Thus the early plantations became heavily concentrated within the western lowlands of the Federated Malay States between the often swampy coastal fringe and the main tin zone at the foot of the western slopes of the Main Range.[4] But as the demand for rubber continued to leap ahead with the growth of the motor-car industry in the West, the planting community began to think of extending cultivation into the adjacent lowlands of western Johore (through which a railway was built between 1904 and 1907), Kedah, and even of eastern Malaya as well.

[1] As late as 1920 64% of the capital in tin was Chinese though with the introduction of more elaborate machinery the Europeans later played a larger role, and by 1936 only 35% of the capital was Chinese.

[2] However, Chinese became important as small-scale planters of rubber.

[3] Various forms of recruitment were used at different times in order to obtain Indian labour for Malayan estates but the practice of assisted emigration was stopped at the instigation of the Indian government in 1938.

[4] See E. H. G. Dobby, 'Some aspects of the human ecology of South-East Asia', p. 48.

Malaysia 87

It was against this background, and spurred on by news of a proposed German-built rail link between Bangkok and the northern Malay states, that the British initiated negotiations which led in 1909 to their acquisition of authority over Kelantan, Trengganu, Kedah and Perlis[1] in exchange for certain financial and other benefits. The four new states came under British protection on essentially the same terms as those originally used in 1874, and, together with Johore, which in 1914 also accepted a similar but not identical formula, gradually became known as the unfederated Malay State (Fig. 7.4).

However, although a major expansion of rubber cultivation did take place in both western Johore and Kedah, the process had not extended in any significant degree into the eastern three-quarters of the peninsula before the post-war slump and the even more serious economic crisis of the early 1930s brought economic expansion virtually to a halt. Thus, notwithstanding the gradual recovery during the later 1930s, Malaya on the eve of the Second World War exhibited a remarkable contrast between the narrow and intensively exploited strip of country lying within about forty miles of the Straits of Malacca, and the much larger but almost completely undeveloped area to the east of the main water-parting.

Within the former, served as it was by the main trunk railway from Singapore to the Siamese border, an excellent road network and regular coastal shipping services linking a string of lesser ports with Penang, Singapore and Port Swettenham, were concentrated over 90 per cent of the country's export production, all its main towns, and approximately three-quarters of its total population, which had increased more than ten-fold during the preceding hundred years. Moreover, and inseparably linked with all the foregoing characteristics, it was in this western zone that the overwhelming majority of the immigrants had made their homes, so that the Chinese alone outnumbered the Malays who in fact accounted for little more than a third of the total population here, though their predominance in eastern Malaya still kept their overall total slightly above that of the Chinese.[2]

In origin this striking difference between western and eastern Malaya

[1] But not over the predominantly Malay area of Patani which remained part of Siam.

[2] The 1931 Census gave totals for Malaya (including Singapore) of 1,934,900 Malays, 1,705,915 Chinese, and 623,224 Indians. But the Malay total included many born in Indonesia, an element which then formed 20% of the Malay total in Perak, 46% in Selangor and 51% in Johore, but only 0·2% and 0·3% in the east-coast states of Kelantan and Trengganu respectively.

D

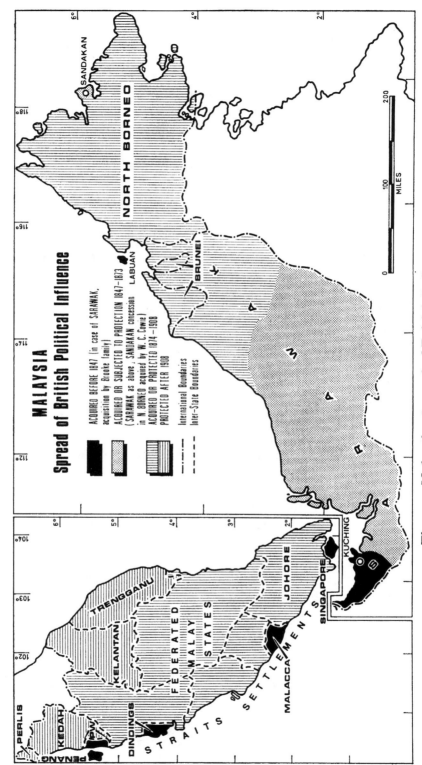

Fig. 7.4. Malaysia: Spread of British Influence

Malaysia 89

was basically a matter of accessibility, for whereas the former was a compact and easily manageable unit looking out onto the bustling maritime highway of the Malacca Straits, the east coast was far removed from the ocean shipping routes from Singapore to Hong Kong or Saigon and, being exposed to the full force of the north-east monsoon, was virtually closed to small craft for nearly half the year. And although a railway had been opened in 1931 through the jungle-covered interior of Pahang to Kelantan in the far north-east, it had come too late to modify the patterns which had evolved during the previous century.

Essentially similar but even more severe problems of inaccessibility also played the decisive part in retarding the development of the territories which lay within the Bornean sector of the British sphere as originally defined in 1824 and, notwithstanding the early acquisition of Labuan, the remoteness of this region from the primary focus of British activity in Singapore goes far to explain both the origin and the subsequent persistence of curious forms of unofficial imperialism in Sarawak and British North Borneo.

Even before the founding of Singapore, the once powerful Malay Sultanate of Brunei had begun to lose control over its more distant outlying territories, and this fact, combined with recurrent rumours of great mineral wealth hidden beneath its dense rain forests, made it a standing temptation to such outside adventurers as James Brooke the founder of Sarawak. Having assisted the Sultan's deputy to crush a Dyak rebellion, Brooke was rewarded in 1841 with a feudal title to a small area around Kuching, over which he thus became the Rajah or subordinate ruler under the Sultan of Brunei. And although Brooke had acted entirely on his own initiative, his determination to clear the coast of pirates gained the support of the British government, and it was in this connexion that he was appointed Governor of Labuan in 1847.[1]

Nevertheless his primary concern remained the improvement of his private domain in Sawawak, a task which both he and his successors viewed in frankly paternalistic terms as being basically a matter of stamping out oppression, putting an end to the Dyak practice of head-hunting, and raising the low level of peasant cultivation. In the process of extending the rule of law the Brookes successively expanded their own territories until these reached almost to Brunei town itself but,

[1] *Cf.* Wang Gungwu, *Malaysia*, p. 131. The two chapters, 'The Nineteenth Century' by Mary Turnbull, and 'Political History 1899–1946' by David McIntyre, in this most useful survey, admirably supplement the standard histories of individual parts of Malaysia, by C. D. Cowan, L. A. Mills, Steven Runciman and K. G. Tregonning.

90 *Essays in Political Geography*

apart from small quantities of gold at Bau in the original south-western corner, no significant mineral wealth was discovered until 1911, when oil was found on the coast at Miri close to the Brunei border.

Though production was never very great and known reserves were largely worked out before the Second World War, the oilfield provided a useful source of revenue, and, being situated in a remote corner of the country, did not interfere with the Brookes' policy of avoiding over-rapid modernization in Sarawak as a whole. However, the practice of encouraging the immigration of Chinese,[1] as a source of dynamism and agricultural expertise which might effect a gradual improvement in living conditions among the indigenous population as a whole, tended to defeat its own purpose, and eventually led to the Chinese gaining a predominant position both in commerce and in small-holder cash crop cultivation, notably of rubber and pepper.

Despite the steady territorial expansion of Sarawak towards the north-east, the capital remained at Kuching in the south-west which was least remote from Singapore, the principal point of contact between Sarawak and the outside world. However, for the corresponding Western encroachment on the opposite side of Brunei, it was Hong Kong which provided the initial jumping-off ground, and the growing disagreement between Brunei and its erstwhile dependency of Sulu which provided the opportunity.

Beginning in 1865 a series of attempts was made by various British, American and Austrian interests to promote the commercial exploitation of the north-eastern corner of Borneo, and directly and indirectly these eventually prepared the way for the formation of the British North Borneo Company. But in view of conflicting claims to the territory, the incorporation of the company under royal charter in 1881 did not take place until after the Governor of Labuan, W. H. Treacher,[2] had negotiated a new agreement with the Sultan of Brunei regarding the area in which it proposed to operate, and the two principal promoters had made doubly sure by obtaining another title to the territory between Pandassan and Sibuko Bay from the Sultan of Sulu.

---

[1] This policy received an early setback with the Chinese rebellion of 1857 which began in the Bau gold-mining area and culminated in an attack on Kuching. Although the Chinese community – reduced by some 3,500–4,000 people – thereafter became more law-abiding, the rebellion intensified local animosities against them, a factor which is still operative today (see below, p. 132). See Steven Runciman, *The White Rajahs*, pp. 124–33.

[2] Treacher later became the first Governor of North Borneo. *Cf.* Wang Gungwu (ed.), *op. cit.*, 137.

Malaysia 91

Rather than attempting to trade on its own account, the Company's policy was to provide the necessary administration, harbours, internal transport facilities and labour supply to attract others to develop the local resources, which were then taxed on its behalf. During the early 1880s its stations were limited almost entirely to the north-east coast, where from 1884 until the Second World War Sandakan served as capital, notwithstanding the subsequent establishment and more rapid growth of new settlements along the western coast, and the expansion of the Company's territory until it adjoined that of Sarawak in the hinterland of Brunei. In contrast to the north-east coast, which was nearer to Hong Kong and almost exclusively concerned with tobacco cultivation until the early 1890s, the west coast had closer links, via Labuan, with Singapore and after 1900 concentrated mainly on the production of rubber, in which it experienced a minor echo of the boom then developing in the Malay peninsula.

This duality of the territory's external links was reflected *inter alia* in the pattern of Chinese immigration, for although the first Chinese, whom the Company introduced into the north-east to make good the shortage of labourers and cultivators, came direct from China via Hong Kong, these were subsequently followed by an influx of Straits Chinese from Singapore, whose smattering of Bazaar Malay gave them an advantage over the mainlanders in establishing themselves as traders. As in Sarawak, the Chinese remained much the largest immigrant community, and although some Indonesian labour began to move into the north-east in the 1920s, there was never any large-scale movement of Indians into either territory.

In the absence of any known mineral resources comparable in scale to the Miri oilfields, British North Borneo, notwithstanding its avowedly commercial *raison d'être*, was even less important economically before 1939 than was Sarawak, while Brunei, the third component in the British Bornean sector, was of almost negligible significance in this respect until the eve of the Second World War when the Seria oilfield – geologically a continuation of that at Miri – began to bring unexpected prosperity to this diminutive Sultanate.

Although the British decision, taken in 1888 at the height of the colonial scramble, to establish protectorates over all these three territories helped to prevent this last surviving fragment of the formerly extensive Brunei domains from complete extinction, it suffered further losses to Sarawak in 1890, which reduced it to a mere 2,226 square miles containing Brunei town and a small surrounding fringe of

92 *Essays in Political Geography*

predominantly Malay countryside.[1] Finally in 1906 Brunei accepted a British Resident on similar terms to those in the peninsular Sultanates though Sarawak and British North Borneo remained respectively under the Brooke and the Chartered Company regimes until the Second World War.

At first sight the declaration of protection in 1888 might be expected to have heralded an intensification of British interest in the north Bornean region as a whole, but in fact such interest amounted to little more than a desire to keep possible rivals away from this southern shore of the South China Sea. And although, in first establishing control over Labuan in 1846, the British had seemed to have acquired an ideal position from which to exert surveillance over Brunei and what later became economically the most important parts of Sarawak and British North Borneo, the steady replacement of the sailing vessel by the increasingly efficient steamship served virtually to eliminate Labuan as a port of call on the Singapore–Hong Kong run. Thus in 1890 continuing decline had led to its incorporation in British North Borneo, and by 1901 its population had fallen to a mere 8,411.

In these circumstances northern Borneo remained even more isolated from the main Straits Settlements ports than was eastern Malaya. And although a few patches of economic activity – all of them accompanied by Chinese settlement[2] – had developed within its otherwise predominantly Muslim coastal fringe, the latter, apart from the narrowly localized oilfields, was generally much less advanced and less densely peopled than eastern – let alone western – Malaya, while the greater part of its hinterland, whose sparse population of animist[3] tribespeople lived by primitive shifing cultivation, was virtually untouched by modern means of transport (Fig. 7.5).

In effect, therefore, so far from eliminating the age-old time-lag between the eastern and western parts of the Malaysian region,[4] the era of improved communication had hitherto served to intensify the

---

[1] *Cf.* Wang Gungwu, *op. cit.*, p. 139. Note also that Brunei had only a very small Chinese population before the development of the Seria oilfield. Even in 1947 Chinese numbered only 8,300, but by 1960 this had risen to 21,795, *i.e.* 26% of the total.

[2] In contrast to Malaya, however, the number of Indians in northern Borneo was minute, partly because the area lay beyond the traditional Indian Ocean sphere of Indian commercial activity and partly because its much smaller rubber production was not dominated by big estates. See note 2, p. 86, above.

[3] Christian missions, though not permitted in Muslim areas, have had considerable success in the animist areas.

[4] See note 1, p. 79, above.

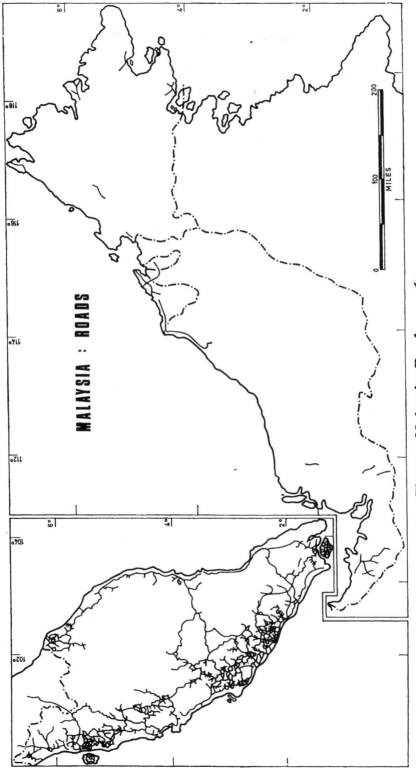

Fig. 7.5. Malaysia: Roads, c. 1960

94 Essays in Political Geography

contrasts, and had given rise to four recognizable zones of successively lower density of population and economic activity, from the highly developed western strip of Malaya, through eastern Malaya and the coastal zone of northern Borneo to the almost completely undeveloped Bornean interior (Fig. 7.6).

This situation in turn produced two inter-related paradoxes. First, although the British Malaysian sphere, having reached its maximum territorial extent in 1914, was geographically centred upon the South China Sea, its demographic and economic centre of gravity lay rather within the immediate peninsular hinterland of the Straits of Malacca. And secondly, while the ten-fold political subdivisions of this sphere, into the Straits Settlements, the Federated Malay States, the six un-federated Malay States of Kedah, Perlis, Kelantan, Trengganu, Johore and Brunei, and the two special protected domains of Sarawak and British North Borneo, bore an obvious relationship to the stages by which British rule had been gradually extended, it was already ceasing by 1914 to have any significant relationship to the four-fold zoning of the area's social and economic geography.

SELF-PERPETUATING FRAGMENTATION, 1826–1942

The practice of creating different types of administrative units at different stages in the process of colonial expansion was not peculiar to Malaysia. Indeed, many parallel çases can be cited in other parts of the British Empire in which the process began with the annexation and subsequent administration under direct colonial rule of small coastal footholds – ideally offshore islands which could be readily held by sea power without incurring extensive commitments on land – and was followed, as opportunity afforded, by the extension of various forms of protection over successively widening areas of the interior. In this sense the protectorate system, which represented a much cheaper form of administration than that of a colony proper, afforded a kind of trial run, well suited to the changing imperial conditions of the nineteenth century. For it served to stake out a claim at a time when rival European powers were seeking to do likewise, and if thereafter it proved successful in fostering profitable commercial enterprise in the territory concerned, it could be followed up by some form of administrative consolidation.

However, whereas in Africa such consolidation usually took the form of an unobtrusive merger of the interior territories with the earlier footholds on the coast, the whole then forming a single compact unit,

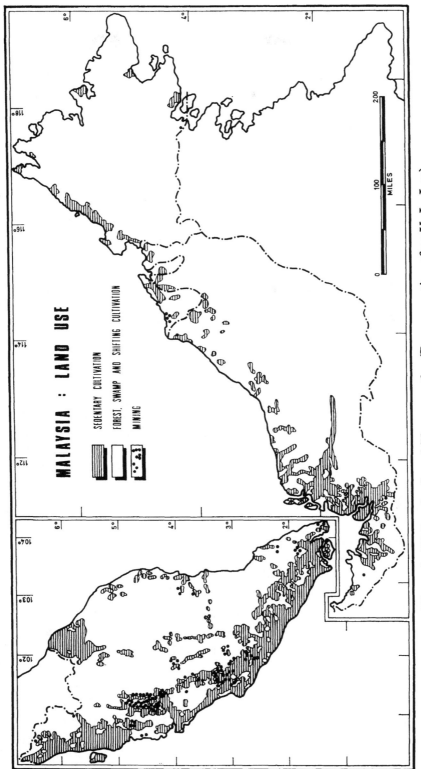

Fig. 7.6. Malaysia: Land Use, c. 1960 (Borneo section after Y. L. Lee)

96 *Essays in Political Geography*

like Nigeria or Sierra Leone, centrally administered from the port-of-entry capital in the original coastal colony, this did not happen in Malaysia, which, on the contrary, remained subdivided into ten separate administrations until the Japanese occupation during the Second World War.

Fundamentally the explanation of this unusual pattern of evolution lies in the failure ever to agree upon what constituted the true *raison d'être* of the British Malaysian sphere. At least from the annexation of Singapore onwards an unresolved conflict existed between what may be called the imperial or sea-route view, and a series of localized views advanced by interested parties on the spot. With the passage of time both the sea-route view and successive local views inevitably underwent significant changes, but arguments advanced in support of particular views at particular times tended to harden into accepted beliefs which persisted long after such changes had rendered them irrelevant. Thus the real nature of the problem eventually came to be obscured in a haze of muddled and parochial thinking, which repeatedly frustrated the efforts of occasional more far-sighted individuals who sought to introduce a measure of administrative rationalization.

As originally introduced by the East India Company, the sea-route policy aimed at opening the route from India to China to British shipping, and although the series of staging posts established for this purpose was also used to develop local trade with the territories through which the route passed, it was of the essence of this policy to keep such territorial commitments to the minimum necessary for the security of the route itself. This can be seen in the extremely restricted area of the original Straits Settlements and also of the two subsequent additions, Hong Kong and Labuan, which were made beyond the Straits after the initiative had passed from Calcutta to London in the 1830s.

With the steady improvements in steamship design, and the opening of the Suez canal in 1869, new strategic factors necessitated successive reappraisals of the sea-route view. Thus in the later nineteenth and early twentieth centuries recurrent fears of a French threat to peninsular Siam and of possible German designs on both sides of the sea route called forth declarations of British interest over various adjacent territories. And although, following the conclusion of the Anglo-Japanese Alliance in 1902, the British appeared to have strengthened their position in the South China Sea, by the time of the Washington Conference of 1921–2 Japan had changed from being a partner to a rival, and the British decided to build the Singapore naval base. Yet here

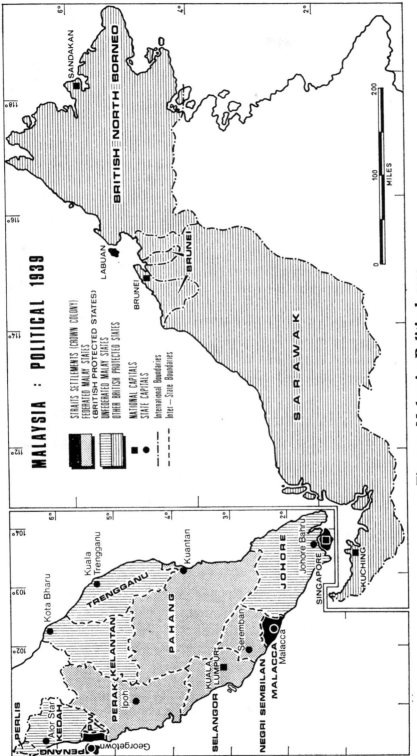

Fig. 7.7. Malaysia: Political, 1939

98   *Essays in Political Geography*

again the emphasis was imperial rather than regional, the primary purpose of the base being to defend India and Australia rather than Malaysia itself, notwithstanding the great and growing economic interests which Britain had meanwhile developed there.[1]

Indeed it is arguable that local economic considerations only succeeded in bringing about any extension of British influence in the Malaysian region when they happened to coincide in time with a consciously felt need in London to reinforce the British hold on the sea route, and although such occasions – as in 1819, 1874, 1896 and 1909 – might have given a superficial impression that local and imperial viewpoints also coincided in purpose, this gradually proved illusory during the years which followed each of the dates in question.

Of the many local views which at different times conflicted in purpose with that of the sea-route view, the first and much the most far-sighted was that of Raffles which led to the founding of Singapore as described on pages 80–1. However, the next decisive British advance in this part of Asia reflected a different kind of conflict, for it was the pressure not of local interests but of British textile manufacturers which led to the Opium War and the related establishment of Hong Kong as a much more effective entrepot for China than Singapore could ever hope to become.

Thereafter, with the string of British staging points completed by the addition of Labuan in 1846, the logical way of co-ordinating control over the sea route would have been to remove the Straits Settlements from British Indian control and to unite it with Hong Kong and Labuan in a single Crown Colony centred in Singapore. But by this time a new and much narrower regional view had emerged among the European community in the Straits Settlements which, though it did seize the opportunity provided by the ending of Company rule in 1858 to petition for separation from India, was concerned above all to prevent an extension of the Indian tariff system into its own free trade area, and to persuade the British government to extend protection over peninsular Malaya in order that Singapore and Penang might expand their trade there to offset the loss of the China entrepot to Hong Kong.[2]

In effect, therefore, the Straits Settlements had begun to develop a kind of expatriate nationalism, arising in characteristic fashion out of

---

[1] Note, however, that the greatest development of British tin and rubber interests was still to come in 1921 when the British decided to build the Singapore base.

[2] *Cf.* Wang Gungwu (ed.), *op. cit.*, p. 134.

Malaysia 99

resentment against its overlords in India and its new rival in Hong Kong, and possessing in 'the maintenance of free trade' a cliché which was hardly less emotive locally than the slogan of 'no taxation without representation' had been in the American colonies. Nevertheless the Straits Settlements only succeeded in becoming a separate Crown Colony on its own in 1867 and in persuading London to agree to the protection of the first Malay states in 1874, as a result of the strategic revolution created by the cutting of the Suez canal between 1859 and 1869. And then, after three decades of rapid expansion in the peninsula, expatriate nationalism began to express itself in yet another and no less blinkered regional view.

For by now the export economy of the peninsular tin zone had assumed a momentum of its own. And although this was still mainly the concern of the Chinese the growing world demand for industrial raw materials, which was beginning to change the whole economic emphasis of colonialism from trade to production, had awakened the British community to the potentialities which the peninsula offered for their own enterprise in both mining and planting. Fundamentally, of course, no conflict existed between the interests of trade and production, and indeed capital derived from the Straits' trade was soon to play as important a role in the development of rubber as it was already doing in respect of tin, both of which in turn were not merely exported through but also processed in, the Straits ports. But, given the prevailing Straits' obsession with the maintenance of free trade, the realization that the cost of providing the infrastructure for an expansion of export production in the peninsula would have to be paid for by export taxes made it a further article of faith that the supposedly divergent interests of traders and producers could not be accommodated within a single political unit.

It seems to have been this clash between different expatriate economic outlooks, and perhaps also the related rivalries of local British officials, rather than any deep concern for the treaty rights of the Malays which seems to have been the decisive factor behind the scheme first proposed in 1893 by local British officials for consolidating the administration of the four protected peninsular states separately from the Straits Settlements, though doubtless their presentation of the proposed Federated Malay States as a protectorate and not a colony made the scheme easier to reconcile with the accepted sea-route view in Whitehall.

In fact, however, the Federated Malay States as set up in 1896 was

100 *Essays in Political Geography*

a rigidly centralized structure in which a kind of overlord Resident, the so-called Resident-General, co-ordinated the 'advice' given to all four Sultans, and himself stood directly under the Governor of the Straits Settlements, acting in his new *alter ego* capacity as High Commissioner for the Federated Malay States.[1] And while this establishment of a *de facto* second colony, informally but effectively co-ordinated with the pre-existing Straits Settlements, might at first sight appear a triumph of the British genius for empiricism and compromise, the practice of make-believe to which it gave rise was an unmitigated disaster.

Thus while the true *raison d'être* of the Federated Malay States was to provide a framework in which British as well as local Chinese economic enterprise could be expanded, a process which it was assumed would indirectly benefit the Malays as well, the impression officially fostered was rather that the Federated Malay States was a Malay land now in process of being modernized, and as such was a totally different country from the cosmopolitan colony of the Straits Settlements.

This official image at first derived a measure of plausibility from the fact that the federated territory, which included Pahang as well as the western mining states but not Johore, contained slightly more Malays than Chinese and was geographically discrete from Singapore, though elsewhere it made marginal contact with the Straits Settlements on the borders of Malacca and Province Wellesley. But between the 1891 and 1901 Censuses the Chinese overtook the 'Malays and other natives of the archipelago' to become the largest single ethnic group in the Federated Malay States, and this alien preponderance was increased by the even more rapid growth of the smaller Indian community.

Nevertheless the process of myth-building continued apace. The former mining town of Kuala Lumpur, which now became the federal capital, was provided with a series of imposing new buildings 'in the modern Moorish style' which, though it could scarcely claim to derive from indigenous Malay architectural tradition, at least contrived to imply that Kuala Lumpur was a Muslim city despite the fact that its population remained predominantly Chinese. Moreover, as befitted the capital of a separate state, Kuala Lumpur had to have its own port, Port Swettenham, appropriately named after the father-figure and first

---

[1] The question of centralization proved to be a controversial issue throughout the existence of the Federated Malay States, but in so far as attempts were made to weaken the influence of Kuala Lumpur they tended merely to strengthen that of Singapore. For a fuller discussion of this problem and for an indispensable critique of British policy in Malaya in general, see R. Emerson, *Malaysia – a Study in Direct and Indirect Rule.*

Malaysia 101

Resident-General of the Federated Malay States, Sir Frank Swettenham, who in 1901 had attained the Janus-like eminence of Governor-High Commissioner in Singapore.

Already before the end of the nineteenth century, therefore, expatriate nationalism had modified the normal colonial trend towards administrative consolidation into producing not one but two rival political units within the Malayan sector of what was in effect a single field of British economic and political influence. Moreover, a further part of this field, in northern Borneo, still remained unconsolidated,[1] notwithstanding the early efforts of James Brooke to bring about a merger between Sarawak and the Straits Settlements in 1857[2] and the local proposal in 1894 that British North Borneo should be federated with Sarawak. Nevertheless the decision of 1906 to appoint a British Resident to Brunei, who was to act under the Governor-High Commissioner in Singapore, represented at least a minor step towards closer co-ordination of British policy in northern Borneo with that in Malaya, and after the four northern Malay states had also come under formal British protection in 1909 as unfederated Malay states their legal position was virtually identical with that of Brunei.

Since, besides the strategic considerations which weighed in London, the local pressure for protecting these northern states – and later for bringing Johore also into line in this respect – had come from a desire to secure a still wider area for British planting and related activities, one might have expected that these states would have been incorporated into the existing Federated Malay States structure. However, the over-centralization of the latter had already come under criticism from the Malay Rulers in 1903, and no such incorporation was attempted at this stage.

Nevertheless, at a time when the completion of the trunk railway between Prai (opposite Penang) and the capitals of the western states of Johore Bharu (opposite Singapore island) was making the political sub-division of the country seem daily more anachronistic, there were many expatriates in Malaya who felt the time had come for a change. It was in these circumstances that in 1912 Arnold Wright and T. H. Reid, two local British residents, put forward in *The Malay Peninsula* a cogent plea for the shedding of illusions and the facing of realities. In particular,

---

[1] The only administrative change to take effect was that Labuan was handed over to British North Borneo in 1890, but in 1906 it was removed from the latter and reincorporated in the Straits Settlements.

[2] *Cf.* Wang Gungwu, *op. cit.*, p. 131.

102 *Essays in Political Geography*

they argued that a basic identity of interest existed between the Straits Settlements, the Federated Malay States and the unfederated states, and that this must not be ignored 'merely to bolster up a system which, though useful in its day, had outlived the conditions which dictated its inception and development. The water-tight compartment system may be good for a ship, but it is bad for a colony.'[1] In short, the whole country should be brought under a single administration.

While in their repeated use of the term Malaya, instead of the official nomenclature which recognized only its several parts, Wright and Reid were distinctly ahead of their time, they made no reference to the Borneo territories, whose geographical remoteness had not been reduced by any improvement in sea communications comparable to that brought about by the railway in the peninsula and so continued to exclude them from popular discussion on the future of British Malaya. But so far as the latter was concerned, it seems probable that the views of Wright and Reid would have gained much wider support but for the intervention of the First World War, which ranked as a major divide in the history of Western imperialism in general and in its specifically Malayan context in particular.

To people of Wright and Reid's generation the growth of commerce and the establishment of 'ordered government and social contentment'[2] provided a self-evident justification of colonial rule and, judged by these standards 'the beacon light of the Federated Malay States shines brilliantly, beckoning (Malaya) on the road she should 'go . . .'[3] But after the war, with its shock to Western complacency and the new insistence on the principle of self-determination, this older view of imperialism began to be replaced by the concept already elaborated by Lugard in Africa, and subsequently incorporated in the League of Nations mandate system, that dependent territories should be held in temporary trust for their own peoples who should meanwhile be assisted economically and educationally in order eventually to run them themselves.

Judged by these criteria, Malaya, in large parts of which the Malays had been pushed into the background by immigrant Chinese and Indians, appeared in a much less favourable light, and although many expatriates continued to accept the old standards, the new outlook became increasingly prevalent in the Malayan Civil Service after the early 1920s. Thus among the latter the belief developed that at all

---

[1] Arnold Wright and T. H. Reid, *The Malaya Peninsula*, p. 349.
[2] *Ibid.*, p. 346. [3] *Ibid.*, p. 344.

Malaysia 103

costs the unfederated Malay States should be protected against any unwanted intrusions of alien forces via the Federated Malay States or the Straits Settlements, and only after the position of the Malays had been generally strengthened *vis à vis* the immigrant communities would it be possible to contemplate any move towards peninsular unification.

Accordingly official policy concentrated upon maintaining the status of the Sultans as heads of the indigenous governmental structure, and bringing more and more members of the Malay aristocracy (but no Chinese or Indians) into the Malayan Civil Service and, at the other end of the scale, on extending the area of Malay Reservations to include all the main paddy regions and assisting the Malay peasant to take up small-scale cash crop production. Meanwhile, in line with the practice dating from 1896 of preferring fiction to fact, the Asian immigrants were regarded mainly as 'birds of passage' who accordingly had no claim to be treated as true citizens of the country.

While it was true that most of the Indians came as labourers and rarely stayed more than three years, a growing proportion of the Chinese was by the 1930s tending to settle permanently, and indeed one such, Tan Cheng Lock, had in 1926 advocated the creation of a united British Malaya in which all who wished to settle permanently should enjoy democratic rights. But it was also true that, as the world depression hit Malaya many unemployed Chinese returned home, and that from 1927 onwards the Malayan Chinese were being subjected to a growing volume of Kuo Min Tang propaganda which on occasion referred to Malaya as China's Nineteenth Province.[1]

It was at this stage that in 1931 the new Governor-High Commissioner, Sir Cecil Clementi, put forward proposals for loosening the administrative structure of the Federated Malay States and establishing a customs union, which together were designed to bring the whole of British Malaya at last into a single system. Moreover Clementi looked ever further afield, and in taking soundings on the possibility of also bringing in the Borneo territories, he appears to have been the first to consider calling in eastern Malaysia to redress the balance of the western part of the sphere.

For Clementi's proposals were aimed not merely at administrative rationalization but also at confirming the paramount position of the Malays *vis à vis* the immigrant population. Not surprisingly, therefore,

[1] Kuo Min Tang influence had been growing among the Malayan (and other South-east Asian) Chinese since the early years of the century.

104 *Essays in Political Geography*

they aroused strong opposition among the British and Chinese commercial communities in both the Federated Malay States and the Straits Settlements on the grounds that they would impair stability and economic efficiency, to which the Straits Settlements added their traditional warning that to tamper with free trade was to undermine their livelihood. Perhaps more surprising was the way in which the Malays of the unfederated states also joined in opposing the proposals, fearing that, notwithstanding the purpose behind them, any closer association with the rest of the peninsula would inevitably increase the danger of alien penetration into their territories.

Whatever the relative merits or demerits of Clementi's proposals, therefore, the negative reaction which successfully emasculated them provided a remarkable demonstration of the staying power of established boundaries. No matter how anomalous the latter may be, provided only that they have time in which to stabilize, they tend to become the accepted frameworks within which political attitudes and economic interests crystallize to produce a condition of politico-geographical ossification. In Malaya's case the First World War provided the necessary time for the mould to set, and it was not until the Second World War that strong enough forces emerged to break it again.

Superimposed upon, but not coinciding geographically with, the communal division between Malays, Chinese and Indians, this long-continued political fragmentation into Straits Settlements, Federated Malay States, and five separate unfederated States – to say nothing of the three Borneo territories – served effectively to prevent the emergence of any all-embracing sense of Malayan – let alone Malaysian – nationality, comparable to that which was developing apace in surrounding areas, including most significantly the Netherlands Indies next door, which, with ten times the population, nevertheless constituted a single political unit.

Instead, each community tended not merely to think in terms of its own sectional interests, but to see these either in narrowly localized terms, or else – more imaginatively but less precisely – in a predominantly extra-Malaysian context. Thus among the Malays the more traditionally-minded thought simply of loyalty to their own Sultan, while many of the younger element dreamed of Pan-Islamic unity or association with Indonesian nationalism. And a not wholly dissimilar dualism existed between those Chinese who continued to think purely of making money in whatever local circumstances they found themselves in, and those whose enthusiasm was fired by the rival ideologies – Kuo

Malaysia 105

Min Tan or Communist – which were contending for the mastery of their homeland.[1]

Seemingly oblivious of these trends, the European community meanwhile took pride in the belief that Malaya was 'a happy country' in which people of different races lived side by side in inter-communal harmony. In so far as this was true – though the depth of the communal feelings which have recently been exposed compels one to re-examine this assumption – it serves only to underline the tragedy of the opportunity which was missed by the British in failing to make any positive attempt at welding these diverse peoples, whom they had been instrumental in bringing together, into a single community which would cohere harmoniously after colonialism had had its day.

To explain this neglect as a deliberate policy of divide and rule is, however, to overstate the case, and indeed there was no need to divide in order to rule. Rather the failure lay in a bland unwillingness to face the facts of time and place and hence, instead of reacting constructively to the momentous changes which were afoot, in taking refuge in what can only be called a policy of benevolent drift.

On the eve of the Second World War, therefore, the British Malaysian sphere, which formed the commercial and geopolitical centre-piece of the Western colonial system in South-east Asia, represented the epitome of that system in both its strength and its weaknesses. Thus, in proportion to either area or population, Malaysia had by far the largest volume of overseas trade in what had meanwhile become the world's greatest single source of tropical produce. Intimately related to its special economic position was the fact that it also had a far higher proportion of Chinese in its population than had any other South-east Asian territory and indeed, with the further inclusion of its substantial Indian community, was the only one in which alien Asians outnumbered the local population.

Moreover, and perhaps more remarkably, just as South-east Asia as a whole was politically divided into a series of rival colonial spheres of widely varying size and importance, so British Malaysia was fragmented into a curiously ill-assorted collection of political units. And as the political divisions of South-east Asia had effectively prevented the Western colonial powers from seeing the problems of this vast region as a whole, the political fragmentation of its focal area had likewise prevented the British from recognizing the common elements in the problems which faced them in the component parts of Malaysia.

[1] *Cf.* Wang Gungwu, *op. cit.*, p. 143.

106　*Essays in Political Geography*

Not the least of these problems, and one which again applied at both the regional and the Malaysian level, was that of providing so lucrative and so exposed an area with adequately co-ordinated defences. Only after the collapse of France had allowed the Japanese a few months before Pearl Harbour to penetrate half-way down the South-east Asian mainland, was the A.B.C.D. front hurriedly put together. But in the conditions of the time this was merely a front without a back as, by the same token, the Singapore base at the strategic focus of the region was a base without a fleet. So a divided Malaysia in a divided South-east Asia faced the Japanese onslaught, and in common division they fell.

OCCUPATION AND RE-OCCUPATION, 1942–6

The swift Japanese seizure of virtually the whole of South-east Asia within a few months of December 1941 was the decisive fact in bringing to an end what K. M. Panikkar has called the 'da Gama epoch' of Western dominance in Asia. For besides administering a devastating humiliation to Western prestige, Japan came also as the self-styled champion of Asia for the Asiatics,[1] and although its activities in China during the preceding decade had raised doubts among some of its neighbours – notably India – about its sincerity in this respect, such misgivings were not widely shared among the indigenous peoples of South-east Asia whose prevailing attitude to China was conditioned by their antipathy to the local Chinese communities in their midst. And while the behaviour of the Japanese armed forces subsequently did much to disabuse the South-east Asians, it was clear to the more far-sighted of Western observers that, although the Allies must expel the Japanese, their military re-occupation of the region could be no more than the prelude to permanent political withdrawal for, on the one hand, the Japanese interregnum had provided a forcing house for South-east Asian nationalism and, on the other, American participation in the War had been accompanied by a growing concern that its allies among the European colonial powers should come to terms with Asian nationalism in the peace which would follow.

On all logical grounds the starting point for any programme of post-war decolonization was the British Indian Empire, incomparably the greatest and most advanced of all the West's dependent territories, and

---

[1] The practice of regarding 'Asiatics' as a derogatory term, and hence of replacing it by 'Asians' did not become popular until after the Second World War.

Malaysia 107

by 1945 a growing body of British opinion, especially in the Labour party, was clearly moving towards the implementation of such a policy. However, so far as South-east Asia was concerned, most of which was much less experienced politically than India, and unlike the latter had been subjected to nearly four years of devastation, turmoil and chaos, British public opinion, while sympathetic to change, was not yet convinced that similar policies to those envisaged for India were immediately applicable here, and the French and Dutch were strongly opposed to anything like such radical measures in the territories for which they were responsible. But whatever the rights and wrongs of these pre-surrender judgments, the American commitment to grant independence to the Philippines in 1946 meant that the whole area between the latter and India would inevitably be caught up in the demand for independence, regardless of the very diverse policies which the Japanese had followed in individual countries during their occupation.

While the interlude from 1942 to 1945[1] was the only period in its history when all South-east Asia was under the control of a single power, the Japanese had attempted, so far as possible, to work within the pre-existing administrative frameworks, in order to avoid any interference with pressing military needs, including the exploitation of local strategic raw materials. Thus, although from an early stage the Japanese sought popular support by making vague promises of independence within the Co-prosperity Sphere, these were mostly expressed in terms of the existing colonial units. Later, as their hopes of a quick victory faded, they began to implement these promises, first in Burma and the Philippines in 1943 and then, in modified form in French Indochina and the Netherlands Indies in 1945.

As always, however, British Malaysia constituted a special case. To the Japanese, as to others before them, Malaya – and in particular Singapore – appeared as the strategic focus of the whole region. For this reason, and also because they considered Malaya to be too politically immature for independence, they initially treated it as Japanese territory, which they proceeded to hold by a policy of divide and rule. Under this the Chinese, particularly those who had shown support for their homeland against Japan, became the main focus of resentment, the Indians, at first handled more cautiously in view of Japan's designs upon their mother country, later suffered severely as the chief source of forced labour, while an attempt was made, at least in theory, to treat

[1] On the Japanese occupation in general, see Willard H. Elsbree, *Japan's role in Southeast Asian Nationalist Movements.*

108 *Essays in Political Geography*

the Malays – and especially the Sultans – as the rightful owners of the country.

This policy towards Malaya was related to the Japanese approach to the Netherlands Indies which, in the early stages of the war, was marked by much uncertainty. For while they did not seriously question the political readiness of Java for independence, when strategic considerations would permit it, they were deeply divided over the desirability of extending this to the politically less advanced outer islands which, moreover, were the principal sources of petroleum and other war materials. In the meantime, therefore, Sumatra was included with Malaya in an army administration; Java was placed under another with its headquarters at Jakarta; and the widely scattered eastern islands, including both Dutch and British Borneo, came under a naval administration based on Makasar.

Strategically sound as the new alignment of Sumatra with Malaya might have been, however, the Japanese attempt to popularize it, by stressing the cultural and linguistic ties between the two and pandering to latent Sumatran jealousy of the Javanese, met with little response in Sumatra and eventually Malaya and Sumatra were each placed under separate military administrations. On the other hand some peninsular Malays, whose relations with the Chinese were becoming increasingly embittered both by Japanese propaganda and by the familiar effect of wartime food shortages in aggravating traditional antipathies between townsmen and countrymen, were less negative in their reaction to the alignment with Sumatra, for it reinforced their tendency to think in terms of closer association with their ethnic kinsfolk in Indonesia.

Such thinking was by no means unwelcome to the Indonesian leaders once the Japanese in the closing stages of the war had recognized the strength of the nationalists and had encouraged them to formulate proposals for an independent Indonesia. Nevertheless, although a clear majority of the Indonesian representatives consulted voted on 10 July 1945 to include both Malaya and British Borneo within the proposed new state, the Japanese finally decided to limit the latter strictly to the area of the Netherlands Indies, and it was on this basis that the Republic of Indonesia was proclaimed by Sukarno, shortly after the Japanese surrender, on 18 August 1945.

Whatever the reason for this last-minute decision by the Japanese, the fact remains that whereas, on balance their policies undoubtedly helped the Indonesian nationalists to consolidate their position in the Netherlands Indies as a whole, the net effect of the occupation in

Malaysia 109

British Malaysia was divisive. For although the Japanese had taken little heed of the old British subdivisions of Malaya, they had retroceded the four northern states to Thailand, administered Singapore as the strategic headquarters separately from the rest of Malaya, bracketed the Borneo territories with eastern Indonesia, and most serious of all, provoked a new intensity of feeling between Chinese and Malays. It was against this unpropitious background that the British returned in September–October 1945.[1]

Nor was this all. The attempt to work out a new British policy towards the Malaysian territories had begun well before the surrender, but by the time the British were in a position to put their ideas into effect an atmosphere of profound uncertainty enveloped almost the whole surrounding region. Thus within South-east Asia itself Indonesia next door was involved in the struggle – which lasted until 1949 – to make good its independence from the Dutch, Burma was in a state of growing tension, and Vietnam already in the throes of the conflict which in one form or another has continued to the present day. And, farther afield, the promise of Indian independence was beginning to split that sub-continent and China was showing signs of reverting to civil war between the Communists and the Kuo Min Tang.

In these circumstances, which entailed the possibility of a whole range of developments of direct concern to one or other of Malaysia's three main communities, the British had to choose between waiting upon events in these neighbouring countries, or attempting so far as possible to isolate the Malaysian situation from its wider geographical context, and pushing ahead with the plans which they had been preparing for it. Understandably they chose the latter course and although, given the rising temper of Asian nationalism, delay was undesirable, the British in their haste misjudged the local situation.

The basic assumption which underlay the British post-war plans for Malaysia was that, unlike their other main possessions in Asia – India/Pakistan, Ceylon and Burma – none of the Malaysian territories as yet possessed any overall nationalist movement. And although the British were surprised on their return to find that certain Malays who had been actively associating with the Indonesian nationalists were now in process of forming the Malay Nationalist Party, and that the MPAJA[2] was apparently preparing to establish a Communist People's Republic,

[1] The British Military Administration was set up in Malaya in September and in northern Borneo in October 1945.

[2] *I.e.* Malayan People's Anti-Japanese Army.

110 *Essays in Political Geography*

they quickly concluded that neither of these movements spoke for more than a minority of either Malays or Chinese, let alone for Malaya as a whole, and accordingly saw no reasons to change the plans which had already been prepared. Thus, after a brief interval of four months in which the more urgent tasks of restoring law and order and organizing material rehabilitation had been set in train, the British announced their new policy in a White Paper in January 1946.[1]

Beginning with a reference to the prewar administrative fragmentation of Malaya, the White Paper went on to assert that

> A stage has now been reached when the system of government should be simplified and reformed. International relations as well as the security and other interests of the British Commonwealth require that Malaya should be able to exercise an influence as a united and enlightened country appropriate to her economic and strategic importance. On a longer view, too, the pre-war system will not lend itself to that political adjustment which will offer through broad-based institutions in which the whole community can participate, the means and prospect of developing Malaya's capacity in the direction of responsible self-government.[2]

To this end, therefore, it proposed to bring the whole of Malaya except Singapore within a single Malayan Union with a centralized administration consisting of a Governor and both an Executive and a Legislative Council. In addition, there would be subordinate administrations for each State and Settlement, while the Sultans would remain as little more than figureheads, to advise on matters pertaining to Malay tradition and religion. To replace the profusion of legal nationalities existing before the war a Malayan Union Citizenship would be created, to which all locally born persons of whatever race, together with immigrants of long standing, would be admitted. Meanwhile, Singapore, implicitly because it was 'a centre of entrepot trade on a very large scale and (had) economic and social interests distinct from those of the mainland', would remain apart, 'at least for the time being',[3] as a separate Crown Colony, with its own Governor and Executive and Legislative Councils. And by a final innovation a Governor-General would be appointed to co-ordinate policies not only in the Malayan Union and Singapore, but also, it was hoped, in all the British Bornean territories as well. For by this time the British Government was negotiating to end

---

[1] *Malayan Union and Singapore: Statement of Policy on Future Constitution,* January 1946, Cmd. 6724.

[2] *Ibid.,* p. 2. [3] *Ibid.,* p. 3.

Malaysia 111

the anachronistic pre-war regimes in Sarawak and British North Borneo,[1] and in July 1946 these latter became Crown Colonies three months after the Malayan Union had officially come into being in April of that year.

THE DIVERGENCE OF SINGAPORE FROM MALAYA, 1946–63

Notwithstanding the severe criticism which the 1946 proposals quickly encountered in many quarters, they represented a well-intentioned – if in some respects an ill-judged – attempt to make up for time lost in the past, and, despite the vastly more difficult circumstances which now obtained, to create with all possible speed a framework in which a Malayan[2] nation could come into being.

In pre-war days the main obstacles to such a development had been the principle of permanent Malay paramountcy and the political fragmentation of the country. And while it would not have been easy to have brought both of these to an end before the war, to attempt to do so now, when an immediate introduction of democratic franchise was envisaged and the winding up of British colonial rule was obviously on the horizon, presented an infinitely more difficult task. For a British withdrawal would leave economic power primarily in the hands of the Chinese and Indian communities, and since together these had been shown by the most recent census (in 1931) to outnumber the Malays, the latter would be faced simultaneously with economic and political inferiority within a country which they regarded as their own, and in most parts of which their special position had been guaranteed by the original treaties of British protection.

The characteristic British response to such a peculiarly intractable problem as this is to compromise, and it was in this spirit that the Malayan Union was conceived. The principle of Malay paramountcy was implicitly abandoned, and new treaties were signed with all the Malay rulers late in 1945 as a preliminary to the publication of the White Paper in January 1946,[3] but the process of administrative

---

[1] On becoming a Crown Colony British North Borneo changed its name to North Borneo. The name was changed again to Sabah in 1963 (see below, p. 123).

[2] In pre-war British expatriate usage 'Malayan' referred to all communities – and not merely to Malays – living in Malaya. It was in this wider sense that the term Malayan should be understood here. However, whereas in prewar days 'Malaya' had included Singapore as well as the peninsula, it now began increasingly to be applied to the latter alone.

[3] See above, note 1, p. 110. The ideas behind this had been presented to the British Parliament in October 1945.

112 Essays in Political Geography

unification was extended only to the peninsula, in which overall the Malays held a numerical lead. By a curious coincidence, as Table 7.1 shows, the Malays in 1931 slightly outnumbered both Chinese and Indians together in the whole of Malaya excluding Singapore, and it seems to have been assumed that, by limiting the Malayan Union to this area, the facts of political arithmetic would give the Malays the necessary confidence to accept all local-born and long-resident immigrant

TABLE 7.1: MAIN ETHNIC GROUPS IN MALAYA, 1931 AND 1947

Area and Census date	Malays (including immigrants from Indonesia)	Chinese	Indians	Total (including others)
All Malaya 1931	1,934,900	1,705,915	623,224	4,365,800
Singapore 1931	71,177	421,821	51,019	559,946
Malaya without Singapore 1931*	1,863,723	1,284,094	572,205	3,805,854
		1,856,299		
All Malaya 1947	2,543,569	2,614,667	599,616	5,448,910
Singapore 1947	115,735	730,133	68,974	940,824
Malaya without Singapore 1947*	2,427,834	1,884,534	530,638	4,908,086
		2,415,172		

* Area included in Malayan Union (1946) and Federation of Malaya (1948).

Chinese and Indians as fellow citizens on terms of political equality with themselves.

Moreover, in the prevailing uncertainties affecting surrounding areas, it could at least be argued that it was best, 'for the time being', to keep Singapore, the strategic focus of British power in South-east Asia, outside the experiment in inter-communal nation-building which was planned for the Malayan Union, and to allow it to advance towards self-government in its own way which, in view of its predominantly Chinese population and its greater sophistication as an international metropolis, might well prove different from that of the Malayan Union.[1]

[1] The difference in the communal composition of the Singapore population from that of the Malayan Union as a whole was referred to in the White Paper (Cmnd. 6724) and was perfectly valid (see Table 7.1). But the communal composition of the population of the main peninsular towns was – and is – almost identical with that of Singapore. See below, note 1, p. 129.

Malaysia 113

Meanwhile the Borneo territories, which by contrast were politically more retarded than Malaya, would be encouraged to take the first steps towards self-government, via what was becoming the normal British colonial practice of creating Legislative Councils with progressively wider unofficial representation.

How long these various roads to responsible government would take in the several parts of British Malaysia it was impossible at this stage to foresee, but the 1946 proposals deliberately kept the way open for future adjustments between them. This was implicit both in the statement that the Governor-General 'will not have any direct administrative functions but he will have power of co-ordination and direction and power to convene conferences on any subject . . . to be attended by British Governors and other British representatives within his sphere of authority', and in the assurance that it was not intended 'to preclude or prejudice in any way the fusion of Singapore and the Malayan Union in a wider union at a later date should it be considered that such a course were desirable.'[1]

It seems, therefore, that the British were already thinking in terms of some form of wider Malaysian grouping as early as 1946. Having accepted the decisive step in respect of India, British opinion was beginning to look ahead to a progressive devolution of power in other parts of the colonial empire and, on the basis of earlier Canadian and Australian experience, the federation of adjacent dependencies appeared to represent a necessary preliminary stage to the achievement of meaningful independence in administratively diffuse areas. Such a possibility had often been mentioned for the West Indies, and comments in the British press soon suggested that a similar approach was being considered for the entire series of British dependencies bordering upon the Straits of Malacca and the South China Sea, including Hong Kong,[2] whose population had fallen from 849,751 in 1931 to less than 600,000 in August 1945, and whose future role *vis à vis* China was becoming increasingly uncertain.

On this interpretation of Britain's long-term aims in the region, the separation of Singapore from the Malay peninsula appeared to make greater sense. For, as the growing point out of which British commercial and territorial interests east of the old Indian Empire had sprung, and the obvious link between the Malay peninsula and both the Borneo territories and Hong Kong, Singapore – in its own insular

[1] White Paper (Cmnd. 6724), p. 3.
[2] *Cf.* F. G. Carnell, 'Closer association in British South-east Asia', p. 13.

114 *Essays in Political Geography*

District of Columbia – seemed marked out by geography for the role of federal capital in any such future grouping. Nevertheless while, alike on administrative, commercial and strategic grounds this arrangement would have self-evident advantages, it was equally clear that in such a federation, the numerical primacy of the Chinese would be further underlined by their even greater predominance in Singapore. If, therefore, the British seriously wished to promote a working partnership between Malays, Chinese and Indians in the Malayan Union, it would be necessary to soft-pedal the question of Singapore and to defer any decision on its future status until such partnership had had a chance to develop in the peninsula, which in the event was precisely what the British did.

However, in the absence of any clear indication of what its role was to be, Singapore was understandably resentful at its separation from the rest of Malaya. For while its entrepot trade and other commercial interests certainly did involve a far wider area than the Malay peninsula, the latter by now constituted much the largest component within its hinterland. And indeed as the headquarters of most of the great Western banks, managing agencies and commercial houses operating in Malaya, and the apex of the Chinese trading system[1] throughout that country as a whole, Singapore was as much the economic capital of Malaya as London was of the United Kingdom.

Within Singapore itself, therefore, its separation from Malaya was seen simultaneously as an act of discrimination against the interests of the entire Malayan Chinese community and as creating a major obstacle to the development of the closer commercial and industrial links with the mainland which seemed to offer the obvious response to the prospect of a relative decline in the entrepot trade, arising from the post-war growth of economic nationalism in neighbouring parts of South-east Asia.

In these circumstances, past experience of the remarkable staying power of arbitrary political divisions in pre-war Malaya suggested that, despite the White Paper's reference to Singapore's exclusion as merely 'for the time being', the likelihood was that henceforth the island would be left permanently as a head without a body. And this impression was not made more palatable by the fact that the only precedent for such a

[1] J. M. Gullick, *Malaya*, p. 112. Gullick's book, and the sections by J. Norman Parmer, 'Malaysia', in G. McT. Kahin (ed.), *Government and Politics in Southeast Asia*, pp. 281–371, and by Victor Purcell, 'Malayan Politics', in Saul Rose (ed.), *Politics in Southern Asia*, pp. 218–34, provide three invaluable complementary accounts of political developments, particularly from the Second World War to the formulation of the Malaysian proposals.

Malaysia 115

division had been under the divide and rule policy of the Japanese, or by the apparent cynicism with which the British had sought to justify the new separation by reference to the entrepot trade while at the same time including the other great entrepot centre of Penang within the Malayan Union.

However, notwithstanding the widespread resentment over the 1946 proposals among Singapore's predominantly Chinese population, it was the opposition of the Malays, based on the contrary argument that the Malayan Union had conceded too much to the Chinese and other immigrants, which eventually led the British to reconsider their policies here.

Owing to the sudden change of Japanese plans in the summer of 1945, which had led to the unexpected exclusion of Malaya from the new Indonesian Republic, the more extreme Malay nationalists of the so-called KRIS movement (People's Association of Peninsular Indonesians) had been left in complete disarray, and indeed the whole situation had been one of the utmost confusion. However, once it had become clear that for the foreseeable future Malaya's destinies would be shaped by London rather than by Jakarta, it was not long before a more moderate and more representative element among the Malays seized the political initiative. It was in these circumstances that in April 1946 Dato Onn, the Prime Minister of Johore, founded the United Malays Nationalist Organization (U.M.N.O.) expressly to oppose the Malayan Union. And when the unexpectedly strong opposition of the Malays called forth equally unexpected expressions of approval from many retired British officials, including the aged Swettenham himself, the tide began to turn, and on 28 February 1948 the Malayan Union was replaced by the Federation of Malaya.

Although the constitution of the latter maintained the principle of strong central administration, it nevertheless restored the pre-war status of the Malay rulers and introduced a new Federal citizenship which applied automatically to virtually all Malays (including Indonesian immigrants) but initially embraced only approximately one-third of the Chinese and Indians domiciled in the country. In effect, therefore, and notwithstanding the reiteration of the British desire that 'progress should be made towards eventual self-government',[1] the creation of the Federation marked a return to the pre-war doctrine of Malay paramountcy. Accordingly, just as the Union had antagonized the Malays

[1] *Federation of Malaya – Summary of Revised Constitutional Proposals*, July 1947, Cmd. 7171, p. 5.

116 *Essays in Political Geography*

so the Federation tended still further to alienate the sympathies of the Malayan Chinese, as quickly became apparent after the outbreak of the insurrection by the Malayan Races Liberation Army in June 1948. For despite its name, the M.R.L.A. was merely a reorganization of the wartime Communist M.P.A.J.A., and 99 per cent of its fighting members were Chinese[1] who, moreover, received their material support from Chinese squatters, most of whom had begun illegally to occupy land on the fringe of the jungle during the Japanese interregnum.

While the Malayan 'Emergency' was only one of the several communist insurrections launched in various parts of South-east Asia in 1948, its distinctive communal overtones at first seemed to spell the end of British hopes of achieving a better relationship between Malays and Chinese. But in fact only a minority of the Chinese gave willing support to the M.R.L.A. and, thanks to skilled anti-guerrilla tactics and an effective programme of squatter resettlement, the insurrection was already on the wane by 1954, though the state of emergency remained technically in force until 1960.

In the meantime the political initiative passed to the emerging U.M.N.O. leadership, which had gained much from its success in getting the Union replaced by the Federation. Moreover, secure in their heavy numerical predominance as Federal citizens, the Malays now began to see the force of the British contention that meaningful independence could not be achieved until they themselves had reached a *modus vivendi* with the other communities, which would make it unnecessary for the British to go on maintaining and periodically readjusting the balance between them, as they had done in 1946 and 1948.

During the immediate post-war period, when it was still the practice to think of the Malayan communal pattern in terms of three main components, there had been some speculation as to whether the Indians – numerically the smallest but perhaps, in the reflected glory of Nehru, politically the most sophisticated – might come to provide a built-in balancing force. But especially after the 1947 census had revealed the severity of the losses which the Indians had suffered during the occupation, the communal problem came to be viewed essentially as a direct conflict between Malays and Chinese.

Symptomatic of this new outlook was the conclusion of the Communities Liaison Committee, inaugurated by the Commissioner-General in 1948, that improved inter-communal relations could best be promoted by combining economic assistance to the Malays with

[1] Saul Rose (ed.), *Politics in Southern Asia*, p. 220.

Malaysia 117

greater political opportunities for the Chinese. But the failure of Dato Onn's attempt to further the second of these aims by admitting Chinese (and Indians) to membership of U.M.N.O. had led in 1951 to his replacement as party leader by Tunku Abdul Rahman, and incidentally also to Dato Onn's becoming chairman of the Rural and Industrial Development Authority (R.I.D.A.) whose main purpose was to promote the second aim.[1]

It was the great strength of the Tunku that he was essentially an empiricist, whose interest lay not in romantic attempts to recreate the real or imagined glories of the past, but in the practical task of building a nation out of the ethnically heterogeneous material that lay to hand. Accepting the new British contention that the essential precondition of independence was the creation of a politically viable nation, he set himself the difficult task of making good the deficiencies in this respect which had resulted from the years of neglect under pre-war colonial rule.

In this task he was greatly assisted by the way in which the void left by the decline of the pre-war Kuo Min Tang movement in Malaya was filled by the emergence of the altogether more constructive Malayan Chinese Association under the leadership of Tan Cheng Lock. (See above, p. 103.) As a life-long supporter of home rule for Malaya on behalf of all who regarded it as their home, Tan had founded the M.C.A. with the aim of promoting Sino-Malay co-operation. But notwithstanding his own background of active participation in politics, he spoke above all for the older generation of peninsular Chinese who, with characteristic pragmatism, had in the past pursued the substance of economic advancement rather than the shadow of politics under colonial rule, and were still prepared to play a secondary role politically in exchange for freedom and security to take the lead commercially.

If, therefore, the Malayan Chinese problem could be solved by giving that community a free hand economically and at the same time using part of the proceeds derived from taxing its enterprise to finance measures designed to close the economic gap between Malays and Chinese, a satisfactory basis existed for co-operation. Thus it was that the U.M.N.O. and M.C.A. leadership, both well schooled in the British tradition of compromise, agreed in 1953 to the political Alliance, which in the 1955 elections won 51 out of 52 elective seats, giving it a working majority over the 47 non-elective members of the Federal Legislative Council.

[1] *Cf.* Gullick, *Malaya*, pp. 113–14.

118 *Essays in Political Geography*

Thereafter, with rising prosperity and the waning of the Communist insurrection, the Federation moved rapidly towards independence which took effect on 31 August 1957. Besides becoming an independent member of the Commonwealth – though not of SEATO – the Federation of Malaya signed a defence treaty with Britain whereby the latter was permitted to lease military bases and to station British and other Commonwealth troops in Malaysia for local and regional defence.

Under its new constitution Malaya remained a federation of nine states and two settlements, and although within each of the former the Malay rulers retained their pre-existing status, provision was also made for them periodically to elect one of their number to act as Supreme Ruler (Yang di-Pertuan Agong) for a term of five years. The Federal Parliament consisted of a Senate with limited powers and a House of Representatives containing 104 elected members, while each of the eleven component units also had its own Legislative Assembly. Islam was declared to be the State religion, but freedom of worship was assured to all, and henceforth all persons of whatever community born in the State would be federal citizens.

Admittedly, certain Malay preferences remained. The new citizenship rules did not apply to non-Malays born before independence, and moreover the Malays were allocated – without time limit – a preponderant share of government scholarships and civil service posts. But, compared with the disabilities from which the non-indigenous communities suffered in most other parts of South-east Asia, these residual survivals of Malay paramountcy seemed unimportant and, as its progress during the next few years was to demonstrate, the new Federation clearly commanded widespread support among all the three main communal groups.

To turn from developments in the Federation to those in Singapore during the fifteen years following 1948 was, however, to see the other side of the coin. For whereas at first this industrious and cosmopolitan city-state, whose wide-ranging view of the world contrasted sharply with the provincialism which had hitherto characterized Malaya, made much the more rapid political progress of the two, the persistent thwarting of its desire for political union with its peninsular hinterland had led by the early 1960s to an explosive sense of frustrated nationalism.

Although the instructions given in 1948[1] to the Commissioner-General of the United Kingdom in South-east Asia suggested that

---

[1] The office of Commissioner-General replaced that of Governor-General in 1948, though the incumbent, Mr Malcolm Macdonald, remained unchanged. By

Malaysia 119

Britain still regarded Singapore in terms of its wider Malaysian context, suspicions within Singapore were intensified by both the change from the Malayan Union to the Federation of Malaya and by the decision to continue to keep Singapore outside. For this reason its Chinese community boycotted the Colony's 1948 elections, which were nevertheless won by the Labour party whose campaign programme had *inter alia* included union with the Federation.

Whatever may have been the justification for the original exclusion of Singapore from Malaya in 1946, the Communist victory in China in 1949, following swiftly after the series of Communist insurrections in South-east Asia in 1948, served to place the whole problem in an entirely new context. Thus, besides apparently underlining the strategic arguments in favour of retaining direct British control over Singapore, it presented the local Chinese, who comprised 76 per cent of the latter's population, with a new dilemma. For, situated at the geographical centre of the nationalist upsurge in South-east Asia, the peoples of Singapore were inevitably moved by similar sentiments, but if their minute island was considered unsuitable for independence on its own, and at the same time was denied membership of the Federation of Malaya, more and more of them would be driven to seek a focus for their loyalties in one or other of the two Chinas which now faced each other across the Taiwan Straits. And while in Singapore no less than in the Federation the commercial Chinese element had no love for Communism as such, the fact that the new People's Republic soon began to cut a far more impressive figure on the world stage than its predecessor had done constituted an appeal to nationalist sentiment which they could not wholly overlook, and was likely to evoke a much less inhibited response among the large proletarian element, which no Singapore politician could possibly ignore.

In these circumstances it says much for the good sense of successive Singapore governments that they continued to seek a solution to the Colony's problems in terms of closer association with Malaya, but throughout the later 1950s growing left-wing agitation and labour unrest in Singapore served only to intensify the Federation's desire to keep it at arm's length and the British resolve to restrict its political prospects to something well short of full independence.

The issue came to a head when, two years after the Federation had

---

the terms of his 1948 appointment he was required to bear in mind that 'in the course of time, some political co-operation may be desirable between the Malayan and Bornean territories'. See Carnell, *op. cit.*, p. 13.

E

120 *Essays in Political Geography*

achieved unqualified independence, the State of Singapore was created in 1959 with internal self-government but with the British still in control of defence and foreign policy, and a joint council of British, Malays and Singaporeans charged with responsibility for its internal security. In the mounting instability which followed, more and more firms began to shift their regional headquarters from Singapore to Kuala Lumpur, and it seemed that, notwithstanding its great geographical advantages, Singapore must inevitably decline in both influence and prosperity.

However, in the first elections held under the new Singapore constitution, Lee Kuan Yew's People's Action Party, which made merger with Malaya the central theme of its campaign, was returned to power and quickly displayed evidence of a new determination to control the situation. From the outset Lee concentrated on promoting a supracommunal sense of Malayan identity within Singapore, *inter alia* by making Malay the 'national' language, despite the predominantly Chinese character of the population, and on seeking to persuade Tunku Abdul Rahman both that the way to solve the Singapore problem was by merger, and that it was in the Federation's as much as Singapore's interest that it should be solved while there was yet time.

Reluctant as the Tunku was to jeopardize the developing but still fragile unity of Malaya, he recognized the problem posed by Singapore but was equally convinced that the addition of its more than a million Chinese to the Federation's carefully balanced population would be politically impossible without a compensating increase in the number of non-Chinese.

Thus it was that in 1961 the Tunku made his first tentative proposal for a still wider Federation of Malaysia, to include, besides Malaya and Singapore, the three territories of Brunei, North Borneo and Sarawak. To this the British, who still retained the controlling hand in Singapore and the Borneo territories, readily agreed,[1] and at the same time the Tunku made a parallel move in external affairs by founding the Association of South-east Asian States (A.S.A.) in which the Federation of Malaysia was to be partnered by Thailand and the Philippines in a joint attempt to foster closer cultural and economic relations within this inner arc of South-east Asia.

In a sense, therefore, the proposed Malaysian Federation represented

---

[1] This meant that control of the Singapore defence installations would be in Malaysian hands, though the 1957 Defence Treaty would remain in force. See above, p. 118.

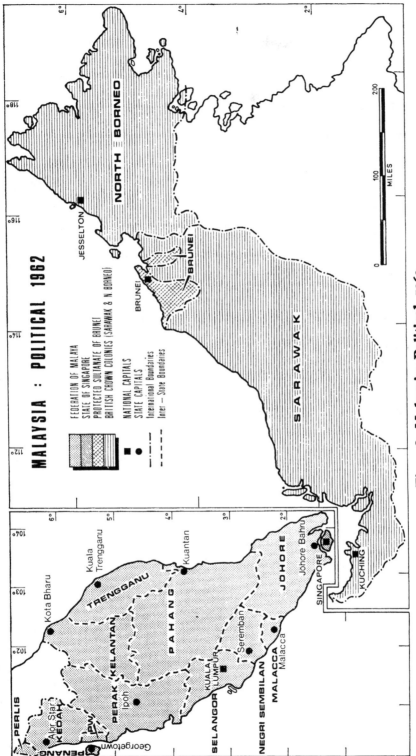

Fig. 7.8. Malaysia: Political, 1962

TABLE 7.2:COMMUNITIES OF MALAYSIAN REGION 1960

Numbers (in thousands) and percentages

TERRITORIES	COMMUNITIES											
	Malays		Borneo indigenes		Total[1] Malaysians		Chinese[2]		Indians[3]		Total Chinese and Indians		Total (including others)
	Number	%	Number	%	Number	%	Number	%	Number	%	Number	%	Number
Federation of Malaya	3461[4]	50	–	–	3461	50	2552	37	773	11	3325	48	6909
Singapore	227	14	–	–	227	14	1231	76	138	8	1369	84	1634
Sabah	23[5]	5	283[6]	62	306	67	105	23	3	1	108	24	455[7]
Sarawak	129	17	378[8]	51	507	68	229	31	2	–	231	31	744
Brunei	45	54	14	17	59	71	22	76	2	2	24	28	84
Total	3885	39	675	7	4560	46	4139	42	918	9	5057	51	9826
Total excluding Brunei, i.e. area included in Federation of Malaysia 1963	3840	39	661	7	4401	46	4117	42	916	9	5033	51	9742
Total excluding Brunei & Singapore, i.e. area included in Federation of Malaysia since August 1965	3613	45	661	8	4174	52	2886	36	778	10	3664	46	8108
Total West Malaysia	3461	50	–	–	3461	50	2552	37	773	11	3325	48	6909
Total East Malaysia	152	13	661	55	813	68	334	28	5	–	339	28	1199

Notes

[1] Refers to ethnic Malaysians, i.e. Malays and Borneo indigenes. [2] Refers to ethnic Chinese.
[3] Refers to ethnic Indians and Pakistanis.
[4] Includes persons born in Indonesia: 311, 5%, and peninsular aborigines: 44, 1%.
[5] Refers to Bruneis. [6] Includes Dusuns: 145, 32%.
[7] Includes Indonesians: 25, 5%. [8] Includes Sea Dyaks: 238, 31%.

Minor inconsistencies due to rounding.

Malaysia 123

the fulfilment of plans apparently sketched out in the terms of the new Governor-General's appointment in 1946, and any thought which there may have been in the early post-war years of also including Hong Kong in such a regional grouping had long since been abandoned in view of the strength of Malay hostility to the Union, and the great influx of mainland Chinese into Hong Kong after 1949.

THE MALAYSIAN EXPERIMENT, 1963-5

In common with the Union of 1946, and the Federations of Malaya of 1948 and 1957, the Federation of Malaysia proposed by Tunku Abdul Rahman was conceived primarily as a piece of political arithmetic. As Table 7.2 shows, the inclusion of Brunei, Sarawak and North Borneo (the last henceforth to become known as Sabah), with their relatively low Chinese percentages of 26, 31 and 23 respectively, as well as Singapore, with its 76 per cent Chinese, would give an overall Chinese percentage of 42 in the new Federation of Malaysia, or only 5 per cent more than that in the existing Federation of Malaya. With the Chinese still clearly in the minority, it did not at the time seem unreasonable to hope that the kind of accommodation between them and the Malays which had proved workable in Malaya would also work in the wider Malaysia. (See Fig. 7.9.)

There were, however, other arguments besides political arithmetic, in favour of bringing the British Borneo territories into the new Federation. Too small and retarded for effective independence as separate entities, their status nevertheless remained an offence to the prevailingly anti-colonial sentiment within South-east Asia, and as such constituted a source of instability. Moreover, since the Japanese occupation and the post-war revolution in air communications,[1] such territories were no longer remote from the outside world and, as events had already shown in Sarawak, these supposedly quiet backwaters offered tempting fishing grounds for subversion.

Largely for these reasons the British had begun by the early 1950s to work towards some kind of closer association between the three Borneo territories but had failed to overcome the obstacle created by the fact that the minute but centrally placed and predominantly Malay Sultanate of Brunei, which had formerly ruled over the other two much

---

[1] With regular air links of at most a few hours' duration between all Malaysia's main centres, the barrier to communications hitherto presented by the South China Sea had been greatly reduced by 1963.

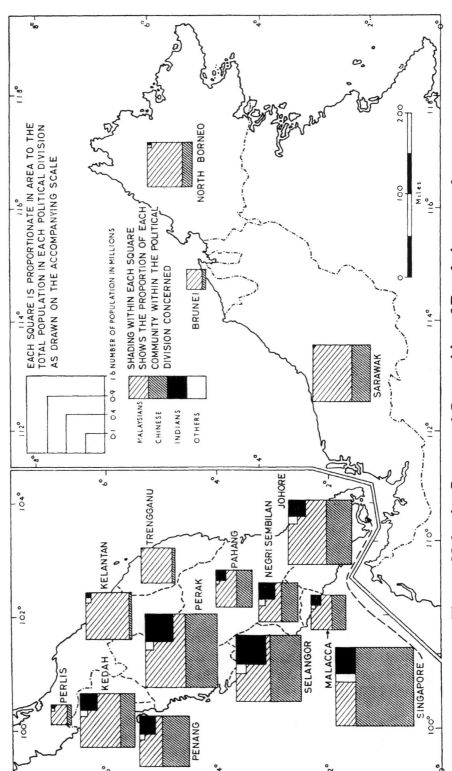

Fig. 7.9. Malaysia: Communal Composition of Population, 1957-60

Malaysia 125

larger and predominantly non-Malay territories, was now, thanks to its oil production, much the richest of the three. While, therefore, neither the indigenous nor the Chinese populations of either Sarawak or Sabah wished to come under a Malay-dominated Brunei, the latter for its part was equally unwilling to associate with them on democratic terms, which inevitably would involve the sharing of its oil revenues and, in view of the ethnic subdivisions within the indigenous Borneo population,[1] would give the Chinese a decisive voice since they would constitute the largest single group in the area as a whole.[2]

In these circumstances, although Sarawak and Sabah had agreed to establish a joint Free Trade Area as from 1962.[3] The inclusion of all three territories in the Malaysian Federation seemed to offer a better way of simultaneously advancing their economic interests and of ending their subordinate political status. But while this view seemed to be shared by the Sultan of Brunei as well as by a majority of opinion in the other two territories, the leader of the Brunei Malay *Partai Rakyat*, A. M. Azahari, staged a rebellion in December 1962 in the hope of keeping the Borneo territories out of Malaysia and bringing them into a separate Borneo Federation, under the Sultan of Brunei and with himself as Prime Minister. In the event, the rebellion, which also aimed at modernizing the political structure of Brunei, and as such enjoyed considerable support among some local Malays, was quickly suppressed with British assistance,[4] and in any case it would never have won general approval in either Sarawak or Sabah, both of which clearly preferred to join Malaysia. But although the Sultan still seemed interested in bringing Brunei in as well, satisfactory terms could not be agreed upon in respect of his status relative to the peninsular rulers and the allocation of oil revenues, and Brunei remained outside.

Viewed retrospectively, this decision by Brunei probably represented a more serious setback to the Federation of Malaysia than was realized at the time. For although Brunei's 83,877 people and 2,226 square miles

[1] A total of some 18 different ethnic groups and sub-groups of indigenes were recognized by the 1960 Censuses of North Borneo and Sarawak, though only 9 of these had more than 10,000 members each. (Details of the two largest, the Dusans and Sea Dyaks, are given in Table 7.2, notes 6 and 8.) This great diversity is basically a reflection of the cultural time-lag of eastern relative to western Malaysia, and more specifically of a low density of population in an area of very poor overland communications.

[2] T. E. Smith, *The Background to Malaysia*, pp. 21 and 43.

[3] *Ibid.*, p. 15.

[4] Made available under the 1957 Defence Treaty with the Federation of Malaya. See above, p. 56.

126 *Essays in Political Geography*

of territory, completely surrounded on the landward side by Sarawak and Sabah, presented no positive problem to Kuala Lumpur, the absence of its oil revenues seriously weakened the final argument in favour of Malaysia – and the one which had the widest appeal in the peninsula – namely that it would add greater diversity to an economy hitherto excessively dependent upon rubber and tin. And indeed, whatever the long-term prospects for development in Sarawak and more especially in Sabah, the inclusion of these without Brunei represented a burden rather than an asset economically for the foreseeable future.

By the same token Singapore, which had been cast, in Tunku Abdul Rahman's phrase, for the role of Malaysia's New York against Kuala Lumpur's Washington, also regretted the absence of Brunei, though from its point of view the whole of northern Borneo was of minor concern compared with the prospect of obtaining unrestricted access to the much larger peninsular market for its own expanding manufacturing industries. In so far as the setting up of a Malaysian 'Common Market' would give Singapore the opportunity to develop as the economic capital of Malaysia, the American analogy was valid enough, but the same cannot be said in a political sense. For whereas in the U.S.A. the citizens of New York play their full part in the political life of the nation, though permanent residents of Washington – and indeed of the entire District of Columbia – have no voting rights on either national or municipal matters, in Malaysia it was Singapore which was to suffer political disadvantage in that it was allocated the disproportionately low share of only 15 seats in the Federal House of Representatives, as against 16 for Sabah, 24 for Sarawak, and 104 for the States of the Malay peninsula.[1] Moreover the retention of a separate Singapore citizenship within Malaysia was designed as a means of restricting the political activities of left-wing Singapore citizens to their own island,[2] and it was also understood that the P.A.P. would not participate in peninsular politics.

In effect, therefore, the terms on which Singapore, with its 76 per cent Chinese and 8 per cent Indian population, was to be admitted into the Federation represented merely a new geopolitical variant of the principle which had underlain the original U.M.N.O./M.C.A. alliance, namely that the Chinese (and Indians) accepted significant political

---

[1] The nine states and two settlements of the Federation of Malaya now became known as the States of Malaya. As noted on p. 132, this has since been changed to West Malaysia.

[2] See Guy Wint (ed.), *Asia – A Handbook* (section on Malaysia by Derrick Sington), pp. 258–9.

Malaysia 127

disabilities in exchange for the opportunity to pursue their economic interests. And, once again, no formal constitutional provision had been made for phasing out the political restraints which were nevertheless designed to provide a breathing space during which the Malays could 'catch up' economically with the two immigrant communities.

Thus, whatever may or may not have been implied in 1946, there was no thought in 1963 of Singapore as capital of Malaysia, and the way in which its remarkable potential as a 'head-link'[1] was politically neglected, in favour of the relatively inward-looking and much smaller Kuala Lumpar, indicated that the *raison d'être* of the new Malaysia was not that of the old British South-east Asia, and that the pattern of its development was to be controlled by the Malays far more than by the local Chinese. Nevertheless many observers, of whom the writer was one, believed that, with regular air links of at most a few hours' duration between all its main centres, the new Federation had good prospects of achieving political as well as economic viability, and that as such it afforded the best available means of completing the orderly decolonization of British South-east Asia.[2]

In fact, however, its birth was stormy and its life, at least in the form in which it was originally conceived, was brief.[3] Notwithstanding the prevailing Afro-Asian sentiment in favour of the speedy liquidation of what remained of Western colonialism, two of Malaysia's closest neighbours, Indonesia and the Philippines, both raised objections to the proposed Federation. And although, following discussions at Manila in June 1963, Malaya, the Philippines and Indonesia agreed to set up a joint consultative body which it was hoped might lead to a confederation of all three states, to be known as Maphilindo, and the inauguration of Malaysia was postponed from 31 August to 16 September to enable the Secretary-General of the United Nations to confirm what had already been demonstrated by the Cobbold Commission,[4] namely, that the majority of the peoples of Sabah and Sarawak wished to join the Federation of Malaysia, the tensions were not thereby resolved and Maphilindo remained a pipe dream.

[1] *Cf.* O. H. K. Spate, 'Factors in the development of capital cities', p. 628.

[2] C. A. Fisher, 'The geographical setting of the proposed Malaysian Federation', p. 114.

[3] See H. F. Armstrong, 'The troubled birth of Malaysia', C. A. Fisher, 'The Malaysian Federation, Indonesia and the Philippines: A study in political geography', J. M. Gullick, *Malaysia and its Neighbours*, and K. G. Tregonning, *Malysia and Singapore*.

[4] *Report of the Commission of Enquiry, North Borneo and Sarawak 1962*, Cmnd. 1954.

128 *Essays in Political Geography*

The declared objections of the Philippines to the Malaysia scheme arose from a long standing claim by the heirs of the former Sultan of Sulu to a substantial part of Sabah, on the grounds, which the British have consistently rejected, that the territory in question was not ceded but merely leased to the predecessors of the British North Borneo Company in 1878.[1] However the past recognition, successively by Spain and the United States, of British protection of all North Borneo seemed to justify Britain's right to dispose of the territory as it thought fit, and in the light of the North Borneo Legislative Council's expressed wish to join Malaysia – to say nothing of the fact that, in its whole pattern of economic and political evolution North Borneo had far more in common with the rest of the latter than with the Philippines – the case for its inclusion in Malaysia was overwhelming. Nevertheless the Philippines remained dissatisfied, and the resultant cooling of relations between Kuala Lumpur and Manila constituted a major setback for A.S.A.

Even more serious, however, was the opposition of President Sukarno of Indonesia who, having already refused the Tunku's invitation to join A.S.A., proceeded also to denounce the proposed Malaysian Federation as a neo-colonialist plot whereby Britain, under the pretence of decolonization, would in fact maintain its control over this focal part of South-east Asia and, in so doing, thwart the legitimate aspirations of peoples in neighbouring lands as well. The formal announcement of confrontation came immediately after the Azahari rebellion in Brunei, but to some who noticed that Sukarno's new line completely contradicted what had been Indonesia's declared policy prior to the satisfaction of its claim to West New Guinea in August 1962, the fact that he now proceeded in 1963 to translate confrontation into military terms, concentrating primarily upon Sarawak and Sabah, suggested that the true explanation of his actions included a desire to incorporate these adjacent territories within *Indonesia Raya* (Greater Indonesia).[2] However, so far from splitting them off from the new Federation, this external military pressure at first served, in classic fashion, to strengthen their allegiance to it.

Nevertheless, the barrage of radio propaganda which accompanied Indonesian military activities, while equally inconsistent, was distinctly more dangerous. For notwithstanding his policy of aligning Indonesia

---

[1] See above, p. 90.

[2] *Cf.* B. K. Gordon, 'The potential for Indonesian expansion', especially p. 381.

Malaysia 129

ever more closely with Peking, Sukarno sought deliberately to inflame anti-Chinese hatred among the Malays and, in thus playing up the racial tensions which it had been the constant aim in their different ways of both Tunku Abdul Rahman and Lee Kuan Yew to reduce, he undoubtedly aggravated the most serious problem facing the new Federation, namely that of achieving a satisfactory relationship between Singapore and Malaya.

Meanwhile Lee Kuan Yew, partly to keep the initiative in politically volatile Singapore, but also apparently from genuine apprehension at the growing emphasis on racialism within the region, went to the opposite extreme of trying to persuade the rest of Malaysia to accept Singapore's non-communal political stance. Thus, contrary to the understanding previously reached with Kuala Lumpur, the P.A.P. contested nine urban seats in the peninsular Malayan elections of April 1964, in effect as a rival to the M.C.A. and, unabashed by its defeat in all but one, went on in 1965 to join with four opposition parties in Malaya and Sarawak in the Malaysian Solidarity Convention, which implicitly aimed at putting an end to the privileged position which the Malays had retained within Malaysia.

In the specific context of Singapore, whose predominantly proletarian Chinese population had no cause to fear the competition of its small Indian and Malay minorities, the P.A.P.'s multi-racialism and democratic socialism represented a model of enlightened self-interest, and its record in socially responsible civic administration effectively gave the lie to the old colonialist myth that the Chinese were interested only in making money. Moreover, since the ethnic composition of the large towns of the Malay peninsula was essentially similar to that of Singapore[1] it was understandable that Lee should have expected the P.A.P. to win strong support in them also. Yet the attitude of the middle and older generations of peninsular Chinese in preferring to stick to the M.C.A.'s well-tried policy, which had enabled them to profit materially from uninhibited capitalist economics in exchange for accepting a secondary role in politics, was no less realistic in the context of Malaya where the Chinese formed only 37 per cent of the total population.

Nevertheless, although Lee had seriously miscalculated, at least in his

[1] 1957 figures: Singapore state, Chinese 75%, Malays 14%, Indians 9%; Singapore municipality, Chinese 78%, Malays 11%, Indians 8%; Kuala Lumpur municipality, Chinese 62%, Malays 15%, Indians 17%, Penang (George Town), Chinese 73%, Malays 11%, Indians 14%; Ipoh, Chinese 67%, Malays 15%, Indians 13 %. See also Fig. 9.

130 *Essays in Political Geography*

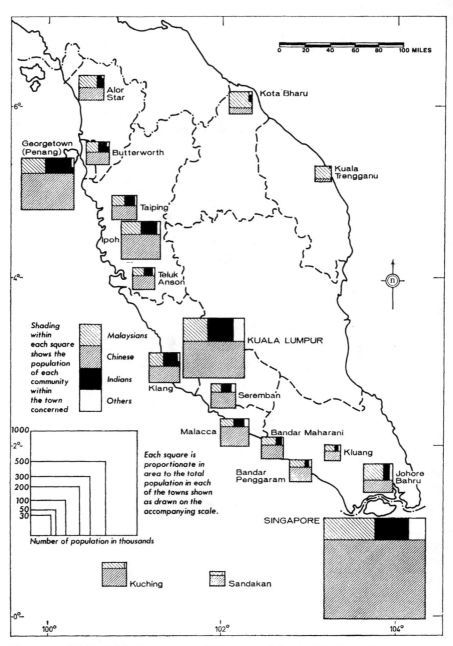

Fig. 7.10. **Malaysia: Communal Composition of Urban Population (in towns with over 30,000 inhabitants 1957–60)**

Malaysia 131

timing, it was evident that the P.A.P.'s policies did exert a strong and growing appeal for the younger generation of peninsular Chinese and indeed of Indians as well. For in contrast to their parents, these were not only Malayan by birth[1] but post-colonial by upbringing, and as such were increasingly reluctant to accept racially restricted opportunities in politics and the public services. In this respect, therefore, time in a united Malaysia was on Lee's side, and a dawning realization that this was so may explain the intensity of the Malay anger against the P.A.P., even though the latter had received a resounding defeat in the peninsular elections.

Be that as it may, a group of Malays led by the new Secretary-General of U.M.N.O. the Indonesian-born Syed Ja'afar Albar, began stirring up anti-Chinese hatred among the Singapore Malays, and after Lee had riposted by forming the Malaysia Solidarity Convention, the tension mounted, during the absence abroad of Tunku Abdul Rahman, to the point where the Malay 'ultras' appeared bent on suspending the constitution in Singapore. It was at this juncture that the Tunku returned and, in great haste and secrecy, insisted on the much less explosive but scarcely less drastic alternative of excluding Singapore from Malaysia, an arrangement which became effective on 9 August 1965.

The Tunku's insistence that Singapore should withdraw was accepted only with the utmost reluctance by Lee Kuan Yew, and had been made without any prior consultation with either Sabah or Sarawak. Not surprisingly, both of these states reacted sharply to the *fait accompli*. For while Kuala Lumpur had presumably sought their participation in the Malaysian Federation primarily to provide counterweights to Singapore's $1\frac{1}{4}$ million Chinese, the Borneo leaders had been persuaded to agree mainly by the prospects of speedier modernization and development which closer association with Singapore and Malaya would bring.

Moreover, whereas to the peninsular Malays it was the Chinese who appeared as the critical element in the communal problem, to the Borneo indigenes fear of the Malays, arising out of traditional resentment against the former overlordship of Brunei, was more deep-seated than their mainly economic jealousies of the local Chinese. Thus for them Singapore had represented a counterweight against excessive Malay predominance, and the summary way in which this balancing factor had been removed suggested that in the newly truncated – or decapitated – Malaysia their own status would be merely that of subordinates

[1] Immigration of Chinese has virtually ceased since the Second World War.

132 *Essays in Political Geography*

to a predominantly Malay Malaya. Particularly in Sabah, where relations with a somewhat smaller Chinese community had been notably less troubled than those in Sarawak,[1] talk of seceding from Malaysia was rife until effectively silenced by the Tunku's denunciation of it as seditious in the face of the continuing military threat from Indonesia.

Nevertheless the ending of confrontation, which, following the fall of Sukarno, was formally agreed upon at the Bangkok meeting of 11 August 1966, did not reduce these tensions. On the contrary, the sudden surge of brotherly sentiments between the Malays and the representatives of the new Indonesian regime served to intensify the Malays' sense of self-confidence *vis à vis* the Malayan Chinese and both the indigenes and Chinese populations of Sabah and Sarawak. In these circumstances, although Malaya at some sacrifice to itself, had begun to make significant contributions to the economic development of both Sabah and Sarawak, the latters' suspicions of Malay motives remained unquieted, as was clearly demonstrated by the events which led to Kuala Lumpur's declaration of a state of emergency in Sarawak in September 1966, and by the results of the Sabah elections in April 1967. Thus, while there seems to be a gradual realization in Sabah and Sarawak that continued membership of a reduced Malaysia is probably now the best available course for both of them – as inevitably it is for the Chinese of Malaya – their original enthusiasm for the Malaysia scheme of 1963 has suffered a setback and, as fear of hostile pressure from Indonesia recedes, the sense of solidarity between the mainland and the Borneo States will need to be strengthened in other ways if it is to survive.

In this connexion the new official nomenclature of August 1966, whereby peninsular Malaya became known as West Malaysia and the two Borneo states as East Malaysia, is symptomatic of Kuala Lumpur's desire to emphasize the common Malaysian cultural affinities of both. But in view of the way in which Singapore's excessive zeal in pressing its version of a 'Malaysian' Malaysia produced the reverse of what was intended in the peninsula, Kuala Lumpur may need to be on its guard against producing a correspondingly hostile reaction in East Malaysia.

[1] See above, p. 90.

Malaysia 133

THE SIGNIFICANCE OF THE SEPARATION OF SINGAPORE FROM
MALAYSIA IN 1965

With the benefit of hindsight it is easy to see the fallacies of the political
arithmetic which underlay the separation of Singapore from peninsular
Malaya in 1946, its continuation in 1948 and 1957, and the belated
attempt to unite the whole of the former British Malaysian sphere in
1963. Thus, in the first place, the very process of juggling with numbers,
attempting to balance one community against another, with or without
the aid of constitutional devices to achieve an equipoise, serves of itself
to keep alive the sense of difference and of rivalry between the communities concerned. And secondly, numbers are of little relevance
except when related to the facts of geographical distribution and
economic function.

In the modern world, in which cities are the pace makers, and the
bigger the city the faster the pace, the gap between the metropolis and
the countryside is tending all the time to widen. And since, in contrast
to the predominantly urban Chinese, the Malays remain even more
markedly rural,[1] it is not surprising that the inclusion in the Malaysian
Federation of Singapore, geographically the summit of the urban
hierarchy of the whole region, could not be politically counterbalanced
by the somewhat smaller total of overwhelmingly rural Malaysians in
Sabah and Sarawak, even though the latter were allocated a disproportionately large share of votes in the Federal Parliament. For the
Borneo indigenes did not form a single group linguistically, nor did they
automatically align themselves with the Malays *vis à vis* the Chinese.
Thus, notwithstanding the fact, already noted on page 123, that the
Chinese remained in a minority in Malaysia as they had been in Malaya,
the situation was nevertheless fundamentally changed in that within
Malaysia they were the largest single community, with 42 per cent,
leaving the Malays in second place with 39 per cent. Moreover, even if
Malays and Borneo indigenes were grouped together, they were still in
a minority with 46 per cent, but the Chinese and Indians together
comprised a majority of 51 per cent.

Nevertheless, although in the event the complications of political
geography compounded the unexpected complexities of political arithmetic, this latter-day attempt to create a single state to embrace the
whole inter-related nexus of the former British Malaysian sphere was

[1] In the total urban population of the Federation of Malaya, the share of the
Malaysians rose from 21% to 23% and of the Chinese from 62% to 64% between
1947 and 1957. That of the Indians fell from 14% to 11%. *Cf.* above, p. 64.

134 *Essays in Political Geography*

not the absurdity born of expediency which some critics have made it out to be, and it ill behoves a British observer to blame either Tunku Abdul Rahman or Lee Kuan Yew for inability to find a workable answer to a problem which the British themselves had done so much to create and so little to resolve.

In his 'unified field theory of political geography'[1] Stephen Jones has suggested a connexion between political idea and political area, via the three links of decision, movement and field. Using this terminology, one may describe the British desire to control the sea route between the Indian Ocean and the China coast as a political idea, translated into action by a series of decisions, which in turn set in train a vast movement not only of trade but also of Chinese and to a lesser extent of Indian migration. But although the original *points d'appui* from which this spreading process of change was induced were linked together by the British in the political area of the Straits Settlements, the persistent conflict of opinion between those who continued to think in terms of the original maritime idea, and those who were concerned with following up the secondary local opportunities to which it gave rise, led to a loss of overall vision and a resultant failure to translate the field of British-induced activity into a coherent political whole. And while, in view of early Chinese activities in Malacca and the nineteenth-century surge of Chinese tin miners into the western Malay states well before the latter came under British protection, the presence of a Chinese community in Malaysia today cannot be regarded simply as a consequence of British rule, it is nevertheless impossible to deny that the policies followed by the British between 1819 and 1942 were primarily responsible for the fact that the Chinese percentage in Malaysia today is many times greater than that in any other ex-colonial territory in South-east Asia.

Whether, if such successors as Swettenham had possessed a breadth of vision comparable to that of Raffles, this most extreme example of the plural society could have been effectively welded into one before the rising tide of Asian nationalism began after the First World War to pull it farther apart, must remain an open question. But with every year which passed thereafter the obstacles became steadily greater, and it is difficult to avoid the conclusion that the point of no return had been passed well before the time came when political responsibility was transferred into Malaysian hands.

Moreover, although immediately after the separation of 1965 it was

[1] S. B. Jones, 'A unified field theory of political geography', p. 115.

Malaysia 135

widely believed that the logic of events would be bound in the long run to bring about a reunification, there is little evidence to suggest that this will happen. If the conjuncture of such eminently reasonable and non-racialist leaders as the Tunku and Lee could not bridge the gap between Malaya and Singapore it is difficult to see what can, and the experience of the last century of Malaysian history provides a depressing comment on the staying power of established boundaries no matter how anomalous these may be.

Indeed the process of adjustment to the new division is already under way, and Singapore is now more separate from the Malay peninsula than it has ever been since the founding of the Straits Settlements. For the Tunku's decision of 1965 produced something which the British had never in their period of control been prepared to concede, namely a completely independent State of Singapore which, as a fellow member of the Commonwealth is now on an equal footing with Malaysia.[1] And although this particular change in status was not of its own choosing, it has given to Singapore a new sense of self-awareness and responsibility for its own destiny. Thus the old sense of frustrated nationalism seems to be largely a thing of the past and although resentment remains over its expulsion from Malaysia, Singapore is looking to the future rather than to the might-have beens of the past.

Meanwhile the separation of 1965, though it may well have averted an immediate catastrophe, has not of itself solved the basic problem of how Malays and Chinese are to live side by side in this critical region at the crossroads of South-east Asia. And if, as now seems clear, this cannot be managed in the context of a single successor state to the British Malaysian sphere, the problem will have to be resolved within a wider context.

To many, particularly among the more racially conscious Malay and Indonesian extremists, the obvious solution lies in a merger between Malaysia and Indonesia. Under such an arrangement, it is assumed that 110 million 'Malays'[2] could safely control their 6 million Chinese and effectively curb any nefarious ambitions of the further $1\frac{1}{4}$ million Singapore Chinese, geographically surrounded if not politically administered by them, and the Malayo-Indonesian realm would then be able to preserve its cultural integrity against alien Chinese pressure.

Yet for all its superficial plausibility this seems a totally unrealistic

[1] On the defence aspects of this see Michael Leifer, 'Astride the Straits of Johroe'.

[2] *I.e.* all indigenous Indonesians and Malaysians.

136 *Essays in Political Geography*

policy within any foreseeable future. A prosperous, respected and independent state like Malaysia does not readily give up its separate identity to become a peripheral province of a neighbour ten times its size but with a visibly lower standard of living, except under the direst pressure, which is certainly not present in this case. And although, if Indonesia now proceeds to put its house in order, its power of attraction may be expected to grow, its supposedly vast natural wealth has been greatly exaggerated and it will be a long time before Indonesian prosperity reaches the level of present-day Malaysia, and the latter will not stand still in the meantime.

Moreover, while it may be feasible – though that does not make it advisable – for Indonesia to pursue a hard line against its own Chinese minority which accounts for less than 3 per cent of that country's population, such a policy would be politically explosive and economically catastrophic if extended to the Chinese 37 per cent in Malaysia, who would not become automatically redistributed over the length and breadth of Indonesia Raya if a merger were to take place.

Finally it is far from clear that the new regime in Indonesia, which has enough problems on its hands for many years to come, has any active interest in a merger, whatever its predecessor may have appeared to desire, and one may assume that Tunku Abdul Rahman has no wish to see the still enviable measure of prosperity and stability which Malaysia has achieved under his guidance subjected to the enormous strains which such a course would inevitably entail. On the contrary, while the Tunku welcomes the growing rapproachement between Malaysia and Indonesia, he apparently wishes this to take place within the wider context of A.S.E.A.N.,[1] in which the great potential weight of Indonesia would be balanced by Thailand and the Philippines, and in which Singapore also could find its proper place.

From every reasonable point of view this would appear to be a far more constructive approach to the problem of the Nanyang Chinese who, though focused in the old British sphere, are present in every country in the region. Taken together, the five members of A.S.E.A.N. contain approximately 88 per cent of the South-east Asian Chinese, though the latter are fairly evenly split into three large clusters, each of around 3 million, respectively in Thailand, Malaysia and Indonesia,

---

[1] *I.e.* Association of South-east Asian Nations, consisting of Indonesia, Malaysia, the Philippines, Singapore and Thailand, set up in August 1967. In effect this grouping represents a combination of those in the previously proposed ASA and Maphilindo groups.

Malaysia 137

together with the smaller total but greatest single concentration of $1\frac{1}{4}$ million in Singapore and less than half a million in the Philippines.

Although the first three of these totals are very similar, the proportions which they represent vary from 36 per cent in post-1965 Malaysia to 12 per cent in Thailand and a mere 3 per cent in Indonesia. Partly for this reason, but also because of very different experiences of racial contact in the past, local attitudes to the Chinese today are equally diverse. Thus, while relations have in general been less than satisfactory in Indonesia, Thailand has achieved a remarkably successful accommodation with its Chinese population and, notwithstanding the recent strains over Singapore, Malaysia, with the highest Chinese percentage of all except Singapore itself, likewise has an impressive record in this respect.

While it would be wrong to seek an explanation solely in these terms, the striking economic advances of both Thailand and Malaysia, in contrast to the dismal showing of Indonesia, are to a significant extent related to the very different degrees in which these countries have respectively harnessed the energies and skills of the local Chinese to serve the national purpose. For this reason, among others, it is to be hoped that the closer association of all three in A.S.E.A.N. may help Malaysia, the small but critically placed central state, to play a more positive role than in past times[1] by serving as a link between Thailand and Indonesia, and that in this process the latter may learn from its neighbours' experience how much is to be gained from encouraging its Chinese population to participate more fully in the national life.

By the same token Singapore, separated from Malaysia and free from the British colonial connexion, should be given every opportunity to play its part within the wider South-east Asian context. As a territorially minute unit, strategically and economically dependent on the goodwill of its neighbours, Singapore, if it is able to earn its livelihood through industry and commerce will menace no-one, but if steadily contracting opportunities should ultimately drive it to desperation the effects of this, given the closeness of the geographical and innumerable personal links, would be bound to spread to Malaysia, as indeed it was feared that a similar malaise would do before 1963.

[1] Notably in the period which saw the rise of Malacca (see above, pp. 78–9). As a Kedah Malay Prince of part Siamese ancestry, Tunku Abdul Rahman is well cast for the role of bridge-builder between Thailand and Indonesia. It is also characteristic of him to seek unostentatiously to learn from history instead of attempting – like Sukarno – to recreate his own version of the supposedly glorious past.

138 *Essays in Political Geography*

Already Singapore's problems are more than difficult. To provide employment for a population which, with an increase of 78·9 per cent between 1950 and 1965, had been growing faster than any other in East or South-east Asia, Singapore had embarked on a major industrial expansion in the expectation of a Malaysian Common Market 10 million strong, and the fading of this hope coupled with the British Government's decision in 1967 to run down its bases and forces, which at present employ 36,000 Singaporeans, will in any case compel it to make drastic changes in its economic plans for the future.

With its external trade hitherto dependent to the extent of approximately one third on the Federation of Malaysia, for which it has always served as the principal port, Singapore remains far more dependent upon Malaysia than the latter is upon it. But while, in view of the animosities that have been aroused in recent years, Malaysia may thus be tempted to press home its considerable advantage in this respect, the overall result in the end could only be a Pyrrhic victory. For better or worse Singapore has been denied its declared wish to identify itself with Malaysia; in the interests of all, alike in Singapore, Malaysia and ultimately in the region as whole, it should not now be treated as a pariah in South-east Asia.

CONCLUSIONS

If one compares the present political map of the Malaysian region with those which have preceded it since British imperialism first began to reshape this part of Asia, one is immediately struck by the way in which Singapore, the original growing point not only of the Straits Settlements but of the whole British Malaysian sphere is left in solitary isolation, while practically all the rest is united in what, geographically speaking, is a successively enlarged Federated Malay States centred today as in 1896 upon Kuala Lumpur.

With the end of empire symbolized by the recently announced running down of British military power in Malaysia and Singapore, the sea route view, which provided the original *raison d'être* of British imperialism here, has lost its meaning, and the age of post-colonial nationalism threatens steadily to undermine the entrepot trade nurtured in the nineteenth-century climate of *laissez faire* and the *pax Britannica*. Thus Hong Kong, which although it formed the culminating point on the sea route was never politically integrated into British Malaysia, now dangles in a far from splendid isolation and daily becomes more

Malaysia 139

dependent on industrialization for its livelihood. Meanwhile Penang and Malacca have been fully incorporated into the Federation of Malaysia, as also has the almost forgotten Labuan, though in a curious way – which aptly reflects the shift from trade to production – the adjacent and oil-rich Sultanate of Brunei has succeeded it as the odd man out of East Malaysia, just as Singapore, now like Hong Kong switching its emphasis from trade towards manufacturing industry, has reverted to being the odd man out of West Malaysia.

Superficially also the territorial extent of the Federation of Malaysia *vis à vis* Singapore symbolizes the triumph of South-east Asian nationalism, in that the extraneous Chinese element controls less than 0·2 per cent of the erstwhile British Malaysian sphere, while the rest of the latter remains under predominantly Malay control, 98 per cent of it in the Federation of Malaysia and the remainder in diminutive Brunei.

Nevertheless the situation is not nearly as clearly resolved as such a view would suggest. For even after the exclusion of Singapore in 1965 the Federation of Malaysia still has the most plural society in Southeast Asia, and furthermore it remains to be seen whether its eastern and western halves can cohere politically in the presence of the rivalry between Malays and Borneo indigenes and in the absence of Singapore as the link and stabilizer between the two. Moreover, given the growing similarity of the problems facing Singapore and Hong Kong, the common dynamism with which both are tackling them, and the possibility that continuing pressure from China may stimulate a new flow of refugee capital from Hong Kong to Singapore and a rethinking of what Hong Kong's future is to be when the lease over the New Territories runs out in 1998, some form of closer association between these two king pins of the old sea route may yet emerge to produce a new style Singapore-Hong Kong axis running diagonally across the centre of South-east Asia.

Whether such a development, were it ever to materialize, would contribute to a better overall accommodation between the local Chinese and indigenous South-east Asians in the region as a whole, or whether it would be regarded as a major source of division and subversive infiltration would depend on many factors, including the future trend of political evolution in China, Hong Kong and the South-east Asian countries themselves, all of which is hidden in as great an uncertainty as that in which decolonization began over twenty years ago.

But if in these circumstances it is still too early to draw any firm conclusions about the wisdom or otherwise of the policies which have

140 *Essays in Political Geography*

been followed, certain observations may nevertheless be made. To decolonize well it is necessary both to have colonized well in the past and to judge wisely the time to begin reversing the process. Whatever may be the British record in other parts of their former empire, their performance on both counts in Malaysia is open to severe criticism, and although both the Japanese occupation and more recently Indonesian confrontation immeasurably complicated their problems, they did so only by aggravating weaknesses which were already there.

To write thus of British policy is not to accuse it of crude economic exploitation or even of deliberate insensitivity to the wishes of the Malays. By purely material standards, and in comparison with the rest of South-east Asia, British Malaysia was – and its successor states still are – outstandingly successful, and even though the Malays have benefited far less economically than the immigrant peoples their standards of living, health and education have nevertheless been very substantially raised, and to a considerable extent this has been achieved by the direct and indirect efforts of these immigrant peoples. But, with the possible exception of the Brookes in Sarawak, those who encouraged the immigration of what ultimately amounted to millions of non-Malaysians did so for their own purposes, as the Malays – who had no say in the matter – remain well aware.

And although the British have come and gone, and their territories particularly in Malaya have more than justified themselves in their final role as the Empire's dollar arsenal, the Malays, alone among the major indigenous peoples of South-east Asia, have been left with no country which they can truly call their own, and hence with no chance of making their own individual adjustment to the challenge of the contemporary world, which in essence is what anti-colonial nationalism, wherever it occurs, is concerned to do. For, given the number and the geographical and functional distribution of the Chinese in their midst, the Malays now have no option – short of indulging in either mass genocide or self-destruction – but to respond to this challenge at a pace and in a manner which cannot be solely of their own choosing, but must be determined to a considerable extent by the more dynamic immigrant community, with which a compromise will have to be painstakingly worked out, as Tunku Abdul Rahman has long been aware.

Moreover, although the Malays have suffered this great deprivation of choice, it is unjust to condemn either the vast majority of Malaysian Chinese for having allowed themselves to be born where they were, or their forebears for exercising the right – which Westerners also treasure

Malaysia 141

– of emigrating to a land of opportunity. In short, so far as the people on the spot are concerned, the conflict is not between right and wrong but between two rights. And, perhaps more to the point, the differences which remain between these two peoples are not so much between different stages of advancement as between age-old ecological adaptations to different environments.

Unfashionable though it may be to say so, the Malays' gracious *andante* tempo of living is as appropriate to the uncrowded humid tropics in which it evolved – and to which it is still restricted – as are the dynamism and resilience of the Chinese to that of the more northerly and intensely congested lands in which they developed over an equally long period before projecting themselves in recent times into South-east Asia.

To end with such comments as these may well call forth the familiar stricture that the academic geographer has nothing to contribute to the problems of everyday life. Yet until these two peoples, who during a century and a half of British rule have come to live side by side in Malaysia, can begin to see themselves in some such terms as these, which give no warrant for the contempt with which each is nowadays increasingly prone to display towards the other, and hence can get away from both the parrot cries of their respective extremists and the pernicious Western half-truth that the Malays must somehow 'catch up' with the Chinese, neither political arithmetic, political economy nor political science will be able to do much to solve their problems.

SELECT BIBLIOGRAPHY

ARMSTRONG, HAMILTON FISH, 'The troubled birth of Malaysia', *Foreign Affairs*, 1963, pp. 674–93.

BROEK, J. O. M., 'Diversity and unity in Southeast Asia', *Geographical Review*, 34, 1944, pp. 175–95.

CARNELL, FRANCIS G., 'Malayan citizenship legislation', *International and Comparative Law Quarterly*, 1952, pp. 504–18.

CARNELL, FRANCIS G., 'Closer association in British Southeast Asia', *Eastern World*, 7 May 1953, pp. 12–14.

COEDÈS, G., *Les états hindouises d'Indochine et d'Indonésie*, Paris, 1948.

COWAN, C. D., *Nineteenth-century Malaya*, London, 1961.

COWAN, C. D. (ed), *The economic development of South-East Asia*, London, 1964.

DOBBY, E. H. G. 'Some aspects of the human ecology of South-east Asia', *Geographical Journal*, 108, 1946, pp. 40–54.

DOBBY, E. H. G., 'Malayan prospect', *Pacific Affairs*, 1950, pp. 392–401.

DOBBY, E. H. G., *Southeast Asia*, London, 9th edition, 1966.

142 Essays in Political Geography

ELSBREE, WILLARD H., *Japan's Role in Southeast Asian Nationalist movements, 1940–1945*, Cambridge, Mass., 1953.

EMERSON, RUPERT, *Malaysia: a study in direct and indirect rule*, New York, 1937.

FIFIELD, RUSSELL H., *The diplomacy of Southeast Asia 1945–1958*, New York, 1958.

FISHER, CHARLES A., 'The geographical setting of the proposed Malaysian Federation', *Journal of Tropical Geography*, 17, 1963, pp. 99–115.

FISHER, CHARLES A., 'The Malaysian Federation, Indonesia and the Philippines: a study in political geography', *Geographical Journal*, 129, 1963, pp. 311–28.

FISHER, CHARLES A., *South-east Asia a Social, Economic and Political Geography*, London, 2nd edition, 1966.

FITZGERALD, C. P., *The third China*, Melbourne, Canberra and Sydney, 1965.

FREEDMAN, MAURICE, 'The growth of a plural society in Malaya', *Pacific Affairs*, 33, 1960, 158–67.

FURNIVALL, J. S., *Netherlands India*, Cambridge, 2nd edition, 1944.

GORDON, BERNARD K., 'The potential for Indonesian expansion', *Pacific Affairs*, 36, 1963–4, pp. 378–93.

GORDON, BERNARD K., 'Problems of regional cooperation in Southeast Asia', *World Politics*, 16, 1964, pp. 222–53.

GULLICK, J. M., *Malaya*, London, 1963.

GULLICK, J. M., 'Resolving racial fears', *The Times Supplement on Malaysia*, 31 August 1966, p. 23.

GULLICK, J. M., *Malaysia and its Neighbours*, London, 1967.

HALL, D. G. E., *A History of South-east Asia*, London, 1955.

HARRISON, BRIAN, *South-east Asia – a Short History*, London, 1954.

HARTSHORNE, RICHARD, 'The functional approach in political geography', *Annals of the Association of American Geographers*, 40, 1950, pp. 95–130.

HERRMANN, A., *An Historical Atlas of China*, Ed. Ginsburg, Norton, with a prefatory essay by Wheatley, Paul, Chicago, 1966.

JONES, STEPHEN B., 'A unified field theory of political geography', *Annals of the Association of American Geographers*, 44, 1954, pp. 111–123.

KAHIN, G. MCT., 'The state of North Borneo, 1881–1946', *Far Eastern Quarterly*, 7, 1947, pp. 43–65.

KAHIN, G. MCT. (ed.), *Governments and Politics of Southeast Asia*, Ithaca, 2nd edition, 1964.

KENNEDY, J., *A History of Malaya*, A.D. 1400–1959, London, 1962.

LEE KUAN YEW, *The Battle for Merger*, Singapore, 1961.

LEE, Y. L., 'Some factors in the development and planning of land use in British Borneo', *Journal of Tropical Geography*, 15, 1961, pp. 66–81.

LEIFER, MICHAEL, 'Politics in Singapore', *Journal of Commonwealth Political Studies*, 2, 1964, pp. 102–19.

LEIFER, MICHAEL, 'Where goes Malaysia now?', *New Society*, 19 August 1965, pp. 23–4.

Malaysia 143

LEIFER, MICHAEL, 'Astride the Straits of Johore', *Modern Asian Studies*, I, 1967.

MCGEE, T. G., 'The Malayan elections of 1959 – a study in electoral geography', *Journal of Tropical Geography*, 16, 1962, 70–99.

MILLS, LENNOX A., *British Rule in Eastern Asia*, Oxford, 1942.

MILNE, R. S., 'Malaysia: a new federation in the making', *Asian Survey*, 3, 1963, 76–82.

PANIKKAR, K. M., *Asia and Western Dominance*, London, 1953.

PARKINSON, C. NORTHCOTE, *Britain and the Far East: the Singapore Naval Base*, Singapore, 1955.

PAUKER, GUY J., 'Indonesia: internal development or external expansion', *Asian Survey*, 3, 1963, pp. 69–75.

PURCELL, VICTOR, *The Chinese in Malaya*, Oxford, 1948.

PURCELL, VICTOR, *Malaya – communist or free ?*, London, 1954.

PURCELL, VICTOR, *The Chinese in Southeast Asia*, Oxford, 2nd edition, 1965.

RATZEL, F., *Politische Geographie*, Berlin and Munich, 3rd edition, 1925.

ROBERTS, GUY, 'East to the Indies', *Geographical Magazine*, 8, 1946, pp. 347–58; 'South to the Indies', *ibid.*, pp. 403–12; 'From Europe to the Spice Islands', *ibid.*, pp. 473–82.

ROBERTS, GUY, 'Making Malaya a nation', *Geographical Magazine*, 9, 1946, pp. 141–50.

ROSE, SAUL (ed.), *Politics in Southern Asia*, London, 1963.

RUNCIMAN, STEVEN, *The White Rajahs*, Cambridge, 1960.

SANDHU, KERNIAL SINGH, 'The population of Malaya – some changes in the pattern of distribution between 1947 and 1957', *Journal of Tropical Geography*, 15, 1961, pp. 82–96.

SINCLAIR, KEITH, 'Hobson and Lenin in Johore', *Modern Asian Studies*, 4, 1967.

SINGH, VISHAL, 'The struggle for Malaysia', *International Studies*, 5, 1964, pp. 221–39.

SINGTON, DERRICK, 'East-West pressures pose hard choice', *The Times Supplement on Malaysia*, 31 August 1966, p. 21.

SMITH, T. E., *Population growth in Malaya*, Oxford, 1952.

SMITH, T. E., *The Background to Malaysia*, Royal Institute of International Affairs, London, 1963 (mimeo).

SOKOL, A. E., 'Communications and production in Indonesian history', *Far Eastern Quarterly*, 7, 1948, pp. 339–53.

SPATE, O. H. K., 'Factors in the development capital cities', *Geographical Review*, 32, 1942, pp. 622–31.

STEEL, R. W., and FISHER, C. A. (eds.), *Geographical Essays on British Tropical Lands*, London, 1956.

TAN, K. C., 'The Federation of Malaysia: some aspects of political geography', Ph.D. thesis (unpublished), University of London, 1966.

TILMAN, ROBERT O., 'Elections in Sarawak', *Asian Survey*, 3, 1963, pp. 507–18.

TILMAN, ROBERT O., 'Malaysia: the problems of federation', *Western Political Quarterly*, 16, 1963, pp. 897–911.

144   Essays in Political Geography

TILMAN, ROBERT O., 'The Alliance pattern in Malaysian politics: Bornean variations on a theme', *South Atlantic Quarterly*, 43, 1964, pp. 60–74.

TREGONNING, K. G., *Under Chartered Company Rule*, Singapore, 1958.

TREGONNING, K. G., *North Borneo*, London, H.M.S.O., 1960.

TREGONNING, K. G., *Malaysia and Singapore*, Melbourne, Canberra and Sydney, 1966.

UNGER, L., 'The Chinese in South-east Asia', *Geographical Review*, 34, 1944, pp. 196–217.

VAN DER KROEF, JUSTUS, 'Indonesia, Malaya and the North Borneo crisis', *Asian Survey*, 3, pp. 173–81.

VLEKKE, B. H. M., *Nusantara: a history of the East Indian Archipelago*, Cambridge, Mass., 1943.

WANG GUNGWU (ed.), *Malaysia*, London and Dunmow, 1964.

Westermanns Atlas Zur Weltgeschichte, Brunswick, 1956.

WHEATLEY, PAUL, *The Golden Khersonese*, Kuala Lumpur, 1961.

WINSTEDT, SIR RICHARD O., *The Malays: a Cultural History*. Singapore, 1947.

WINSTEDT, SIR RICHARD O., *Malaya and its History*, London, 1949.

WINT, GUY (ed.), *Asia – a Handbook*, London, 1965.

WRIGHT, ARNOLD and REID, THOMAS H., *The Malay Peninsula*, London, 1912.

WURZBURG, C. E., *Raffles of the Eastern Isles*, London, 1954.

OFFICIAL PUBLICATIONS

Malayan Union and Singapore: Statement of Policy on Future Constitution, Cmnd. 6724, London, H.M.S.O., 1946.

Federation of Malaya – Summary of Revised Constitutional Proposals, Cmnd. 7171, London, 1947.

British Dependencies in the Far East 1945–1949, Cmnd. 7709, London, H.M.S.O., 1949.

Singapore Constitutional Conference, Cmnd. 9777, London, H.M.S.O., 1956.

Report of the Commission of Enquiry, North Borneo and Sarawak 1962, Cmnd. 1794, London, H.M.S.O., 1962.

Malaysia. Report of the Inter-Governmental Committee 1962, Cmnd. 1954, London, H.M.S.O., 1963.

Malaysian heritage, Ministry of Culture, Singapore, 1962.

Report of the Economic Aspects of Malaysia by a Mission of the International Bank for Reconstruction and Development, under the Chairmanship of Mr Jacques Ruett, Government Printing Office, Singapore, 1963.

Indonesian Aggression against Malaysia, Ministry of External Affairs, Malaysia, Kuala Lumpur, 1964.

A Plot Exposed, Cmd. 12 of 1965, Malaysia, Kuala Lumpur, 1965.

The Problem of 'Malaysia', Embassy of the Republic of Indonesia, London, 1964.

Malaysia 145

CENSUS REPORTS

British Malaya. A Report on the 1931 Census and Certain Problems of Vital Statistics, by C. A. Vlieland, London, 1932.

Malaya. A Report on the 1947 Census of Population, by M. V. Del Tufo, London, 1949.

1957 Population Census of the Federation of Malaya, 14 vols., by H. Fell, Kuala Lumpur, n.d.

State of Singapore, Report on the Census of Population 1957, by S. C. Chua, Cmd. 19 of 1964, Singapore 1964.

Sarawak. Report on the Census of Population taken on 15th June 1960, by L. W. Jones, Kuching, 1962.

Brunei. Report on the Census of Population taken on 10th August 1960, by L. W. Jones, Kuching, n.d.

North Borneo, Report on the Census of Population taken on 10th August 1960, by L. W. Jones, Kuching, 1962.

Malaysia Buku Rasumi Tahunan (Official Year Book), Kuala Lumpur annual.

8

Ceylon:
Some Problems of a Plural Society   B. H. FARMER

This short essay is concerned with divisions in Ceylonese society which are marked by language and religion. For reasons of space it deals only marginally and incidentally with caste divisions, even though these are of great importance, not least in modern politics,[1] and at certain periods in Ceylon's long history, notably in the late nineteenth century, have been in some ways more divisive than language and religion.[2] The author, in choosing his subject matter in this way, is fully aware of the fact that, as a geographer, he may be accused of selecting only those socially plural phenomena which differ significantly from area to area (as do language and religion in Ceylon) and of omitting those which, because their variation is stratigraphical rather than geographical (as is caste in some sense, though there are many complications), are less susceptible to mapping and to other geographical techniques. It does appear to be true that the predilection of geographers for phenomena that vary spatially – one might almost say their vested interest in such phenomena – can lead to serious misinterpretations. For example, there was a tendency at the time of the Spanish Civil War to 'explain' the troubles of Spain in terms of the regionally fissiparous nature of Iberia, whereas in fact the Civil War had its origins in tensions far more complicated than those associated with regional centrifugality.[3]

But this essay must not degenerate into yet another exposé of what geographers cannot, or at any rate do not do. And certainly in the Ceylon case it has been religion and language, those eminently mappable phenomena, that have been the principal causes of recent dissensions, even though the problem has been complicated by caste and class. Moreover, whatever his concern here, the author, geographer though he

---

[1] See, for example, Bryce Ryan, *Caste in Modern Ceylon*, New Brunswick, N.J., 1953, especially pp. 199–200, 275–82 and 330–1; W. Howard Wriggins, *Ceylon: Dilemmas of a New Nation*, Princeton, 1960, especially pp. 25–6, 136, 152 and 158; B. H. Farmer, 'The social basis of nationalism in Ceylon', *Journal of Asian Studies*, 30, 1965, pp. 431–9.

[2] B. H. Farmer, *Ceylon: A Divided Nation*, London, 1963, pp. 48–50.

[3] *Cf.* W. G. East, *Mediterranean Problems*, London, etc., 1940, pp. 176–89, where a more comprehensive and balanced view was taken.

148 Essays in Political Geography

is, can at least claim to have examined the two last-named phenomena elsewhere.[1]

One final point must be made by way of introduction. Again for lack of space, this essay will assume familiarity with the main elements in the physical and economic geography of Ceylon,[2] especially with the clear physical contrast of Low Country with Up Country and Wet Zone with Dry Zone; and with the much less clear economic contrast between peasant and export sectors, now grown to overlap to such an extent, in the Wet Zone at any rate, as to make it increasingly hard to apply the time-worn concept of a dual economy – and still less to apply the notion of dual *economics* put out by J. H. Boeke and others of his school.[3]

THE FACTS OF PLURALITY IN CEYLON

According to the Census of 1953 the 'race and nationality' of the people of Ceylon were as shown in Table 8.1.[4]

TABLE 8.1: CEYLON: COMMUNITIES IN 1953

Citizens of Ceylon:

Sinhalese, Low Country	3,464,126	
Sinhalese, Kandyan	2,157,206	
Total Sinhalese		5,621,332
Ceylon Tamils		908,705
Ceylon Moors		468,146
Malays		28,736
Burghers		43,916
Others		20,678
Non-Citizens of Ceylon:		
Indians		984,327
Pakistanis		5,749
Europeans		5,886
Others		11,162
TOTAL		8,098,637

[1] B. H. Farmer, *op. cit., passim.*

[2] See, for example, B. H. Farmer, 'Ceylon', in O. H. K. Spate, *India and Pakistan,* 3rd edition, London and New York, 1967.

[3] J. H. Boeke and others, *Indonesian Economics: the Theory of Dualism in Theory and Practice,* The Hague, 1961.

[4] *Census of Ceylon, 1953* [Preliminary abstract], Colombo, 1953, Table 1, with corrections kindly supplied to the author by the Director of Census and Statistics.

Ceylon 149

Figures for 'race and nationality' at the Census of 1963 are not available at the time of writing, though the total population of Ceylon in 1963 has been given[1] as 10,624,507. On the basis of this increase of 31·2 per cent over the 1953 figure, which immediately highlights one of the island's principal and most intractable problems, the approximate strength of the main communities in 1963 has been estimated in Table 8.2.

TABLE 8.2: CEYLON: COMMUNITIES 1963 (ESTIMATED)

Citizens of Ceylon:

Sinhalese, Low Country	4·5 millions	
Sinhalese, Kandyan	2·9 millions	
Total Sinhalese		7·4 millions
Ceylon Tamils		1·2 millions
Ceylon Moors		0·6 millions
Non-Citizens of Ceylon:		
Indian Tamils		1·3 millions

Notwithstanding the official terminology, the author prefers the term 'community', which carries, or ought to carry, no implication of a race in the genetic sense, for, whatever the Sinhalese and their fellow-inhabitants of Ceylon may or may not be, they are certainly not pure races, biologically speaking. It will also be noted that the Census of 1953 classifies non-citizens by nationality, whereas the author's rough estimates for 1963 single out the numerically most important community, namely the Indian Tamils, most of whom are non-citizens.

The geographical distribution of the principal communities in Ceylon in 1953 is shown in Fig. 8.1, which follows the Census Districts of that year. It will be noticed that the Low Country Sinhalese are mainly concentrated in the lowland parts of the Wet Zone in the south-western sector of the island, though there are substantial minorities Up Country and, with the resettlement of the Dry Zone,[2] in some Dry Zone districts, especially those adjacent to the Wet Zone. The Kandyan Sinhalese, on the other hand, are dominant in the Up Country districts, as might be expected from their name; though in no district are they as markedly predominant as are the Low Country Sinhalese in the lowland Wet Zone, while in the tea-planting districts in the central and highest part

[1] *Census of Ceylon, 1963, Preliminary Report*, published as Ceylon Government, Gazette Extraordinary No. 13703, 19 July 1963.
[2] See B. H. Farmer, *Pioneer Peasant Colonization in Ceylon*, London, etc., 1957.

150 *Essays in Political Geography*

of the highlands they form less than 50 per cent of the total population. The Ceylon Tamils dominate the northern districts and, to a somewhat lesser extent, the eastern and north-western districts, as Fig. 8.1 clearly shows; they also form considerable minorities in many other parts of Ceylon, notably in the Colombo District and in districts west and north of the capital. Ceylon Moors are widely scattered, but are proportionately most numerous along the east coast, where locally, in fact, they are the dominant community, and along the north-west coast. The group referred to in the 1953 Census as 'Indians and Pakistanis' is overwhelmingly composed of non-citizen Indian Tamils; and Fig. 8.1 shows very clearly their concentration in the planting districts, where locally, as in Nuwara Eliya District, they constitute a majority, and, to a lesser degree, in the lowland Wet Zone.

PRE-COLONIAL PLURALITY

It is sometimes stated or implied that a plural society is the social accompaniment of a dual economy; and since the latter is, almost by definition, a product of colonialism, it is implied that a plural society also has followed some imperial flag. There are, of course, numerous instances of the association of a plural society with a colonial dual economy: those of Mauritius, Fiji, British Guiana, and the Caribbean generally, spring readily to mind. But, as Carl Troll has recently reminded us,[1] with widely chosen examples, not however including Ceylon, some elements in social plurality are pre-colonial. Indeed, social pluralism would have differentiated, and perhaps scarred, the fair face of Ceylon even if there had been no colonial experience at all. The paragraphs that follow will, in fact, suggest that some at least of Ceylon's lamentable communal disharmony springs neither from colonialism, nor from the mere propinquity of two or more communities in a relatively small space. The roots of the trouble lie deeper.

The two main communities concerned in the story of pre-colonial plurality in Ceylon were the Sinhalese, not yet differentiated into 'Low Country' and 'Kandyan', and the Ceylon Tamils, though the Ceylon Moors were also *in situ* in pre-colonial times. It is idle to enquire which came first, the Sinhalese or the Tamils, if the question implies that a whole community arrived, ready-made, as it were, on the beaches, and kept itself identifiable and inviolate in spite of the incursion of the other;

[1] Carl Troll, 'Plural societies of developing countries—aspects of social geography', Presidential Address to the 20th International Geographical Congress, London, 1964.

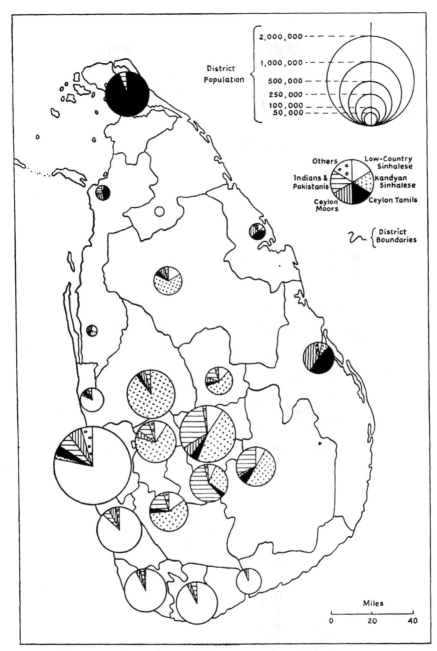

Fig. 8.1. Ceylon: size and communal composition of District population according to the 1953 Census

The area of each circle is proportionate to the population of the District which it represents. The area of each sector of a circle is proportionate to the population of the community it represents. (No attempt has been made to subdivide the small circle for Vavuniya District, where population is 5 per cent Low-Country Sinhalese, 11 per cent Kandyan Sinhalese, 67 per cent Tamil, and 8 per cent Indian and Pakistani.)

152 *Essays in Political Geography*

though the question has been asked with just these implications, and even answered, according to the communal affiliation of the enquirer. It is more sensible, but still not particularly profitable, to enquire which language, in an ancient form, was spoken the earlier in Ceylon. Tamil is a tongue descended from ancient Dravidian roots, as are other languages now spoken in southern India, like Malayalam, Telugu and Kannada; while Sinhalese is essentially an Aryan language, though with later borrowings from Tamil, sprung from the same linguistic roots as the present languages of northern India. It seems clear that some Aryan-speaking group, perhaps a very small one, reached Ceylon by sea some centuries B.C., thus over-leaping or by-passing the Dravidian-speaking lands of India, which may then have stretched much farther north than at present, and establishing an outpost of Aryan speech at the extreme southern tip of the Indian sub-continent. Thereafter, as one distinguished authority has recently put it, it may well have been that 'the higher culture, including the languages, brought to these regions by the Sinhalese as well as the Tamils, was adopted in varying degrees by the people of a Stone Age culture who were there before their arrival. Thus, the vast majority of the people who speak Sinhalese or Tamil today must ultimately be descended from those authochthonous people of whom we know next to nothing'.[1] Moreover, from historical evidence and from the study of place-names it is clear that, particularly in the northern Dry Zone and along the east and north-west coast, the frontier between Sinhalese and Tamil speech has shifted back and forth across the map, so that the people of a given village may at one time have considered themselves Sinhalese, at another time Tamils. Again, a number of Sinhalese castes (notably the Karāva, fishers and Salāgama, weavers and later cinnamon-peelers) are thought to have come from southern India where they must presumably have spoken Tamil, Malayalam or some other Dravidian tongue; and comparatively recently aboriginal Veddas have been 'Sinhalized'.

In other words, there is no more room in Ceylon for any sort of pure race theory than there is in Europe; and it is every whit as legitimate and pertinent to ask 'How Tamil are the Sinhalese?' and 'How Sinhalese are the Tamils?' as to ask 'How Welsh are the English?'. But this has not prevented the rise of myths of origin, especially among the Sinhalese, which tend to savour of racialism.[2]

[1] S. Paranavitana, 'Aryan settlements: the Sinhalese' in S. Paranavitana (ed.), *University of Ceylon History of Ceylon*, Vol. I, Pt I, Colombo, 1959, p. 96.

[2] See, for example, E. F. C. Ludowyk, *The Story of Ceylon*, London, 1962, Chapter 1.

Ceylon 153

Whatever the early history of Ceylon and whatever the truth behind surviving mythology, it is clear from the *Mahavamsa*,[1] a chronicle apparently written by a Buddhist monk about the fifth century A.D., that there were by that time recognizable Sinhalese and Tamil communities, and that the two had already been in conflict. Already Tamils had captured Anuradhapura, the ancient and sacred capital of the Sinhalese, while the Sinhalese king Dhatusena (A.D. 460–78) is praised by the chronicler for driving out the Tamils and entering the city as a victorious conqueror.

A millennium and a half ago, then, Sinhalese and Tamil, recognizing each other as such, were in Ceylon, and in conflict. But it is important, as already hinted, not to ascribe the conflict merely to propinquity, or to the struggle of two dynasties (of a sort so common in India) who might equally well have been both Sinhalese or both Tamil. For, although for long periods it seems clear that the Sinhalese and Tamil communities lived peaceably, even symbiotically, together, there was always, from those early days onward, what E. F. C. Ludowyk has called a 'special quality of hostility' ready to be called forth in times of difficulty and stress.[2] Primarily this quality arose, and still arises, from the special view that the Sinhalese held and still hold of their island as Sri Lanka (Holy Lanka) and of themselves as the chosen people of the Buddha who according to legend, prayed as he entered *nirvana* 'In Lanka, O Lord of gods, will my religion be established, therefore, carefully protect him[3] with his followers, and Lanka'. Perhaps the Sinhalese became aware that, with the Hindu revival on the mainland, they were a Buddhist people cut off from their religious roots in northern India, just as they were an Aryan-speaking people cut off from their cultural and linguistic, and they would add their racial, roots in northern India. Certainly there came to be a triple intertwining, unique in the Indian sub-continent, of language, religion and national survival for, given the strength of the Sinhalese feeling about themselves and their almost Jewish sense of destiny, it does not seem too strong a term to speak of them, from quite early times, as a nation. And it was against the Tamils, the principal historic threat to all elements in the triple strand, that the 'special quality of hostility' could be evoked. Later, moreover, the

---

[1] Available in English translation: W. Geiger (trans.), *The Mahavamsa or the Great Chronicle of Ceylon*, new edition, Colombo, 1950.

[2] E. F. C. Ludowyk, *op. cit.*, p. 65.

[3] The word 'him' refers to Vijaya, the legendary founder of the Sinhalese, who is said to have landed in Ceylon on the very day in which the Buddha entered *nirvana*.

154 *Essays in Political Geography*

Sinhalese, after the collapse of their Dry Zone civilization, were able, rightly or wrongly, to cast the Tamils in the role of destroyers of the ancient and the sacred.[1]

It seems fair to say, without bias in favour of the Tamils, that they did not and do not feel the same *special* hostility towards the Sinhalese, except as a reaction to the behaviour of the latter. The Ceylon Tamils, as Hindus, are in the Hindu eclectic tradition, and do not feel themselves to be defenders of the faith or, given the existence of the Dravidian mass of southern India, to be defenders of a language or 'nation' otherwise doomed to disappear.

CEYLON'S COLONIAL EXPERIENCE

Notwithstanding the case that has been made out for the depth and long-standing nature of the potential feeling of hostility between the Sinhalese and Ceylon Tamil communities, it is undoubtably true that the social scene in Ceylon has been complicated during the colonial period in such a way as to introduce fresh elements of plurality and to exacerbate inter-communal tensions, and developments since the return of independence have also played their part.

One of the notable consequences of Ceylon's 'four hundred and fifty years of foreign rule' has been the differentiation of Low Country from Kandyan Sinhalese. It was to be expected in any case that there would be some ecologically-based social difference between Sinhalese living in the lowlands of the Wet Zone and Sinhalese living in hill villages Up-Country; but it was long years of contact with the Portuguese, the Dutch, and the British before 1815 that did most to set the Low Country Sinhalese apart from the Kandyans of the hills and the interior of the Dry Zone. Though events after 1815, when the Kandyan Kingdom was absorbed by the British, tended to blur the distinction, it remains true that the Kandyans are on the whole more conservative and retain more of their traditional social structure, and that they at the same time feel themselves superior, not least as guardians of Sinhalese culture and religion, to the Low-Countrymen who have intruded into their domain.[2]

The colonial period also saw the intrusion into Ceylon of completely

---

[1] It is true that the Tamils were invaders, but it seems likely that political collapse, owing something but not everything to Tamil incursions, followed by the coming of malaria, rather than the physical destruction of irrigation works and buildings, lay behind the collapse. See *inter alia*, Rhoads Murphey, 'The ruin of ancient Ceylon', *Journal of Asian Studies*, 16, 1957, pp. 181–200.

[2] B. H. Farmer, *Ceylon: A Divided Nation*, pp. 18–20.

Ceylon 155

new elements in the population, following the familiar pattern of association between a dual economy and a plural society. By far and away the most numerous community thus intruded into the Ceylon scene was that made up of Tamil labourers who were brought in to work first on coffee plantations, and later on estates growing tea and rubber, and whose descendants, the 'Indian Tamils', are now more numerous than the 'Ceylon Tamil' descendants of pre-colonial immigrants from South India. Their concentration in the planting districts has already been noted. In spite of the fact that Ceylon and Indian Tamils share a basic common language and a common Hindu culture, there has been relatively little contact between these two communities. This has undoubtedly been due in part to the geographical separation of their respective areas of concentration, but it also owes a great deal to differences of caste and economic status: the Indian Tamils hail for the most part (so far as one can discover, though the censuses of Ceylon do not collect statistics by caste) from the great pool of mainly Harijan landless labourers to be found in Madras. Only since 1956, and at times of communal stress, have the two Tamil groups really made moves towards the presentation of a common front to the Sinhalese, and these moves in turn have provoked extreme nervousness among the latter.

Because of their heavy concentration in the planting districts the impact of the Indian Tamils has fallen most heavily on the Kandyan Sinhalese. Though many thousands of Indian Tamil estate labourers live at high altitude, where Sinhalese villages were never founded, some of them occupy hill-tops immediately above Kandyan Sinhalese villages, as around Kandy itself, and consequently earn some of the opprobrium that descends on the estates for occupying land that would otherwise be available for the expansion of village fields. Moreover, there have been other causes of friction, for example, allegations that Indian Tamils have been acquiring Sinhalese village land.[1] Largely under Kandyan Sinhalese pressure, then, most Indian Tamils, who had been enfranchised by the so-called 'Donoughmore' constitution of 1931 and who tended in a number of constituencies to elect members of their own community, were in effect disenfranchised by two of the early enactments of independent Ceylon, namely the Citizenship Act No. 18 of 1948, which limits Ceylon citizenship to those who can claim it by descent or who can acquire it by registration, and the Indian and

[1] See, for example, *Report of the Kandyan Peasantry Commission*, Sessional Paper 18 of 1951, Colombo, 1951, p. 258.

156 *Essays in Political Geography*

Pakistan Residents (Citizenship) Act No. 3 of 1949, which lays down procedure for registration that has made it very difficult for Indian Tamils to become citizens of Ceylon.[1]

The problem of the 'stateless' remainder of the Indian Tamil community has, of course, been a bone of contention between India and Ceylon and, for many years, weary and inconclusive negotiations have dragged on. In December, 1964, however, Mrs Bandaranaike, then Prime Minister of Ceylon, concluded an agreement with Shri Lal Bahadur Shastri, Prime Minister of India, under which 525,000 Indians were to be repatriated, 300,000 to be absorbed by Ceylon, and the remainder of the 'stateless' were to be the subject of further negotiations. Already, however, it has been reported that there has been friction because of the uncertainty of the Ceylon's government's intentions as to the citizenship rights and enfranchisement of the 300,000 to be absorbed. It should also be noted that although there has been a tendency for the Sinhalese proportion of the estate labour force to rise steadily, it is not easy to see how nearly half the Indian labourers now in Ceylon could be withdrawn without damaging production on the estates, which is so vital to the country's economy in so many ways.

Space forbids more than a mere mention of other communities introduced during the colonial period. These include the so-called 'Indian Moors',[2] never so well-accepted by the Sinhalese as the older Muslim community known as the Ceylon Moors; the Burghers, some of whom claim pure European descent from Dutch settlers; and the Europeans.

Another notable consequence of colonial rule in Ceylon, especially during the British period, was the movement of population within the island in such a way as to lead to new patterns of distribution which, in some cases, heightened the danger of intercommunal clashes in times of stress. Thus the Portuguese expelled the Moors from their territory in about 1620, partly no doubt because they identified the Ceylon Muslim community with the Moors of Iberia, and partly because they found on their arrival that the Muslims were politically strong, so much so that, but for the Portuguese arrival, Ceylon might have become a sultanate like that other area of near-Sinhalese speech, the Maldives. The expelled Moors then settled in Kandyan territory, notably on the east

---

[1] This was indeed the intention; only about 100,000 citizens have in fact acquired that status by registration.

[2] Trouble between Kandyans and Indian Moors indeed sparked off the 1915 riots, the aftermath of which gave a number of Ceylonese leaders that taste of a British jail so essential to the image of a successful nationalist.

Ceylon 157

coast round Batticaloa, thus contributing to the high proportion of Muslim population that gives the coast some of its particular ethnic flavour.

More important from the point of view adopted in this essay was the fact that, with the rise of educational standards in the north after the concentration of a good deal of missionary endeavour there, and under the sheltering umbrella of the *pax Britannica*, educated Ceylon Tamils spread to almost all parts of Ceylon geographically, and to almost all sectors occupationally, especially however in such branches of the government service as the railway, the post office, and the Public Works Department, though a much smaller number of Sinhalese moved into Tamil areas. The consequence was the insertion of pockets of Ceylon Tamil population almost everywhere, but especially in the towns, bringing Sinhalese and Tamil into contact, and providing highly exposed minority groups at times of communal trouble. Further, in course of time there came to be bitter jealousy among some Sinhalese who, rightly or wrongly, claimed that the Ceylon Tamils had more than their fair share of jobs in government service. This jealousy was to grow all the more bitter after independence, with the rise in population and in unemployment, especially among would-be white-collar workers.

The beginnings of the recolonization of the Dry Zone, dating from colonial times and continued at an accelerated rate after independence,[1] were also to provide a source of communal trouble. In some places Sinhalese were put into what it was claimed were traditionally Tamil areas, while some political parties took the view that, given the great agrarian pressure in the Wet Zone, it was only reasonable that an overall view should be taken of the colonization problem, and that there should be no sanctity about traditional areas of settlement. Moreover, the work preparatory to colonization tended to involve large, deracinated labour forces which rather than peasants or colonists, proved in 1958 to be easily provoked by the inflammatory speeches of communal agitators.[2]

It remains to consider the effect of constitutional developments during British times, the long and rather dull story of which has often been told.[3] What is relevant to the present discussions is the question whether the British, when they instituted communal constituencies and representation by way of recognizing communal divisions, thereby strengthened those very divisions. This is a difficult question on which

[1] B. H. Farmer, *Pioneer Peasant Colonization in Ceylon.*
[2] See Tarzie Vittachi, *Emergency '58*, London, 1957, pp. 43–68.
[3] See, for example, Sir Charles Jeffries, *Ceylon – The Path to Independence*, London, etc., 1962.

158 *Essays in Political Geography*

the last word will not be said for a long time. The author's own tentative conclusion has already been recorded elsewhere:

> The basic dilemma that confronts representative government in a country riven by communal differences is here plain for all to see: territorial electorates, drawn with no eye to the distribution of communities, mean rule by the majority community with no safeguard for the minorities, while safeguards for the minorities inevitably deepen the divisions of the nation along communal lines.[1]

Possibly, however, the most important effect of colonial rule is to be found in the nationalist reaction to it. The first wave of nationalism in Ceylon,[2] which carried the country to independence, was generated in the thin English-speaking upper lamina of Ceylonese society which contained, it should be said, a number of enlightened individuals, including Mr D. S. Senanayake, who saw clearly the vision of a united nation, at least so far as the Sinhalese and Ceylon Tamils were concerned, though it was during the period in which this wave was dominant that the citizenship laws hostile to the Indian Tamils were enacted. There followed a second wave, much more tempestuous than the first, which was generated among the Sinhalese-speaking, Buddhist middle-class in the villages. This was the class which felt most cogently the force of the traditional intertwining of language, nation and religion, and hence was especially likely to feel the need to establish Sinhalese as the sole national language in association with a Buddhist revival and in opposition to the Tamils. It was this same class, moreover, which, besides being most affected by the Buddhist revival connected with Buddha Jayanti, the 2500th anniversary of Buddha, was exceptionally liable to feel economic frustration, against both the English-speaking and the Tamils, during a period of mounting unemployment particularly for those who aspired to white-collar jobs, and was also subject to the 'majority-in-a-minority' complex already mentioned. On all of these complicated and inter-woven motives Mr S. W. R. D. Bandaranaike played in order to gain power in 1956 and, in so doing, he necessarily, though perhaps not deliberately, exacerbated them. The results in terms of communal emotions and violence are all too well known, and in terms of the plurality of society in Ceylon they will be felt far into the future.

[1] B. H. Farmer, *Ceylon: A Divided Nation*, p. 56.
[2] B. H. Farmer, 'The social basis of nationalism in Ceylon', *Journal of Asian Studies*, 30, 1965, pp. 431–9.

CONCLUSION

It is no part of the argument of this essay to claim that Ceylon is unique in the fact that its social plurality and communal tensions have roots that are pre-colonial and characteristics that derive from other factors than mere propinquity. But it can legitimately be claimed that there is something special, at least in the context of South and South-east Asia, in the view that the Sinhalese take of themselves and of the Tamils, especially the Ceylon Tamils. Certainly the model suggested for Burma, Thailand and Malaya by the late F. G. Carnell, whose untimely death will be deplored by all seriously concerned with South and South-east Asian studies, does not exactly fit the Ceylon case. Carnell saw the history of plural societies in these countries in terms of three phases.[1] In the first phase, before the nineteenth century, 'such cultural fusion as took place was by conquest and miscegenation' though outlying groups retained their traditional culture unimpaired. In Ceylon, however, it is arguable that, while there was far more miscegenation than modern communalism allows, it was the traditional relationship of Sinhalese to Tamil, not isolation or remoteness, that kept the cultures of both substantially unimpaired. In Carnell's second phase, in the nineteenth century, a flood of immigration added new elements to the plurality of society, but there was little mobility of persons or ideas because of 'the slow growth of communications'. Ceylon, of course, had its flood of immigrants, but they remained separate from the Sinhalese in spite of, and not because of propinquity; meanwhile the growth of communications took Low-Countrymen to Kandyan territory and Ceylon Tamils almost everywhere. It was in the third phase of Carnell's model, after the 1930s, that urbanization, economic mobility and education led to increasing contact between communal groups, to increasing competition and to increasing communal disharmonies accentuated by the Japanese occupation. Clearly, and quite apart from the absence of any Japanese occupation in Ceylon, this model does not explain the rise of second-wave nationalism in Ceylon, or its revival, in a new economic context, of ancient grievances going back to early relations between Sinhalese and Tamil and to the traditional Sinhalese view of themselves.

[1] F. G. Carnell, 'Ethnic and cultural pluralism in Burma, Thailand and Malaya', *Ethnic and Cultural Pluralism in Intertropical Communities*, Report of the 30th Session of the International Institute of Differing Civilizations, Lisbon, 1957, Brussels, 1957, pp. 407–22, especially pp. 409–10.

9

The Problem of Nagaland

ULRICH SCHWEINFURTH[1]

When the 'map war' in the Himalayas came into prominence in 1962, there was some suspicion that the Chinese advance towards Assam, and in particular down the Lohit valley, might have been planned with knowledge of the unrest prevailing for several years in the nearby Naga Hills. This suspicion was subsequently confirmed, and it is now known that there have been overtures from the Chinese side to contact the Nagas, and at least twice before 1962 Chinese parties are said to have entered Naga territory.

In attempting to trace the background to this situation the author, whose interest in the Naga question is a by-product of his studies of the Himalayas and adjacent regions, proposes to emphasize three main themes. These are, first the lack of knowledge of the outside world about the Nagas and their country, secondly, the nature of the Naga question today as a typical example of the problems arising from the process of decolonization in many parts of the world and, thirdly, the significance of the Naga question in the wider context of international rivalries in Asia.

THE NAGAS AND THEIR COUNTRY

The remoter parts of the Asian continent rank among the least known areas of the globe, and the lack of cartographical data is ample proof of the difficulties of the terrain. But this is only one example of the problem which arises here. Those who seek information about the Naga Hills quickly discover how little has been written about this area, a point which is well illustrated by referring to a few standard geographical works. Thus, for example, Krebs, in his treatise *Vorderindien und Ceylon* (1939), considers the Naga Hills to belong to *Hinterindien* and therefore feels relieved of the duty to deal with them, and a similar attitude is adopted by Spate in his *India and Pakistan* (1960). Both these authors

---

[1] The author wishes to express his indebtedness to Professor J. H. Hutton and to Lt. Col. and Mrs F. N. Betts for information and critical comments without which this paper could not have been written.

162 *Essays in Political Geography*

of well-known text-books about the Indian sub-continent, therefore, in a way provide substance to the Nagas' claim to have nothing whatsoever to do with India. Fisher, in his recent treatise on *South-east Asia* (1964), makes some reference to the Nagas of Burma, but as his book is based on the political units of South-east Asia, only the Nagas of the Burmese Union lie within his scope and in this context the Naga country is a very marginal area indeed. Even the *Encyclopaedia Britannica* (1964 edition) is remarkably brief in its treatment of the Nagas and the Naga Hills, and references in scientific journals are few, the best available being from anthropologists. But the promising beginnings of a much-needed exploration of the Naga Hills came to an abrupt end with the outbreak of the Second World War.[1]

The Nagas have hitherto achieved no prominence in world politics, and indeed have had neither the opportunity nor the desire to participate in international affairs. Whatever may be suggested to the contrary by small-scale maps, the Nagas live in very difficult country between the Brahmaputra in Assam and the Upper Chindwin in northern Burma. Extending as far south-west as Imphal in Manipur and as far west as Haphlong at the edge of the Khasia-Jaintia plateau, they are spread over an area of some 200 by 400 miles. This country, which is not yet fully explored, is peripheral to the Indian Union and marginal to the Union of Burma. The practice in many books and atlases of showing the Indian sub-continent separately from South-east Asia is not very helpful to those seeking an understanding of the Naga country as a whole, and no maps exist which could be called reliable for the Naga area in its entirety.[2]

This hill country, so difficult of access, now carries the international boundary between India and Burma, but it may be safely assumed that this line is little more than a fiction of the political map. All these hills are loosely known as the Naga Hills, a term which is not fully adequate and indeed rather misleading since it was for some time applied to a much smaller administrative unit. The hills rise steeply from the valley of Assam to culminate in summit levels of between 9,000 and 13,000 feet, as for example in Mt Japyo (9,734 feet) near Kohima, and Mt Sarameti (12,663 feet) on the Indo-Burman border.

All this country is off the beaten track, rugged, steep and the reverse

[1] Reference should in particular be made to the former Assam Government series of monographs by J. H. Hutton, T. C. Hodson, and J. P. Mills.

[2] It is noteworthy, however, that during the period of British rule surveyors accompanied most expeditions into unexplored territory and these old maps are surprisingly reliable so far as they go. (Betts)

The Problem of Nagaland 163

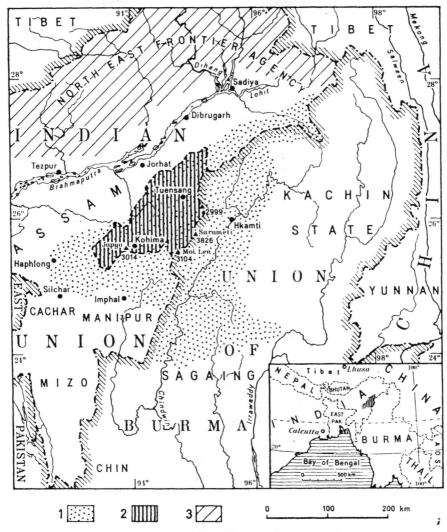

Fig. 9.1. 'Nagaland' and area inhabited by Nagas
1 Area inhabited by Nagas
2 'Nagaland' as defined as State of the Union of India
3 Area claimed by Chinese People's Republic
For note on sources see p. 176.

164 *Essays in Political Geography*

of inviting, but because of its very inaccessibility it affords a refuge. The Nagas, who have lived here for many centuries,[1] now number about 500,000 within the Indian Union, of whom only 350,000 are included within Nagaland, the sixteenth state of the Union, and there are another 90–100,000 in Burma, though it must be stressed that all these figures are only approximations.

The Nagas comprise some twenty tribes which are further subdivided into local groups, and these – despite a strong sense of 'Nagahood', which is also shared by the Nagas of upper Burma – do not always live in perfect harmony with one another. Inter-tribal and inter-village strife was formerly of frequent occurrence, and obvious indications of this can be seen in the characteristic position and features of Naga villages, which are situated on ridges or spurs, high above the valleys and difficult of access, and very heavily fortified with trenches, fences and guardhouses. On the steep slopes below the ridges are the cultivated lands, usually consisting of dry rice fields worked according to a rather advanced form of shifting cultivation, though the Agamis have a highly developed form of staircase irrigation with rice terraces not unlike those of the Ifugao in the Philippines. The valleys, usually narrow and highly malarial, are normally left to the jungle and hence form barriers to communication, though in some areas they are used for wet-rice cultivation, in which case they may also provide means of communication during the dry season.

The Nagas are wholly distinct racially, linguistically and culturally from the plains people, by whom they have never been dominated and whom indeed they despise. They fiercely resent any attempt to intrude into or control their domain. Fiercely independent, and hungry for the status-giving heads, they found the plains people easy prey for their hunting activities, and the tea plantations in the nearby Assam plains a heaven-sent quarry for heads. Not surprisingly, therefore, the plains people have always regarded the Nagas as fierce warriors, and the latter have accordingly been respected – or feared – by the outside world. In their turn the Nagas have been proud of their reputation as head-hunters, and it may be assumed that traces of this behaviour still survive in the remoter parts of the hills. This reputation for savagery provides, of course, another reason why the Naga Hills have remained so little known.

Since rather more has come to be learned about the Nagas, especially

[1] Ptolemy records the Nagas in their present position in the second century A.D. ($\pi \varepsilon \zeta \grave{\iota}\ \tau \tilde{\eta} \varsigma\ \gamma \varepsilon o \gamma \zeta a \varphi \acute{\iota} a \varsigma$: VII, II, 18).

The Problem of Nagaland 165

as a result of anthropological explorations, speculation has increased regarding their earlier affinities. It now seems to be reasonably well established that the Nagas belong to a group of people speaking Tibeto-Burmese languages, but varying greatly among themselves. The nearest related peoples occur in scattered groups in the mountain country between Assam, Burma and Yunnan. Probably all of these must be regarded as representatives of old palaeo-mongoloid stocks, perhaps once of common origin, and deriving, according to some experts, from the north-western parts of China. These peoples may subsequently have split up and developed distinctive characteristics in different habitats. However, there also appear to be other interesting relationships between the Nagas and the Dyaks of Central Borneo and some of the hill peoples of the Philippines (see, for instance, Hutton, 1965).

In the mountain country to the north of the Assam valley, particularly that which forms the southern slopes of the Assam Himalayas, there are other distinctive hill tribes which show certain similarities to the Nagas. Space permits only a brief reference to one of these, namely the Apa Tanis, a tribe confined to one small valley in the Subansiri system. Although they had been heard of before,[1] their valley was not discovered until the early 1940s, and it is to von Fürer-Haimendorf and to Graham Bower that we owe most of our present knowledge of this most interesting hill tribe. These people remained undiscovered in their secluded valley owing to the nature of the country, whose remote valleys, rough topography, and impenetrable tropical jungle, together with the bad reputation which these tribes had always had in the nearby Assam plains, kept them undisturbed from the interference of the outside world and so preserved them more or less untouched until the present day.

THE ASSAM FRONTIER REGION UNDER THE BRITISH

The British approach to all the Assam frontier problems was one of expediency. The tribal areas produced next to no revenue, and had to be financed from money drawn from the plains. Thus, unless either raiding, as in the nineteenth century, or defence considerations, as during and after the Second World War, made some sort of administration absolutely necessary, governments were most reluctant to sanction any advance. It was this outlook which led to the piecemeal annexation of the Naga area, and hence to its administrative fragmentation.

[1] See Verrier Elwin, *India's North-East Frontier in the Nineteenth Century*, Bombay, 1959, pp. 189–203.

166 *Essays in Political Geography*

Everywhere the process followed much the same kind of sequence. The tribes nearest the plains were controlled to stop raiding; then – sooner or later – the frontier had to be pushed forward to protect them from their wilder neighbours beyond; and so on, at least in the Naga Hills, until peaceful contact and occasional punitive expeditions had so conditioned the unadministered tribes that they could be absorbed peacefully and without military assistance. To sum up briefly, there were three administrative zones: first, the one nearest the plains which was regarded as being fully administered, and was subsequently called the 'Naga Hills District'; secondly, a belt of partly administered country ('control area') into which British officers made sporadic visits rather in the nature of expeditions; and thirdly, the remoter hills which remained unadministered. There were punitive expeditions in 1879, followed by a peace concluded in 1880; and between 1917 and 1919 operations were conducted against Tuensang. But the principle of British administration, once it was assured that there would be no more raids into the plains, was to leave the Nagas to themselves.

From about 1910 onwards a succession of Deputy Commissioners took command, namely Hutton, Mills and Pawsey, who proved to be extremely well chosen. Notwithstanding the warlike traditions of the Nagas, these men managed to rule them effectively with a very small number of British personnel. The backbone of the administration was made up of the Naga chiefs themselves, the Naga village councils, and the *dobashis*, who were nominally interpreters but in fact native aides of high integrity and capacity. In addition to these, the Deputy Commissioner himself acted, in Graham Bower's phrase, as a sort of benevolent High King, functioning simultaneously as adviser, protector and administrator, who could be called upon for help, but who only intervened when native institutions failed to settle disputes. This procedure suited the Nagas' temperament and very largely accounted for the system's success. When the Japanese penetrated into Burma during the Second World War, the hills south of the Assam valley became an operational area. The Japanese forces pressed forward as far as Kohima and Imphal, investing the latter from March to June 1944 before being effectively stopped at Kohima.[1] During this time the British administration, though it was interrupted and disturbed, never broke down entirely and following the British success at Kohima, it was quickly functioning again having meanwhile retreated into the jungle. Thus the Nagas did not actually pass out of British control, and furthermore the British suc-

[1] See A. Swinson, *Kohima*, London, 1966.

The Problem of Nagaland   167

ceeded in enlisting their co-operation against the Japanese. Without this help from the Nagas, Kohima would have fallen into Japanese hands, and the way into the plains of Assam would have been thrown open. Nevertheless the Nagas were witnesses of this great shock administered to British rule in India, and for the first time they came into possession of a large stock of modern weapons, obtained first for defence purposes from the British and later by collecting arms left behind in considerable quantities on the battlefields. Thereafter, doubtless because of all that had recently happened, the Nagas did not feel entirely obliged to give these weapons up, and it may safely be assumed that there would have been trouble between at least some of the Nagas and the British, had the latter remained as rulers in India. But events now began to move in another direction.

Peace and contentment for the Naga people were achieved during the British period by cultural and political isolation, which in effect meant isolation from India. This was precisely what the majority of the Nagas desired but this did not lessen the difficulties of the British officers in charge, who had to look to the future.

Between the two World Wars there was a period of general advancement. American Baptists had established missionary schools at Impur, and the Nagas, being an intelligent people, were quick to benefit from them, especially the Ao Nagas in the vicinity of Impur. The influence of the missionary and the government schools furthered the spread both of English and of literacy in the Naga languages. Today 60 per cent of the Nagas are Christians and the Christian faith has certainly had a detribalizing effect. But on the other hand it is also an important unifying factor behind the present demand for independence, for the adoption of Christianity created another barrier against the Indians in the plains. In this context it is significant that, soon after independence, the Indian government expelled the missionaries from the Naga areas. In Burma there were no missionary schools among the Nagas, and there the latter remain tribal and animistic to this day. But on the Indian side of the border the influence of missionary and government schools had awakened a new sense of self awareness among the Nagas.

When in 1929 the Simon Commission investigated, with an eye to forthcoming constitutional changes in India, the 'Naga Club'[1] impressed it with their outright refusal to accept an Indian government as successor to British rule. Their leaders made it abundantly clear that, if the British were to withdraw, the Nagas wished to revert to the status

[1] See Patterson, 25.10.1962.

168 Essays in Political Geography

they had enjoyed before the British arrived, namely that of an independent people, free to decide their own destiny. In no circumstances would they agree to be governed by plains people, whom they regarded as militarily, socially and religiously inferior to themselves. The cleavage along the foothill zone, a true natural divide which also marked a decisive racial, cultural and linguistic boundary, was absolute.

The Simon Commission recognized these differences. In 1937 it declared the Assam Frontier Districts, which included the Naga Hills, to be an Excluded Area, that is an area excluded from the scope of the central and provincial legislatures. The principle of different treatment was resented by the Indians as reflecting upon their administrative competence, but in fact it was not new and the same system had formerly been applied to other problem areas.

INDIAN INDEPENDENCE AND THE CREATION OF NAGALAND

In possession of large quantities of modern weapons after the Second World War, the Nagas – particularly the Western Angamis of Khonoma who have always constituted some of the most powerful villages – were not in a hurry to give them up, especially as the transfer of sovereignty from Britain to India was now impending. The powerful position of the Western Angamis caused their eastern neighbours considerable concern when it became clear that the British really were going. Certain groups of Nagas who had a chance to become all-powerful under these conditions now demanded immediate independence, while others wanted a temporary link with India to provide an opportunity in which to consider independence later, and still others wanted a British mandatory state. Two official plans for such a mandate were in fact put forward (the so-called Reid and Copland Plans), one of which envisaged a kind of confederation of several similar states including the frontier tribes of Burma, to form a frontier tract which could be built up with a view to eventual independence. This plan was in fact sanctioned by Sir Winston Churchill, but was later vetoed by the new Labour government.

In the event, however, the Nagas themselves concluded the 1948 Agreement with the Indian government, which on the face of it gave them all that they could have wished for, including in the ill-fated Clause Nine a prospect of independence. In this connexion, it is worthy of note that, when Indian independence did come into effect on 14 August 1947, A. Z. Phizo, the leader of the Naga independence movement, declared his village, Khonoma, independent from India.

The Problem of Nagaland 169

Unfortunately the prospects of a workable agreement foreshadowed in 1948 were not fulfilled. From the outset the Nagas resisted the attempts of the Indian government to turn them into 'co-operative citizens' of the Union. Bearing in mind their profound disregard for all strangers, and for plains people in particular, it could easily have been foreseen how the Nagas would react to any approach by the Indian government designed to teach them a lesson which, in the event, was precisely how the attitude of the Indian government appeared to the Nagas.

In January 1951 Phizo called for a plebiscite to demonstrate popular support for the demand for independence, but his approach to the United Nations was of no avail. In December 1951 Prime Minister Nehru met the Naga National Council which had meanwhile been established, but refused its demand. In 1953 when Nehru and U Nu, then Prime Minister of Burma, met in the frontier area and wanted to address the Nagas at Kohima, the Nagas staged a dramatic walk-out. The subsequent reports in 1954 of killings of Nagas in Free (unadministered) Naga Territory by Indian Army personnel marked the beginning of the upheaval, and by 1956 the Indian Army was fully deployed against the Nagas.[1]

Press reports are scanty and for various reasons not always reliable, and stories of cruelties have been reported from both sides. During the course of the events described above, there was established besides the N.N.C., which aimed at complete independence, the more moderate Naga People's Convention under the leadership of Dr Shilu Ao. By a policy of appeasement the N.P.C. in September 1957 achieved under the Kohima Convention the separation of the Administrative District of Naga Hills from Assam State. This new administrative unit was composed of the old British Naga Hills District and the Tuensang Frontier District[2] which was taken out of the North-east Frontier Agency. The new unit was now called the 'Naga Hill Agency' and was placed directly under the authority of the President of the Indian Union.

This conciliatory move on the part of the Indian government did not, however, satisfy the more determined elements among the Nagas. Again, in July 1960, fifteen Naga leaders, headed by Dr Ao, appeared before the Indian Prime Minister with a petition for further autonomy. An independent state within the framework of the Indian Union, and containing roughly 350,000 inhabitants, was thereupon proposed, with the

[1] Professor J. H. Hutton – in private communication – thinks that the burning of administered villages marked the beginning of the unrest.

[2] Hence the name of the Naga Hills and Tuensang Act (1957) under which this arrangement was put into effect.

170   *Essays in Political Geography*

Governor of Assam to become the Governor of the new state as well, though the latter was also to have its own Chief Minister. A change in the Indian constitution, dated 18 August 1962, raised Nagaland with all formalities to become the sixteenth state of the Indian Union.

From the Indian side this offer implied a considerable recognition of the Nagas' struggle for their independent way of life, and indeed it contained everything the Nagas could hope to obtain from Delhi. On 1 December 1963 Nagaland was officially inaugurated as the sixteenth – and also the smallest – state of the Indian Union, containing 350,000 out of the Indian Union's 500,000 Nagas, and having its capital at Kohima, a town whose population numbered some 5,000 in 1951.

This development, however, did not change the attitude of the more determined Nagas. Moreover there are strong tribal ties between the moderates and the so-called 'hostiles' or 'rebels', and in addition the sense of Nagahood, which seems to be shared by the Nagas of the Union of Burma, is strong. Late in 1962 Phizo and four other Naga leaders approached the United Nations again to raise the possibility of a union of the Nagas and other hill peoples alien to the Indians, a proposal which recalled the former British plans referred to on page 168.

THE DEMAND FOR NAGA INDEPENDENCE

While it could certainly be argued that the state of affairs achieved by the creation of Nagaland should have satisfied the Nagas, especially in view of the many substantial material advantages which membership of the Indian Union confers, the experience of recent years shows that matters of this kind are not solved by clear reasoning alone. The cleavage between plains people and hill people here seems complete, and it has been so aggravated during the past decade of hostilities that any solution other than complete independence may prove unacceptable to the Nagas.

Furthermore the latter may point to other examples in the world of today which appear to bear out their claim. Why should not Nagaland ask for independence when Ruanda Burundi or Gambia are allowed to take independence for granted simply because of their rather peculiar colonial past? If Ruanda and Burundi, which were merely pockets of the former German East Africa, had not been handed over to the Belgian Congo after the First World War in a straightforward colonial transaction typical of its time, they would never have gained the kind of prominence that they have today, and both would doubtless have

The Problem of Nagaland 171

become parts of Tanzania by now, instead of being regarded as independent nations. Compared with these, and other similar examples among the newly independent states of Africa, the Nagas' claim for independent nationhood would appear to be substantial.

The Naga leaders have achieved much in the way of improvisation during the years of war, and in so far as information is available their organization appears to be efficient. To establish an independent Nagaland they would certainly need help from outside, but as outside help is common practice these days it would doubtless be available for the Nagas. They cannot go back to the jungle, nor do they wish to do this after their experience of recent years. But after all that has happened they will be reluctant to accept help from the most obvious source.

Meanwhile, the fact remains that the Indian government has proved unable to end the war and to establish peace, whether by political accommodation or by sheer force and military action. There is some hope that under the regime of the new Prime Minister of India a new approach might be made to the Naga problem, but here one can only await further developments. The conditions put forward by the 'hostiles' show that the latter are fully conscious of the success of their now more than ten years' war, and in this they are strengthened by the attitude of the moderates who have made it clear that they will not be used against their 'hostile brothers', and indeed would be willing to step down from their positions in the Nagaland administration to make way for a new settlement with the Indian government.

In most current discussion of the Naga problem far too little heed is paid to the fact that there are also approximately 100,000 Nagas on the Burmese side of the frontier. This so-called Sagaing District of northern Burma is unadministered, and no influence is felt there today from far away Rangoon. In the British days a nominal administrative delimitation was believed to run right through the hills, and with the independence of both India and Burma this line has become an international boundary, though the Nagas, who still live on both sides of it, have at no time been asked what they think about this arrangement. When Burma decided to leave the Commonwealth the line acquired even more of an international status, and this situation provides an argument in support of the Nagas' claim that they simply cannot surrender to a mere change in administration.

It is usual nowadays to give former colonial administrative units the status of independent nationhood, but there is very little consideration of how these units came into being, or how their delimitation was

172 *Essays in Political Geography*

arranged. As a matter of fact many of the lines in question were drawn in some European capital with a ruler on the desk, when the countries concerned had not yet been explored. But the delimitations so agreed upon were quickly put on the map, and there they have remained. In the author's opinion the way in which these colonial delimitations have been accepted by the newly independent states of today, and in some examples already fiercely defended against questioning, is the most dangerous legacy which the colonial past has left behind.

In the case of Nagaland this colonial legacy has so far resulted in more than ten years of unrest, which is not less deplorable simply because so little has been heard about it. As has been noted above, there has been one attempt, by Nehru and U Nu in 1953, to find a common policy towards the Naga Hills frontier tract, but the outbreak of unrest among the Kuo Min Tang forces then roaming in eastern Burma interrupted the meeting and led to its premature end.[1] The topic has never since been taken up between the two governments concerned.

It may thus be assumed that there exists no effective international boundary dividing the Naga peoples in India from those in Burma, and therefore that in the event of strong pressure from the West they could always quietly recede to the east where the hills and jungles of northern Burma would provide abundant shelter. There is now ample evidence that these inner parts of the Naga country are beyond the effective control of the governments which claim responsibility for them. There is thus abundant scope for determined guerrilla leadership, and here the Nagas have proved their determination. Their guerrilla strength is said to number 40,000 disciplined men of high morale, the effectiveness of whose organization can be gathered from the apparent ease with which certain people have for many years been channelled in and out of the 'rebel'-held territory. It would seem in short that there is no justifiable reason for regarding the problem presented by the Nagas as purely an internal problem of the Indian Union.

From the Indian point of view, Assam and the surrounding hills are areas of concern in relation to many unsettled problems, and as these areas are now frontier zones *vis à vis* China they are especially sensitive. The lack of basic knowledge of the country concerned adds to its potential danger. The Chinese moves in 1962 have already gravely weakened the Indian position in so far as the show-down was naturally noticed by all the hill tribes most immediately concerned.

There is no apparent indication of any awareness by the Burmese

[1] See H. R. Tinker, *The Union of Burma*, London, 1961, p. 356.

The Problem of Nagaland 173

government of the development in the north of the country, though to the Chinese the unrest in the Naga Hills is no doubt of interest for it affords opportunities to put pressure on both the Indian and the Burmese governments should the need arise. Moreover, it provides the further opportunity to act as champion of a national independence movement, which is especially welcome here since it lies in an inaccessible and unknown region close to the Yunnan border of China itself. Thus the setting exists for creating endless trouble, as the last ten years have all too clearly shown. In this connexion it is perhaps surprising that the Naga leaders have so far kept their hands free, a fact which tends to confirm their desire for genuine independence, as also did their offer to help the Indian government against the Chinese in 1962.

Furthermore the Chinese might attempt to use the 'Naga War' to discredit the Indian government as neo-colonial or neo-imperialist, as in their eyes the Indian reluctance to grant independence to the Nagas is merely an attempt to maintain the former British colonial empire, and in so far as it was only under British administration that the Naga country was ever attached to India there is some substance in the Chinese argument.

In general the Naga unrest is symptomatic of the softening-up along China's southern marches by national independence movements, which is also occurring in Laos and Vietnam and perhaps in northern Burma. This process keeps China's opponents busy while China, not itself openly involved, can sit on the fence and await the outcome in relative comfort. The unrest among the Nagas means instability in a very sensitive corner of the Asian continent, a corner which is not of minor importance because so little is known about it. On the contrary, it is now the meeting place of the international boundaries of Burma, India and East Pakistan, and it suffers from a particularly high degree of political instability since these areas are all so remote from the administrative centres which are respectively responsible for them.

The Chinese proposal for a confederation of hill states provides another example of how the Chinese take up proposals from the colonialist past whenever it suits their interests to do so. No doubt the aim is to establish a cordon of small states, a sort of satellite confederation whose members could easily be played off one against another by the power in command of the Asian Heartland. While there cannot be much doubt that China holds the main initiative in this corner of Asia it is not the only country which has attempted to fish in these troubled waters. That Pakistan has evidently found this a useful place in which to annoy India

174 *Essays in Political Geography*

has been confirmed by reports that guerrillas, having been trained in Pakistani territory, have been sent back into the Naga Hills. This information provides further evidence of the danger of regarding the Naga problem as a purely internal affair of the Indian Union.

CONCLUSION

Now that large-scale all-out war seems fortunately to be regarded as too dangerous to be used as a political weapon, subversive activities and guerrilla warfare appear in practice to have taken its place. For this kind of war scarcely known areas are particularly inviting. Decolonization has presented the world with many new problems arising from the fact that many of the newly established nations, immediately after gaining their independence, have tended to resort to policies similar to those of which they accuse the former colonial powers. The resultant problems are inherent in so far as aspirations for national independence are not confined simply to the ex-colonial administrative units to which sovereignty has been transferred.

When such problems of decolonization arise in an unknown or scarcely explored country the stage is set for endless trouble, which can all too easily be taken up and used in the wider context of the great world confrontation. The Naga problem is a case in point: a scarcely known people in a little-known country, situated in between the two greatest Asian powers, whose relations have been profoundly changed by the ending of the Western dominance of Asia. Although still a kind of no-man's-land, the Naga country is bound increasingly to attract the attention of its larger and more powerful neighbours. For this reason it deserves fuller consideration, for the acquisition of basic knowledge, as fundamental and precise as possible, is the first step towards the achievement of a peaceful and lasting solution.

POSTSCRIPT

Since this paper was written a cease-fire has been achieved between the Indian government and the Naga 'rebels', which took effect from 6 September 1964. This was meant as a first step towards negotiations and it has subsequently been prolonged as discussions on certain proposals have continued.

The Problem of Nagaland 175

SELECT BIBLIOGRAPHY

BOWER, U. GRAHAM, *Naga Path*, London, 1951.

BOWER, U. GRAHAM, *The Hidden Land*, London, 1953.

BOWER, U. GRAHAM, *The Naga Problem*, Institute of Race Relations, London, 1962.

BUTLER, MAJOR J., *Travels and Adventures in the Province of Assam: During a Residence of 14 years*, London, 1855.

ELWIN, VERRIER, *India's North-East Frontier in the Nineteenth Century*, Bombay, 1959.

EMBREE, J. F. and DOTSON, L. O., *Bibliography of the Peoples and Cultures of Mainland Southeast Asia*, Yale University, Southeast Asia Studies, New Haven, 1950.

Encyclopaedia Britannica, Vol. 16, p. 59, 1963.

FISHER, C. A., *South-east Asia*, London, 1964.

FISHER, C. A., 'The Chinese threat to South-east Asia: fact or fiction ?', *Royal Central Asian Journal*, 51, 1964, pp. 251–67.

FÜRER-HAIMENDORF, C. VON, 'Through the unexplored mountains of the Assam–Burma border', *Geographical Journal*, 91, 1938, pp. 201–19.

FÜRER-HAIMENDORF, C. VON, *Die nackten Nagas*, Wiesbaden, 1946.

FÜRER-HAIMENDORF, C. VON, *Gluckliche Barbaren*, Wiesbaden, 1956 (*Himalayan Barbary*, London, 1955).

HODSON, T. C., *The Naga Tribes of Manipur*, London, 1911.

HUTTON, J. H., *The Angami Nagas*, London, 1921.

HUTTON, J. H., *The Sema Nagas*, London, 1921.

HUTTON, J. H., 'The mixed culture of the Naga tribes', *Journal of the Royal Anthropological Institute*, 95, 1965.

INDISCHE BOTSCHAFT BONN, Bulletin 8.4.1954; 11.7.1957; 25.9.1957; 8.10.1960.

KAUFFMANN, H. E., 'Landwirtschaft bei den Bergvölkern von Assam und Nordburma', *Zeitschrift für Ethnologie*, 66, 1936, pp. 16–111.

KAUFFMANN, H. E., 'Kurze Ethnographie der nördlichen Sangtam-Naga (Lophomi), Assam', *Anthropos*, 34, 1939, pp. 207–45.

KREBS, N., *Vorderindien und Ceylon*, Stuttgart, 1939.

KUNSTADTER, P. (ed.), *Southeast Asian tribes, minorities, and nations*, Princeton, New Jersey, 1967.

MILLS, J. P., *The Lhota Nagas*, London, 1922.

MILLS, J. P., *The Ao Nagas*, London, 1926 (pp. 429–40: Hutton, J. H., 'A bibliography of the Naga Hills, with some adjacent districts').

MILLS, J. P., *The Rengma Nagas*, London, 1937.

MILLS, J. P., 'The Nagas', *Civilisations* 3, 1933, pp. 355–9.

PATTERSON, G. N., 'Recent Chinese policies in Tibet and towards the Himalayan border states', *China Quarterly*, 12, 1962, 191–202, London.

PATTERSON, G. N., *Peking versus Delhi*, London, 1963.

PATTERSON, G. N., 'The Naga Problem', *Journal of the Royal Central Asian Society*, 50, 1963, pp. 30–40.

SCHWEINFURTH, U., 'Nagaland', *Aussenpolitik*, 13, 1962, pp. 853–7.

SMITH, W. C., *The Ao Naga tribe of Assam*, London, 1925.

176   *Essays in Political Geography*

SPATE, O. H. K., *India and Pakistan*, London, 1960.
SWINSON, A., *Kohima*, London, 1966.
TINKER, H. R., *The Union of Burma*, London, 1961.
YOUNG, G., *The Nagas – an Unknown War*, London, 1962.

CARTOGRAPHIC SOURCES

Atlas of South-east Asia, London, 1964.
Karta Narodna Hindostana, 1 : 5,000,000, Moscow, 1956.
Karta Narodna Indokitaya, 1 : 5,000,000, Moscow, 1959.
Ethnolinguistic groups of mainland Southeast Asia, compiled by Human Relation Area Files, Yale University, Southeast Asia Studies, New Haven, Conn., 1964.
South-east Asia, 1 : 6,000,000, Edinburgh, 1964.

10

Minority Unrest and Sino–Soviet Rivalry in Sinkiang, China's North-western Frontier Bastion, 1949–1965

MICHAEL FREEBERNE

INTRODUCTION

During the 1950s, when it was claimed by the Chinese that the East Wind was prevailing increasingly over the West Wind, Sino-Soviet relations were generally warm and a high degree of co-operation existed at all levels, although it is now clear that the seeds of conflict were sown in this period. On the surface, therefore, between October 1949, when the People's Republic of China was founded, and 1960, inter-state rivalries were minimal in the vast Central Asian borderlands of Sinkiang.

In recent years, however, the apparently monolithic structure of the Communist bloc has undergone a remarkable, almost precipitous metamorphosis, which the departure of Khrushchev has left unchecked. China is no longer prepared to occupy a subordinate position relative to the U.S.S.R., and indeed has emerged as a rival contender for the leadership of the Communist world.[1] This change is reflected in events which have occurred in the last few years along the Sino–Soviet frontier in Sinkiang. Essentially internal political upheavals, based according to the Chinese upon a background of Kuomintang and imperialist associations, have been superseded by an inter-state struggle which has itself produced both domestic and international repercussions. The significance of this latter phase can only be appreciated properly against the background of the internal political turmoil of the fifties, and the history of Sino–Soviet relations in this disputed region, beginning with the nineteenth century eastwards penetration of Soviet influence, which involved constant fluctuations in the control exercised by the two nations, and culminated in the Ili Revolt of 1944–5. But for reasons of length, this paper is confined to the post-1949 period.

A peculiarly difficult geographical environment, which though often

---

[1] Compare the *Jen-min Jih-pao* editorial of 27 February 1963, 'Whence the differences? A reply to Thorez and other comrades.' See also the comments by Saul Cohen, *supra*, p. 65.

178 *Essays in Political Geography*

harsh is not altogether without both physical and strategic compensations, is considered by way of introduction, together with recent demographic and economic trends.

Sinkiang occupies a vast region of some 627,000 square miles, about one-sixth of the total surface area of China. The region, situated as it is in the far north-west, is extremely remote, being roughly a thousand miles inland from the country's eastern seaboard, and overlapping a segment of Mackinder's 'Geographical pivot of history', which he later termed the 'Heartland'. Within recent years changes have taken place whereby the earlier advantages of isolation have been effectively dissipated by the development of inter-continental ballistic missiles and by the fact that Sinkiang shares with the Soviet Union a boundary of approximately 1,500 miles in length. (Fig. 10.1)

Lofty mountains, the Tienshan, separate two great depressions, the Tarim Basin in the south, and the Dzungarian Basin in the north. The Tarim Basin, which is almost completely surrounded by mountains, covers over half the area of Sinkiang, and includes the Takla Makan Desert. Throughout arid and semi-arid Sinkiang an adequate supply of water is essential for permanent settlement. Oases fringe the Tarim Basin, Kashgar, Yarkand, Khotan and Aqsu being among the most important. Glacial meltwaters from the surrounding mountains and underground water resources help to supplement the low rainfall.

North of the Tienshan, the Dzungarian Basin is lower in altitude, and less arid conditions support more extensive pastures. Unlike the Tarim Basin this region is orientated towards the Soviet Union. Agriculture depends upon irrigation almost everywhere in Sinkiang, with pastoralism more common north of the Tienshan.

Sinkiang is rich in mineral resources, including oil and uranium. With the exception of Taching, Karamai and Tushantze possess the largest oil reserves so far discovered in China, and there are probably considerable reserves south of the Tienshan. Coal, and low grade iron ore are widely distributed, with coal reserves totalling 3,000,000 million tons. Economic deposits of barite, copper, gold, gypsum, halite, jade, lead, mica, molybdenum, sulphur, tungsten and zinc have also been discovered.

Among the most significant of the frontier characteristics is the ethnic diversity of Sinkiang, whose population includes representatives of a dozen or more different peoples as shown in Table 10.1.

In an article in *Population Studies* the author has described recent events, in terms of rapidly altering demographic characteristics, which

Sino–Soviet Rivalry in Sinkiang 179

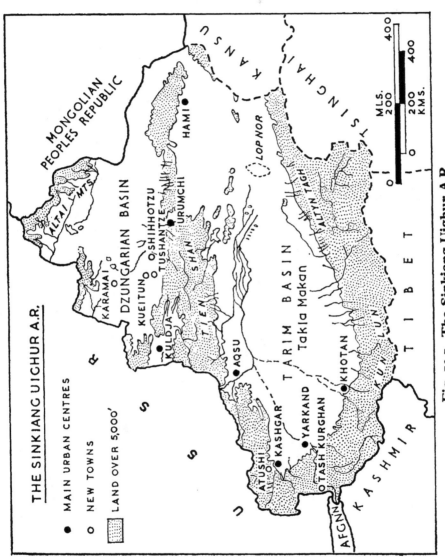

Fig. 10.1. The Sinkiang Uighur A.R.

180   *Essays in Political Geography*

have resulted from economic, social and political changes occurring within the Region.[1] Briefly, the main arguments may be summarized as follows. First, in sixteen years the population of Sinkiang has more than doubled, growing from 3·7 million to about 8 million; this increase was achieved mainly through state-organized immigration of Han Chinese from China proper. Secondly, the large-scale immigration is reflected by modified age–sex ratios, the marital condition and the ethnic composition of Sinkiang's population. Most important, the marked rise in the number of Han Chinese has obvious political implications, for in 1949 there were only between 200,000 and 300,000 while now there are

TABLE 10.1: ETHNIC COMPOSITION OF THE POPULATION
OF SINKIANG, 1953

A.	Turkic peoples	
	Uighurs	3,640,000
	Kazakhs	475,000
	Khalkhas (Kirghiz)	70,000
	Uzbeks and Tartars	13,000
B.	Chinese peoples	
	Chinese	300,000
	Huis (Dungans)	200,000
C.	Mongols	120,000
D.	Manchus, Sibos, etc.	20,000
E.	Tadjiks	15,000
F.	Russians	13,000
G.	Others	8,000
	TOTAL	4,874,000

Source: *Central Asian Review*, 4, 1956, p. 434.

about 3,000,000, and the real figure may be considerably larger as a result of undisclosed immigration. The increase in the number of Chinese, together with the minority and economic policies of the central government, have combined to bring Sinkiang more and more within the sphere of effective Chinese control. Thirdly, associated with economic planning and especially with the redistribution of Chinese industry, there has been a pronounced growth of urbanization, and hence the creation of easily controlled nodes. Finally, the distribution of population has fanned outwards in keeping with developments in the agricultural and pastoral sectors, particularly the reclamation of new lands, the extension of irrigation, and the settling of pastoral nomads.

[1] Michael Freeberne, 'Demographic and economic changes in the Sinkiang Uighur Autonomous Region', *Population Studies*, 20, 1966, pp. 103–24.

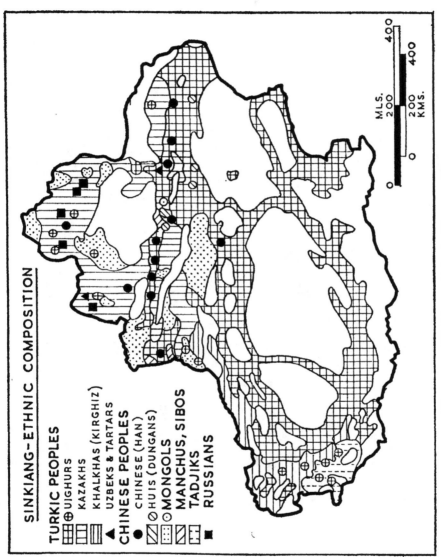

Fig. 10.2. Sinkiang Ethnic Composition

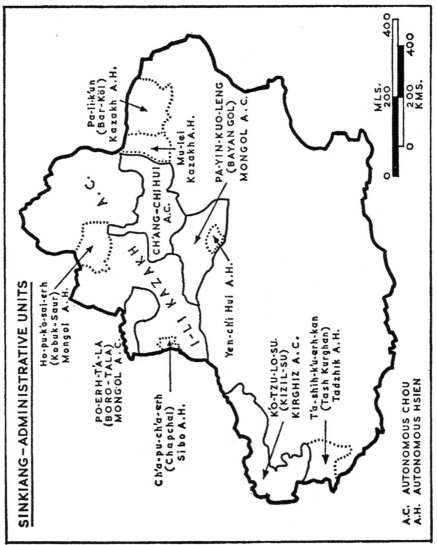

Fig. 10.3. Sinkiang Administrative Units

One of the conclusions reached in the *Population Studies* paper was that the Chinese will probably intensify attempts to settle and develop Sinkiang along these lines in order to protect their interests in the area. The strong racial affinity of Sinkiang's population with that of adjacent Soviet territories must influence worsening Sino–Soviet relations, as former co-operation is replaced by deepening tension, and as the ethnic, cultural and religious ties of the peoples on both sides of the frontier are affected by the large number of immigrant Han Chinese. In spite of the increase in Han population, Sinkiang is the only Autonomous Region where the minorities are not outnumbered by the Hans.

MINORITY UNREST IN SINKIANG, 1949–60

The Growth of Local Nationalism, 1949–55 In the first six years following the 'liberation' of Sinkiang in September of 1949, and before Sinkiang Province became the Sinkiang Uighur Autonomous Region a number of mass movements were launched by the Chinese. These nation-wide movements included the campaigns for resisting the United States and aiding Korea; for the suppression of counter-revolutionaries; for the reduction of rent and fight against despots; the 3-anti and 5-anti movements; and land reform. A common feature of these movements was the fervour and ruthlessness with which the respective aims were pursued. Such tactics were |probably ill-advised in a peripheral territory, as resentment against the methods employed by the Chinese and minority cadres contributed to the spread of local nationalism which was causing grave concern to the government by 1954.

Initially counter-revolutionary activity was widespread as 'United States–Chiang agents, native bandits, despots, reactionary Party backbone elements, reactionary Taoist leaders . . . took the opportunity to fabricate rumours, commit arson and murder' in the early stage of the 'liberation'.[1] The struggle against counter-revolutionaries was intensified in 1951, when the Deputy Commander of the Sinkiang Military Division, Tao Shih-yueh, claimed 'unanimous support' from the minority nationalities as well as the People's Liberation Army forces regarding 'measures for suppression'. But Tao was forced to caution that 'hidden enemies are utilizing old relations [and] old friendship . . . for winning over . . . a few backward elements'.[2] Had the unanimous

[1] Kao Chin-chun, 'Achievements in political and judicial work in Sinkiang in the past five years', *Sinkiang Jih-pao*, 30 September 1954.
[2] N.C.N.A. (New China News Agency), Sian, 7 April 1951.

184 Essays in Political Geography

support actually existed, and had the trouble been confined only to a few backward elements, it is unlikely that the campaign would have been pressed with such severity or that it would have lasted for as long as it did. Similarly, the Provincial Chairman, Burhan, referred to the attempts of 'the imperialists and their running dogs . . . to set one nationality against another nationality . . . by spreading rumours and fostering splits'.[1] Late in 1951 a report stated that although the counter-revolutionaries had suffered severe blows there remained a small number 'determined to be hostile to the people and continuing to carry on sabotage'.[2]

Undoubtedly there was frequent anti-Chinese sabotage. At the same time, even in the early 1950s, there was perhaps an ulterior motive behind the way in which China's military forces were deployed, for the Chinese were extremely sensitive about the integrity of their border. One description, for example, tells of a 24-hour, round-the-year watch by a chosen garrison in the Pamirs in defence of the fatherland. Ostensibly the function of this 'patriotic detachment' was 'to prevent the imperialists' and Kuomintang 'from entering the fatherland'.[3] Could it be that as early as 1952 the Chinese suspected that the U.S.S.R. might become the real threat to its north-western border?

As a result of the mass movements mentioned above, it was claimed that 'social order had become completely stabilized throughout Sinkiang by the end of 1952'. While conforming with the assessment that the country largely set its house in order between 1949 and the beginning of the First Five-Year Plan in 1953, Kao's assertion distorts the actual situation in Sinkiang for, writing two years later, he had to admit to the continued existence of counter-revolutionaries and criminals, engaged in 'theft, arson, murder, and sabotage of production'.[4]

The Chinese clearly anticipated a degree of local opposition from the many national minority groups, which was expressed actively through supporting and engaging in counter-revolutionary activities. They assumed, however, that their minorities policy, and their plans for establishing regional autonomy, backed by the presence of the People's Liberation Army would accommodate or at least contain all manifestations of minority nonconformity.

In any event, local autonomy or no, concern over emerging local nationalism increased during 1954. 'The main question is that survivals of ideas of great nation chauvinism and narrow nationalism still

[1] N.C.N.A., Sian, 7 April 1951.
[2] N.C.N.A., Urumchi, 26 November 1951.
[3] N.C.N.A., Urumchi, 21 July 1952. [4] Kao Chin-chun, *op. cit.*

exist'.[1] Again, in his speech on minority unity in February 1955, Burhan blamed the growth of local nationalism on the devious measures of the ubiquitous imperialists who 'even put on the cloak of religion, to carry out activities of rumour spreading, sabotage and the deception of the masses in an attempt to undermine our revolutionary unity'.[2]

Sinkiang Province becomes the Sinkiang Uighur Autonomous Region The official reason for the creation of the Sinkiang Uighur Autonomous Region in October 1955 was that 'it will enable all nationalities there to enjoy the full right to administer their own affairs ... This will promote unity among and within the various nationalities, deepen their patriotism and internationalism and inspire them to build socialism with yet greater enthusiasm'.[3] Unlike the position of the Soviet Republics, which in theory are allowed to opt out of the Union, an important distinction exists in that Sinkiang is regarded as 'an inseparable part of the Chinese People's Republic'.[4] In the light of subsequent developments in Sino–Soviet relations it is particularly significant that an additional function of the Autonomous Region was 'to consolidate national defences'.[5]

Throughout 1956 and 1957 there was a further intensification of the anti-counter-revolutionary struggle as well as a continued development of local nationalism. Apparently counter-revolutionaries had 'infiltrated into every nook and cranny'.[6] No opportunity to threaten stable government escaped them, and rural sabotage was rife, as in the case of the Hotien 'uprisings' in December 1954 and March 1956.[7] Contemporary Chinese sources revealed the omnipresence of the resistance to the present government, sometimes an expression of dislike of Chinese hegemony, sometimes of Communism, and, probably often, of Chinese Communism. Towards the end of 1957 the Urumchi Public Security Bureau arrested a group of counter-revolutionaries, 'bitterly hostile towards the people'. They included Li Hung-chung, charged with forming the 'China Peasant Party' in April 1957, which plotted the staging of 'armed uprisings in a vain attempt to overthrow the people's regime'.[8]

An indication of the blatant nationalism which had appeared even

[1] *Sinkiang Jih-pao*, Urumchi, 30 May 1954.
[2] *Sinkiang Jih-pao*, Urumchi, 25 February 1955.
[3] N.C.N.A., Peking, 30 September 1955.
[4] *Ibid.*
[5] N.C.N.A., Urumchi, 21 September 1955.
[6] *Sinkiang Jih-pao*, Urumchi, 26 May 1956.
[7] *Sinkiang Jih-pao*, Urumchi, 23 September 1956.
[8] *Sinkiang Jih-pao*, Urumchi, 13 November 1957.

186 *Essays in Political Geography*

before the inauguration of the Autonomous Region was given by the Secretary of the Sinkiang Communist Party Committee, Saifudin, at the Party Congress meeting in September 1956. Some local nationalists had openly 'advocated the establishment of a union republic or an autonomous republic'.[1] During the rectification campaign which followed Mao Tse-tung's speech *On the Question of the Correct Handling of the Contradictions among the People* it was stressed that 'it is entirely essential to emphasize the need of opposing the trend of local nationalism . . . After this campaign the unity of the different nationalities is bound to grow in solidarity and strength'.[2] This was an obvious necessity when 'some people clamour for "national independence", for the formation of "Eastern Turkistan", the establishment of a nationalities party, and the exclusion of Han cadres and Han people'.[3] The growth of local nationalism was described by Saifudin as 'remarkable in some places, and (it) has become the most dangerous ideological trend of the present time . . . revealing (itself) to a serious extent'.[4] Saifudin emphasized that 'since last year (1956) seriously erroneous trends, including opposition, discrimination, and insults against Han people have appeared among cadres and intellectuals of the local nationalities. Some ultra-nationalists have even tried to "oust" all Han people from Sinkiang . . . These are hateful and execrable acts of treason and counter-revolutionary views'.[5]

A paroxysmal burst of activity ushered in the Second Five-Year Plan in 1958, the year of the 'great leap forward' and the establishment of the communes. Driven relentlessly by the administration, minority opposition stiffened and local nationalism took on a more coherent form during 1958 and 1959.

In an article entitled *Marxism versus Nationalism in Sinkiang – A Major Debate*, Hsia Fu-jen answered the call for a republic within the Chinese Union by citing Lenin who advocated a monolithic state founded on the basis of democratic centralism. 'The object of socialism is not to separate the nationalities from one another but to draw them together so that they may be fused together'.[6] Hsia criticized the way in which exclusive measures were advocated by those with nationalist sympathies even within the Party, 'they want a "national" socialism

---

[1] N.C.N.A., Peking, 25 September 1956.
[2] *Jen-min Jih-pao*, Peking, 1 November 1957.
[3] N.C.N.A., Urumchi, 30 November 1957.
[4] *Jen-min Jih-pao*, Peking, 26 December 1957.
[5] *Ibid.*
[6] *Kuang-ming Jih-pao*, Peking, 10 April 1958.

Sino-Soviet Rivalry in Sinkiang 187

from which all Han people are barred'. He then went on to describe the quite remarkable manifestations of which those near the Party were capable: 'They cry, "We want our own Karamai" . . . They have even tried to evacuate the several tens of thousands of Han residents from Urumchi in order to "nationalize" the city. They falsely accuse Han people and cadres of being "colonists" '. As for those nationalists who are not communists they 'declare that they want "national independence" alone and not socialism'.[1] One individual allegedly went as far as to say 'Sinkiang does not need Han people, and Sinkiang should belong to us; *if we do not have enough people, we can call back Uighurs and Kazakhs from the Soviet Union*'.[2] Meanwhile other nationalists 'cherished the hope of international tension and the occurrence of the Hungarian incident to enable Sinkiang to achieve "independence" '.[3]

Some months later in the Hotien area, the Kotzulosu Kirghiz Autonomous *Chou* and around Aqsu, it was claimed that 'a big victory' had been won against local nationalism. Success was greatest, however, in the Ili Kazakh Autonomous *Chou* where an anti-Party group led by a Kazakh, Chia-ho-ta, Governor of the A.C., was 'thoroughly smashed' after attempting to establish an 'independent kingdom'.[4] Likewise a 'decisive victory' in the Kashgar Special Administrative District defeated an attempt to set up an independent republic.[5]

Five leading nationalists were exposed during the combined conference of the Sinkiang Regional Committee of the C.P.P.C.C. and the Sinkiang Islamic Federation, which met between August 1958 and March 1959. Together they had undermined national unity, attempting 'to give away Sinkiang to imperialism', and sabotaged socialist construction,[6] hoping that this would eventually lead to the establishment of an 'Islam Republic'.[7]

If the Chinese reports are to be believed, the local nationalists were hardly lacking in ambition, and one of them was quoted as follows: 'As soon as I hold state power, I shall drive the Kazakhs to Altai and Tacheng; drive the Hui people and the Sibo people to Tarim Gobi; drive the Mongol people to Yenki, and forcibly assimilate the Tatar and Tadjik people'.[8] Indeed, the pent up frustration of some minority

[1] *Ibid.*
[2] *Sinkiang Jih-pao*, Urumchi, 28 May 1958. Italics added.
[3] N.C.N.A., Urumchi, 26 June 1958.
[4] *Kwang-ming Jih-pao*, Peking, 11 September 1958.
[5] *Sinkiang Jih-pao*, Urumchi, 5 September 1958.
[6] *Sinkiang Jih-pao*, Urumchi, 10 March 1959.
[7] *Sinkiang Jih-pao*, Urumchi, 11 March 1959.
[8] *Ibid.*

188   *Essays in Political Geography*

leaders knew no bounds: 'There are even individuals who hold the illusion of "the third World War", and entertain the reactionary plot of making a "final reckoning" with us in the future'.[1]

Generally, there was little specific mention by the Chinese of local nationalism and counter-revolutionary activity during 1959. If non-Chinese accounts of events occurring in Sinkiang have any foundation, this represented a deliberate attempt by the Chinese to obscure the actual and grave situation, and indeed economic difficulties and frequently admitted opposition to the communes would have provided the Chinese with sufficient cause to wish not to broadcast any signs of minority unrest. The relatively innocuous crimes of three counter-revolutionaries executed in January 1960 prompted especially stern editorial comment: 'there are still some remnant counter-revolutionaries who refuse to repent, refuse to reform, and dare to take the kindness of the people for weakness and molest them. They hate bitterly every achievement and every victory in our socialist construction . . . (and) turn more violent and vicious'.[2]

It is possible, therefore, that such harsh words were provoked by events other than those surrounding the three unfortunate counter-revolutionaries, for an outside report based on evidence supplied by a refugee from Sinkiang who reached Pakistan revealed that four Moslem leaders had precipitated a revolt of 10,000 young people in Hotien on 20 March 1959, immediately after the Tibetan uprising. A prison was attacked, 600 prisoners released, fifty Communist officials killed, and grain stocks seized. Within six days the revolt was crushed by reinforcements sent from Urumchi.[3]

According to refugees reaching Hong Kong late in 1959 the situation was 'like that in Tibet'. Strong troop reinforcements had arrived in Sinkiang to crush a fresh anti-Communist rebellion and to promote Communist reforms.[4] At the same time Urumchi radio admitted that the inauguration of the communes had been delayed in certain areas owing to opposition among demobilized Chinese who had been given land.[5]

In August 1959 an article from *Sinkiang Hung Chi*, Number 17, was reproduced in the *Sinkiang Jih-pao* in which it was announced that the extensive and penetrating struggle against local nationalism, dating from

---

[1] *Sinkiang Jih-pao*, Urumchi, 11 March 1959.
[2] *Sinkiang Jih-pao*, Urumchi, 26 January 1960.
[3] *Le Monde*, 9 June 1959.
[4] *Giustizia*, 16 January 1960.
[5] *The Scotsman*, 4 December 1959.

Sino–Soviet Rivalry in Sinkiang 189

December 1957, had ended in a rout.[1] A sanguine assessment of the tranquil political, economic and social scene was to undergo a severe buffeting in the opening years of the succeeding decade, however, for China as a whole suffered severe economic setbacks to the formidable progress achieved during the 1950s, Sino–Soviet relations entered a new phase of growing enmity, and local nationalism took advantage of these conditions and found fresh coherence and vitality.

Immediately before the virtual cessation of Chinese news sources relevant to internal political unrest in Sinkiang which took place in 1960, there was an apparent toughening in Chinese policies, and the Second Session of the First Party Congress of the Sinkiang Uighur Autonomous Region demanded that 'Party committees at various levels . . . must insist on placing politics in command'.[2] This was a curiously strident note to be sounding at much the same time as Saifudin made his optimistic speech to the Second Session of the Second National People's Congress: 'Following the struggles 'against bourgeois rightists, local nationalism, and rightist opportunism, immense changes have taken place in the ideology of the broad masses of cadres and the people, enabling them to further elevate their communist consciousness, strengthening the solidarity among all nationalities to a great extent and greatly increasing the revolutionary and constructive zeal among cadres and the people'. Saifudin was at pains to stress the 'unprecedentedly excellent situation' which had emerged 'in the political and economic front'. Yet, in view of the contemporary resolution of the Party Congress, perhaps Saifudin overstated his case, and in fact he made a significant admission that there was one critical factor hampering large-scale socialist construction in Sinkiang, namely a shortage of man-power. Seen in a rather different light, especially in view of the minority unrest Saifudin's statement assumes a more sinister role for, as he pointed out, man-power is 'one of the most important elements' not only in 'construction' but also in 'revolution'. Innocent enough at face value, from the minority point of view there is the ominous historical precedent of the swamping of other geographical areas, notably Inner Mongolia, by Han Chinese. 'Thanks to the special concern shown by the Central Committee, and the assistance provided by the fraternal provinces and regions, solution of this problem has also begun.'[3]

[1] *Sinkiang Jih-pao*, Urumchi, 22 August 1959.
[2] *Jen-min Jih-pao*, Peking, 28 March 1960.
[3] N.C.N.A., Peking, 5 April 1960.

190 *Essays in Political Geography*

SINO–SOVIET RELATIONS IN SINKIANG, 1949–62

After Saifudin's report in April 1960, there is virtually a total absence of Chinese reports about internal political unrest in Sinkiang. Contrasting with the frequent and comparatively frank accounts of the type already surveyed, there was an abrupt shift in emphasis so as to stress the economic progress, unity, and happiness of the many nationalities, and to hide internal tensions, as it were, by default. Not least because of the marked difference in the tone of the description of events in Sinkiang, accounts of the post-1960 period must be handled with care and a measure of scepticism. The lack of reports of domestic disturbances does *not* mean that the minority population had been transformed overnight into a uniform, conformist group, dazzled by the excellence of, and subservient to, Party policies.

Rather the silence may be attributed to both local and national economic difficulties, particularly serious in 1960 and 1961; to growing Chinese discomfort with regard to the way in which Sino–Soviet relations were developing; and to awareness of the potentially inflammable situation which might result if, for whatever reason, the closely related ethnic groups on either side of the international frontier should attempt to join forces with each other.

Early Co-operation Some two years after the founding of the People's Republic of China the Sino–Soviet Friendship Association claimed a membership of 80,000 in Sinkiang alone. The Association was especially active in the Ili Special District, an area contiguous with the Soviet Union, which had almost half the total number of provincial members (36,814). At a time when 'the Government foiled a plot of anti-Soviet and anti-revolutionary elements for an armed rebellion', the Association was busy organizing study groups 'formed of activists . . . to study the various advanced construction experiences of the Soviet Union, and the various policies of the Communist Party and the State'. This work was 'inseparably linked with the very great assistance that we received from the Soviet Cultural Association for Foreign Countries'.[1]

Educational aids were supplied by the Soviet Union to help the work of the Association, which organized 16 'after-work propaganda and music-dance teams' in the Ili area; these teams were composed of 110 performers, 215 music lovers, and 170 propaganda activists. The dances and plays were usually about Russian construction work and life in the

[1] *Chun Chung Jih-pao* (*Masses Daily*), Sian, 7 November 1951.

Sino–Soviet Rivalry in Sinkiang 191

Chinese People's Liberation Army. By such means the local population became 'systematically acquainted with the Soviet Union'. Defects were admitted, however, particularly as 'insufficient contact is established between education in internationalism and in patriotism, which is to be corrected in the future'.[1]

Even in this early phase of intimate Sino–Soviet contact the Chinese were peculiarly sensitive about the safety of their frontiers, and there was frequent reference to the defence of the fatherland. For example, accounts describe the work of the People's Liberation Army and Public Security Corps 'in safeguarding the frontier of the fatherland'.[2]

Apart from the fact that there was a population of over 23,000 Soviet citizens living in Sinkiang in 1953, chiefly in Ili, Tacheng, Altai and Tihwa, and working in agriculture and handicrafts,[3] the main reason for Soviet interest in the province was initially economic. (That is, on the assumption that Russia was prepared, at least for the time being, to forego all territorial ambitions.) Until 1955 there were four Sino–Soviet Joint Stock Companies, established in 1950 and 1951 to extract non-ferrous and rare metals, to extract and refine petroleum, and to organize and operate civil airlines. Meeting to celebrate the third anniversary of the Sino–Soviet Non-Ferrous and Rare Metals Company, the acting General Manager for the Soviet side described the project as a 'distinguished example of the close economic co-operation between the Soviet Union and China'.[4] Similarly, when the Sino–Soviet Civil Aviation Company inaugurated the service between Tihwa (Urumchi) and Kashgar in September 1953, it was stated that 'the opening of this airline will promote the political, economic and cultural interflow between the frontier and the hinterland'.[5] And, after the transfer of Soviet shares, the Sinkiang Petroleum Company was termed a 'pledge of Sino–Soviet Friendship'.[6] In October 1954 it was decided that the agreements were to be terminated as from 1 January 1955, and that the value of the Soviet holdings was to be repaid in the course of several years, in the form of normal export commodities.[7] Later the Chinese alleged that the Soviet Union had received the lion's share from

[1] *Ibid.*
[2] N.C.N.A., Urumchi, 15 October 1952; *Sinkiang Jih-pao*, Urumchi, 30 September 1954.
[3] N.C.N.A., Urumchi, 8 April 1953.
[4] N.C.N.A., Urumchi, 7 January 1954.
[5] China News Service, Peking, 23 September 1953.
[6] N.C.N.A., Urumchi, 25 September 1955.
[7] N.C.N.A., Peking, 12 October 1954.

192 *Essays in Political Geography*

these joint undertakings, especially where strategic minerals were involved.

Whether or not there is any foundation for this charge, it appears to be a churlish way of acknowledging the very considerable technical aid which the U.S.S.R. gave to the Chinese in Sinkiang. For example, in agriculture, improved wheat and cotton strains were introduced; advice and equipment given for anti-locust work, soil and water conservation, and animal husbandry; technical assistance was provided in prospecting, mining and processing of minerals; and further aid was made available in industry and communications.

One of the most striking and perplexing instances of Soviet assistance was the projected Lanchow–Urumchi–Alma-Ata Railway, which was to have been completed by 1959,[1] 'with a view to strengthening mutual economic and cultural ties'.[2] At first progress was rapid and enthusiasm high, so much so indeed that it was announced in 1958 that a widescreen colour film, *Alma-Ata–Lanchow*, had been completed. 'The film treats the building of the railway as a symbol of the friendly co-operation between China and the Soviet Union'. But the showing of the film was premature, as it is unlikely that the line extends beyond the oil-refining centre of Tushantze even today.

Throughout the opening years of the 1950s there was a steady expansion of trade between Sinkiang and the Soviet Union. In 1950 70 per cent of the goods imported from the U.S.S.R. were consumer goods, but when the Chinese completed the Tienshui–Lanchow Railway there was a shift of emphasis, and industrial equipment and supplies accounted for about 70 per cent of the imports by 1952. This 'proved to be strong support for the construction of the province'.[3] Wool constituted one of Sinkiang's major exports, and cattle, furs, hides, grain, oil-seeds and dried fruit were exported via the province, in exchange for building materials, tractors and other machinery.[4]

A certain amount of educational aid was provided by the U.S.S.R., and reference was made to a Russian Language institute, although no location was given.[5] Assistance in public health was also provided, and in late 1955 and early 1956 the entire property and equipment of two Russian hospitals, the first in Urumchi and the second in Ining were handed over to China. At the former celebrations the Director of the

[1] *Ta Kung Pao*, Hong Kong, 1 January 1957.
[2] N.C.N.A., Peking, 12 October 1954.
[3] *Ta Kung Pao*, Tientsin, 24 May 1953.
[4] N.C.N.A., Peking, 21 September 1955.
[5] N.C.N.A., Urumchi, 22 March 1956.

Sino–Soviet Rivalry in Sinkiang 193

Public Health Department 'greeted the impressive ceremony as marking the unbreakable friendship between the people of China and the Soviet Union'.[1]

Cultural exchanges were also arranged. Performances given by artists from Kazakh, Uzbek and Kirghiz Soviet Socialist Republics between September and November 1955 were watched by over 200,000 people.[2] A youth delegation from the Kazakh Soviet Socialist Republic 'visited factories, schools and farms and was warmly welcomed wherever it went'.[3] About the same time 'a Sino–Soviet friendship hall was opened in the new oil centre of Karamai on 23 June to mark the immense aid given by the Soviet Union to Sinkiang's petroleum industry. In the past seven years the Soviet Union has supplied 240,000 tons of up-to-date oil prospecting, drilling, extraction and refining machinery and 500 experts'.[4]

One of the most significant features of Sino–Soviet co-operation in Sinkiang was the forced attempt to introduce a comradely, even a personal touch into what can only be seen as a political and economic marriage of convenience. Great play was made of two incidents where the normal bounds of duty were exceeded. In the first of these 'two Soviet specialists, Kuznitsin and Kovalyev, were cited at a ceremony here on 28 September (1958) for internationalism displayed in risking their lives to rescue a Chinese interpreter [from drowning]. The citations from Premier Chou En-lai . . . expressed thanks for their selfless heroism.' Saifudin, in presenting the citations said that 'this glorious and worthy deed fully reflected the deep friendship of the Chinese and Soviet peoples, and a high level of internationalism'.[5]

The second incident was reported under the heading of 'Flower of Sino–Soviet Friendship Blooms', and told of a desperate and successful attempt to save the life of the Soviet Consul in Urumchi, Tapashen.[6] An emotional account described the warm personal relationships which were established between the Russian Consul and the Chinese doctors and nursing staff.

Indeed, the inhabitants of Sinkiang were exhorted to 'love not only our own socialist country but also the Soviet Union and all other socialist countries'.[7] After all, was this not 'the age of socialist construction

[1] *Sinkiang Jih-pao*, Urumchi, 31 January 1956, and 17 February 1956.
[2] N.C.N.A., Urumchi, 4 November 1955.
[3] N.C.N.A., Urumchi, 20 May 1958.   [4] N.C.N.A., Karamai, 25 June 1958.
[5] N.C.N.A., Urumchi, 30 September 1958.
[6] *Sinkiang Jih-pao*, Urumchi, 3 August 1960.
[7] *Jen-min Jih-pao*, Peking, 27 June 1958.

194 *Essays in Political Geography*

when the world peace camp ¦headed by the Soviet Union is unprecedentedly powerful'?[1] And yet it is more than likely that one of the major obstacles to Sino–Soviet co-operation was found in precisely the realms of personal relationships, and that racial traits of a more obvious nature than those distinguishing Han Chinese from the minority peoples of Sinkiang, tended to magnify ideological and economic differences between China and the U.S.S.R.[2]

Be this as it may, there was to be little mention of Russian aid after 1960, when Nu-ssu-je-ti, Secretary-General of the Sinkiang Uighur Autonomous Region Sino–Soviet Friendship Association, stated that economic, social and cultural achievements 'are indivisible from Soviet aid and the selfless labour of Soviet experts'. He concluded: 'This great and profound friendship . . . closely unites 850 million people', affecting 'the fundamental interests of world peace and human progress. While the East Wind blows stronger and the West Wind declines steadily in the sixties, the Sino–Soviet alliance enters its second decade. . . . Let us unreservedly continue to strengthen and consolidate the friendship and unity of China and the Soviet Union, [and] learn humbly from the experience of the Soviet Union in revolution and construction.'[3]

Assuming that Nu-ssu-je-ti's calculations were representative of the official government views regarding the state of Sino–Soviet relations at the turn of the decade it will be seen that the administration was in for a rude awakening.

The Lull Before the Storm, 1960–61 As from the beginning of 1960 it is necessary to rely on largely second-hand, more varied, more fragmentary, and perhaps in some cases more dubious, sources, in attempting to trace the development of political unrest in Sinkiang. At least the Chinese reports already used have the merit of consistency, though their terms of reference must be remembered constantly, impregnated as they are with Chinese Marxist thinking. It was noted earlier that Chinese sources are less productive after 1960, as it was obviously realized by the Chinese that Sinkiang was in a peculiarly vulnerable situation should they be unable to stem the rising minority discontent and inter-state tensions. Granted the poverty of available sources, it is still possible to follow developments in Sinkiang in broad outline.

The suppression of information makes it impossible to confirm the

[1] *Sinkiang Jih-pao*, Urumchi, 11 March 1959.

[2] Michael Freeberne, 'Racial issues and the Sino–Soviet dispute', *Asian Survey*, 5, 1965, pp. 408–16.

[3] *Sinkiang Jih-pao*, Urumchi, 14 February 1960.

rumour that heavy fighting between Chinese and Tibetans in western Tibet had spread into Sinkiang.[1] The same applies regarding a report reaching East Berlin in February 1962, about an uprising intended to establish an independent republic; apparently the revolt had been put down in December 1961, when some five hundred minority leaders were arrested.

The Disturbances of 1962 Rioting flared up in mid-1962, centred on the capital of the Ili Kazakh Autonomous *Chou*, Ining, and Tacheng, another border town roughly 200 miles distant. The local population felt that their standard of living compared unfavourably with that of their ethnic counterparts on the Soviet side of the border. In particular, a food shortage had been aggravated by the export of foodstuffs to the U.S.S.R.

Spasmodic outbreaks occurred in which local cadres were beaten up. An especially dangerous situation was created when minority crowds gathered in front of the Soviet consulate in Ining, and asked for Soviet weapons to aid them in achieving independence from the Chinese. The Soviet Consul refused assistance, and ordered the crowds to disperse.

Meanwhile there was an exodus involving an unknown number of families out of Sinkiang and across the border into the Soviet Union, where the minorities were housed, fed and given work. Some of the escaping minority nationalities may have come from Tushantze, the oil-refining centre, which was seriously affected by the disturbances, in which oil tankers were sabotaged, and where oil output declined by at least 25 per cent.[2]

Eventually increased food supplies were made available and order was restored by September. Although the Chinese sealed the border, efforts were still made to cross it.

The Chinese then took the extreme measure of closing the Russian consulates in Ining, Tacheng and Urumchi. Some thought that this was because the Russians had actively promoted unrest in Sinkiang.[3] The same source transmitted stories reaching Gantok that Sinkiang was 'seething with a series of bloody revolts against the Chinese dictatorial rule triggered off by Kazakh insurgents with the active support of all other nationalist communities'.[4] There were reports of heavy Chinese casualties, sabotage to bridges and supply lines, and widespread arson

[1] *New York Times*, 4 June 1960.
[2] *Sunday Telegraph*, London, 2 June 1963.
[3] *Indian Express*, 3 January 1963.
[4] *Ibid.*

196 *Essays in Political Geography*

and looting. 'Many of the rebels were using Russian weapons',[1] and it was even rumoured that the Russians were co-ordinating minority forces. These same disturbances may have been partially responsible for the Sino–Indian cease-fire in Ladakh and the North-east Frontier Agency, which occurred about the same time.

A further large-scale revolt took place in the Sinkiang–Tibetan border region, according to the Chairman of the Nationalist Chinese Commission for Mongolian and Tibetan Affairs, Tien Chiung-chen; again extensive Chinese casualties were claimed.[2]

The pattern of events during 1962 outlined above had emerged quite clearly by the middle of 1963, but many months elapsed before open mention of trouble in Sinkiang was made either by the Chinese or the Russians.

SINKIANG AND THE SINO–SOVIET DISPUTE

Sinkiang made its official entry into the arena of the Sino–Soviet dispute in the form of Chinese accusations which were part of a lengthy article, written jointly by the editorial departments of *Red Flag* and *Jen-min Jih-pao*, and dated 6 September 1963. The article was the first of several commenting on the open letter from the Central Committee of the Communist Party of the Soviet Union of 14 July 1963. The relevant passage ran as follows:

> In April and May 1962, the leaders of the C.P.S.U. used their organs and personnel in Sinkiang . . . to carry out huge-scale subversive activities in the Ili region and enticed and coerced several tens of thousands of Chinese citizens into going to the Soviet Union. The Chinese Government lodged repeated protests and made repeated representations, but the Soviet Government refused to repatriate these Chinese citizens on the pretext of 'the sense of Soviet Legality' and 'humanitarianism'. To this day this incident remains unsettled. This is indeed an outstanding event, unheard of in the relations between socialist countries.[3]

With these words the Chinese thus confirmed the rumours that the U.S.S.R. had been actively engaged in promoting disturbances on Chinese territory.

The U.S.S.R. responded obliquely when on 20 September it issued counter-charges to the effect that 'beginning with 1960, Chinese service-

---

[1] *Sunday Telegraph*, London, 2 June 1963.
[2] Taipeh Radio, 17 January 1963.   [3] *Peking Review*, 13 September 1963.

Sino–Soviet Rivalry in Sinkiang 197

men and civilians have been systematically violating the Soviet border. In the single year of 1962, more than 5,000 violations of the Soviet border from the Chinese side were registered. Attempts are being made to "develop" some parts of Soviet territories without permission.' In addition, Western news sources quoted 'Russian officials' who claimed that roughly 50,000 minority Moslems had crossed into the adjacent Soviet republics since mid-1962, and that during the previous eight weeks the flow had increased. Despite their consternation, the Russians had organized a resettlement scheme for the refugees, who wished to escape religious persecution and 'measures of colonialism'.[1] In this way the Russians suggested that enticement and coercion would have been unnecessary to precipitate what had been, in fact, a spontaneous influx of population. There followed a carefully prepared press and radio campaign designed to convey an impression of the harsh conditions prevailing in China.

For instance, four refugee denunciations were published together under the title of 'Eye-witnesses Accuse'. The contributions were written by a peasant, a teacher, a writer, and an ex-official and a Party member. There is always the possibility that such accounts may have been deliberately planted in the Soviet press, or at least embellished by the editor; even so, they are still important. The strangely articulate and politically perceptive peasant, for example, condemned the 'barrack-like surroundings' of the commune, where the peasants had their 'spoons, buckets, cups and plates' taken away from them. Not that it was the intrinsic value of these articles which mattered. 'The main danger lies in something else . . . because of the splitting activities of the Chinese Government, because of their deliberate anti-Soviet policy, the working people of China have been deprived of material and technical assistance from the Soviet Union.'[2]

The teacher stated that Soviet citizens in Sinkiang found life especially difficult. 'Their position is now that of outcasts: they have no voting rights; they cannot hold any responsible offices; they are not permitted to participate in the social life of the country.' The four refugees indicated that anyone expressing pro-Soviet sympathies was immediately labelled a 'revisionist', and ran the risk of being sent to a labour reform camp; and they were unanimous in their condemnation of the anti-Soviet policy of the Chinese leadership.[3]

[1] Tass, Moscow, 20 September 1963; Reuter, Moscow, 6 September 1963; *New York Times*, 7 and 8 September 1963.

[2] Moscow Radio, and *Komsomolskaya Pravda*, 20 September 1963.

[3] *Ibid.*

198 Essays in Political Geography

Another letter from a Soviet Uighur, Usman Mamyetov, who had once lived in Sinkiang but was now working on a Soviet collective described how 'the Chinese authorities who spread untrue stories about the situation of the nationalities in the Soviet Union, themselves openly persecute the so-called "national minorities". . . . Many of us who have relatives and loved ones in China are very concerned about their fate. Hundreds of our countrymen who openly express their sympathy for the Soviet people are thrown into labour correction camps which are, in fact, concentration camps with cruel regimes. One of these terrible camps is situated not far from our section of the Soviet–Chinese border.'[1] Besides setting up concentration camps, the Chinese are said to have evacuated non-Chinese families from frontier villages.

A few days later the same newspaper contained reports that Chinese border guards fired on refugees fleeing to Russia in 1962. These incidents were described by an inhabitant of a mountainous region between Sinkiang and Kazakhstan. 'Last year dozens of families fled. . . . The people were wasted by hunger, dressed and shod in all kinds of inconceivable rags and worn footwear. Chinese border guards fired at them, but they kept coming all the same.'[2]

Perhaps *Kazakhstanskaya Pravda*'s greatest *coup* at this time was the publication of information supplied by an ex-Major-General of the Chinese People's Liberation Army, Zu Leng Tai Yeh Fu (Zunun Taipov), who had fled to the Soviet Union three years previously. Taipov claimed that 'the notorious Chinese agricultural communes [had] burst like soap bubbles. . . . The order was given to the military commander from Peking: if the communes collapse you will be answerable for it with your head. In fact many did answer with their heads for the stupid adventurism of the Chinese pseudo-politicians.'[3]

Even more sensational was Taipov's account of a massacre which occurred in the Ili Kazakh Autonomous *Chou* in May 1962. Apparently forty local inhabitants were refused a hearing when they applied for papers to go to the Soviet Union. A crowd of some 300 minority tribesmen gathered in front of the local Party headquarters. 'According to [Taipov], machine-gun fire started up from through the windows of the building, and from the army headquarters opposite an even thicker hail of bullets was aimed at the group.' Cries from the wounded rang out: 'Punish these power-crazed madmen', and when 'the crowd scattered,

---

[1] *Kazakhstanskaya Pravda*, 22 September 1963.
[2] *Kazakhstanskaya Pravda*, 26 September 1963.
[3] *Kazakhstanskaya Pravda*, 29 September 1963.

Sino–Soviet Rivalry in Sinkiang 199

there remained only a few dozen corpses of men, women and children, as evidence of the Chinese Communist leadership's failure to realize its plan for the national minorities.'[1]

Other contemporary reports were carried by *Pravda* (23 September 1963) and *Literaturnaya Gazeta* (26 September 1963). It was maintained 'that hundreds of Uighurs, Kazakhs and Kirghiz had been thrown into what are virtually concentration camps and that Peking is bent on "Sinifying" Sinkiang and sealing it off from the U.S.S.R. To this end the Kazakhs, Uighurs and Kirghiz are forbidden to correspond with their relatives in the U.S.S.R. and are being forcibly resettled in the interior of China, while streams of Chinese from the central and eastern parts of the country take their place.'[2]

Articles which appeared in the Kazakhstan press must have been especially successful in aggravating anti-Chinese opinion, in view of the ethnic ties involved. The Soviet propaganda campaign served the dual function of dissociating the minorities from the Chinese policies and in particular of discrediting the Communist Party's minority policy. By way of an answer the Chinese did all in their power to broadcast the idyllic existence enjoyed by her national minorities, and to prove that 'the nationalities policy of the Chinese Communist Party was great and correct, and so were the three red banners of the general line, the big leap forward and the people's commune'.[3] It is unlikely that it was pure coincidence that the Chinese accusation of coercion was preceded by a comprehensive report on *the good life* of China's national minorities.

The account 'painted a glowing picture of the end of discrimination, of newly acquired political rights and the strengthening of national unity, contrasting the present with the exploitation and oppression practised by the "imperialists". It referred to the numbers of autonomous units set up at the various levels and to the high positions held by Saifudin and the Panchen Lama. It pointed to the numbers of minority functionaries and to the role of the minorities in state affairs and in local government, underlining the fact that proportionately they have more representatives in the National People's Congress than the Hans. It reiterated that religious freedom was guaranteed; and, finally it claimed that China was "a big socialist family of nationalities, all of them united on the basis of equality and mutual cooperation and working for their common progress." '[4] The most striking feature of all this publicity was the

[1] *Ibid.*
[2] *Central Asian Review*, 11, 1963, pp. 431–2.
[3] N.C.N.A., Urumchi, 24 December 1962.
[4] N.C.N.A., 29 August 1963.

200 *Essays in Political Geography*

proliferation of reports about the Ili Kazakh Autonomous *Chou*, the focus of the 1962 disturbances.

Economic and cultural improvements were given particular prominence and, for example, it was claimed that Taipov's 'burst-bubble communes' had helped to achieve a situation where 'there has been almost a glut of grain, meat and milk throughout the autonomous region',[1] in fact the proverbial land flowing with milk and honey. An item written some months later, which referred specifically to the predominant Uighur minority, might be regarded as typical of the official attitude towards all minorities for it was claimed that 'if they (the Uighurs) could turn the trees in the world into pens and the water of all the rivers into ink, they would never be able to write down all the favours the Chinese Communist Party has done them!'[2]

A state of constant friction along the Sino–Soviet border in Sinkiang has persisted since the events of 1962. A source published in Taiwan stated that: 'In spring 1963 some 8,000 officers and men of the Sinkiang Production and Construction Corps escaped to Russia.' As a result 'Peking sent a great number of "reliable" officers and men selected from various places to Sinkiang to seal the border and prevent escapes.'[3] Because of the trans-border movements the frontier defences were gradually strengthened along both sides.

Despite this, Wang Su-nan claimed that the border was penetrated from the Soviet side in May 1963. Wang, differing from other commentators, suggested that it was only after the 'Ili incident' of 1962 that the Deputy Commander of the Sinkiang Military Zone, Zu Leng Tai Yeh Fu defected with some of his men. 'These fugitives are now settled in Tashkent, receiving training and equipment from the Russians. They were organized into the "East Turkistan Government Army" and "Sinkiang Liberation Youth Corps". In May 1963 they attacked Ili and Tacheng, destroying Chinese Communist production installations and once engaged in hand-to-hand (fighting) with the Chinese Communist troops.'[4] Wang's account is, it must be noted, the sole description of specific overt aggression; nor did he disclose the source of his information. Wang also stated that 'in autumn, one battalion of the fourth agricultural division stationed in Ining fled to Russia with weapons.'[5]

---

[1] N.C.N.A., 20 September 1963. See Michael Freeberne, *op. cit.*, *Population Studies*, 20, 1966, pp. 103–24, on some of these advances.

[2] *Kuang-ming Jih-pao*, Peking, 30 April 1964.

[3] Wang Su-nan, 'Moscow-Peking conflict in Sinkiang', *Chinese Communist Affairs*, 1, 1964, pp. 1–5.

[4] *Ibid.*   [5] *Ibid.*

Rather vague Soviet newspaper accounts appeared about this time telling of 'Russian frontier troops having recently taken part in a major operation along the border'. Soldiers were on duty for many hours in the mountainous frontier areas of the Kazakhstan Republic. It was obvious from the reports that 'at least one of their tasks was to prevent "frontier violators" from entering Soviet territory.'[1] According to one source, 'the main Russian worry appears to be to prevent the infiltration of agents from China. Earlier this year [1963] *Kazakhstanskaya Pravda* described the capture of five "especially dangerous" men trying to cross the frontier into Russia.'[2]

The build-up of Russian and Chinese military strength continued steadily. 'Since August, the Soviets have moved four . . . crack divisions from Eastern Europe to be deployed along the Chinese frontier.'[3] Wang Su-nan also claimed that 'in autumn 1963, Moscow amassed more than 150,000 troops along the Sino–Soviet border. These troops included units from Eastern European Russian satellites, jet bombers and missile units'.[4] Late in December 'the Soviet military command secretly air-lifted two of its best paratroop divisions from Moscow to Alma-Ata, the capital of Kazakhstan.'[5]

To counteract these movements the Chinese 'shifted large numbers of troops from Kwangtung and Kiangsi provinces, opposite Formosa, and from the Indian border to reinforce their already heavily manned garrisons' and 'China's No. 1 soldier, Marshal Lin Piao, "now spends most of his time at the frontier", a high official recently told a visitor to Peking.'[6] Wang Su-nan gave some idea as to how the Chinese troops might have been deployed 'According to reliable sources, the Chinese Communist regulars are organized in mixed units, with the regiment as the basic independent unit. They number more than 120,000 troops (excluding the Production and Construction Corps) in Sinkiang. They seal the 1,500-kilometre long Sino–Soviet border. Troops are heavily concentrated along the 600-kilometre long borderline from Tacheng to Chaosu and in the area to the west of Altai and Shufu and are deployed 25 miles deep. In the troop concentration areas, underground fortresses, gun emplacements and strong fortifications have been built. A high tension power transmission system has been set up linking the

---

[1] *Kazakhstanskaya Pravda*, August 1963. (See *Sunday Telegraph* 23 August 1963. Precise date of *K.P.* item not given.)

[2] *Sunday Telegraph*, London, 23 August 1963.

[3] *The Dominion*, Wellington, 2 January 1964.

[4] Wang Su-nan, *op. cit.*

[5] *The Dominion*, Wellington, 2 January 1964.   [6] *Ibid.*

202 Essays in Political Geography

area between Tacheng and Shufu. A missile base has been set up in the east of [the] Pamir Plateau, near Khorog. Radar stations have been built in Ili and Artush, keeping watch on the "rocket city" in the Balkhash desert and jet bomber sites on the Russian side.'[1] Again Wang fails to disclose his sources; whilst this fact does not automatically invalidate his description of Chinese installations, it does mean that the material quoted must be treated with extreme caution.

The need for relying on unsubstantiated and somewhat tenuous information underlines the difficulties in attempting a geopolitical analysis of an inaccessible part of the globe, where first-hand observations are virtually unobtainable. An obvious parallel with the Soviet Union during the 1930s exists; reports were compiled and frequently disbelieved and yet later events proved the general outlines described to be relatively accurate. Similarly it is possible to piece together a comparatively reliable picture of happenings in Sinkiang, and indeed in China at large.

Towards the end of 1963 Tom Stacey of the *Sunday Times* 'made an extensive tour in the flash-point area of Russia's eastern border with Sinkiang', and so one eye-witness account became available. In broad outline his lengthy comment bears out the tortuous description above. 'Probably not less than 100,000 refugees (half the smallest estimate I was given) have now crossed the border, after a series of anti-Chinese uprisings among the Muslim inhabitants of Sinkiang over the past three years, in which Russians or Soviet Central Asians appear to have played a significant part.'

Stacey then provided the following fresh information: 'the Soviet "Auto-Transport Trade" organization has been disbanded in the Chinese frontier area. This little-known network had representatives in all or most of the main towns on the Chinese side of the border along not only the three roads but also the numerous mule or bactrian camel trade routes through the mountains.'

Stacey continued by describing events in the Ili area, his report coinciding with those already quoted. Of the incidents in Uch Turfan and neighbouring Aqsu he wrote: 'Here the Russian representative was accused by the Chinese of having supplied arms to insurgents who last year rose and killed several Chinese officials and possibly soldiers, and then escaped in droves into Soviet Kirghizia.'[2]

According to Stacey 'the fiercest spontaneous uprising seems to have taken place [in 1962] at Chuguchak, to the north. Here Kazakhs were mainly involved. According to one version they attacked government

[1] Wang Su-nan, *op. cit.*   [2] Tom Stacey, *Sunday Times*, 8 December 1963.

Sino–Soviet Rivalry in Sinkiang 203

offices and a Chinese army barracks. Here, and among the Altai mountains northward, the number of Kazakhs crossing was put at 40,000.'

Stacey concluded by quoting a Russian description of the eastern frontier of the Pamirs as 'the quietest border of Soviet land, with eternal friendship binding the Chinese and Soviet peoples'.[1] This was written in 1954. The situation some ten years later was greatly changed, and 'in January 1964, the Russian Communist Party Central Committee in Kazakhstan reported that the Chinese Communists committed more than 5,000 border violations in 1963, mostly in connexion with pursuit of escapees.'[2]

In 1954 the Chinese had published a map which showed parts of Kirghizia, Tadjikistan and Kazakhstan as far as Lake Balkhash, as well as the Pamirs, within the borders of China.[3] Late in February 1964 a joint Sino–Soviet Boundary Commission was set up to delimit the border between China and Russia. 'From Moscow the Russians were reported to want to confine their discussions to minor adjustments only, while the Chinese hoped for a wholesale review of frontier claims.'[4] Again, 'in Peking communist diplomatic sources . . . said the talks were "relatively unimportant" and could not be construed as inter-state negotiations'.[5] The fighting tone of the letter from the Central Committee of the Chinese Communist Party, to the Central Committee of the Communist Party of the Soviet Union, dated 29 February 1964, seems to confirm the Chinese interpretation, and a revealing summary – Chinese style – of events happening along the Sino–Soviet border as a whole, but referring in all probability to Sinkiang especially, was presented. 'The government of the People's Republic of China has consistently held that the question of the boundary between China and the Soviet Union, which is a legacy from the past, can be settled through negotiation. . . . It has also held that, pending such a settlement, the status quo on the border should be maintained. *This is what we have done over the past ten years or more. Had the Soviet Government taken the same attitude, both sides could have lived in amity along the border and preserved tranquillity there.* . . . With the stepping up of anti-Chinese activities by the leaders of the C.P.S.U. in recent years, the Soviet side has made frequent breaches of the *status quo* on the border, occupied Chinese

---

[1] *Ibid.*

[2] Wang Su-nan, *op. cit.*

[3] Liu Pei-hua, ed., *Chung-kuo chin-tai chien-shih* (*A short History of Modern China*), Peking, 1954, p. 253.

[4] *Far Eastern Economic Review*, Hong Kong, 26 March 1964.

[5] *The Times*, London, 10 March 1964.

204 *Essays in Political Geography*

territory and provoked border incidents.'[1] This reference to the *occupation* of Chinese territory was a fresh emphasis. 'Still more serious, the Soviet side has flagrantly carried out large-scale subversive activities in Chinese frontier areas, trying to sow discord among China's minority nationalities to break away from their motherland, and inveigling and coercing tens of thousands of Chinese citizens into going to the Soviet Union.'[2]

The Chinese letter continued in bitter terms: 'Among all our neighbours it is only the leaders of the Communist Party of the Soviet Union and the reactionary nationalists of India who have deliberately created border disputes with China.'[3] Most significantly, the Chinese stated: 'The delegations of our two governments started boundary negotiations in Peking on 25 February 1964. *Although the old treaties relating to Sino–Soviet boundary are unequal treaties, the Chinese Government is nevertheless willing to respect them and take them as the basis for a reasonable settlement of the Sino–Soviet boundary question.*' Magnanimously, the Chinese concluded: '*If the Soviet side takes the same attitude as the Chinese Government, the settlement of the Sino–Soviet boundary question . . . ought not to be difficult, and the Sino–Soviet boundary will truly become one of lasting friendship.*'[4]

Despite the above Chinese assertions, trouble along the Sinkiang border continued. A news item, dated 7 April 1964, read: 'An official of Russian Kazakhstan reported a mass exodus of the Uighur and Kazakh population from China, (AFP).'[5] The next day *Tass* announced 'the Chinese side has been for some time continually and systematically violating the Soviet Chinese border and often in a crude and provocatory form'.[6]

FRONTIERS: A PROBLEM OF PEACE

June 1964 saw the publication by the International Affairs Press in Moscow of a book by B. M. Klimenko, *Frontiers: A Problem of Peace.* The main argument of the book is that it is essential to avoid aggression in the nuclear age when contemplating changes in 'historically formed' frontiers. In spite of 'repeated violations, some of them amounting to barefaced provocation, the Soviet Union took the initiative in consultations regarding certain sectors of the frontier between the U.S.S.R.

[1] *Peking Review*, 8 May 1964. Italics added.   [2] *Ibid.*
[3] *Ibid.*   [4] *Ibid.* Italics added.
[5] *Far Eastern Economic Review*, Hong Kong, 16 April 1964.
[6] *Ibid.*

Sino–Soviet Rivalry in Sinkiang 205

and the Chinese People's Republic . . . particularly since the Twentieth Party Congress of 1956, the Soviet Government, having greatly extended its frontiers during the War, has carefully refrained from transfrontier excursions. . . . *But the possibilities cannot be excluded that circumstances might impel it to revert to its earlier methods.*'[1]

A further historical inference which may have caused the Chinese some embarrassment was made by Mr Khrushchev in Moscow on 15 September 1964, during an interview he gave to a Japanese parliamentary delegation. Khrushchev stated that the Chinese Emperors had deprived the 'Uighurs, Kazakhs, Kirghiz and other peoples of their independence', implying that the Chinese required force to subdue their minority nationalities.[2]

There was considerable speculation as to whether or not the downfall of Khrushchev would result in an improvement in Sino–Soviet relations, and initially a number of Russian moves indicated that the new leadership wished to facilitate a *rapprochement*. For instance, issue Number 10 of *Mezhdunarodnaya Zhizh* (*International Affairs*), which was released to the press on 21 September 1964 included a controversial article on the Sino–Soviet boundaries. Normally an English language edition of *International Affairs* follows about a fortnight after the Russian edition, but in this instance the English language edition was delayed, and subsequently published without the article on frontiers. The author of the disputed article was N. M. Khvostov, an editor of the authoritative *Diplomatic Dictionary*. Significantly, as the *Central Asian Review* has pointed out, whereas in his article Khvostov insists that the frontier treaties between Tsarist Russia and China were *not* unequal, 'the article on Sino–Soviet treaties in Volume III of the *Diplomatic Dictionary* clearly implies that at the time of publication (1964) the Soviet Government was prepared to admit that they were unequal'.[3]

Whether or not the Russians showed signs of genuinely wishing to come to terms with the Chinese, the latter remained adamant, and the Russians were accused of 'trying to poison the relations among the various nationalities of [the Ili Kazakh Autonomous *Chou*] in order to undermine [China's] national unity . . . constantly creating border incidents and attempting to disrupt production in the border areas.'[4] These

[1] B. M. Klimenko, *Frontiers: A Problem of Peace*, Moscow, 1964. Quoted in *Central Asian Review*, 13, 1965, pp. 2–3. Italics added.
[2] *Soviet News*, 22 September 1964.
[3] Editorial, *Central Asian Review*, 13, 1965, p. 1. A summary of the Russian *International Affairs* article is found on pp. 89–91.
[4] *Peking Review*, 11 September 1964.

206 *Essays in Political Geography*

charges reiterated the accusations made in some detail to delegates attending the Second Session of the Fourth People's Congress of the Ili Kazakh Autonomous *Chou* held in Ining between 26 and 29 August 1964, when Irhali, Chairman of the *Chou* declared that the outstanding political and economic achievements had been registered in spite of sabotage by the Khrushchev revisionist clique.[1]

A few weeks later Saifudin declared at a rally held in Urumchi to celebrate National Day that 'if the Khrushchev revisionists dare to stretch out their evil hands to invade and occupy our territory they will certainly be repulsed by the people of the various nationalities in Sinkiang and by the 650 million Chinese people.'[2] Similarly at the Regional People's Congress which met between 22 October and 1 November the delegates unanimously agreed that 'Sinkiang is an inalienable, sacred part of our great motherland. We do not want an inch of other's land, nor shall we allow others to take even an inch of our land. Any base attempt to undermine the unity of our motherland and the great unity of the nationalities of China is doomed to failure.'[3] Again, at celebrations marking the tenth anniversary of the Kotzulosu Kirghiz Autonomous *Chou*, Iminov, Vice-chairman of the Sinkiang Uighur Autonomous Region, stressed that as the *Chou* was situated in the border region that the local inhabitants 'should redouble their vigilance and be ready to crush any subversive and sabotage activities by the imperialists, reactionaries and modern revisionists'.[4]

Obviously, however, the Russians take a rather different view of the situation. They fear that the Chinese are anxious to do other than simply preserve the *status quo*, and in fact see Chinese activity in Sinkiang as a manifestation of an 'absurd demand for a re-examination of the state boundary of the U.S.S.R. in favour of China.'[5]

Thus the border dispute remains unresolved, and a seemingly perpetual tension predominates in the frontier zone of Sinkiang. An explosive situation has developed in a relatively short period of time, a fact which is underlined by a *Jen-min Jih-pao* editorial marking the fifteenth anniversary of the Sino–Soviet Treaty of Friendship, Alliance and Mutual Assistance. There is something of a hollow ring about the assertion that 'no force on earth can possibly undermine the great friendship forged between our two peoples in the long years of revolutionary

[1] N.C.N.A., Ining, 2 September 1964.   [2] N.C.N.A., 1 October 1964.
[3] N.C.N.A., Urumchi, 6 November 1964.
[4] N.C.N.A., Artush, 5 December 1964.
[5] B. N. Ponomaryov, ed., *The International Revolutionary Movement of the Working Class* (Reference in N.C.N.A., Moscow, 28 February 1965).

Sino–Soviet Rivalry in Sinkiang 207

struggle', especially in view of the 'still present shadows over the relations between China and the Soviet Union.'[1]

But, for the most part, the Russians have refrained from public polemic since the departure of Khrushchev, and, with immediate reference to Sinkiang, China largely held her fire during the first half of 1965, only to resume with a barrage of invective as the tenth anniversary celebrations of the founding of the Autonomous Region drew near.

Among those who condemned the activities of the Khrushchev revisionist clique were Saifudin, the Region's Chairman; Wang En-mao, First Secretary of the Sinkiang Regional Committee of the Chinese Communist Party; Vice-Premier Ho Lung, Member of the Political Bureau of the Central Committee of the Chinese Communist Party and Head of the Central Delegation attending the anniversary celebrations; and Hsieh Fu-min, Chairman of the National People's Congress Nationalities Committee. Noticeably, Hsieh was the only one to refer to a 'handful' of 'local nationalists and other counter-revolutionaries working in the service of revisionism',[2] while the other three associated revisionism with imperialism. For example, speaking on the eve of the festivities Wang En-mao 'condemned the Khrushchev revisionist clique for its subversive and disruptive activities in Sinkiang, which, he said, "are an important part of the joint anti-China scheme of the Khrushchev revisionist clique, the United States imperialists and the Indian reactionaries." '[3]

More precise details of the alleged crimes of the Khrushchev revisionists were provided by Saifudin in a lengthy article published in *Jen-min Jih-pao*. These 'renegades from communism and lackeys of imperialism' (compare Ho Lung's 'Traitors to the proletariat'),[4] were charged with 'harbouring a deep-seated hatred', 'carrying out constant subversive and sabotage activities', and 'increasingly spreading rumours and slanders and making virulent attacks on us.'[5]

Specifically, first, the Khrushchev revisionists 'slander our [socialist] revolution as "alien to Marxism-Leninism", a "chauvinistic movement" and a "movement at the expense of the minority nationalities".' Secondly, the revisionists 'slanderously charge that Sinkiang [has seen] "no development in industry" after liberation, that "its agriculture has gone bankrupt" and that "the people's livelihood there is in a state of poverty".'

[1] N.C.N.A., Peking, 14 February 1965.
[2] N.C.N.A., Peking, 2 October 1965.
[3] *Peking Review*, 8 October 1965.
[4] N.C.N.A., Urumchi, 30 September 1965.
[5] *Jen-min Jih-pao*, Peking, 30 September 1965.

208 Essays in Political Geography

Finally, the revisionists 'slanderously allege that Sinkiang is China's "colony", that a policy of "deception and national discrimination" was practised, etc., in an attempt to undermine and disrupt our national unity.' Saifudin warned, however, that 'whatever subversion and sabotage the Khrushchev revisionists may attempt in the future they will not succeed and will only meet with still more shameful defeats'.[1]

As if to underline this last assertion, the Chinese now characterize Sinkiang as a 'solid bastion'.[2] 'The Sinkiang Uighur Autonomous Region is a fortified frontier and a great wall in defence of our motherland. In the storm of struggle, it will for ever stand majestically on the western frontier of our motherland.'

CONCLUSION

What, then, are the salient geopolitical lessons which emerge from this discussion of political upheaval and Sino–Soviet rivalry in the borderlands of the Sinkiang Uighur Autonomous Region?

First, the resurgence of Chinese power within a marginal area at a time of strong central government. This historical 'ebb and flow' of Chinese influence and authority in the far north-west has been analysed dramatically by Owen Lattimore. Now Chinese power waxes strong. But the contemporary phase is different from its predecessors in its totality[3] for, in the long run, the Chinese aim at the complete assimilation of, and political and economic control over, an area which they consider to be an integral part of China, whereas previously it was more a case of establishing domination over an essentially colonial territory. The scale of the Chinese onslaught has never before been so all-embracing, especially in respect of the immigration of Han Chinese, the consequent efforts to swamp the minority peoples, and the strategic build-up to secure and maintain China's position against internal and foreign pressures. Moreover, the Chinese find themselves driven up against the Russian presence which controls the adjacent lands of Soviet Central Asia more firmly than at any period in the past.

Secondly, the continuance of a further, if more recent, historical pattern is reflected in the struggle for hegemony between China and the U.S.S.R. Since the eastwards shift of the Russian centre of gravity during and since the nineteenth century, the two countries have intrigued in

---

[1] *Jen-min Jih-pao*, Peking, 30 September 1965.

[2] N.C.N.A., Urumchi, 30 September 1965; and N.C.N.A., Peking, 29 September 1965.

[3] Michael Freeberne, *Population Studies, op. cit.*

Sinkiang; but it must surprise some Marxist thinkers that naked power politics enter into the relationships between the two leading communist nations.

Thirdly, there is the catalytic nature of the indigenous peoples of Sinkiang. Although the Chinese claim that the lives of their minorities have been improved immeasurably, as in the case of the settling of pastoral nomads, it is precisely the quality and degree of *real* change, if any, that is in doubt. Certainly the mass movements across Sinkiang's troubled frontier would suggest that the wandering habit is far from lost, nor is it likely that conditions along Sinkiang's frontier will become sufficiently stable within the foreseeable future for a peaceful development of these lands by their native population to result.

Finally, in no circumstances is it possible to agree with either Mehnert's thesis that: 'Today Sinkiang can scarcely be regarded as a seriously disturbing element in the relationship between Moscow and Peking,'[1] or Jackson's view of the entire Sino–Soviet borderlands as constituting 'zones of co-operation and stabilization'.[2] Some years ago Fisher warned, almost prophetically, 'Central Asia is ceasing to be a power vacuum, and although it will certainly be many years before its isolation is decisively broken down, the possibility of exploiting some of the strategic advantages implicit in its position as the pivot of Asia can no longer be discounted. Whether in these circumstances, and especially if important minerals are discovered there, Russian and Chinese interests will coincide, remains to be seen. *But, in so far as past history is any guide, there would appear to be considerable room for divergence.*'[3]

Indeed the Sinkiang borderlands are likely to provide a semi-permanent stage for Sino–Soviet rivalry, not only because of the arguments already pursued concerning the mercurial national minority inhabitants and inter-state relations, but also because of the strategic location of Sinkiang which forms part of a vast Asiatic crescent of potential and actual tension and conflict, stretching from Korea and the Far East possessions of the Soviet Union westwards to include Mongolia, Sinkiang itself, and south and east through Kashmir and the Himalayan lands of Tibet, Nepal, Sikkim and Bhutan.

[1] Klaus Mehnert, *Peking and Moscow*, London, 1963, p. 273.

[2] W. A. Douglas Jackson, *Russo-Chinese Borderlands*, Princeton, 1962, p. 110.

[3] C. A. Fisher in *The Changing World* (Ed. W. G. East and A. E. Moodie), London, 1956, p. 591. Italics added.

11

The Evolution of the Boundary between
Iraq and Iran
VAHÉ J. SEVIAN

INTRODUCTION

This study is limited to a factual account of the role of politico-geographical factors in the evolution of the present Iraq–Iran boundary. The historical background embraces four centuries of hostile relations between the Persian and the then Ottoman Empires, before the demarcation of their common boundary, which runs from the Caucasus down to the Arabian Gulf,[1] was finally achieved in 1914 on the eve of Turkey's participation in the First World War. Throughout this period imperial ambitions, political aspirations, and strong religious discords between the two neighbouring empires, sharing a common faith but separated by schism, overrode geographical, ethnic, linguistic and economic considerations.

Frontiers were only vaguely described in the international instruments which followed each act of hostility between the two empires. This state of affairs continued until about 1850, when improved geographical knowledge of the region made possible a more accurate description of the 2,000-kilometre-long frontier. The slow evolution to the present stabilized alignment necessitated a further period of patient mediation from Great Britain and Russia, in consideration of their own interests and objectives within their respective zones of influence. The frontier was demarcated in 1913–14 by a mixed Frontier Commission comprising representatives of Great Britain and Russia and the two neighbouring countries directly involved.

Controversial conditions of local significance still occasionally occur. Difficulties are experienced in Iraq from interference with the regime of frontier streams from Iran, and with the discovery of oil in the bed of the Arabian Gulf a new problem exists, since it has become necessary to extend the sea frontier into the Gulf. The territorial waters have thus been extended from three to twelve nautical miles and the continental shelf demands due consideration. Occasionally Iran demands the shifting to midstream of the estuarine frontier, the Shatt-al Arab, the only

---

[1] More familiarly known in the West as the Persian Gulf.

212 *Essays in Political Geography*

outlet to the open sea of land-locked Iraq. This frontier, fixed according to politico-geographical considerations, runs along the low water mark on the Iranian shore, leaving the estuary within Iraq's sovereignty. However, there are two exceptions in that the frontier runs midstream, and follows the *thalweg* over short distances, thus providing anchorage facilities to two Iranian ports.

International co-operation in the making of this frontier, despite strong antagonism between the two great powers, gave stability for the first time in four centuries to both Iraq and Iran, the former having succeeded in this region to the then Ottoman Empire.

THE EVOLUTION OF THE BOUNDARY FROM THE SIXTEENTH TO THE EARLY NINETEENTH CENTURY

An early mention of the boundary between the Ottoman and Persian Empires was made during the reign of Sultan Selim I (1512–20). The Ottomans claimed that the annexation by Persia of Armenia, the Caucasus, Kurdistan and Iraq was a violation of their eastern frontiers. Schismatic discords between the two empires of common faith were embittered by the massacre of Sunnis in Baghdad, then under Persian Shia rule, and by the massacre of Shias in the Sunni Ottoman Empire. Furthermore, strong imperial rivalry aggravated the relations between the two empires. Hostilities broke out in 1514, and Sultan Selim I, victorious at the battle of Chaldiran (1515) annexed Eastern Anatolia and Kurdistan. However, he did not exploit fully his victory, but directed his army elsewhere, capturing and adding Egypt to his empire in 1517 and obtaining from the Caliph the surrender of the spiritual and hereditary title of Caliph to himself and to his heirs, an arrangement which lasted until 1924.

Following the Ottoman invasion of Persia by Sultan Solaiman I[1] and the capture of Baghdad, a Treaty of Peace and Friendship was concluded in 1535. Hostilities were resumed a few years later. These ended to the Ottomans' advantage, in spite of their campaigns for holding their vast empire extending as far as Vienna. Following the hostilities a new Treaty of Peace was concluded in 1555. The Sultan declared that there should be 'peace between the two states as long as the Persians did not break it, and the Governors of the frontier provinces would be instructed to protect pilgrims bound for the Holy Cities within the Ottoman Empire'.

---

[1] *I.e.* Solaiman the Magnificent.

The Evolution of the Boundary between Iraq and Iran 213

A few years later, and following a new state of war, a Treaty of Peace was signed in 1568 on the basis of the Declaration of 1555. Soon afterwards Turkey invaded Persia in 1587, capturing Tabriz and Baghdad, and annexing parts of Iraq Ajami, Luristan and Khuzistan. A Treaty of Peace was signed at Constantinople in 1590, by which treaty Persia ceded Tabriz, Shirwan with its ports on the Caspian, Georgia and Luristan to Turkey.

Two more treaties following hostilities ending to Persia's advantage were concluded in 1613 and 1618. In 1639, after the re-capture of Baghdad and its district by the Ottomans, the first *Treaty of Peace and Demarcation of Frontiers*[1] between the two empires was signed at Zohab. Under the terms of this treaty, the Ottomans allocated to either belligerent localities and sites along a short strip in the isthmus extending from the Black/Caspian Seas to the Arabian Gulf. It was the first milestone towards the gradual shaping of the present boundary during the subsequent three centuries.

A period of calm followed. Turkey in agreement with Russia, under a treaty for the partition of Persia concluded in 1724 on the mediation of France, invaded the Caucasus and Persia, at that time under Afghan rule. A treaty to Turkey's advantage was signed at Hamadan in 1727, whereby Persia abandoned to Turkey a large part of her western provinces and the Caucasus. Protection was guaranteed to Persian pilgrims of Shia sect proceedings to the Holy Cities held by the Ottomans belonging to the Sunni sect. Further, Persia undertook to prevent the excursion of brigands into the country between Basra and Baghdad. But peace did not last long. Hostilities were resumed and were followed by short-lived treaties, the first signed at Baghdad in 1732 and the second at Constantinople in 1736. Ganja, Tiflis, Erivan, Nakhischevan, and other places north of the river Aras were ceded to Turkey, the river being considered the boundary between the two countries. To the south of the river, Tabriz, Ardelan, Hamadan, Kirmanshah and Luristan remained to Persia. Consulates were to be established at Constantinople and Isfahan. Clauses for the protection of Persian pilgrims to the Holy Cities were included as in the previous treaties.

After defeating the Afghans in 1743, Nadir Shah of Persia resumed war with Turkey upon the Sultan's refusal to accept the new Ja'fari sect founded by the Shah. Previous treaties were superseded by the *Treaty of Peace* concluded in 1746 at Kerden between Kazvin and Tehran. The treaty re-affirmed *inter alia* that the previous treaty concluded

[1] Boundary treaties are italicized.

214 Essays in Political Geography

in 1639 'shall be maintained as valid by the two governments and the frontiers and limits fixed by that treaty shall be preserved on the same footing, and that there shall occur neither change nor alterations of the principles enunciated therein'. It was stated in the Appendix to the treaty that 'the limits and frontiers, established under Sultan Murad IV (Boundary treaty of 1639) shall be verified and the frontier commanders shall abstain from measures detrimental to friendship'. The clause that 'Persian pilgrims may go to the Holy Cities . . . in full security and tranquillity' was repeated here.

A second long period of calm ended with the last Turko–Persian war of 1821–2 which in turn was followed in 1823 by the first *Treaty of Erzrum*. The preamble to the treaty states its basic principle, namely that the stipulations of the Treaty concluded in 1746 respecting 'the ancient boundaries and limits of the two empires and the former agreements relating to pilgrims . . . are considered valid and are to be strictly observed. The slightest deviation from the engagements therein shall not be permitted and the amity between the two powerful States shall be for ever preserved'. Furthermore, the first article of the treaty stipulates that 'the two High Powers do not admit each other's interference in the internal affairs of their respective States. The Persian Government shall now no more allow herself to interfere in any way in the districts of Baghdad and Kurdistan within the frontiers of the Ottoman Empire . . . nor to assume any authority over the present and former governors of these countries'. It was also agreed that, should the tribes on either side of the frontier cross the boundary for a summer or winter residence,[1] arrangements should be made regarding the payment of the customary tribute, the rent of the pasture lands and other claims.

Thus ended three centuries of hostilities between Turkey and Persia. However, difficulties were not over. On many occasions sporadic armed aggressions brought Turkey and Persia to the brink of war and increased the distrustful attitude between them. It took another century with many vicissitudes before the frontier was finally demarcated, so at last ending the vagueness of the description of the frontier in an uncharted region which began with the treaty of 1639 and was re-affirmed and maintained in the subsequent frontier treaties of 1746 and 1823.

---

[1] This practice still continues, since the boundary line divides a country inhabited by people of the same race and faith.

THE PERIOD OF BRITISH AND RUSSIAN MEDIATION

Early in the nineteenth century, notwithstanding their mutual rivalries, Great Britain and Russia, having in mind their own interests and objectives within their respective zones of influence, began moving towards a common recognition of the need for a definitive boundary between Turkey and Persia. Through their good offices, further hostilities between these two neighbouring states were averted, and persevering mediation eventually resulted in 1914 in a final demarcation of the boundary. A mixed Boundary Commission with representatives from the mediating powers was set up in 1843 for the demarcation of the boundary, but no results were obtained from it. The neighbouring countries were brought together again through mediation and, as a result, a new *Treaty of Erzrum* was concluded in 1847. Omissions and gaps in earlier treaties relating to the description of the boundary line were less evident in the new treaty. Two main points were included: 'the Persian Government abandons all claim to the City and Province of Sulaimani [a Kurdish district in Northern Iraq] and formally undertakes not to interfere with or infringe the sovereign rights of the Ottoman Government over the said province'. Also on its part 'the Ottoman Government formally recognizes the unrestricted sovereignty of the Persian Government over the city and port of Muhammara [now Khoramshahr], the island of Khizr [Abadan], the Abadan anchorage, and the lands on the eastern bank – that is to say, the left bank – of the Shatt-al-Arab' (Article 2).

The treaty also states: 'Further, Persian vessels shall have the right to navigate freely without let or hindrance on the Shatt-al-Arab from the mouth of the same to the point of contact of the frontier of the two Parties' (Article 2). It was also agreed that the 'Two Contracting Parties having by the present waived their other territorial claims undertake forthwith to appoint commissioners and engineers . . . for the purpose of determining the frontiers' (Article 3); that a fair settlement should be made 'of damage suffered by either Party since the acceptance of the friendly proposals drawn up and communicated by the Mediating Great Powers' (Article 4); and that Turkey should undertake 'to accord the requisite privileges to enable Persian pilgrims, in accordance with the former treaties, to visit the Holy Places in the Ottoman dominions in complete safety without vexatious treatment of any kind' (Article 7).

In addition, the appointment of consuls was stipulated in Article 7. Both Parties agreed to 'adopt and enforce the necessary measures to prevent and punish theft and brigandage on the part of the tribes and

Fig. 11.1. The Iraq–Iran Frontier

The Evolution of the Boundary between Iraq and Iran 217

peoples settled on the frontier' . . . and also the 'tribes the suzerainty over which is not known shall be left free . . . to choose once for all and specify the localities which they will henceforward always inhabit' (Article 8).

Continuous disagreements between the Turkish and Persian Commissioners appointed for the delimitation of the boundary prevented a new Mixed Boundary Commission from working between 1848 and 1851, and after that the Crimean War (1854–6) and the Anglo-Persian War (1856–7) interrupted work on the delimitation of the frontier. Twelve years were spent by the mediating powers in surveying and making a map – *La Carte Identique* – of a wide strip of country running along the eventual line of the frontier. This brings us to 1869. Many discrepancies in the maps and the adoption of different scales (1 : 84,000 down to latitude 36°, and 1 inch to one nautical mile from latitude 36° to the Gulf), were corrected and settled before the mediating powers informed the two neighbouring states that 'the future line of boundary was to be found within the limits fixed on the maps and they should themselves make out the line'. In case of non-agreement 'the points of dispute should be referred to the decision of the Governments of Great Britain and Russia'. This decision of the mediators was soon accepted by Persia but Turkey's agreement was delayed until 1875.

DEVELOPMENTS DURING THE TWENTIETH CENTURY

Insurrections in the Balkan and in Crete and two Serbian Wars were followed closely by the Turco-Russian War of 1876–78, and then by a long period of inactivity. In 1911, by the terms of the Protocol of Tehran, both parties agreed on the formation of a Commission to meet at Constantinople in order to establish the boundary line separating the two countries in a spirit of sincere impartiality; after which, a technical commission would merely have to apply the definite delimitation on the spot, based on the clauses of the Treaty of Erzrum concluded in 1847. It was also stipulated in the Protocol that in case 'the two Parties fail to agree . . . in order to completely settle the question of the delimitation of the frontier' the case should be submitted to the Hague Court of Arbitration. In this connexion meetings were held and, in November 1913, the *Protocol Relating to the Delimitation of the Turco-Persian Boundary* was signed at Constantinople between Great Britain, Persia, Russia and Turkey. The Protocol, after 'recapitulating the progress up to the date of negotiations', gave a clear definition of the frontier line to

218 *Essays in Political Geography*

be demarcated. It defined the duties of the Commission, the arbitral powers of the British and Russian Commissioners 'in the event a divergence of opinion raised either by Turkey or Persia' (Article 4). It was also stipulated that any part of the frontier once delimited 'shall be regarded as finally fixed and shall not be liable to subsequent examination or revision'. (Article 5.) Further, Turkey agreed that 'the concession granted' by Persia 'to William Knox D'Arcy and now being worked . . . by the Anglo-Persian Co. Ltd. . . . shall remain in full and unrestricted force throughout the territories transferred by Persia to Turkey'. (Article 7.)

As regards the demarcation of the estuarine frontier described in the Protocol (Article 1), it is stated that 'From the point where the land frontier joins the Khayin (a branch of the Shatt-al-Arab) the frontier shall follow the course of the Shatt-al-Arab as far as the sea, leaving under Ottoman sovereignty the river and all its islands therein, subject to the following conditions and exceptions'. These are: (*a*) a few islands shall belong to Persia, (*b*) the modern port and anchorage or Muhammara (now Khoramshahr) 'shall remain within Persian jurisdiction . . ., the Ottoman right of usage of this part of the river shall not, however, be affected thereby, nor shall Persian jurisdiction extend to the parts of the river outside the anchorage'. The description by the Mixed Commission of the delimitation of the estuarine boundary confirms the above: 'elle (la frontière) suit le niveau des basses eaux[1] de la rive gauche du Chatt-el-Arab rive d'Abadan', and after allocating a few islands to Persia, states again, 'elle (la frontière) se confond de nouveau avec la ligne du niveau des basses eaux'.

In spite of the clear definition of the estuarine boundary, sporadic claims are raised by Iran[2] on Iraq's sovereign rights over the Shatt-al-Arab, the only access of land-locked Iraq to the open sea. Iran's claims are for joint control over the navigation in estuarine waters and the shifting to midstream of the present boundary line.

The demarcation of the boundary from the Gulf to Ararat was begun soon after the conclusion of the Protocol of Constantinople and was completed in October 1914. The boundary remains unchanged up to the present day save for small rectifications. The first was made in the region north of and beyond Iraq when the *Turco-Iranian Agreement of 1937* slightly adjusted the original boundary at three places.[3]

---

[1] It should be noted that the estuary is subject to tidal influence.

[2] These reflect changes in the political atmosphere.

[3] 'The Turkish-Iranian Boundary'. Two notes by G.R.C. in *Geographical Journal*, 91, 1938, pp. 57–9; and 92, 1938, pp. 149–50.

The Evolution of the Boundary between Iraq and Iran 219

The other rectification was also made during the same year. When after the conclusion of the First World War Iraq attained statehood, Iran 'felt she was no longer legally obligated to the past Treaties and Agreements between Persia and the Ottoman Empire'.[1] Numerous unfriendly acts along the land frontier and in the estuary compelled Iraq in 1934 to lodge a complaint with the League of Nations. After many deliberations and direct negotiations, the *Boundary Treaty of 1937* was concluded between Iraq and Iran.[2] Both Iraq and Iran agreed that the Protocol of Constantinople of 1913, together with the Minutes of the Meeting of the 1914 Boundary Delimitation Commission, 'shall be deemed valid and binding' and 'the frontier between the two States shall be as defined and traced by the Commission' (Article 1.) Under the terms of the Treaty, Iraq conceded to Iran for anchorage facilities the sovereignty over a strip of some six kilometres in the Shatt-al-Arab opposite Abadan, by transferring to the *thalweg* the boundary running along the low water mark on the Persian bank (Article 2.) Conditions in estuarine waters are illustrated in Fig. 11.2 which shows the various sections of the estuary where the boundary runs respectively along the low water mark on the Persian side, at midstream, and along the *thalweg*.

Many rivers and streams flow from Iran across the boundary demarcated in 1914 between the Ottoman Empire and Persia. All of these have their headwaters in Persia, thus making Iraq, which succeeded the Ottoman Empire in this region, dependent on Iran for its water resources along its eastern boundary. In some instances, the boundary follows the *medium filum aquae* of the streams, while in other instances it intersects them. With one exception no provision was entered in any of the various treaties or agreements between the two neighbouring states on the apportionment of the waters of the streams, nor was any reference made to the rights acquired from time immemorial.

The exception mentioned above concerns the Guanguir, which is a small frontier stream. The Boundary Commission decided in 1914 that the waters of the stream 'shall be divided into two halves, one half shall belong to Mendeli [in the Ottoman Empire] and the other half to the people of Soumer [in Persia]'. It was agreed that the execution of the decision should be 'left to the local experts'. Bearing in mind possibilities of disagreement between the two neighbouring countries over the fair application of the decision, the Commission ruled that any such

[1] Mohamed Alwan, *The Iraq–Iran Frontier – A Case Study*, Washington, D.C., 1960.

[2] 'The Iran-Iraq Boundary Treaty, 1937'. Note by A. S. E.-S. in *Geographical Journal*, 93, 1939, pp. 541–2.

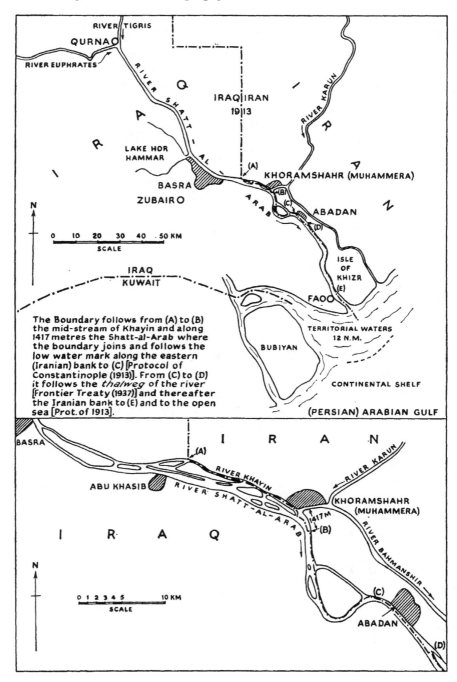

Fig. 11.2. The Present Estuarine Frontier between Iraq and Iran

The Evolution of the Boundary between Iraq and Iran 221

differences be handled through diplomatic channels. Moreover, the British and Russian Commissioners thought that their Consuls-General at Baghdad could lend their assistance in case of divergence of opinion regarding the application of this arrangement. This clause has not been made use of in spite of recurrent difficulties in obtaining a fair distribution of the Guanguir waters.

The small plains in the region through which the present international boundary line runs have been divided between the two neighbouring countries, and the difficulties created by partitioning such geographic regions of similar physical and social character were unavoidable. Increased withdrawal of water across the border, particularly during the low water period of the streams, is carried out without consideration of the consequences of such action to the areas on the other side of the boundary line. Thus agricultural life is improving and being extended on the eastern side of the boundary at the expense of the lands on the western side (in Iraq), where agricultural life and rural conditions are disrupted from time to time, and possibilities of development are seriously affected.

Finally the occurrence of oil in commercial quantity in the Arabian Gulf, which forms a vast area of continental shelf, presents new politico-geographical problems to the countries bordering the Gulf. In November 1958 Iraq extended the limit of its territorial waters from three to twelve nautical miles, so that the Iraq-Iran sea boundary, though not finally delimited at the present time, has been extended well into the Gulf.

RETROSPECT AND CONCLUSIONS

In the past the concept of the boundary did not have the same significance which it has today, and many diverse peoples crossed and occupied for varying periods the region where the present boundary line runs.

From the middle of the fourteenth century the political ambitions of the Ottomans were aimed at conquests in Europe, but in 1529, at the time when besieged Vienna was relieved, Persia resumed hostilities against Turkey's eastern provinces. Here, however, the Ottomans were victorious and Persia was invaded and Baghdad occupied in 1534.

The Ottoman and Persian empires were the two great rivals in the territories which comprise the vast isthmus extending from the Black and Caspian Seas in the north to the Arabian Gulf in the south. Recurrent hostilities between them kept fluid the limits of the territories under their alternate occupancy. In 1639 a small section of the frontier

222 *Essays in Political Geography*

along the central part of the country was vaguely defined and this was reaffirmed subsequently in 1746 and 1823. Later, in 1847 Turkey's sovereignty was recognized over part of Kurdistan now in north-east Iraq, and that of Persia over the country east of the Shatt-al-Arab, the estuary of the Euphrates-Tigris.

Religious antagonism between the two empires was never appeased. The possession by the Sunni Ottomans of the Holy Cities in Mesopotamia, which were highly venerated by Shia Persians, was a source of continuous political friction. Every treaty concluded between the two neighbours included a clause for the safe travel and prevention of molestation to Persian pilgrims proceeding to the Holy Cities.

Ethnic and linguistic considerations were set aside when Persia abandoned her claim over the western part of a Kurdish region inhabited by Mohammedan Sunnis and in return obtained from the Ottomans access to the Shatt-al-Arab through a region inhabited by Arab Shias. Kurdistan was divided between Ottomans and Persians to be split again between Turkey and Iraq when the latter achieved independent nationhood. In the delta of Shatt-al-Arab, an Arab region was divided between the two neighbours. Thus the mitigation of political antagonism was made at the expense of ethnic and linguistic considerations.

Owing to an unaccommodating climate the Ottoman Turks were unable to settle large colonies of their own people in the Mesopotamian plains in order to strengthen and justify their hold over them. And this situation was aggravated by the heterogeneous population of Turkey itself, the deterioration in the administration of their vast empire, and the smallness of their numbers. Thus the few elements which remained were gradually absorbed by the Arabs.

No economic requirements could justify either neighbour pursuing a policy of extending into and holding permanently regions which differed ethnically from it, nor was there in either case any justification for doing so on grounds of population pressure.

Imperial ambition brought the Ottomans to the centre of Europe, thus precluding them during the height of their power from obtaining greater success in the east, which might have resulted in a very different political map of the Near East. Persia's aggressiveness is easier to understand. Its western frontier regions, inhabited by Persians, were under direct menace from any warlike power which settled as a neighbour, and the desire to possess the Holy Cities in the Mesopotamian plains represented a standing temptation. To counteract Persia's ambitions in this respect, Turkey relied on military rather than political measures.

The Evolution of the Boundary between Iraq and Iran 223

In the north the boundary follows the watershed forming the eastern limit of the Tigris basin, but in the centre and south it has no such natural basis, and on its way to the estuary it cuts across the numerous lesser basins of the Tigris tributaries, whose headwaters are thus left in Iran. Lack of agreement between Iraq and Iran in respect of all but one of these international streams gives rise to friction and prevents sound economic development of the many basins thus partitioned by the border line facing in opposite directions for their development.

The estuary with its complex boundary line (Fig. 11.2) serves the oil ports of Abadan in Iran and Fao in Iraq as well as a large region in Iran and the entire hinterland of Iraq. The limits between the territorial and contiguous waters of the two neighbouring states are now extended well into the Gulf.

To conclude, it must be stressed that imperial ambitions and religious antagonism were for three centuries the two main causes of the recurrent wars between the two powerful empires. The shaping of the concept of the boundary and its final demarcation necessitated another century during which the diplomacy of Great Britain and Russia played an important role with both the Ottomans and Persians.

Land boundaries are not perfect and the present boundary is no exception. Goodwill has overcome difficulties, but what of the future? Present-day economic complexities and interdependence, inequitable distribution of natural wealth, nationalist and racial consciousness all present problems whose solution here will continue to demand the most careful attention.

SELECT BIBLIOGRAPHY

ALWAN, MOHAMED, *The Iraq-Iran Frontier—A Case Study,* Washington D.C., 1960.

A. S. E.-S. (ELWELL-SUTTON, A. S.). *The Iran-Iraq Boundary Treaty 1937.* Note in *Geographical Journal,* 93, 1939, pp. 541–2.

G.R.C. (CRONE, G. R.), Two notes in *Geographical Journal,* 'The Turkish-Iranian Boundary', 91, 1938, pp. 57–59, and 92, 1938, pp. 149–50.

HAMMER, J. de, *Histoire de l'Empire Ottoman depuis son origine jusqu'à nos jours, traduit de l'allemand par J. J. Hellert,* 18 vols., Paris, 1835–43.

HUREWITZ, J. C., *Diplomacy in the Near and Middle East,* 2 vols.

Medjmouai Mouahedat (Turkish Treaty Series), 5 vols.

NORADOUNGHIAN, G., *Recueil d'Actes Internationaux de l'Empire Ottoman,* 4 vols.

RYDER, COL. C. H. D., 'The Demarcation of the Turco-Persian Boundary in 1913–14'. *Geographical Journal,* 66, 1925, pp. 227–42.

Encyclopaedia Britannica.

12

The Geographical Background of the Jordan Water Dispute

MOSHE BRAWER

One of the aspects of the Palestine Problem, which has recently taken a serious turn and attracted much international attention, is the Jordan water dispute. On the one hand Israel has completed a project which enables it to draw large quantities of water from the river, while on the other hand Syria has embarked on a project designed to cut off the headwaters of the Jordan to prevent them from reaching Israel. The dispute is basically a direct result of long-standing Arab–Israel hostility, and not a genuine clash of interests. It is, however, essential to acquaint oneself with some facts concerning the water resources and water problems involved, as well as some of the intricacies of prevailing conditions in the frontier areas through which the Jordan runs, in order to understand the issues involved. The quantities of water in dispute seem very small when compared with those involved in other similar and recent disputes, for example that between Pakistan and India, or with the dimensions of water projects in other parts of the Middle East, for example, the Nile or the Tigris and Euphrates, but they are nevertheless of considerable importance in the region through which the Jordan runs.

ISRAEL'S WATER PROBLEM

Israel suffers from a serious shortage of water. It should be remembered that well over half the area of the country has an average annual rainfall of less than 8 inches, with considerable fluctuations in the annual quantity of precipitation. Years in which the total rainfall is well below 8 inches in the southern half of the country are quite common. Thus the total rainfall at Beersheba, for example, was only 1·5 inches during the rainy season of 1962–3, though the average for that area is 8 inches. Further, the rainy season is short, not exceeding four months, and the number of rainy days is small, especially in the southern half of the country, where most of the precipitation falls in a few short rainstorms. The average annual number of rainy days in Beersheba is 27, while over about half the area of the country it is less than 20.

The rapid increase in the population of Israel over the last 18 years

226 *Essays in Political Geography*

(from about 900,000 at the end of 1948 to 2·7 million at the end of 1966) and the great expansion of irrigated areas (from about 65,000 acres in 1948 to 350,000 acres in 1966) have made great demands on the limited water resources of the country. A substantial and continuously increasing part of the funds invested in development projects has been placed at the disposal of the various national and private bodies entrusted with meeting the water requirements of the population. The great expansion in tapping, control and utilization of the various available water resources did not catch up with the rapidly increasing consumption. It was, therefore, necessary to legislate a special 'Water Law' which nationalized all water resources and imposed strict control and heavy restrictions on water consumption. A system of water rationing was instituted in agricultural as well as in industrial and household consumption. Each village or farm has its annual water ration, which it can only exceed by special permission from the Water Authority. Each household, farm, factory, workshop or similar unit must have a water meter which is read by inspectors at intervals of three months. Use of water above the ration is subject to a fine, or payment at a high rate (three times the normal price of water) for the quantity used in excess of the allocated quota. Wasting water is an offence punishable by heavy fines. A leaking tap is one form of water waste, and the owner of such a tap is liable to a fine. Water installations in flats, houses, backyards, workshops, and fields are inspected from time to time and offenders of the water economy regulations punished. A continuous propaganda campaign on the radio, in the press, on billboards, and in various other forms, under the motto 'Don't waste a single drop', is intended to make the population appreciate the scarcity of water and bring about maximum economy in its use. All these measures have considerably reduced the water consumption *per capita* especially in urban households. However, the total annual water consumption of Israel has been rising from year to year with the increase in population and the expansion of agriculture, especially in irrigated areas.

Israel is already exploiting a very high percentage of its potential water resources. In this respect it has attained one of the most advanced standards in the world. With the exception of the waters of the Jordan, the rights to which are disputed by neighbouring countries, Israel had, in 1962–3, already reached a stage where it tapped and used well over 80 per cent of its potential water resources. Almost the entire output of perennial streams and springs, as well as all available groundwater, (in the search for which nearly the whole area of the country has been

Geographical Background of the Jordan Water Dispute 227

thoroughly combed by the most modern methods and equipment), goes towards meeting the country's water requirements. Groundwater in several densely inhabited areas in the coastal plain has, in recent years, been subjected to over-pumping, a development which was unavoidable in view of three successive years (1960–3) of low rainfall. Increasing quantities of storm run-off water and flows in seasonal streams, which are few each winter and generally last for only a few days, are directed into reservoirs to augment the available water supply. The same applies to the greater part of the urban sewage which is purified in special plants and put to useful purpose in agriculture and industry. Both storm run-off waters and sewage are used increasingly to enrich groundwater resources.

The total quantities of water which Israel can hope to master and put to use, from resources entirely under its control (excluding the Jordan), is approximately 1,400 million cubic metres. This includes 450 million cubic metres from perennial streams and springs, nearly 700 million metres from groundwater, 100 million cubic metres from storm run-off waters and seasonal streams and 130 million cubic metres by purifying urban sewage. The total water consumption of the country exceeded 1,200 million cubic metres in 1962 and is expected to approach 1,500 million cubic metres in 1968. With the expected increase in population from 2·7 million at the end of 1966 to 3 million by 1970 and the planned expansion of the irrigated areas, especially in the arid south, to 400,000 acres, the consumption of water will rise within the next five to six years to 1,700–1,800 million cubic metres per annum. This requirement can be met only by drawing on a substantial part of the waters of the river Jordan. Since all other available resources are being exploited almost to the utmost, the plans to develop Israel's economy, and especially its agriculture, will very soon reach stagnation point unless the water supply can be augmented by large quantities of Jordan water.

This situation was foreseen several decades ago when the first extensive development plans for Palestine were considered. It gave rise to ideas and plans to divert the Jordan into the arid areas which lie west and south of its valley. Most famous among these is the 'Lowdermilk Plan' which was produced in the early forties of this century. Shortly after the establishment of the state of Israel, and in view of the large influx of immigrants into the country, plans were laid down for using the waters of the Jordan for development purposes. These plans, which for political, military and practical reasons underwent fundamental

228 *Essays in Political Geography*

changes, led to the building of the 'National Water Carrier', which was completed and put into operation in April 1964, for the purpose of bringing the waters of the Jordan from the shores of the Lake of Galilee to the arid plains of the northern Negev. The dispute with the neighbouring Arab states, especially Syria, over the waters of the Jordan arose as soon as work started on a diversion canal in 1953. It reached a critical stage in the spring of 1964 when the Israelis began drawing off large quantities of Jordan waters.

THE RIVER JORDAN

The Jordan is a small river, one of the smaller perennial rivers of the Middle East. Upon being faced with a rapid stream of greyish water 30 to 40 yards wide, the average tourist cannot hide his disappointment, as from reading the Bible he had imagined the Jordan to be a large, quiet and beautiful river. However, the river holds a key position in the future development of Israel and perhaps also of the neighbouring kingdom of Jordan.

The Jordan is formed by the union of three main head streams near the village of Sde Nehemia, about two and a half miles inside the extreme northern border of Israel, at 270 feet above sea level. These three head-streams are the Dan, the Banias (in Hebrew–Nahal Hermon) and the Hasbani (Nahal Snir). The course and behaviour of these head-streams have become an important factor in the development of the Jordan water dispute.

The Dan is the largest and most steady of the head-streams of the Jordan. It is fed entirely by springs, and carries only a negligible quantity of run-off water during the rainy season. The sources of the Dan are inside Israeli territory, though only within a stone's throw of the Syrian boundary, and their average annual discharge amounts to 240 million cubic metres, with only comparatively small seasonal and annual fluctuations. Thus during March–April, when the volume of discharge is highest, the average flow is 10·7 cubic metres per second, while during September, when the output is generally lowest, it is 7·3 cubic metres per second. Over the last twenty years the maximum annual discharge (1949–50)[1] was 285 million cubic metres while the minimum annual discharge (1961–2) was 217 million cubic metres. The fact that the rate of discharge of the Dan springs is high even during the summer months is of considerable importance in a region

[1] The hydrological year in Israel runs from the beginning of October.

Geographical Background of the Jordan Water Dispute 229

where the output of many springs during the height of the dry season tends generally to dwindle to a small fraction of their discharge during the rainy season. The flow of the Dan is confined to Israeli territory.

A number of springs at the foot of Mount Hermon near the Syrian village of Banias are the sources of the second head-stream, itself also called the Banias. These springs are situated about 1,200 yards in a straight line from the Israeli boundary, and the Banias flows for about a mile on Syrian territory before entering Israel a short distance south-east of the village of Dan. The average annual volume of discharge is 120 cubic metres (about half that of the Dan) of which 85 per cent is provided by springs and the rest by run-off water during the rainy season, from the south-western slopes of Mount Hermon. The seasonal and annual fluctuations in the volume of discharge of the Banias are much greater than those of the Dan. The average flow for a winter month may reach 16 cubic metres per second but at the height of the dry season this average may come down to 2 cubic metres per second. The maximum annual discharge recorded over the last twenty years was 148 million cubic metres (1944–5) while the minimum annual discharge was 81 million cubic metres (1960–1). So far, almost the entire waters of the Banias have been reaching Israel, only a very small part being used in Syria. Work on the diversion of the Banias to prevent its flow into Israel began in the summer of 1964.

The Hasbani is largely a seasonal stream. Its head is well inside Lebanon, at the north-western foot of Mount Hermon, about thirty miles from the Israeli border. The upper part of the Hasbani carries water only during rainy periods in winter. It is only from the village of Hasbaya, twelve miles from Israel, that it becomes perennial, and the quantity of discharge of its springs is small and subject to considerable seasonal fluctuations. As it approaches the Israeli boundary more perennial springs feed the Hasbani, the most important of which are the Wazan springs, some two and a half miles from the Israeli boundary. Before entering Israel, two miles west of the village of Dan, the Hasbani flows for about one and a half miles on Syrian territory, thus entering Israel from Syria and not directly from Lebanon. Some of the waters of the Hasbani are used in Lebanon, especially for irrigation purposes during the summer months; however no information on the amounts used is available.

The Hasbani brings into Israel, at its confluence with the other head-streams of the Jordan, an average annual volume of 153 cubic metres of water. Between 60 and 70 per cent of this water comes from perennial

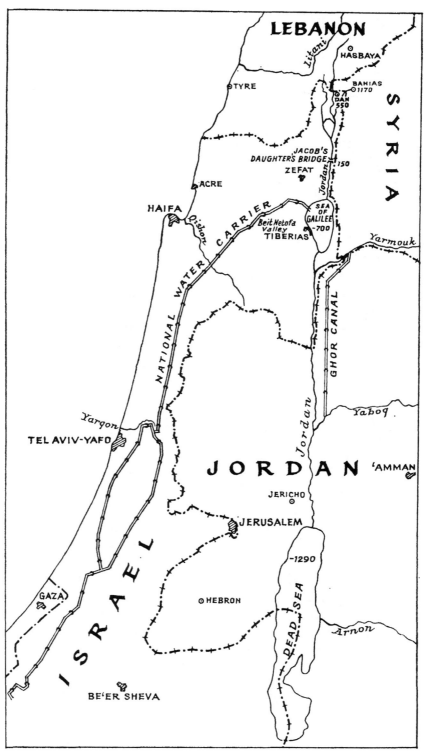

Fig. 12.1. The Jordan Basin

Geographical Background of the Jordan Water Dispute 231

springs and the rest from seasonal streams and run-off water during the winter and spring. Thus the seasonal and annual fluctuations in the volume of discharge are very great and, while during rainy periods in winter the Hasbani carries large quantities of water, its volume towards the end of the summer is very small. During a winter month with heavy rains the average monthly flow may reach 20 cubic metres per second but for September this average dwindles to a mere 1·4 cubic metres. The maximum annual discharge of water reaching the Israeli border for the last twenty years was 236 million cubic metres (1947–8) while the figure for the minimum year (1960–1) was 63·5 million cubic metres. Works to prevent the flow of most of the Hasbani waters into Israel were due to start in Lebanon early in 1965.

Another head-stream of the Jordan which comes from Lebanon is the Bureighit, but its volume is small and much of its water is used for irrigation in the Ayoun valley in Lebanon. It carries very small quantities of water into Israel and these only during the winter months. It contributes towards the waters of the Jordan only an average of 5 million cubic metres annually. *Thus the Jordan starts on its way, at the confluence of its head-streams, with an average annual volume of approximately 520 million cubic metres of water.*[1]

The northernmost part of the Jordan valley is known as the Huleh valley. Up to 1955 the shallow lake Huleh, about five square miles in area, together with adjoining swamps, occupied most of the southern part of this valley. Some two miles below the confluence of its head-streams the Jordan entered and got lost in the Huleh swamps and lake. Here a number of springs and seasonal streams, coming down from the highlands bordering on the valley in the east and west, brought into the Jordan over 100 million cubic metres of water but the net gain of the river on its emergence from lake Huleh, at the southern end of the valley, was small, owing to heavy losses of water by evaporation. The lake and the swamps were completely drained in the mid 1950s and turned into rich farm land. This resulted also in the saving of about 60 million cubic metres of water previously lost by evaporation. At present the Jordan flows through most of the Huleh valley in two artificial canals which also drain the springs and seasonal streams of this valley, and provide water for irrigating it. These merge later into a single canal which leads the Jordan out of the Huleh valley. Near Jacob's Daughters' Bridge (Gesher Benot Yaakov) the Jordan re-enters

[1] Some of the waters of these head-streams are used by villages, in the extreme north of Israel, before they reach the Jordan.

232 *Essays in Political Geography*

its natural channel, and from here to the Lake of Galilee it is a torrential stream flowing in a narrow ravine.

The slope gradient of this section of the river is considerable. At Jacob's Daughters' Bridge the normal surface of the river is about 150 feet above sea level while the surface of the Lake of Galilee is nearly 700 feet below sea level. The river thus descends nearly 850 feet over a distance of ten miles. Over its entire course of 180 miles from the neighbourhood of Dan (Sde Nehemia) to the Dead Sea the river descends about 1,600 feet; thus more than half this total descent takes place over the short section just above the Lake of Galilee. This section has, therefore, become an obvious choice for a hydro-electric power station and other development projects.

The Lake of Galilee, with a maximum depth of 160 feet, is a thirteen-mile-long fresh-water lake covering an area of sixty-five square miles. Its average volume of water is 4,600 million cubic metres. The Jordan brings into the lake an annual average of 580 million cubic metres of water, which is about 50 million cubic metres more than before the completion of the drainage of Lake Huleh and its swamps. Numerous springs rise on the bottom of the lake, the waters of some having a high chlorine content. Seasonal streams also bring large quantities of water into the lake during the rainy season, but with clear skies on almost three hundred days in the year and high temperatures during eight months, the average for July and August being 86°F., loss of water by evaporation from the surface of the lake is very great. In the total balance the Jordan emerges at the southern end of the lake with a net loss of 30–40 million cubic metres of water. Its average annual volume of discharge at the exit from the Lake of Galilee was 515 million cubic metres before the draining of Lake Huleh, and has risen now to an average of about 550 million cubic metres. It is perhaps worth mentioning here that this quantity of 550 million cubic metres represents in fact the maximum average annual total that Israel can ever hope to draw from the Jordan. This quantity of water equals the volume of discharge of the Nile at Aswan in nineteen hours during an average September day, or the discharge of the Tigris over forty-five hours, on the average, in April or May. The waters of the Jordan enter the Lake of Galilee with a salinity content of 80 milligrams per litre, but on leaving the lake at its southern end this salinity content has risen to nearly 300 milligrams per litre,[1] which makes the water useless for irrigation in the citrus belt and for the growing of many plants. The

[1] In 1963, following three successive dry years, it rose to 360 mg. per litre.

Geographical Background of the Jordan Water Dispute 233

salinity problem is being solved by capturing the main springs at the bottom of the lake, which yield salty water, and leading them out of the lake through special pipes, so that they do not mix with the water of the lake.

Five miles south of the Lake of Galilee the Jordan receives from the east its largest tributary, the Yarmouk, which drains much of south-western Syria. The Yarmouk almost doubles the annual volume of the Jordan, into which it brings an average annual quantity of 480 million cubic metres of water. However, the Yarmouk is subject to extreme seasonal fluctuations, for although it carries much water in winter and spring it is only a small and slow brook from May, or even April, to November. In February, which is generally the month of maximum discharge, the Yarmouk may carry as much as 40 per cent of its total annual flow, but in each of the summer and autumn months when water is most needed in this region, it carries only 3–4 per cent of its annual discharge. The Kingdom of Jordan has already put into operation the first stage of a plan to store and divert the waters of the Yarmouk into the Ghor Canal for use in irrigation projects in the arid lower Jordan valley.

From its confluence with the Yarmouk to its entry into the Dead Sea, sixty miles further south, the Jordan meanders extensively through thick beds of soft calcareous marls which cover the arid lower Jordan valley. Here it receives numerous tributaries, the great majority of them seasonal streams (*wadis*) which carry water only on a limited number of days each winter. The few perennial tributaries are small and contribute very little towards the total volume of water which the Jordan carries into the Dead Sea; indeed they do not even make up for the loss of water, through evaporation and dissipation, which the Jordan sustains in its lower course. The Jordan provides the Dead Sea with an average annual quantity of nearly 1,000 million cubic metres of water, though this average covers considerable seasonal and annual fluctuations. The maximum annual discharge recorded over the last thirty years near the entrance to the Dead Sea was 1,650 million cubic metres in 1942–3, whereas the minimum was 648 million cubic metres in 1933–4. All the waters which the Jordan and a number of other streams and springs bring into the Dead Sea are lost through evaporation, which is very extensive, from the surface of this sea. Besides being the lowest basin on earth this is also an exceptionally hot and dry region.

All development projects concerning the Jordan are planned to harness the river or its tributaries above its junction with the Yarmouk.

234 *Essays in Political Geography*

Israel needs the waters of the Jordan mainly in order to irrigate the northern part of the dry Negev and to supply the requirements of the growing population of that region. As the area in which the Jordan waters are most wanted is some 300 to 800 feet above sea level, it would suit Israel best to draw these waters as high up the Jordan valley as possible, or at least before the river plunges into that part of the valley which is several hundred feet below sea level. However, before we deal with the Israeli project for the waters of the Jordan, let us look at the position of the boundaries in the frontier areas through which the river runs, and the problems which they raise.

BOUNDARY PROBLEMS

The Jordan being the only comparatively large perennial water source within the borders of the Holy land it obviously became a major factor in any modern plan to develop the country, or parts of it, whether agriculturally by means of irrigation or industrially through the use of electricity. As far back as 1905 an engineer by the name of N. Wilbush, who spent about a year studying the Jordan and its valley, produced a plan to exploit the waters of the river for the production of hydro-electric power and for large-scale irrigation. He realized that in the long run the Jordan itself could not solve the water problems of Palestine, and suggested that large quantities of water be drawn artificially into the Jordan from the well-watered area of southern Lebanon, by diverting the river Litani into the Hasbani head-stream of the Jordan. In this way the volume of water in the Jordan would be more than doubled. This idea was subsequently brought forward several times in other plans, and was last included in 1955 in a general project for the full utilization of the waters of the Jordan region produced by the American engineer, John S. Cotton. The Lebanon which, with its comparatively high rainfall, is amply provided with water resources, still utilizes only some 12 per cent of the waters of the river Litani, which has a larger annual discharge than the Jordan, leaving the rest to flow into the Mediterranean.

Some of the development projects involving the Jordan produced in the years preceding and immediately after the First World War attracted the attention of senior officials in the British administration, established in Palestine after the war. They were quick to realize the importance of the Jordan for the future development of the country. When the question arose of defining and demarcating the boundary

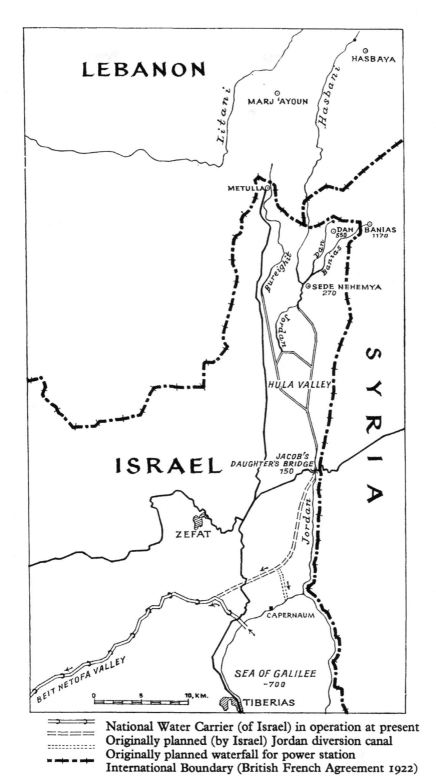

→→→ National Water Carrier (of Israel) in operation at present
= = = Originally planned (by Israel) Jordan diversion canal
.... Originally planned waterfall for power station
▬·▬·▬ International Boundary (British French Agreement 1922)

Fig. 12.2. The Upper Jordan Valley

236 *Essays in Political Geography*

between Palestine under the British Mandate, and both Lebanon and Syria, under the French Mandate, the British refused the convenience of having much of the boundary run along the course of the Jordan and through the two northern lakes of Huleh and Galilee, although this would have been an easily recognizable physical boundary which would have saved much demarcation work. Instead, the British insisted on including in Palestine as much as possible of the head-waters of the Jordan, and both banks of the river itself, as well as the whole of lake Huleh and the Lake of Galilee, and were prepared to make concessions to the French in other parts of the Middle East in order to secure this requirement. The British–French Boundary Agreement between Syria and Palestine signed early in 1922[1] and the demarcations of the boundary accordingly achieved this aim. This remained (and remains, theoretically at least, to the present day) the boundary, between Lebanon and Syria on the one hand and Israel on the other, after the respective departures of the French and the British from these countries.

It was agreed in 1922 to have both the springs of the Dan and the Banias within Palestine. The French, however, insisted that by placing the sources of the Banias in Palestine an important road leading from south-west Syria to Beirut would be cut. This brought about the shifting of the boundary originally agreed upon by some 1,200 yards to the south-west in favour of Syria, thereby resulting in the existing situation in which the springs of the Banias are within Syrian territory a short distance from the Israeli boundary, though the British refused to accept this position as final. The above-mentioned agreement states: 'The British Government shall be free to re-open the question of re-adjusting the frontier between Banias and Metallah. . . .'[2] Thus, of the three head-waters of the Jordan, only the Dan, the largest and most important, remained entirely within Palestine and is now, therefore, within Israel.

From the vicinity of Banias southwards the boundary runs along the lower slopes of the highlands which rise east of the Huleh valley, leaving the entire area of the valley inside Israel. Before Lake Huleh was drained the boundary ran 200–500 yards east of the lake, so that even its eastern shores were in Israel. From Lake Huleh to the Lake of Galilee the boundary runs a short distance, varying from 50 to 400 yards, east of the river Jordan and almost parallel to it. (Fig. 12.2). The

---

[1] The report was published by H.M. Stationery Office, Cmd. 1910, London, 1923. [2] *Ibid.*, p. 7.

Geographical Background of the Jordan Water Dispute 237

position of the boundary here, as well as further south along the north-eastern shores of the Lake of Galilee, makes it quite obvious that the intention of the boundary makers in 1922 was to grant Palestine full legal ownership of the Jordan and its lakes so that there should be no necessity to obtain the consent of any other country for any project to utilize the waters of the river. The narrow strip east of the Jordan was never in fact controlled by the British Mandatory Authorities, nor has it been by the Israelis, but the boundary definitely placed both banks of the Jordan inside Palestine and now, therefore, inside Israel. Since the Palestine War of 1949 the Syrians and Israelis actually face each other across the section of the Jordan between the Huleh valley and the Lake of Galilee, despite the fact that this area was made into a demilitarized zone in the armistice agreement signed between both countries in 1949. Thus along this section the river has formed the actual separation line between Syria and Israel ever since 1949.

Along the north-eastern shores of the Lake of Galilee, from the entry of the Jordan into the lake to a point called Messifer, about halfway down the eastern shore, the boundary runs along the shore parallel to and at a distance of 10 metres from the edge of the lake, so that a narrow 10-metre wide strip of land east of the lake became Palestinian (now Israeli) territory. The British–French agreement of 1922 laid down that the position of the boundary at 10 metres from the edge of the lake should be maintained 'following any alterations of level consequent on the raising of its water owing to the construction of a dam on the Jordan. . . .'[1] This actually means that, should the lake rise, the boundary will be pushed further east so that the distance of 10 metres between the edge of the lake and the boundary is preserved. There is no provision in this agreement for the case of the fall and shrinkage of the lake, which is what is going to happen when the Israeli National Water Carrier comes into full operation. This is why the Israelis press for a new and full demarcation of the boundary on the north-eastern shores of the lake before the substantial fall in the surface of the lake takes place, while the Syrians refuse to allow such a demarcation.

From Messifer southwards the boundary turns eastwards away from the shores of the Lake of Galilee into the neighbouring highlands, including in Palestine (now Israel) a strip of land 1,500–2,500 yards wide on the east of the lake, down to its southern end. This slightly wider strip of Israeli territory continues further south to the right (northern) bank of the river Yarmouk, so that the area east of the Jordan

[1] Cmd. 1910, London, 1923.

238   *Essays in Political Geography*

between the southern shores of the Lake of Galilee and the lower course of the Yarmouk is Israeli territory. (Fig. 12.1)

For its last five miles before its junction with the Jordan the Yarmouk forms the northernmost part of the boundary between Israel and the Kingdoms of Jordan. From the confluence of the Jordan and the Yarmouk the Israeli–Jordanian boundary runs for about forty miles downstream along the Jordan before turning westwards, thus leaving the river entirely inside Jordanian territory down to its entry into the Dead Sea. It should, however, be borne in mind that until 1946 the area of the Kingdom of Jordan was subject to the same British Mandatory rule as was Palestine, so that the lower Yarmouk and the full length of the Jordan were both under the same supreme political authority.

The Palestine War, the establishment of the state of Israel, containing over 76 per cent of the area of British Palestine, and the armistice agreements between Israel and the neighbouring Arab states together created a new situation. The fact that the Syrians actually hold small strips of Palestinian territory in the upper Jordan valley has brought sections of the eastern bank of the Jordan and shores of the Lake of Galilee under their control. Further, the Syrians are not prepared to accept the arrangements of the British–French boundary agreement of 1922, which was designed to keep Syria away from the Jordan and its lakes. Moreover, Syria does not recognize the state of Israel and is hostile towards it, and the greater part of the lower Jordan is now entirely within the kingdom of Jordan, whose attitude towards Israel is similar to that of Syria. All attempts to bring Israel and its Arab neighbours to an agreed division of the Jordan waters or to a common plan for their utilization have so far failed. In 1955 a scheme, the *Unified Water Plan for the utilization of the Jordan–Yarmouk River System,* was evolved by a special representative of the United States government, Mr Eric Johnson, who acted as mediator between Israel and its Arab neighbours. The principal feature of this scheme, which is now known as the 'Johnson Plan', was the equitable distribution of the waters of the Jordan and the Yarmouk among the riparian states. After prolonged negotiations the scheme was approved by both Arab and Israeli technical experts, but was then rejected on political grounds. According to this plan, Israel was entitled to 40 per cent of the combined waters of the Jordan and the Yarmouk, that is about 400 million cubic metres per year.

Geographical Background of the Jordan Water Dispute 239

ISRAEL'S JORDAN PROJECT

The original Israeli plans for the utilization of the waters of the Jordan chose the vicinity of Jacob's Daughters' Bridge as the starting point of the diversion canal. (Fig. 12.2) This point, about 150 feet above sea level, is just below the exit of the Jordan from the Huleh valley, where its volume is increased by the waters of some springs and seasonal streams, and where the terrain west of the river presents less difficulties than further up or down the river. From here the greater part of the water was to have been raised, by means of a large pumping station, about 350 feet to the Beith Netofa valley, which is 500 feet above sea level. The Beith Netofa valley was to have been turned into a big reservoir for the storing of Jordan water during the winter rainy season when water consumption is low, to be used in summer when consumption is high. Thus the water stored during the winter in the Beith Netofa reservoir would, during the summer, have augmented the quantities then directly available from the Jordan. From the Beith Netofa valley the water would have run, by gravitational flow, through a number of tunnels and a 100-mile long pipe (108 inches in diameter) to the northern fringe of the Negev, to be distributed from there in much smaller pipes to various parts of this arid region.

A much smaller part of the Jordan water than that raised to the Beith Netofa valley was to have been diverted from the vicinity of the Jacob's Daughters' Bridge into another canal which would have run down to the Lake of Galilee. This canal was to be graded in such a manner that a waterfall, nearly 600 feet high, would have been formed just before it reached the Lake of Galilee. As mentioned above, there is a difference in height of 850 feet between Jacob's Daughters' Bridge and the Lake of Galilee. The electricity generated by this waterfall could have provided not only the power for raising the waters of the Jordan to the Beith Netofa valley, but also the requirements of the towns and villages of eastern Galilee. Thus the Jordan would have provided not only the water for irrigating the dry south but also the power to pump the water to its destination. Work on this plan started in September 1953, but had to be abandoned in view of strong Syrian objections. Force was used to prevent the building of the diversion canal in the vicinity of Jacob's Daughters' Bridge, or at any other point between the Huleh valley and the Lake of Galilee. After this had resulted in a number of serious military clashes the matter was brought to the United Nations Security Council which in view of the danger of

240 *Essays in Political Geography*

further hostilities between Syria and Israel, resolved that the work in the demilitarized zone in the neighbourhood of Jacob's Daughters' Bridge, should be stopped.

Faced with the failure of the conciliation efforts by the United States government's 'Johnson Plan' and the approach of a serious water shortage brought about by the rapid growth of the population and the expansion of the economy, Israel was forced to introduce basic changes in its original plans and produce a modified project which would be much less exposed to interference from Syria. Work on this new project started in 1956 and reached completion in the spring of 1964. In this project, known as the *National Waters Carrier*, the waters of the Jordan are pumped from the north-western corner of the Lake of Galilee, about four miles inside Israeli territory, to the Beith Netofa valley. The fact that the surface of the Lake of Galilee is nearly 700 feet below sea level entails the raising of the Jordan waters nearly 1,200 feet to the Beith Netofa valley, as against 350 feet under the original project. The present Beith Netofa reservoir is only a small operational one, as by damming the southern outlet of the Lake of Galilee it was made into a reservoir for the winter flow of the Jordan. From the Beith Netofa valley the water runs, as originally planned, down to the Negev. Under the present project no electric power is derived from the Jordan so that the pumps which raise the Jordan waters are operated by oil. Thus the water drawn from the Jordan is at present almost three times as costly as it would have been under the original plan. Further, the water pumped from the north-western corner of the Lake of Galilee has a much higher chlorine content than the waters of the Jordan at Jacob's Daughters' Bridge.

The only advantage of the new project over the original one is that total loss through evaporation will be much smaller. By turning the Beith Netofa valley into a reservoir for the waters of the Jordan, substantial quantities of water would have been lost through evaporation and seepage into the ground. Now that the Lake of Galilee is to perform this function the loss will be avoided, as by storing large additional quantities of water in the lake, evaporation from its surface will not increase. In the Lake of Galilee it will also be possible to store much larger quantities of water than in the Beith Netofa valley, and to store not only from the rainy season to the dry season but also from a good year to a bad year. However, the high cost involved in operating the National Water Carrier in its present form, combined with the problem of salinity, outweigh the advantages of the use of the Lake of Galilee

Geographical Background of the Jordan Water Dispute 241

as a reservoir for the Jordan waters. It is therefore hoped to return to the original plan when the political situation will permit.

When operating at full capacity, the pumping station on the shores of the Lake of Galilee will draw about 350 million cubic metres of Jordan water per year. This, together with 1,400 million cubic metres which Israel hopes to master by exploiting to the utmost all its other water resources, should meet the requirements of the increasing population and expanding agriculture up to 1974–5. By then it is hoped to overcome the difficulties of sea water desalination. Work on a common U.S.–Israeli project to solve the economic and scientific problems of desalination of sea water was begun in 1964.

It should be pointed out that, of the four countries of the Jordan drainage basin, only the kingdom of Jordan and Israel are in real need of the Jordan waters. Lebanon is a well-watered country and has at its disposal water resources much in excess of its maximum requirements. Of its potential water resources, other than the Jordan (Hasbani), it is at present exploiting about 25 per cent. Syria has substantial water resources, only a small part of which are fully exploited, east of the Anti-Lebanon and Hermon highlands, in the neighbourhood of the region of the upper Jordan. It still has a long way to go before it will require most of the potential water resources, other than the Jordan (Banias), of its south-western region, which borders upon Israel. The kingdom of Jordan is taking its share of Jordan water by drawing continuously increasing quantities of water from the Yarmouk. When its Yarmouk project reaches completion it will have diverted for its own use the entire flow of the Yarmouk which, on the average, constituted 45 per cent of the total discharge of the lower Jordan, though a substantial part of this water will be lost by evaporation and seepage. The kingdom of Jordan is still far from tapping efficiently many other, though much smaller, water resources, and it was estimated in 1964 that the kingdom of Jordan utilized only 30–40 per cent of its potential water resources other than those of the Jordan.

Full use of the Jordan for irrigation and production of electricity can be achieved only by the co-operation of all the states of the Jordan basin. Through such co-operation, these states could benefit much more than by the individual projects already in operation or planned for the future. Thus, by the diversion of the Yarmouk into the Lake of Galilee, which would become the storage reservoir for the waters of Yarmouk, the kingdom of Jordan could utilize 25–30 per cent more water from this source than it could get from the present Yarmouk

242   Essays in Political Geography

project. The individual projects of the riparian states entail considerable waste of water and potential energy, which this arid region definitely cannot afford. Further, the expense involved in building the individual schemes is far higher than a common project would cost, so that by doing it individually more is invested and less gained from the Jordan than if all concerned had undertaken to co-operate. Thus it is by co-operation and not by competition that the states of the Jordan basin can get the river to make its maximum contribution towards the solution of their water and energy problems.

The factors underlying the Jordan water dispute are, as mentioned, primarily political ones, and can only be fully appreciated against the general background of the Palestine problem and the state of Arab–Israeli relations.

SELECT BIBLIOGRAPHY

AVITZUR, S., *Water Power in Israel*, Tel Aviv, 1964.

GOLDSCHMIDT, M. J., The Flow of the Jordan River at Allenby Bridge (unpublished), Jerusalem, 1947.

Hydrological Annual Reports, Government of Israel – Ministry of Agriculture, Tel Aviv, 1950–63.

IONIDES, M. G. and BLAKE, G. S., *Report on the Water Resources of Transjordan*, London, 1939.

Israel's Water Problem, Geography Department, Hebrew University, Jerusalem, 1956.

Israel's Water Projects, Tahal (Israel's Water Authority), Tel Aviv, 1963.

OREN, O. H., *Physical and Chemical Characteristics of Lake Tiberias*, Tahal (Israel's Water Authority), Tel Aviv, 1957.

PRUSHANSKY, Y., *Water in Israel*, Jerusalem, 1963.

SCHATTNER, I., *The Lower Jordan Valley*, Jerusalem, 1963.

Water Measurements 1938–1947, Government of Palestine – Water Commissioner, Jerusalem, 1947.

13

The Case of an Indeterminate Boundary:
Algeria – Morocco ANTHONY S. REYNER

French occupation of Algeria, which began in 1830, was not part of a systematic plan for a North African Empire. France vacillated for several years before she began colonization along the coast and pacification in the interior. Moroccan raids continued until 1844, when Marshal Bugeaud's victory on the shores of the Isly led to the Tangier Convention which intended to fix the border of French Algeria with the sovereign Sultanate of Morocco.[1] Before 1844, no defined lines comparable to boundaries between Western nation-states existed in North Africa. Only natural features or zones of fluctuating width separated traditional areas. Such Western concepts as country or nation hardly applied to Morocco in the course of its long history as an independent state.

Morocco's temporal-spiritual rulers – Berbers, converted to Islam and intermarried with Arabs – never felt the necessity for accurate delimitation. Their early treaties with Europeans concerned trade, not territory. The Sultans' domain was a community of believers which was neither static nor exclusive, rather than a definite territory. Morocco's neighbours were of similar origin, and of the same religion. Everyone's first concern was to expand *dar al Islam*, the world of Muslin faith, at the expense of *dar al harb*, the world of Infidels. At times they received help from *dar al solh*, the tributary non-Muslim peoples.[2]

EVOLUTION OF THE BOUNDARY

Unfortunately, the first effort to establish territorial limits with Morocco was restricted to a vague statement that 'the boundary should remain the same as when Algeria was under Turkish domination.' Conflicts

---

[1] A. G. de Lapradelle, 'La déclaration concernant le Maroc', in *Revue générale de droit international publique* (Paris, 1904), p. 719. The French text of the Tangier Convention, published in the *Bulletin des Lois*, 1844, No. 1158, and ratified on 26 October 1844, can be found in *British and Foreign State Papers*, Vol. 32, p. 1202.

[2] A. S. Reyner, 'Morocco's international boundaries: a factual background', *The Journal of Modern African Studies*, 1, 1963, p. 313.

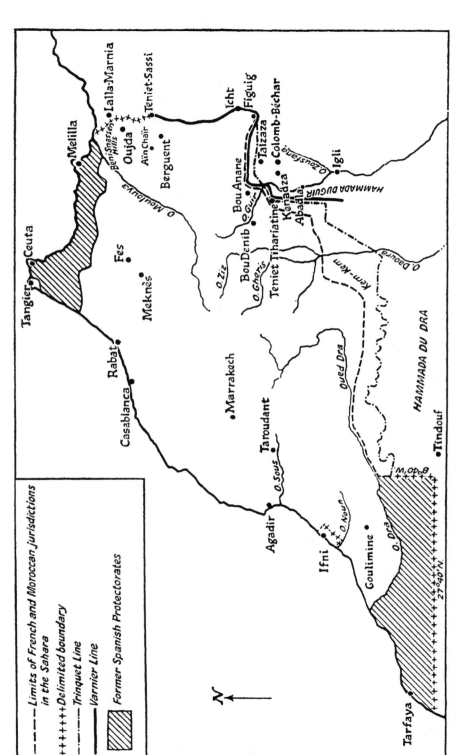

Fig. 13.1. Boundaries of Morocco

The Case of an Indeterminate Boundary 245

continued and required a more definite delimitation. As a result, the 1845 Treaty of Delimitation signed at Lalla-Marnia precisely described 165 kilometres (102·5 miles) of boundary from the mouth of the Oued Adjeroud (Oued Kiss) on the Mediterranean to the hill of Teniet-el-Sassi, located at approximately 34° 06′ N. and 01° 38′ W. in the Saharan Atlas.[1]

In addition to the water courses of the Oued Adjeroud and specified tributaries, the boundary followed or connected fixed cultural and geographical features. Most are even today easily identified on medium- and large-scale topographical maps. The boundary traverses an area which is fairly densely settled by farmers north of the Tlemcen hills, and only sparsely populated by sheep-raising nomads on their southern slopes. As a supplement to the physical description of the segment 'from the sea to the beginning of the desert', the 1845 Treaty enumerated tribes under Algerian and Moroccan administrations.

In the desert to the south and south-west of Teniet-el-Sassi, the Treaty attempted to define the two sovereignties by authority over enumerated tribes, rather than by territorial delimitation.[2] Apart from dividing specified 'Kessours' between France and Morocco, the 1845 Treaty actually re-established a frontier zone instead of creating a boundary line.[3]

As French control spread southward into the Sahara, clashes with tribes under allegiance to Morocco led to a re-examination of the frontier question. Local French officials declared the concept of a 'frontier' indefensible. As a result, on 20 July 1901, a protocol signed in Paris extended the boundary southward from Teniet-el-Sassi (Teniet-ess

---

[1] *Cf.* Art. 3. The French text of this Treaty of Delimitation, ratified on 6 August 1845 at Tangier, is reprinted in *British and Foreign State Papers*, Vol. 34, p. 1287.

The French Ministry of War chose the mouth of the Oued Adjeroud (or Oued Kiss) instead of that of the Moulouya, which had been the traditional eastern frontier of Morocco. Once the border between the Tingitanian and Caesarean Province of Roman Mauritania, the Moulouya had subsequently been the scene of conflict between Tlemcen and Maghreb al Aqsa (Morocco) for the possession of Oujda. Between 1529 and 1830, the Moulouya had separated the empires of Morocco and Turkey. Cf. Henri Terrasse, *Histoire du Maroc*, Casablanca, 1950, II.

[2] The dependent tribes of Morocco were the M'béia, Beni-Guil, Hamian-Djenba, Eumour-Sahra, and the Ouled-Sidi-el-Cheikh-el-Gharaba, while those of France were the Ouled-Sidi-el-Cheikh-el-Cheraga and all of the Hamian except the Hamian-Djenba.

[3] Ksour, plural of Ksar – a fortified desert village. The villages of Yiche (Iche or Ich) and Figuigue (Figuig) were in Morocco, while Ain-Safra, S'fissifa, Assla, Tiout, El-Abiad, and Bou-Semghoune were in Algeria.

246 Essays in Political Geography

Assi) to Guir (Ghir) south of (Colomb-) Béchar.[1] This protocol provided for the establishment of military and customs posts along the limits of territory controlled by both powers. In the central section, the boundary was defined again by tribal areas rather than by geographical features. As a result, it is virtually impossible to trace the 1901 line from Teniet-el-Sassi to Figuig even on detailed maps. Official cartographers, however, have been remarkably consistent in representing this vaguely defined segment.[2]

The immense difficulties involved in the establishment of customs and guard posts in this inhospitable area led, on 20 April 1902, to an 'Accord . . . between the Chiefs of the two Missions . . . charged . . . by the Protocol . . . (of) 20 July 1901'. France and Morocco then consolidated their authority in the territory from the mouth of the Oued Kiss to Figuig and abrogated the provisions of the 1901 Protocol requiring guard and customs posts south of Teniet-el-Sassi with the exception of Figuig. This Accord created areas of joint authority along the boundary, thus returning to the 'frontier' concept of the nineteenth century. A second Protocol signed in Algiers on 7 May 1902 elaborated on this concept.[3]

Unfortunately, conflicts continued and French military forces occupied Oujda and Beni Snassen in the north as well as Aïn Chaïr, Bou Anane, Boudenib and Berguent in the south-east. The 'Accord relative to the Frontier Region', of 4 March 1910, returned these posts to Morocco and definitely established French control over the territory of the Doui Menia and Oulad Djerir in the Colomb-Béchar–Kenadsa–Abadla region. Varnier, the French High Commissioner in Oujda, was entrusted with the execution of this Accord. He recognized the difficulties in the Figuig–Colomb-Béchar area, where tribal limits were used

[1] Protocol of Paris (Execution of Treaty of 1845; South-west Algeria) was ratified on 16 December 1902. British and Foreign State Papers, 101: 458.

[2] From Teniet-Sassi the boundary followed a straight line south-south-westward for approximately sixteen miles before turning south-south-eastward for an additional eight miles. The extension southward followed cultural rather than natural features to the Oued Bou Arjam south of the Bab Brazzi Basin. From here, the boundary continued along the Oued Bou Kalkal south-eastward for approximately twenty miles before falling into a geometric pattern. A series of straight lines was utilized as far as Iche which was closely circumscribed. South of Iche, on to Figuig, the boundary was highly irregular but followed physical features exclusively, e.g., the ridge of the Djebel Abiene plus several *wadi* courses. The next major segment, the Colomb-Béchar–Kenadsa–Abadla salient, was defined according to the Protocol by (a) the tribal limits of the Doui Menia and Oulad Djerir, (b) the Oued Telzaza (Talzaza), and (c) the Oued Guir to a point 15 kilometres north of the village (Ksar) of Igli.

[3] *Cf. British and Foreign State Papers*, 101: 430 and 434.

The Case of an Indeterminate Boundary 247

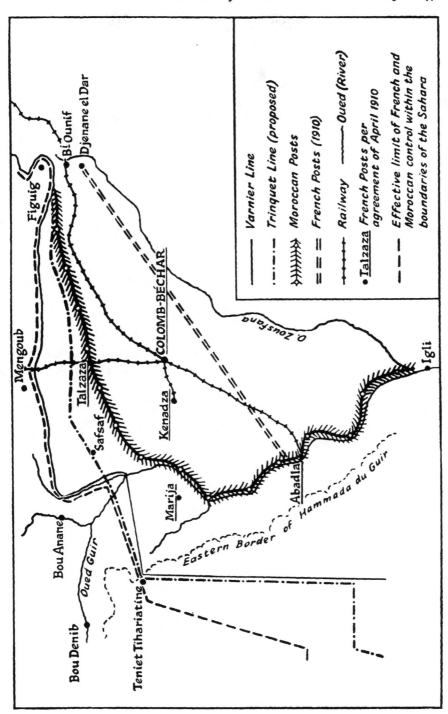

Fig. 13.2. Boundary South-West of Figuig

248 *Essays in Political Geography*

for boundary delimitation, and endeavoured to create a 'realistic' line. His studies led to the creation of the 'Varnier Line' which was sanctioned by a French Ministerial Decree of 21 March 1912.[1]

From Teniet-el-Sassi to south of Figuig, the 'Varnier Line' and the 1901 Protocol boundary were identical. From Figuig westward, however, the 'Varnier Line' was established to the north and west of the former boundary, thereby adding several hundred square miles to Algeria. According to *La Semaine en Algérie* the 'Varnier Line' passed approximately 4 kilometres south of Ain Chaïr to Dar Jorf Krolfi and to Teniet Tihariatine. Most of the Hammada du Guir was thus included in Algeria. On 26 March 1914, however, the Council of Ministers amended the boundary in this area by reducing the limits of the 'Cercle de Colomb-Béchar' to the eastern border of the Hammada du Guir.[2]

The 'Treaty of Protection of 1912' merely referred to the 'natural frontiers' of Morocco and did not affect the established boundaries. Furthermore, no agreements existed for the remaining segment between the Hammada du Guir and Spanish Sahara. In 1938, the so-called 'Project Trinquet', while recognizing the 'natural limits' of Morocco as being the Oued-Noun, Djebel Bani, and the Kem-Kem plateau, proposed a line much further to the south. According to this plan the boundary was to pass south of the Oued Dra and the Kem-Kem (south-western section of the Hammada du Guir) to include certain tribes (Aït Yribel, Ida, *etc.*) in Morocco. The French government rejected this proposition. The Moroccan government, nonetheless, subsequently seized upon it as a basis for Moroccan claims to the Sahara.

In spite of this lack of boundary definition in the south-west, most French sources tacitly admit that the southern border of Morocco stopped at the north cliff of the Hammada du Dra. It is interesting to note that French maps of Morocco used this boundary as the 'limite de la zone de sécurité'. In contrast, French maps of Algeria showed the boundary along the northern cliff of the Oued Dra. (The Franco-Spanish treaty of 1912 placing the 'Southern Protectorate of Morocco' under Spanish administration did establish the boundary between the two protectorates along the Oued Dra from the Atlantic to Algeria.)

In addition to this discrepancy in the representation of the administrative boundary in the south and south-west, there have also been variations shown in the south-east. As pointed out, the 'Varnier Line' originally placed the greater part of the Hammada du Guir in Algeria

---

[1] *Revue générale de droit international public*, 17, Paris, 1904, p. 43d.

[2] *La Semaine en Algérie*, No. 48, p. 31.

in 1912. By 1914 the limit was moved eastward to the eastern edge of the Hammada. Again in 1950 the 'Varnier Line' was moved westward close to, but not coinciding with, the 1912 position. For example, the original 'Varnier Line' passed 4 kilometres south of Aïn Chaïr. The last French maps showed the line much farther to the south. Moreover, the Algerian 'Oued Dra Line' has had several versions for the section between the Oued Dra and the 'Varnier Line'. Further, French mapping authorities were highly inconsistent and used both the 1901 Protocol boundary and the 'Varnier Line', for example, as recently as 1953.[1]

THE CHARACTERISTICS OF THE BOUNDARY

The Algeria–Morocco boundary has been demarcated from the Mediterranean south to Teniet-el-Sassi, a distance of some 102 miles (165 kilometres), to the apparent satisfaction of both governments. The 1845 Treaty is the basis for this segment.

From Teniet-el-Sassi southward, the boundary was created by the 1901 Protocol of Paris supported in part by the supplemental Accords of 20 April 1902 and 7 May 1902. Modifications (the so-called 'Varnier Line') were unilaterally carried out in 1912, 1914, and 1950 and perhaps at other dates. This delimited sector should be considered as comprising two segments, namely (a) Teniet-el-Sassi–Figuig (about 200 miles) and (b) Figuig – southward to the Oued Guir about 205 miles. Each of these will be considered briefly.

(a) While Morocco has stated that no fixed boundary exists south of Teniet-el-Sassi, claims for a 'Greater Morocco' generally follow the 1901 Protocol boundary as far south as Figuig. Morocco may not accept the present boundary in a *de jure* sense, but no claims to 'Algerian territory' appear to have been advanced in opposition to the boundary.

(b) South of Figuig, however, the situation is most complicated. The Algerians claim Moroccan agreement to the 1901 Protocol boundary and the 'acceptance' for forty years of the 'Varnier Line' as the French did before them. The French were not consistent in their 'acceptance' of either line. Both lines appear on fairly recent official maps. Of course, Moroccan claims to the Sahara are so extensive as to render academic any discussion of the merits and validity of the two lines.

The final segment of the Algeria–Morocco boundary, approximately 425 miles, has apparently no legal basis. French sources indicated the

[1] Government Maps of Morocco and Algeria, Nos. 28394 and 28395.

Fig. 13.3. Greater Morocco

The Case of an Indeterminate Boundary 251

'natural limits of Morocco' by the Hammada du Dra, the Kem-Kem, and the Hammada du Guir referred to as 'limite de la zone de sécurité'. At the same time, official French maps of Algeria showed the Oued Dra as the boundary.

In view of these discrepancies and Morocco's territorial claims which extend as far as the Senegal River, it was not altogether surprising that Morocco invaded the Algerian Sahara immediately following the departure of the French in July 1962. Within a year, skirmishing along the indeterminate desert frontier and elsewhere developed into a full-scale war.

In the autumn of 1963, the Organization for African Unity persuaded Algeria and Morocco to sign a cease-fire agreement. Since then, the Organization has endeavoured to bring about a settlement of territorial disputes which have disturbed the peace in the western Sahara and hindered the development of its rich mineral resources. To date, however, in spite of some progress, a definitive boundary between Algeria and Morocco still remains an ideal rather than a reality.[1]

[1] In 1964, following the withdrawal by both powers, Algeria and Morocco re-established railway connexion along the Mediterranean.

14

Politics and Transportation
The Problems of West Africa's Land-locked States
DAVID HILLING

In his Presidential address to the Institute of British Geographers in 1960, Professor W. G. East, talking on 'The geography of land-locked states', made reference to only one potential African example, the Central African Federation. It is a measure of the rapidity with which the political map of Africa has changed that in western Africa there are now five land-locked nations, namely the republics of Mali, Upper Volta, Niger, Chad and Central Africa.

The independent nations of West Africa can be divided into two groups. First, there are those which crystallized around the original European coastal 'colonies' such as Gambia, Senegal, Ghana and Dahomey. (Fig. 14.1) Secondly, there are the territories which resulted from the break-up of the extensive interior regions of French West and Equatorial Africa. The land-locked states now being considered fall into this second category. A further distinction can be drawn between those territories, mainly British, in which the communications networks evolved in isolation from those of the adjacent areas (*e.g.* Ghana, Sierra Leone and Nigeria) and the French area of control in which there was some attempt to integrate the communications of the coastal and inland territories.

That the French made this attempt was a reflection of their desire to tap the wealth of the Sudanese zone. Since the Niger River, the natural artery of French West Africa, entered the sea in British Nigeria, and the Senegal River is only of limited value for navigation, the development of the area had of necessity to be geared to a programme of railway construction. This took the form of a series of lines from the coast towards the river Niger. The through link from Dakar via Bamako to Koulikoro on the Niger was completed in 1924, almost forty years after construction started. The line inland from Conakry, which was begun in 1900, reached Kouroussa on the navigable upper Niger in 1914. The Abidjan-Niger railway, in the Ivory Coast, had been extended to Bobo-Dioulasso in Upper Volta by 1934 and to Ouagadougou by 1954, but was never extended to the Niger itself. Similarly, the Benin–Niger line

254 Essays in Political Geography

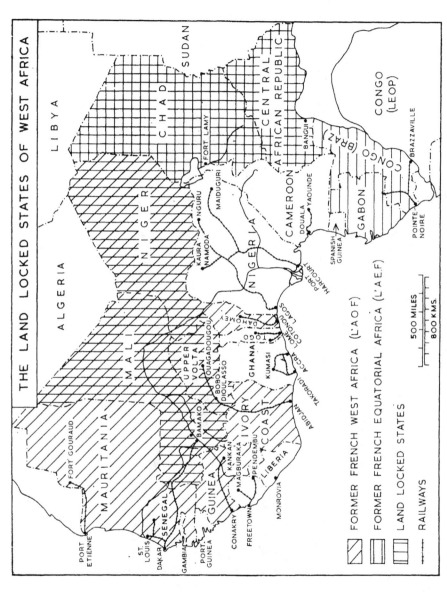

Fig. 14.1. The Land-locked States of West Africa

Politics and Transportation 255

was gradually built northwards from Cotonou between 1900 and 1936, but was not extended beyond Parakou in central Dahomey. Thus only two of the new land-locked nations, Mali and Upper Volta, have through rail links with the coast.

All of the West African states, coastal and interior, however, find that their boundaries, drawn with an almost complete disregard for the pattern of indigenous societies, cut across many of the natural economic routes. Since they are all predominantly primary producers, their prosperity depends on their ability to engage in external trade, particularly overseas, and the land-locked states, therefore, are at a severe disadvantage. The problems of certain of these states in trying to overcome their locational disadvantages are the subject of this essay.

MALI

The union in 1959 of Soudan and Senegal as the Federation of Mali was a logical outcome of French administrative policy in their West African territory, and also of geographic and economic fact, for with the rail link from Koulikoro to Dakar there had developed a close inter-dependence between the two territories. (Fig. 14.2) Soudan, with an area of 465,000 square miles and a population of 4·1 millions (1960), as compared with Senegal's 77,000 square miles and a population of 2·9 millions, was by far the poorer unit, being dependent on the railway to the Senegalese port for the export of groundnuts, its main cash crop, and for the import of all manufactured goods. In response to this trade the port of Dakar set aside part of the port area for the sole use of the Soudan transit traffic. In 1959, 80 per cent of the Soudan's external trade passed through Dakar. Exports from the Soudan by this route amounted to 95,000 tons and imports to 164,000 tons.[1] While the Dakar–Niger railway had never made a profit, Soudanese trade provided an important percentage of the total revenue. Senegal, on its part, had grown to rely heavily on the Soudan for its main food import, rice, and as a market for its manufactured products, which in 1959 amounted to £18 million.

During the first year of Federation it became obvious that there existed a personality conflict between the more radical Modibo Keita of Soudan, a supporter of close union and non-aligned foreign policy, who had little inclination for French domination in economic matters, and Leopold Senghor of Senegal, the supporter of a looser form of federation

[1] *West Africa*, 22 June 1963, p. 687.

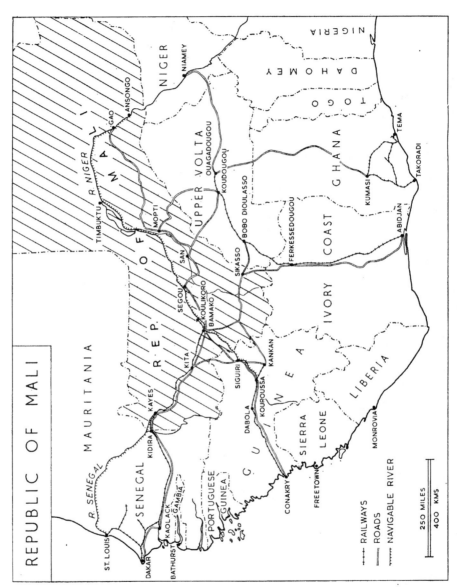

Fig. 14.2. Republic of Mali

Politics and Transportation 257

and the retention of more definite links with France.[1] These differences led in August 1960 to the withdrawal of Senegal from the Federation and the closing of the railway line. Soudan, with no choice but to 'go it alone', assumed the name Mali and made the break complete by severing all transport links, road, rail and air, the last only briefly, with Senegal. The fanaticism with which this was carried out was evident by the taking up of the frontier section of the railway line near Kidira. There can be no doubt that Mali suffered considerably as a result of this disruption of its normal trade pattern. Markets were temporarily lost and the cost of living rose steeply. That the country was able to survive at all was a measure particularly of the drive and ability of the Minister of Trade, Mr M'Doure, who in a matter of months effected the complete reorganization and redirection of the country's trade.

The most direct alternative route to the sea was by road or river to Kouroussa in Guinea, and thence by rail to the port of Conakry. The upper stretches of the Niger are, however, navigable for only part of the year, the roads are poor, and the Conakry–Niger railway is badly aligned, slow and of limited capacity. Moreover, Conakry, the terminal port, would have been unable to cope adequately with the increased traffic, and it would have taken considerable time and very great capital expenditure to develop the route sufficiently to handle all of Mali's external trade. Thus, although Mali's political outlook was closer to that of Guinea than that of neighbouring Ivory Coast, the rather longer but more efficient Abidjan–Niger railway route was adopted because of the speed with which it could be put into use. Discussions were held with Guinea on the possibility of extending the railway from Kouroussa to Bamako but such a long term project could not fill the immediate need to maintain existing trade.

The most convenient railhead on the Abidjan–Niger route was Bobo-Dioulasso, 350 miles from Bamako, the capital of Mali, and from the most productive agricultural area in the country. An emphasis had of necessity, therefore, to be placed on extensive road improvement and massive investment in road transport. A fleet of over 400 lorries and road tankers, many of them purchased with a long term loan from Krupps, was used to handle the traffic to the railhead. The Abidjan–Niger railway encouraged the traffic by offering preferential rates so that the cost of the road/rail haul compared favourably with the cost by

[1] T. Hodgkin and R. Schachter, *French Speaking West Africa in Transition,* 1960.

258　*Essays in Political Geography*

other routes. By the end of 1961, the 'Priority Plan' in association with the Ivory Coast ensured that the new route was working smoothly. The Guinea route and also a much longer route through Nigeria were looked upon as reserve routes. The traffic of the Abidjan–Niger railway increased by 34·2 per cent from 1960 to 1961, and 85 million ton/kilometres were attributed to Mali transit trade. While the Senegalese ports of Dakar and Kaolack worked well under capacity, Abidjan increased its trade from 1·7 million tons in 1960 to 2·4 million tons in 1961. It can be seen, therefore, that the problems of the land-locked states are not without economic effect on their coastal neighbours.

The creation in December 1960 of the Union of African States (Ghana–Guinea–Mali Union) led to renewed consideration during 1961 of the possibility of extending the Guinea railway to Bamako and the route was surveyed by Soviet technicians. However, with the Ivory Coast route working efficiently, there was no great urgency apparent in these moves.

In June 1963, following the 'African Summit' Conference at Addis Ababa, the Senegal–Mali frontier was reopened. Whilst this was a reasonable economic and political move it remains to be seen how much of the traffic will find its way back to the Dakar route. The efficient organization of the Ivory Coast route enables it to compete favourably with the Dakar route, especially for the southern and eastern regions of Mali. Furthermore, there has been heavy capital investment in roads and vehicles. In December 1964 it was reported that the weekly Dakar–Bamako rail traffic was still only about three-quarters what it had been before the rupture four years earlier.[1] Since Mali has increased its external trade over the same period there is the suggestion that the Abidjan route is retaining a good share of the trade. It is naturally to Mali's advantage that it is no longer dependent on any single route to the coast and, with the possible establishment at a later date of a more efficient route through Guinea, it will have coastal links through neighbours with widely divergent political views, a not unwise precaution.

NIGER

Niger, a country of 459,000 square miles with a population of just over three million, has no great natural resources, but like the other land-locked states, sees in improved routes to the coast the key to economic development. With no through rail links to the sea, Niger has the

[1] *Industries et Travaux d'Outremer*, December 1964, p. 1060.

Politics and Transportation 259

choice of road haulage, either to the Dahomeyan railhead at Parakou or to Kaura Namoda.

TABLE 14.1: NIGER: ROAD & RAIL DISTANCES TO PORTS
(all distances in miles)

	Road	Rail	Total
Zinder–Lagos	162	700	862
Zinder–Cotonou	765	265	1,030
Niamey–Cotonou	401	265	666
Niamey–Lagos		No direct route	

Thus, while for the Niamey region and the west of the country the Parakou/Cotonou route is the shortest, and indeed the only practical route to the coast, the rail link to Lagos is obviously more convenient for the Zinder–Maradi region in the east. (Fig. 14.3) By far the most important export in terms of value and tonnage is groundnuts (114,000 tons in 1964) and the main producing region is located between Zinder and Maradi and the Nigerian border. The natural export route, therefore, is through Lagos.

During the 1950s a rapid increase in Nigerian internal traffic led to considerable congestion on the railway and consequent delays in the transport of Niger's groundnuts. Further problems arose with regard to the transfer of currency between Niger in the Franc zone and Nigeria in the sterling zone. The *'Organization Commune Dahomey–Niger des chemins de fer et des transport'* (O.C.D.N.) was established with the express purpose of developing the alternative route to the coast through Dahomey, using the port of Cotonou. Thus came into being *Opération Hirondelle*, by which Niger traders were compelled to export groundnuts from November to June each year by the all-franc route to Cotonou. Similarly, all imports for a nine-month period were to come into Niger from Dahomey. The road from the railhead at Parakou was improved and bituminized to take the increased traffic, and a bridge was constructed across the Niger between Gaya and Melanville. The cost of transport by the Dahomey route, particularly for the east of the country, was much higher than by the Nigerian route, and the traders were compensated so that they did not lose by the enforced use of the longer route. There was, however, a saving in foreign exchange. A secondary effect of the enforced routing through Dahomey was the gradual emergence of a group of transport operators in Niger, where formerly there had been almost complete dependence on Nigerian-owned transport.

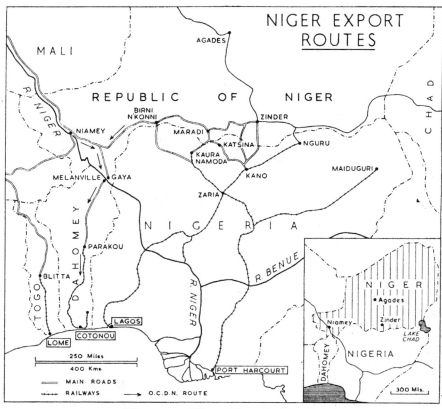

Fig. 14.3. Niger Export Routes

With *Opération Hirondelle*, the traffic on the Dahomey route increased rapidly, as can be seen from the table below.

TABLE 14.2: TRAFFIC ON THE DAHOMEY ROUTE
(All figures in tons)

	1953–4 Eastern Niger	1953–4 Western Niger	1959–60 Eastern Niger	1959–60 Western Niger
Imports	4,470	—	12,571	16,117
Exports of groundnuts	4,700	—	23,650	5,641
Regional total	9,170	—	36,221	21,758

Apart from the need to subsidize the transport on the Dahomey route, the poor port facilities at Cotonou were a definite restriction on the total tonnage that could be handled. It is for this reason that Niger

Politics and Transportation 261

was unable to rely completely on the Dahomey route, and half to two-thirds of the groundnut crop continues to be exported through Lagos. Plans have been considered for extending the Parakou railway to Kandi, with a branch to Niamey. Such a line would have obvious advantages for the south-western part of the country, but would still leave the Zinder–Maradi region far nearer the Nigerian railheads.

That Niger would be unwise to depend solely on one route has been demonstrated by the case of Mali. Furthermore, events of the last few years have indicated that although Niger and Dahomey are associated as members of the Conseil d'Entente (which also includes the Ivory Coast and Upper Volta) political differences are able to develop all too rapidly. The change of government in Dahomey in October 1963, with the deposition of President Maga, a close personal friend of Niger's President Diori, created considerable mutual antipathy and the possibility that Dahomey may reject the Entente. During 1964 a definite crisis arose in relations between the two countries over the ownership of the island of Lette in the Niger river.[1] Dahomeyans employed in the Niger Civil Service were expelled, and Dahomey threatened to take the question to the Organization for African Unity. These political troubles had economic repercussions. While the railway was not closed to Niger, the port of Cotonou was, and Niger had to fall back on the Nigerian route. The Benin–Niger railway has always made a deficit and relies heavily on the Niger traffic for revenue. So also did the port of Cotonou. In the first seven months of 1964 the railway traffic was down 60 per cent on the same period in the previous year. It was not until January 1965 that the two states came together again at a meeting of the Entente and issued a statement that 'fraternal relations' were to be restored.

In the meantime, however, Niger showed that it intended to develop the Nigerian route. Thus, during 1964, it was planned to re-lay 225 miles of the Niamey–Zinder route with bitumen. A.I.D. funds amounting to $1·5 million were obtained for the improvement of the Dungass to Damthiao route and for making a new road from Dungass to Maigatari on the Nigerian frontier.[2] This new route will make possible the use of motor transport where at present camels are used, and will give Niger a third good route, in addition to Maradi–Katsina and Zinder–Kano, which are already reasonable roads, to the Nigerian railheads.

At Cotonou, a new deep-water port was due to come into full commercial operation during 1965. This port has been designed with a

[1] *West Africa*, 23 January 1965, p. 83.
[2] *Industries et Travaux d'Outremer*, August 1964, p. 776.

262   *Essays in Political Geography*

capacity of 450,000 tons a year and it is estimated that at least 25 per cent of this would be Niger transit trade.[1] Thus the economic viability of the new port is to a large measure dependent on the Niger traffic and there seems every possibility that when 'fraternal relations' are restored, great efforts will be made to attract trade back to the Dahomey route. It may even be that the economic factors will accelerate the political reconciliation. Like Mali, Niger has several workable export routes, and is in the far more satisfactory position that its external trade is not over dependent on any one of its coastal neighbours.

CHAD AND THE CENTRAL AFRICAN REPUBLIC

In the break-up of the former French Equatorial Africa two land-locked states were created, the Republic of Chad and the Central African Republic. (Fig. 14.4) These are respectively 496,000 and 238,000 square miles in area and have populations of 2·8 and 1·3 millions. Of all the land-locked states of western Africa, Chad and Central Africa have the least satisfactory existing routes to the sea, and, with the possibility of economic asphyxiation in mind, it is hardly surprising that great efforts are being directed toward *désenclavement*.

During the colonial era there developed the '*Route Fédérale*' linking the interior regions with the coast at the Congo port of Pointe-Noire. This route utilized the 320 mile Congo–Ocean railway from Pointe-Noire to Brazzaville and over 800 miles of the Congo and Oubangui rivers to Bangui. Fort-Lamy, a further 600 miles from Bangui, could only be reached by road during the dry season, or by way of the river Chari from Fort Archambault during the rains. The inefficiency of this, the only effective route to the coast, is reflected in the cost of articles in the two interior territories. Thus in the Central African Republic most goods are double the Pointe-Noire price, and in the case of a heavy article such as cement the cost may be trebled. Added to the cost factor is the limited capacity of the river service and also of the single-line Congo–Ocean railway. On the attainment of self-government in 1959, the *Agence Transéquatoriale des Communications* (A.T.E.C.) was established to administer the route and maintain some form of effective cooperation between the four territories concerned, namely Chad, Central Africa, Gabon and Congo (Brazzaville). The A.T.E.C., a public body with financial autonomy, is responsible for regulating traffic and tariffs on all sections of the route. It is therefore responsible for the ocean

[1] *Industries et Travaux d'Outremer*, July 1964, p. 631.

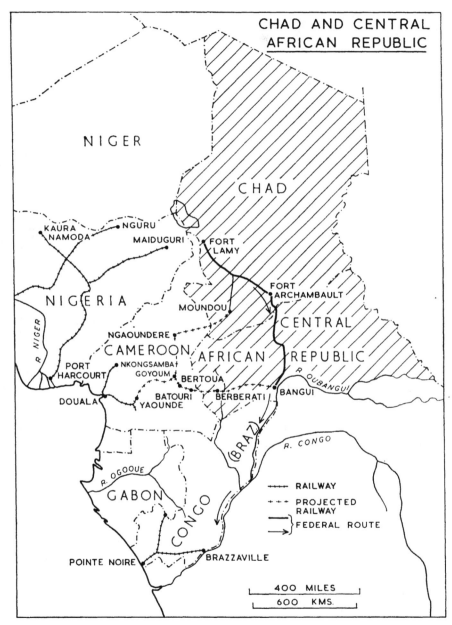

Fig. 14.4. Chad and Central African Republic

264 Essays in Political Geography

port of Pointe-Noire, the river ports of Brazzaville and Bangui, the Congo–Ocean railway, river navigation on the Congo–Oubangui system and, since January 1965, for the road axes from Bangui to Fort-Lamy and from Dolisie (Congo) to N'Dendé (Gabon).

Since 1959 the route has, wherever possible, been improved and the tonnage handled at Pointe-Noire has increased from 584,634 tons to 1,437,411 tons. The port, already working at over 80 per cent capacity in 1959, is now working at full capacity and vessels are having to wait for berths. Extensions which will give the port an extra two berths are now under construction. Since 1962, when the rail-link with M'Binda on the Gabon border came into operation, the Congo–Ocean traffic has been increased yearly by an extra one million tons of manganese from the mines at Moanda. The closing by the Congo (Leopoldville) government of the pipeline by which petroleum was formerly taken from Matadi to Leopoldville and Brazzaville has made it necessary to rail the oil from Pointe-Noire. In spite of increased locomotive and rolling stock, this extra traffic has put considerable strain on the railway. The two interior states depend on this route for almost all their external trade, which in 1963 amounted to 123,500 tons of imports and 46,800 tons of exports, and it is not surprising, therefore, that they are searching for alternative routes both to lower transport costs and also to make possible increased trade.

There has been considerable difference of opinion regarding the most suitable solution of Chad's transport problem. As early as 1930 a Douala–Chad railway was proposed, this in fact being but an extension from the existing Douala–Yaoundé line. Such a line, it was envisaged, would make possible the economic development of the central Cameroun area and also the Moundou region of Chad, and had the support of the Douala Chamber of Commerce and the traders of Fort Lamy. Oubangui-Chari, however, favoured a rail line northwards from Bangui to Chad and the continued use of the Federal Route. In Chad, where a section of opinion has always seen the country as 'a victim of the Federal Artery', [1] the main hopes have become centred on the trans-Cameroun railway. The initiative for this line, an extension from Yaoundé to Ngaoundéré, has been taken by the Cameroun government, but the interest and active participation of the interior states has been sought, and the studies of the economic feasibility of the line have envisaged traffic from Chad and Central Africa consequent upon further

[1] V. Thompson and R. Adloff, *The Emerging States of French Equatorial Africa*, Palo Alta, 1960, p. 137.

Politics and Transportation 265

extensions. In 1958 the *Société Civile d'Études du Chemin de Fer Douala–Chad* (S.E.D.O.T.) was established and in 1961 it became a public utility. A meeting of the leaders of Cameroun and Chad at Garoua in March 1962 led to the setting up in November of the same year of a co-ordinating committee. Early in 1963 European funds were negotiated for the first stage of the work, and with additional assistance from A.I.D. the contract for the first section of the track, 185 miles from Yaoundé to Belabo, was signed in August 1964. Construction work started in October 1964. Meanwhile, at the Chad office of the co-ordinating committee, preliminary studies are being pursued for the eventual extension of the line from Ngaoundéré, the Cameroun terminus, to Chad.

The Cameroun government has always thought of the rail extension as a preliminary to the economic development of the central and northern savanna of the country. With this in mind, and also with the idea of tapping traffic from the land-locked states, the route approximates closely to that originally advocated in the 1930s, by way of the Sanaga valley to Goyoum, and then northwards via the Pangar valley to Ngaoundéré. This route follows the most convenient line of least gradient and also brings the line within relatively easy reach of the interior republics.

While the details of the remainder of the route have not been finalized it would seem that Chad is thinking in terms of an extension of the Cameroun railway from Ngaoundéré to Moundou, a distance of 250 miles. Certainly the government's road improvement programme, with an emphasis on routes converging on Moundou, suggests that this town will become the railhead. An alternative possibility would be a link with the Nigerian railway, which, with its now completed extension to Maiduguri, comes to within 100 miles of Fort-Lamy, the Chad capital. However, at the present time no serious consideration is being given to a rail link with Nigeria, although there are plans for the improvement of the road to Maiduguri and the construction of a bridge to replace the ferry across the Lagone river, which would certainly permit greater ease of access to the Nigerian railhead. The capital cost would obviously be greater in the case of the link with Ngaoundéré (250 miles) but, since in both cases two-thirds of the extension would be in the territory of the coastal neighbour, considerable co-operation would be necessary and presumably international financial assistance would be sought. The Moundou–Douala line would provide the shorter route to the sea and would have the further distinct advantage of being entirely within the franc zone. For Fort-Lamy traffic the trans-Cameroun route would have

266 *Essays in Political Geography*

little cost advantage over the Nigerian route, but for the Moundou region itself it would be cheaper by about half.[1]

For the country as a whole there would seem to be on balance very little to choose on economic grounds between the two routes. The Cameroun government, for its part, has always expressed interest in the Equatorial Customs Union, leading eventually to closer political union, and sees its port of Douala as the natural outlet for the trade of the entire region. From Chad's point of view either the Nigerian or the trans-Cameroun route would have advantages over the present lengthy, inefficient and costly haul via Pointe-Noire, which not only increased the overland distance but also that of the ocean transport to Europe, the ultimate destination of most of the produce of Chad.

The existence of the trans-Cameroun link will not be without its effect on the other coastal states. The Congo (Brazzaville) will hardly be enthusiastic for a scheme that will take to Douala the trade now passing through Pointe-Noire and will deprive the Congo–Ocean railway of some £500,000 revenue every year. Likewise, the expected traffic from Chad was one of the important economic justifications for the construction of the Nigerian railway extension to Maiduguri, and while the trans-Cameroun route will not be completed for some years it is bound eventually to take trade that Nigeria might have expected to handle. It remains to be seen whether or not the use of the new route will be enforced by legislation, but at least with its completion Chad will possess varied trade routes and a through rail link with the sea. The completion of the line will in all probability serve to strengthen the political ties which already exist between French-speaking neighbours, and the emphasis on the Cameroun rather than the Nigerian route is in itself a reflection of political as well as economic considerations.

The territory which now comprises the Central African Republic has never suffered from the same degree of *enclavement* as Chad. The lack of marked topographic barriers and the existence of a dense river network, albeit seasonal, made the Oubangui-Chari region a natural route and trading centre. In the inter-war years the territorial government created a road system far superior to that in the rest of French Equatorial Africa and developed in particular the road links with Cameroun to the west. Like Chad, however, Central Africa depended mainly on the Federal Route for its external trade, but had the advantages that it was nearer the sea, that Bangui, its capital, was the main port on the axis and that one-third of its roads were open all year.

[1] *Industries et Travaux d'Outremer*, May 1964, pp. 431–2.

Because no great road haul is necessary, transport costs for the Central African Republic are less than for Chad, and the drawbacks to the route are mainly in its limited capacity. Under A.T.E.C. river navigation has been greatly improved by dredging and the removal of rock obstructions, and at Bangui the river quays and storage areas have been greatly extended.[1] These improvements have made possible an increase in traffic and the consideration of even further extensions to the installations.

TABLE 14.3: EXTERNAL TRADE OF CENTRAL AFRICAN REPUBLIC AND CHAD

(All figures in tons)

| | 1959 | | | 1963 | | |
	C.R.A.	Chad	Total	R.C.A.	Chad	Total
Imports	75,200	14,900	90,100	83,400	40,100	123,500
Exports	30,300	14,100	44,400	22,900	23,900	46,800
Total	105,500	29,000	134,500	106,300	64,000	170,300

The Central African Republic has demonstrated neither the same interest nor degree of urgency in the trans-Cameroun route as Chad. The obvious preference of the Chad government for the Cameroun route has, however, made it necessary for Central Africa to abandon its proposals for a Bangui–Fort-Lamy rail route. Furthermore, because construction work on the trans-Cameroun line has already started, it has become inevitable that Central Africa should think seriously of a link in that direction. Thus in April 1963 a joint Cameroun/Central Africa Commission was established to study possible routes to the sea. The most favoured route at present is a line from Bangui through Betoua, Batouri and Berberati to link with the trans-Cameroun line in the region of Goyoum. This would bring Bangui within 840 miles of the sea at Douala as compared with 1,060 miles by the combined river/rail route to Pointe-Noire. The trans-Cameroun route would have distinct advantages. The present trans-shipments from road to river and river to rail would be eliminated, and the ocean freight distance to Europe reduced. This would have the effect of lowering the cost of all imports. The construction of the railway across the potentially rich forest regions of Haute Sangha and Lobaye would almost certainly stimulate economic development in those southern provinces, the only forest area in an otherwise savanna country.

[1] *Ibid.*, December 1964, pp. 1043–8.

268 *Essays in Political Geography*

Thus, while no definite arrangements have yet been made, it is likely that the Bangui–Goyoum railway will be constructed once the Cameroun line is completed. The effect of this can only be to weaken further the political ties inherited from the colonial Equatorial Federation, represented in the Federal Route, and strengthen association with the Cameroun Republic. In this way Cameroun may assume an increasingly important, even dominant role in equatorial African politics whereas it has hitherto been the outsider.

CONCLUSIONS

What general conclusions can be drawn from this brief consideration of some of West Africa's land-locked states? Overseas contacts have become an increasingly vital factor in economic growth in the developing countries, and the land-locked states are having to increase the capacity of their trade routes to avoid economic stagnation. In some cases existing routes have been improved and in others new arteries created. The general inadequacy of the West African communications network makes competition for the limited facilities between neighbouring states inevitable. During the colonial period the federal organization of French West and Equatorial Africa meant that such friction as occurred was internal, but with the attainment of independence there has developed an understandable hyper-sensitivity on questions of national sovereignity, and competition has become a matter of political rivalries. All too frequently political tensions between interior and coastal neighbours have developed, sometimes for no other reason than conflict of personalities, and the economic repercussions have been serious. In the case of both Mali and Niger normal trade routes have been completely disrupted.

Following their long history as French colonial possessions, the land-locked states, with the exception of Mali, have continued since independence to be associated with the French community and the franc monetary zone. There has been a tendency, for practical reasons, to seek links with French-speaking rather than English-speaking neighbours. Thus Niger and Chad have developed routes respectively through Dahomey and Cameroun and look upon the routes through Nigeria, although possibly shorter and more economic, as secondary or reserve. With the ephemeral character of political associations the land-locked nations are wise, for economic as well as political reasons, to diversify their links with the sea, for '. . . nations, like individuals, do not relish

Politics and Transportation 269

being wholly beholden to their neighbours',[1] and in the context of the land-locked country it is expedient not to become over dependent on any one neighbour.

The interior states have continually to reconcile political factors with economic and geographical considerations. From the economic point of view it should be their aim to develop transport links which will reduce transfer costs on imported and exported commodities to a minimum, although with the desire to stimulate development in hitherto unproductive regions some of the routes may initially be uneconomic. In the face of political influences such economic considerations have not always been given the attention they deserve.

Ultimately, the transportation problems of the land-locked states will be solved only by large-scale regional co-operation. The ease with which political associations can be severed, as evidenced by examples in this essay, makes it reasonable to assume that the necessary co-operation will be most fruitful and most stable where it is founded on basic economic projects involving the active participation of adjacent countries.

POSTSCRIPT

Since this essay was prepared early in 1965 certain of the details have been rendered inaccurate by subsequent events. The Mali–Senegal link has become fully operative again. The new port at Cotonou was opened in August 1965 and is well able to handle Niger's trade. Recent events in Nigeria have led to the disruption of the rail services and an inability to handle even her own traffic to the coast. Changes of government in a number of the territories concerned have served to strengthen the general conclusions of the essay.

[1] W. G. East, 'The geography of land-locked states', *Transactions of the Institute of British Geographers*, 28, 1960, p. 17.

15

The Ewe Problem:
A Reassessment   B. W. HODDER

The case of the Ewe in West Africa is often used to illustrate the difficulties arising from the drawing of former colonial boundaries through homogeneous tribal territories. Here, it is frequently suggested, is a classic instance of such a boundary, drawn originally on wholly arbitrary grounds, and calling now for early revision. The Ewe problem today is believed by many observers to be a central factor in the strained relations between the two neighbouring states of Ghana and Togo. The international boundary between them, especially where it passes through Eweland, is held to be a chief cause of constant friction, interrupting trade, leading to accusations and counter-accusations about the smuggling of arms and subversive elements, and also giving rise to hardship on the part of those communities who normally cross the border for seasonal labour or other temporary visits.

The main historical facts about the Ewe problem are well-known and require only the briefest mention here. Lying between the Volta and Mono rivers, and stretching inland from the coast for over eighty miles in places, the Ewe have been divided between the British, Germans and French in varying ways since the end of the nineteenth century (Figs. 15.1, 15.2, 15.3). First, as a result of negotiations between the British and German colonial powers, about four-fifths of Eweland was incorporated into German Togo and one-fifth into the British Gold Coast. Secondly, after the conquest of German Togo by British and French forces in 1914, Eweland was redistributed so that some three-fifths were now in British territory and two-fifths in French territory. Thirdly, after the First World War, yet another adjustment was made, the French area being extended westwards to include the entire coastline of former German Togo. As a result of the formal mandate agreements, Eweland was divided into three political elements: two of them under the British (in the Gold Coast and in British-mandated Togo) and one under the French (in the French-mandated territory). After the Second World War, the two mandated areas continued to be administered by the British and French respectively as trusteeship territories of the United Nations. Fourthly, and finally, the British trusteeship territory

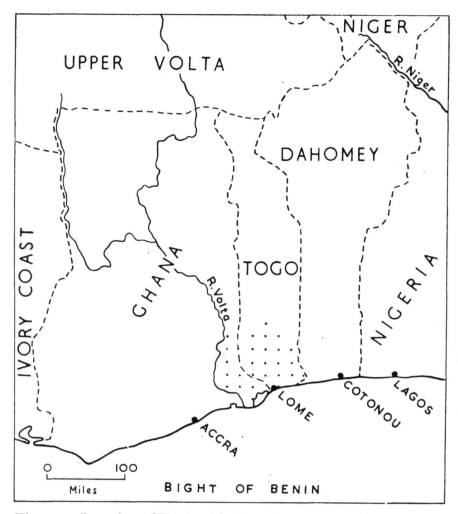

Fig. 15.1. Location of Eweland in West Africa. The area inhabited chiefly by Ewe-speaking peoples is dotted

was incorporated into the new independent state of Ghana in 1957, and in 1960 the former French Togo became an independent republic. The Ewe, then, after a most complicated and chequered political history, are today divided between the two independent republics of Ghana and Togo.

A great many solutions to the Ewe problem have been advanced in the past, but today only two radically opposed ideas receive any wide support. The first of these solutions is expressed in Ghana's view that the Ewe problem can only be solved by extending Ghana's boundary

The Ewe Problem 273

eastwards to include all of present-day Togo. Only in this way, it is claimed, can all Ewe be united within the framework of one national state. As the former President Nkrumah himself expressed it, 'the artificial barriers which have irritated and annoyed us and our kinsmen on the other side all these years and which led to the initiation of the Ewe unification movement can only be removed by the total integration of Togoland with Ghana into a quite indivisible nation'.[1] Union between Ghana and Togo, according to the official Ghanaian view, is 'inevitable'.[2] More recently (February 1965) it was stated in Ghana that talks had been taking place between the governments of Ghana and Togo 'to remove the imperialistic border drawn to divide sisters and brothers';[3] and it is argued that 'if we of this generation want to demonstrate Ghana's quest for African unity and world peace, borders separating kith from kin should be removed'.[4] The other solution, believed to be currently favoured by many Togolese, is the extension westwards of Togo's boundary to include all of the former British-administered trusteeship territory. This move would reunite, so it is claimed, about four-fifths of the Ewe.

It is not proposed here to go fully into the arguments for and against these two main viewpoints. The Ewe problem is a long and complicated story, capable of many conflicting interpretations, and no summary statement of the situation could do it justice. It is possible, however, to make three points by way of a brief contemporary re-assessment; and significantly, these points seem to be relevant not only to the Ewe question itself, but also to a host of similar questions occurring in many other parts of the African continent today.

THE EWE POPULATION

There seems little doubt that earlier published material has tended greatly to misrepresent the statistical basis of the Ewe problem. According to Hailey, there were in 1956 some 400,000 Ewe in the Gold Coast, 227,000 in British Togoland, and only 175,000 in French Togo.[5] Another estimate showed the Ewe in 1955 as numbering 376,000 in the Gold Coast, 139,000 in British Togo and 176,000 in French Togo.[6] Most

---

[1] Statement at Ho (Ghana), November 1959.
[2] *Daily Times*, Lagos, 21 December 1960.
[3] *West Africa*, 15 February 1965, p. 212.
[4] *Ibid.*
[5] Lord Hailey, *An African Survey: Revised, 1956*, London, 1957, p. 354.
[6] U.N./T.C./T./1206/Add. 1, 21 October 1955.

274 Essays in Political Geography

available data suggest, indeed, that only between one-fifth and one-third of the Ewe live in Togo, giving Ghana a very strong numerical advantage over its eastern neighbour in its Ewe population. Whether such a division of the Ewe between the two present states is true is clearly an important issue, because it is largely on the basis of such figures that a number of writers have come out in support of Ghana's aims to solve the Ewe problem by integration with (or annexation of) the Togo Republic. In fact, however, there are firm grounds for suggesting that there is something approaching a rough balance in the numbers of Ewe on the two sides of the present international boundary.

The most recent census figures for Togo[1] indicate that previous censuses and estimates, as they were accepted by the French authorities, greatly underestimated the total population figures. While allowing for the generally tentative nature of African population statistics and for the passions aroused both by the break-up of the European empires and by the desire for African independence, it is still significant that Togo registered a population increase of some 25 per cent in 1960, her year of independence. This increase was particularly notable in the southern Maritime Region, populated predominantly by Ewe. In Ghana, on the other hand, no such dramatic increase in total population has been recorded. Assuming the validity of the Togo census – and all the evidence suggests that this census was reasonably accurate – then all population data in the years immediately preceding independence tended to underestimate the population of Togo; and this fact to some extent accounts for the new relative significance of the Ewe component on the Togo side of the boundary between Ghana and Togo.

But far more important, a comparative analysis of the methods of classifying the ethnic composition of the population in the two territories concerned reveals that in Togo the French trusteeship administration after the Second World War always tended to present ethnic data in such a way as greatly to underestimate the Ewe population in Togo. In 1945 the Ewe population in French Togo was given officially by the French authorities as 417,749.[2] By 1951, however, the figure was given by the French authorities to the Fourth Committee of the United Nations General Assembly as only 290,000;[3] and four years later, in 1955, the figure was only 176,000.[4] This apparent drop in the number

[1] *Le recensement général de la population du Togo (hors communes)*, Lome, 1961.
[2] *Le Togo Français*, Lome, 20 June 1945.
[3] U.N.Doc.A/C.4/195 of 4 December 1951.
[4] U.N./T.C./T./1206/Add. 1, 21 October 1955.

of Ewe from 417,749 in 1945 to 176,000 in 1955 was in fact due largely to the adoption by the French authorities of a new system of classification which redefined the term 'Ewe' in a much narrower sense than formerly. Various sub-groups of the Ewe – the Minas, Ouatchis and Ahoulans – were now statistically isolated in a way that was not adopted across the border by British authorities in the Gold Coast or in British Togo; indeed, the Ghana census makes no mention at all of the Minas, though they originated in southern Ghana. The result was that during the ten years after the Second World War the Ewe population in what is now Ghana rose steadily, whereas in Togo the official number of Ewe fell by over half; and this was due mainly to differences in methods of ethnic classification on the two sides of the boundary.

The crux of the matter clearly lies in the meaning given to the term 'Ewe'. If in fact the ethnic data are classified in Togo according to the way the Togo Ewe themselves interpret the term 'Ewe' today – and incidentally in the way Ghanaian statisticians interpret the term on their side of the international boundary – then the latest census figures published show that the total number of Ewe in Togo in 1960 was some 600,000, or about the same as the estimate for Ghana in that year. In Togo the term 'Ewe' for the purposes of political identification means more than the 'Ewe Proper', just as the term 'Yoruba' means for all practical purposes very much more than simply the 'Yoruba Proper'. It also means more than the 'Ewe-speaking peoples' in the sense adopted by the Ethnographic Survey of Africa.[1] In Togo the term 'Ewe' in the context of the Ewe problem means also the Minas, the Ahoulans, the Ehoue and the Ouatchis. This last group is often left out of any discussion on the Ewe, yet the name Ouatchis means literally 'from Nuatja', a town in north-eastern Eweland and the commonly accepted dispersal centre of the Ewe people. Certainly the Ouatchis think of themselves as Ewe in the context of the Ewe problem; and to exclude them from any consideration of the Ewe as a politically identifiable group is as unrealistic as to leave the Ife Yoruba out of a discussion of the Yoruba of south-western Nigeria and south-eastern Dahomey.

Most interpretations of the Ewe problem today, then, seem to rest upon misleading statistical material, reflecting the lack of common criteria adopted by post-war British and French administrations for defining the term 'Ewe'. Here, indeed, is an instance of what is believed to be a common situation where the significance of a community in relation to

[1] M. Manoukian, *The Ewe-speaking Peoples of Togoland and the Gold Coast*, London, 1948.

276 *Essays in Political Geography*

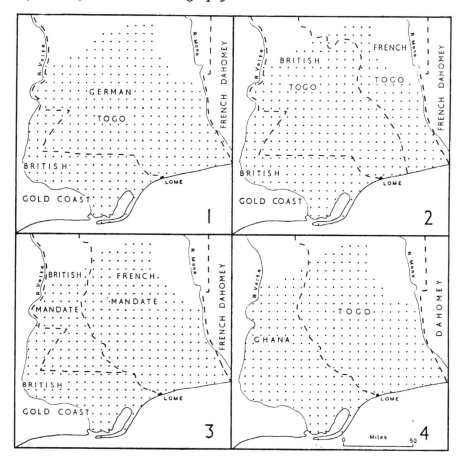

Fig. 15.2. **Changes in international boundaries passing through Eweland (represented by the dotted area)**
1 The pre-1914 position
2 1914–1919
3 1919–1957 (mandate and trusteeship areas identical)
4 Present position

an international boundary cannot really be understood simply by an exercise in statistical classification and mapping. The area of Ewe identity as it refers to the question of boundary study can only satisfactorily be determined in the field. Only by an *ad hoc* examination of the situation on the ground can any real understanding be reached of the Ewe as a politically homogeneous group. The area over which the Ewe call themselves Ewe for the purposes of political action is not the same as the area inhabited by the Ewe 'tribe'. As K. M. Barbour has pointed out, 'the term tribe is capable of several meanings: it may be used for

The Ewe Problem 277

a group of persons who speak the same language and observe a generally similar pattern of dress and customs, or it may mean all the persons who acknowledge a common political head, whether they are culturally identical or not'.[1] Nor is the term 'Ewe' in the context of the Ewe problem the same as the area over which some other single criterion, such as any one form of social organization, is found to operate. Indeed, it is one of the limitations of boundary studies in many parts of Africa that too much dependence has often to be placed upon an interpretation of communities and their distributions made by ethnographers, linguists or social anthropologists for strictly limited and specialist purposes. This is not to criticize such studies; for as any human geographer who tries to work in tropical Africa soon finds out, his debt to social anthropologists in particular is very great indeed. The point here is rather that we cannot accept uncritically the ethnographer's, linguist's, or social anthropologist's definition, interpretation and distribution of a community as *necessarily* accurate in the context of boundary studies.

BOUNDARY RE-ADJUSTMENT

Any objective examination of the Ewe problem makes it difficult to avoid the conclusion that neither of the two solutions already mentioned is acceptable; the present international boundary through Ewe territory must remain where it is.

It is admitted that the various international boundaries through Eweland appear always to have been drawn on arbitrary, even irresponsible grounds. Today it is still possible to argue that the present boundary is manifestly unsatisfactory in that it has constituted, and indeed still constitutes, a hardship to certain small elements of the Ewe population on either side of the border. The All-Ewe petition to the United Nations in 1947, for instance, listed three districts, three towns and thirteen farms that were split by the boundary, as well as the names of some 350 persons who were said to live on one side of the boundary and whose farms lay on the other side.[2] It is also worth pointing out that whereas the eastern half of Eweland includes the entire core region of the Togo Republic today, the western half constitutes only a peripheral region within the Republic of Ghana. For Togo this is an especially serious weakness. Lome is a good example of a capital lying right against an

[1] K. M. Barbour, 'A geographical analysis of boundaries in inter-tropical Africa', in K. M. Barbour, and R. M. Prothero, (eds.), *Essays on African Population*, London, 1961, pp. 314–15.
[2] U.N.T./A.C. 1947.

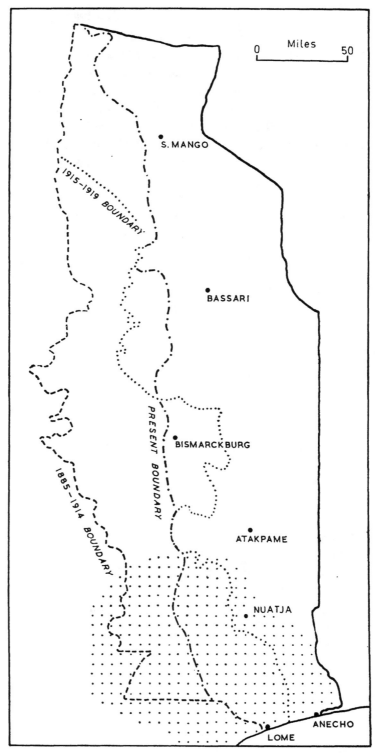

Fig. 15.3. The changing western boundary of Togo

The Ewe Problem 279

international boundary, the government offices and main official resi-
dential area lying but a few hundred yards from the Ghana border.

As far as being responsible for friction and irritation between Ghana
and Togo today is concerned, some observers would go so far as to
claim – though there appears to be no real evidence to support this contention – that the assassination of the former President Olympio of Togo
in 1963 resulted directly from the unsatisfactory nature of the international boundary. As *The Times* expressed it, 'the truth may be that
President Olympio was a martyr to the unreal boundaries drawn by
former colonial powers in Africa, careless of tribal unities or even of
economic realities'.[1]

On the other hand, any kind of boundary adjustment here would set
a precedent for wholesale agitation for boundary changes throughout
West Africa. For almost without exception the state boundaries of West
Africa are drawn on similarly unsatisfactory grounds from a strictly
geographical point of view. The Ewe question is by no means unique;
it has simply attracted more international interest than have similar
questions in other parts of the region. Ghana's western boundary with
Ivory Coast, for instance, cuts through Sanwi and Nzina territory; and
to the north the B'Moba, Konkomba and Kotokoli, and to the east the
Fon and Yoruba are similarly split by international boundaries. Any
attempt to re-draw boundaries today 'would have to deal with all the
former difficulties, together with the certainty that any unrequited loss
of territory would almost certainly provoke political troubles far more
serious than those it was hoped to remedy'.[2]

Moreover, as far as the Togo–Ghana boundary is concerned, the bulk
of it does already take into account the distribution of the larger tribal
groups: indeed, it was because the Dagomba, Mamprussi and Gonja
groups in the former British-administered Togo wished to be reunited
with their kinsmen to the west that British Togo was eventually incorporated into Ghana. At the 1956 referendum in British-administered
Togo the Ewe people in the south of that territory voted in great majority
against union with Ghana; but – again as was to be expected – the more
numerous non-Ewe in northern British Togo voted for union with Ghana,
giving a clear majority for union.

Again, there is a tendency to exaggerate the homogeneity of the so-
called ethnic or tribal groups in Africa today. It is often forgotten that
the desire for unification among the Ewe – the idea of Eweland as a
distinct and homogeneous unit – is in reality of European origin. As

---

[1] *The Times*, London, 14 January 1963.　　　[2] Barbour, *op. cit.*, p. 323.

K

280 *Essays in Political Geography*

Manoukian has pointed out, there has never been any political confederation of the Ewe sub-tribes; and it seems 'to have been left to the European administration to begin welding together of the sub-tribes into larger centralized groups, and to the effects of European rule to create a national Pan-Ewe consciousness'.[1] A strongly organized Pan-Ewe movement for political unification of the Ewe under a single administration, which is supposed to command widespread support, is now a thing of the past. It was in any case really representative only of those Ewe who lived in the larger towns or very close to the border and originated as a serious movement with a few British-educated and French-educated Ewe towards the end of the Second World War; and this timing was determined by the closing of the boundary by the Vichy Government during the war period, when for the first time the boundary was made to act as a barrier. Furthermore, the close association of the two parts of former German Togo with Britain and France over more than thirty years inevitably and irrevocably imposed important differences upon the two territories, and these differences make the idea of unification today much less of a practicable proposition. Different official languages, cultures and systems of education developed in the two Togos; and unlike the British the French did not include the indigenous culture and language in their school curriculum. Clan and family ties were weakened by the difficulties of exchanging visits across the border. However arbitrary the boundaries might originally have been, their very existence tended increasingly to separate the peoples of the two territories.

Finally, and perhaps most important, there is no factual basis whatsoever for interpreting as synonymous the causes of Ewe unity and national unity. Concerning Ghana's arguments, the Ewe problem by itself can never be legitimate justification for annexing the territory of a people, three-quarters of whom are not Ewe at all, and many of whom are likewise 'separated' from their kinsmen in Dahomey and Upper Volta. Similarly, the Ewe problem by itself is no justification for extending Togo's boundary westwards to include the entire area of former German Togo. Not only would this still leave an important minority of Ewe in Ghana, but such a move would mean splitting once again the Dagomba, Mamprussi and Gonja peoples.

[1] Manoukian, *op. cit.*, p. 4.

A BASIS FOR CO-OPERATION

It is contended that the solution to any problems arising from the present international boundary through Eweland must lie, not in the manipulation of the boundary, nor in the annexation of the smaller weaker country by the larger more powerful country, but in the development of some form of co-operation between the neighbouring states in the fields of social and economic, if not political, endeavour.

Between Ghana and Togo the possibilities of some such form of co-operation are obvious: much closer trading links, joint tariff regulation, the reduction of visa and travel requirements, and the improvement of all forms of communication between the two countries. Furthermore, Ghana's Volta Scheme at Akosambo could then develop as the natural power centre for the whole Volta valley, and the abolition of the boundary as a social and economic barrier would re-establish the traditional mobility of labour across it.[1]

Much is heard of the need for co-operation among African states today. Probably most observers would agree with President Nyerere's statement that 'in the sphere of boundaries, as in all others, we must start our quest for African unity from the facts of our historical inheritance',[2] and further, that 'we must use the African national states as instruments for the re-unification of Africa, and not . . . as tools for dividing Africa'.[3] Yet it is unfortunately true that the recent trend in Ghana and Togo, as in many other African states, has too often been towards the more parochial forms of nationalism and away from co-operation at any level. Indeed it is significant that the Ghana–Togo boundary was never so much of a barrier as it has become since both countries achieved their independence. During the colonial period, as Austin points out, 'the weight of imperial power on each side held the position steady, and the border remained open, subject to customs and visa requirements, except when the European states quarrelled among themselves'.[4] Furthermore, the difficulties of achieving effective social and economic co-operation between Ghana and Togo, while at the same time preserving the susceptibilities of national sovereignty, need no stressing. Yet it is perhaps in this very context that the Ewe problem can act as a link between the two countries. In this sense it is possible

[1] D. Austin, 'The uncertain frontier: Ghana–Togo', *Journal of Modern African Studies*, I, 1963, p. 141.

[2] J. Nyerere, 'A United States of Africa', *Journal of Modern African Studies*, I, 1963, p. 2.

[3] *Ibid.*, p. 6.   [4] Austin, *op. cit.*, p. 143.

282 *Essays in Political Geography*

to view the divided Ewe not as a problem but as an opportunity, providing a common and realistic basis for co-operation between neighbouring African states.

SOME WIDER CONSIDERATIONS

As R. W. Steel has pointed out, political geographers have so far given relatively little attention to Africa.[1] There is an urgent need for research, including the examination of the geographical and historical aspects of boundary making, especially, as Steel suggests, 'at a time when changes of political control are focusing attention on both the strength and weakness of some of the inter-territorial and internal boundaries drawn in the past, often when little was known of the geographical conditions of the areas and peoples through which they passed'.[2] A contemporary re-assessment of the Ewe problem in West Africa does indeed emphasize the need for conventional academic approaches in trying to achieve any full understanding of the problems associated with the Ghana–Togo boundary.

Yet at the same time there seems equally to be an urgent and practical need for geographers to give some attention to the opportunities for different forms of closer association between states created by such boundaries. Both in our thinking and writing on the problems of boundaries dividing existing tribal territories or ethnic communities in Africa we may need to question two sets of assumptions. The first of these comprises the assumptions which we apparently make about the nature of the tribe or ethnic community in terms of its extent, numbers, composition or homogeneity; while the second includes those which relate to the significance of such boundaries. It is still too commonly assumed, for instance, that effective national unity is the essential prerequisite of effective international co-operation, so that the Ewe problem is viewed solely as a centrifugal force working *against* the growth of national unity and so, inevitably, as a source of contention between the two countries.

Yet there appear to be several cases in Africa where the arbitrary nature on all geographical grounds of a political boundary matters not a jot to the people living on either side of it. Certainly this seems to be true nowadays of the Ewe question. The Ewe now seem perfectly content to leave the boundary where it is, and have no strong desire for Ewe

[1] R. W. Steel, in R. W. Steel and R. M. Prothero, eds., *Geographers and the Tropics: Liverpool Essays*, London, 1964, p. 15.

[2] *Ibid.*, p. 15.

The Ewe Problem 283

unity as such. The Ghanaian Ewe think of themselves first as Ghanaian and secondly as Ewe; similarly, the Togolese Ewe think of themselves first as Togolese. What these people object to is not that they live in one country rather than another. What they *do* object to is that they are cut off from their kinsmen and sources of seasonal labour every time the boundary is closed by one of the two governments concerned. This boundary has now (1965) been closed continuously since February 1963.

The need here, as in many other parts of Africa, is not to concentrate attention solely on the geographical analysis of former colonial boundaries; nor is it a matter of redrawing the political boundaries more in accordance with 'geographical realities'. The need, rather, is to study ways of ensuring that boundaries function as the territorial limits of administrations and not as barriers to all movement and contact between states. While all the realities of the specific situation as outlined above support the argument for leaving the boundaries as they are, they do at the same time underline the need for larger regional groupings for the purposes of social and economic development. Political geographers would seem here to have an important practical role to play in examining and analysing the prospects for co-operation between states, such as the East African Federation and the Organization for African Unity, and interpreting such issues as the divided Ewe as one of the very bases of co-operation.

16

Nationalism, Regionalism and Federalism:
The Geographical Basis of Some Conflicting Political Concepts in East Africa   B. W. LANGLANDS

INTRODUCTION

The intention of this essay is to portray the political geography of East Africa by examining from the standpoint of the geographer the political issues which are of greatest concern to the people of the area. Undoubtedly the most fundamental issue facing the politicians of East Africa is that of creating a national interest to replace the tribal particularism of the traditional systems of government which had been cultivated during the colonial era. At the same time, the strength of regional differences within the various states of East Africa must be recognized, for these are often important in the manipulation of political forces in each country and in the drafting of their constitutions. In contrast, there is throughout Africa a desire to associate internationally as part of a Pan-African ideal, of which the creation of the Organization of African Unity is a manifestation. As a step towards achieving this ideal, the East African states might move towards a closer union between themselves, a move which would necessitate a suppression of local nationalisms.

It is possible to see in the area forces of nationalism, regionalism and federalism in some measure at variance with each other. This is not to suggest that a major clash of interest exists. It is possible that a strong state idea can be built up on the basis of balancing regional interests to the benefit of the whole state, and also that a federation can be created from the co-operation of three political units each with a strongly developed local nationalism. The political landscape in East Africa is undergoing a rapid process of change, but while all these forces for change have a basis in the political organization of the land area, some have their origin in areal differences and others have their effect in creating new areal patterns. East Africa, therefore, deserves to be considered as a distinct political realm, for here there exists a set of interrelated political issues in a general setting of geographical uniformity.

286 *Essays in Political Geography*

THE STATE AND THE NATION IN EAST AFRICA

The political map of Africa is usually regarded as the creation of the imperial powers. In particular, the essentially arbitrary political units of eastern Africa are the product of British, German, Italian, Belgian, Portuguese, Egyptian and Ethiopian imperial influences of the nineteenth century, though minor changes have taken place in their boundaries during the present century. Within this setting many of the boundary lines are the product of administrative convenience, and their definition has seldom taken the interests of the indigenous people into account. With the exception of Zanzibar, under the rule of an alien sultan, only the people of Buganda had a centralized political organization with a territorial basis on the eve of colonial rule. This special position of Buganda and Zanzibar had been recognized by the formulation of special treaty agreements to control the British jurisdiction over them. In Buganda particularly, a clearly defined state idea could be recognized in pre-colonial days.

The three main states of East Africa, Kenya, Uganda and Tanzania[1] are not in any sense logical creations arising from the distinctiveness of their areas or from the expressed wish of their peoples, but represent combinations of different geographical landscapes occupied by a great number of socially different communities each with their own local loyalties and possessing little in common, whether culturally, historically or economically. These political units have recently become independent sovereign states with full powers to determine their own future and the same is true of all but one of their nine neighbouring political units. Yet, however illogical these state creations may have been, there is little evidence of a willingness to rectify the deficiencies. The union of Tanganyika and Zanzibar and the desire for a federation are exceptions to the more general rule that the boundaries are accepted as the inheritance of the new states and regarded as sacrosanct. Thus the state area is given, and it is assumed that if anything has to change it is the attitude of the people, not the area. The importance of ethnic factors is expected to lessen, and it is assumed that new loyalties will be built up.

The common characteristic of the states of eastern Africa, with the exception of Somalia, is that each is populated by groups of people of

[1] Tanzania is the name adopted in 1964 for the combination of Tanganyika and Zanzibar in a united republic. For convenience the names for the separate units have been retained in this essay in so far as it deals with the period before 1964.

Nationalism, Regionalism and Federalism 287

ETHNIC GROUPS OF EAST AFRICA

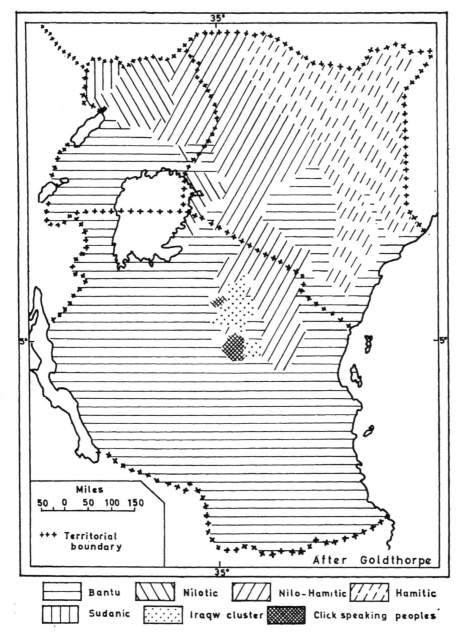

Fig. 16.1. Ethnic Groups of East Africa

288 *Essays in Political Geography*

different ethnic origins, and it is in all cases the policy of their nationalist leaders to instil a spirit of national unity. The ethnically heterogeneous nature of the East African countries may arise from a grouping of tribes mainly of one racial stock, as in Tanganyika, where the people are predominantly Bantu, or from a juxtaposition of different African stocks, as in Uganda, where Bantu, Nilotic, Nilo-Hamitic and Sudanic strains meet. Greater heterogeneity arises from the introduction of non-African peoples, such as Arabs, Indians, Europeans and Somalis. In some cases these various peoples may occupy discrete areas, while in other instances they may be identified with particular social positions. Although a few examples of cultural assimilation can be recognized, each state faces the need to weld together a nation out of a heterogeneous group of peoples possessing different cultural attitudes. It is now becoming customary to minimize tribal attachments, and educated people make an effort to think in national terms, but it must be recognized that under the colonial regime ethnic differences had been bolstered by the application of a system of local government to fit them. In each territory district governments were tribally based, and in Kenya it was legally impossible to acquire land in a 'Native Land Unit' which was not of one's own tribe. Nowhere was there an effort to create a national consciousness, and indeed in Tanganyika, even up to the eve of independence, attempts were made to strengthen tribal ties to counter the growing power of a national political party.[1]

Nation building is now an important part of state policy. At the same time, the dangers of excessive nationalism are realized and comparisons with nationalism in Europe resented. In eastern Africa only Somalia appears as a nation state in which a common ethnic origin, common language, common religion and common traditions provide the basis for a national consciousness.[2] Here the political appeal is for the expansion of state boundaries to include all the Somalis in one nation state. Such a national force is necessarily at variance with that of the poly-ethnic state for whom any secession of territory must invite the disintegration of the entire state.

NATIONALISM IN TANGANYIKA

Of all the East African territories in 1963 Tanganyika had the most fully developed national consciousness. In part, this reflected Tanganyika's

[1] R. C. Pratt, 'Multiracialism and local government in Tanganyika', *Race*, 2, 1960, p. 33.

[2] See for instance S. Touval, *Somali Nationalism*, Cambridge, Mass., 1963.

Nationalism, Regionalism and Federalism 289

longer independence and the presence of a nationally organized political party which emerged before independence, and indeed the earlier independence of Tanganyika was achieved because of the greater unity which existed. The fostering of a spirit of national unity did, however, depend upon more favourable circumstances, for regional and social differences had been far less marked than those which existed elsewhere. Although there are a great many tribes, probably about 120, tribal animosities are few. The very multiplicity of tribes could be interpreted as a source of strength since no single large tribe was able to dominate the whole and to insist upon a federal form of government in order to preserve its identity.[1]

Of the twenty-two tribes with more than 100,000 people only the Sukuma number more than a million and this group itself is a federation of fragmented chiefships located in the interior of the country and is not especially prosperous. Of the other tribes, some, such as the Chagga and the Haya, are intensely proud of their own institutions, but the fact that there are many medium sized tribes has prevented any one from dominating. It may also be significant that of the large tribes only the less advanced Iraqw are not of Bantu stock, while the group with strongest regional interests, the Nilo-Hamitic Masai, number less than 100,000. Further, none of the large tribes lives near the capital city, and most of the political leaders have been drawn from the small tribes. The Chagga and the Haya, as the most prosperous peoples with strong traditional loyalties, live near to the northern and north-western borders, but there is no evidence of separatism in these parts.

Another factor contributing to the unification of Tanganyika has been the presence of a *lingua franca* which has been adopted as a national language. Swahili, which is widely known, is the official language of parliament, and is commonly used for legal proceedings and official pronouncements. Although Swahili is also used in Kenya it is only extensively used on the coast, while in Uganda only a small proportion of the people understand it and there is a prejudice against using it.

These various factors favoured the earlier development of a national political party, the Tanganyika African National Union, which gathered strength on a policy of independence and national unity. This political party came to dominate the political life of Tanganyika which was run as a one-party state with T.A.N.U. representatives being the only ones in the central government, and also with party supporters leading the

[1] S. A. De Smith, *New Constitutions in the Commonwealth*, London, 1964, p. 236.

290 *Essays in Political Geography*

district councils and trade unions. Because Tanganyika had achieved this degree of solidarity a note of impatience could be detected in the attitudes of its politicians at the lack of similar success in the neighbouring countries.

REGIONALISM IN UGANDA

In Uganda local loyalties have remained strong, though some progress is being made in creating a national consciousness. The colonial rulers found in four parts of the country an established system of rule by chiefs which was strengthened by the policy of indirect rule. Under the independence constitution, room is allowed for local feeling to express itself, but in some areas it is finding expression outside the law.

The presence of local patriotism hinges upon a variety of circumstances. First is the ethnic complexity of the country. The largest tribe, the Ganda, contains about one-sixth of the total population and is nearly twice as numerous as the next largest, the Iteso. In addition, the Ganda are located at the centre of the country and are dominant in the capital. The variety of ethnic types is considerable, comprising the Nilotic Lango (364,000), Acholi (285,000), Alur (123,000), Jophadola (101,000) and Kumam (61,000); the Nilo-Hamitic Iteso (525,000), Karamojong (132,000) and Sebei (37,000); and the Sudanic Lugbara (236,000) and Madi (80,000). Differences also occur within the Bantu group between those with a centralized political system focusing upon the personality of the ruler, such as the Ganda (1,045,000), Nyankole (519,000), Toro (208,000) and Nyoro (188,000) and those without strong rulers like the Kiga (460,000), Gisu (329,000), Konjo (107,000) and Amba (33,000). The Soga (502,000) occupy an intermediate position. At least thirteen of these groups dominate in a district of their own.

An additional two districts, West Nile and Bukedi, consist of an amalgamation of minor groups, in one of which (Bukedi) rioting, as a result of ethnically based grievances, occurred in 1962. A policy of favouring the minor groups by allowing them district administrative status, as had been displayed by the Democratic Party in relation to Sebei, would threaten the continuance of these two districts. Already district administration has virtually collapsed in the Konjo and Amba areas of the kingdom of Toro where these two groups are agitating for the establishment of a Ruwenzururu district.

A second factor associated with the strength of regionalism is the multiplicity of languages, itself a product of ethnic diversity. In the

POLITICAL DIVISIONS OF UGANDA

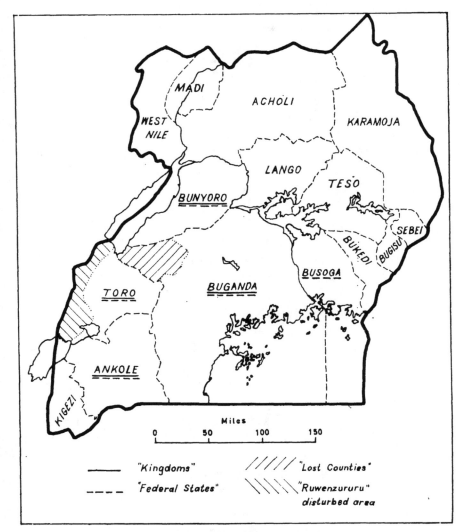

Fig. 16.2. Political Divisions of Uganda

absence of Swahili, with the northern parts of the country unable to accept Luganda and with English spoken by less than 10 per cent of the people, Uganda lacks a national language. For the purposes of an adult literacy campaign primers have been prepared in twenty languages. Requests to increase the number of languages used in broadcasting beyond the thirteen already in use have been declined by the minister on the grounds that broadcasting in so many languages serves to divide

292 *Essays in Political Geography*

the nation instead of uniting it.[1] For similar reasons the possibility of offering languages other than English and Luganda for examination purposes has not been pursued.

A third factor making for local differences is religion. According to a sample census between 50 and 60 per cent of the population are Christian and 5 per cent Muslim. Moreover the Christian group is itself divided into Roman Catholics and Protestants, with the former rather more numerous than the latter. This division has taken on a political significance since the Democratic Party clearly appealed to the Roman Catholic community for its support, and this was especially so in those parts of northern Uganda where Italian missionary influence was strong. The D.P. had at least two members of parliament from Bukedi, Acholi and West Nile, where Roman Catholicism is well established, and also from Ankole and Kigezi where Roman Catholic and Protestant influences are more evenly matched. It is possible that the Uganda People's Congress received some benefit from supposed Protestant connexions for Protestant dominance tends to coincide with support for the U.P.C. in Lango. On the other hand, in Buganda, the most Christianized part of Uganda, other forces of particularism are stronger than religion.[2]

In addition, a few special issues heightened the importance of regional differences. In particular, a long-standing dispute between Buganda and Bunyoro has existed over the question of administration of the so-called 'Lost Counties', that is the northern part of Mubende which had been taken from Bunyoro and given to Buganda at the time of the establishment of colonial rule. Bunyoro had expected a more sympathetic treatment from the D.P. and hence supported that party.[3] Similarly some support was given to the D.P. in the kingdoms of Toro, Bunyoro and Ankole in the expectation that that party would be more likely to grant them a federal status equivalent to that of Buganda.

Thus the D.P. benefited from support of various factional elements. In the elections of 1962 it won 27 seats against the U.P.C.'s 41. Later defections took place, initially from those areas where local issues had accounted for the election of D.P. supporters, and subsequently representatives from the Catholic areas changed their party allegiances.[4]

[1] A. Nekyon, *National Assembly Proceedings*, 20 November 1962.

[2] G. F. Engholm, 'The Westminster model in Uganda', *International Journal*, 18, 1963, p. 469.

[3] As a result of a referendum these countries are being returned to Bunyoro in 1965.

[4] In December 1964, the opposition was seriously weakened by the defection of its leader.

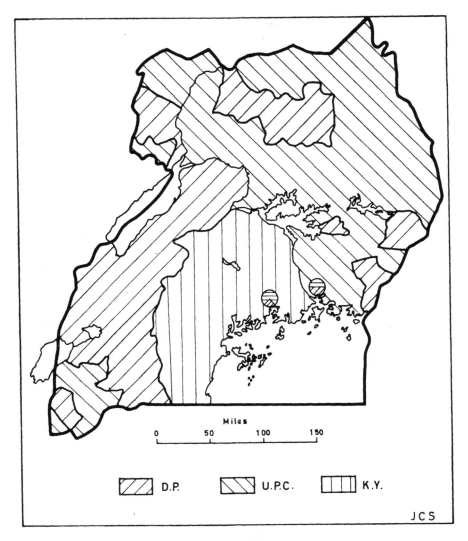

Fig. 16.3. Uganda Election 1962

It is also significant that during the first year of the U.P.C. government the D.P. lost control of all of the district councils in which it had formerly been strong, namely Ankole, Kigezi, Bunyoro and Sebei. The U.P.C., which has always presented itself as a national party, thus increased its control in the centre and in the districts.

294 *Essays in Political Geography*

THE UNIQUENESS OF BUGANDA

The treaty arrangements between the United Kingdom and the Kingdom of Buganda always gave the latter a special position in Uganda, and even under the 1962 constitution it still functioned as a privileged region. This distinctiveness is in some respects more than tribalism, and the leaders of the area, although commonly branded as neo-traditionalists, have shown a remarkable ability to adjust to new situations.[1] This special position of Buganda has been described as that of the 'single advanced enclave, which refused to be treated as a province of the new state on a level with other provinces'.[2] This 'advanced enclave' owes much to its economic prosperity which in turn is dependent upon favourable geographical circumstances, and upon the fact that a centralized state has existed for thirty-five generations and had produced a strong monarchical system supported by an efficient administrative machinery. The kingdom of Buganda has, therefore, more of the attributes of a state in terms of contiguity, homogeneity, historical continuity and coherence of social customs than has the larger political unit of which it forms a part.

The problem facing the colonial administration had been to incorporate this special area into a unitary state. In the process of evolution towards independence Buganda had declared its intention to secede. Although such a move was impossible since so much of the polity of Uganda as a whole is located within the Buganda domain, such declarations as this have been instrumental in preserving for Buganda powers in the independent Uganda which are stronger than those possessed by any other area. The parliament of Buganda, the Lukiiko, now exercises considerable authority over the police, education, justice and revenue collection, and in addition it functions as an electoral college nominating the representatives for Buganda in the National Assembly. Thus, in order to accommodate the political importance of Buganda, Uganda has been obliged to adopt a non-unitary constitution.

Although under the constitution the traditional Kingdoms, Buganda, Bunyoro, Toro and Ankole are technically federal states, as also is Busoga which has now elected an hereditary ruler, the privileges and powers of these other units are all much less than those of Buganda and none may act as electoral colleges. Ten other administrative districts

---

[1] D. A. Low, *Political Parties in Uganda 1949–1962*, Athlone Press, Commonwealth Papers No. 8, London, 1962.

[2] A. I. Richards, 'Constitutional problems in Uganda', *Political Quarterly*, 33, 1963, p. 363.

Nationalism, Regionalism and Federalism 295

exist, most of which have elected non-hereditary heads of state, but these are not considered to be federal units. Uganda professes to be a semi-federal state, with one unit having a considerable autonomy so that Buganda now, as in the past, has something of the appearance of a state within a state.

Potentially there is some liability of conflict between the central government and the government of Buganda, and occasional crises have already arisen. The participation of a number of Ganda in the cabinet, and the election of the Kabaka as the first President of Uganda has served to lessen the tension. Nevertheless, the survival of the nation depends upon a balancing of central and regional forces and, although it is clear that the consolidation of the regional strength of Buganda is contrary to the ideal of national solidarity, some recognition of the unique position of Buganda has been necessary. Fortunately, now that many issues are being resolved, many leading people of Buganda are devoting their services to the affairs of the central government and speak forcefully for the cause of national unity.[1]

In quite another sense Buganda is unique; that is, that although the attachment of the Ganda to their ruler and to their traditions provides the motivating force for their strength, the power of Buganda depends upon more than tribalism. Even without counting the people of Bunyoro descent in Mubende, there are about 400,000 non-Ganda dispersed throughout the kingdom. These are predominantly migrants from Rwanda and Burundi, together with lesser numbers of Alur and Lugbara from the north-west, and Hima herdsmen from Ankole. In addition, there are Luo employees in factories and the railways, and Asian traders in small commercial centres outside Kampala. Some of these people are short-term migrants, but many have become permanent residents.

Although there have been occasional and localized tensions, a high proportion of the long-term immigrants have identified themselves with the aspirations of the Ganda. Many have become land-owners or tenant cultivators, and some have acquired a Kiganda name and are generally fully assimilated into local society. Potentially this substantial body of non-Ganda could provide a discordant political element, but except in

---

[1] See for instance S. J. L. Zake, *The K.Y.-U.P.C. Merger*, Kampala, 1963, p. 3. Initially the first government of independent Uganda depended upon a coalition of political parties including the U.P.C. and the Kabaka Yekka, a Buganda movement. Late in 1964 the K.Y. withdrew from the coalition and some Ganda minister resigned, though a major breach was avoided. Since the defection of D.P. members to the U.P.C. the government is no longer dependent upon K.Y. support.

296 Essays in Political Geography

Mubende, where the Ganda have failed to assimilate the Nyoro, there is little evidence that this is so.[1] A further indication that the Ganda can adopt a non-tribal view is revealed in the election of an Indian and a northern Ugandan to the Lukiiko, and by the nomination of the only European to the National Assembly as a Buganda representative. This reveals a lack of parochialism which is unusual in the country as a whole, and indicates a willingness to think on a level that transcends the tribe.

REGIONALISM IN KENYA

The extent to which regional interests were written into the independence constitution of Kenya reflects some of the conditions present also in Uganda. The main difference lay in that fact that the regions enshrined in the constitution were special administrative units only recently created, so that there was no tradition either in terms of customary practice or of colonial administrative machinery. Further, one main political party, the Kenya African Democratic Union, was more strongly identified with 'majimbo-ism', the elevation of regional government status, than was the case in Uganda. In so far as most regions consisted of an amalgamation of tribes, this regional movement must be regarded as a superior force to tribalism. In effect the first constitution was unitary in form but it assumed great complexity in its provisions designed to preserve regional powers.[2] The constitution provided for the election of a series of Regional Assemblies with extensive powers; a House of Representatives with 117 seats elected by the constituencies and an additional 12 special members; and a Senate of 41 seats whose main function was to oversee the fair operation of the constitution.

In order to safeguard the interests of the regions a change in the constitution required a 75 per cent vote in the House of Representatives, and a 90 per cent vote in the Senate, or a 66 per cent vote on a referendum. The main political support for the regions centred upon the K.A.D.U. party, which was a consortium of representatives of the lesser tribes whose main motivating force had been a fear of domination by Kenya's two largest tribes, the Kikuyu and the Luo, which had combined politically to form the Kenya African National Union. In the

[1] See D. Apter, *The Political Kingdom in Uganda*, Oxford, 1961. Apter thinks that the D.P. received support from immigrants in the 1961 elections, but there is no reason to believe that this was so in 1962.

[2] The constitution was so complex that few people can seriously have believed that it would work. See D. A. De Smith, *op. cit.*, p. 301. Constitutional amendments were proposed late in 1964 which led to the dissolution of the K.A.D.U. opposition.

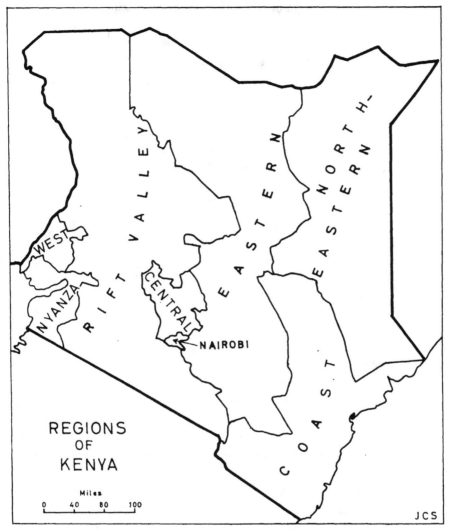

Fig. 16.4. Regions of Kenya

event K.A.N.U. won the election immediately prior to independence and has since shown little concern for the needs of the regional governments. Thus although the forces of regionalism were strong enough initially to play a major role in shaping the constitution, they are now in eclipse, and a political party is in control anxious to establish a united national outlook.

The regional divisions of Kenya were established following the recommendations of a commission of enquiry,[1] and ultimately depend upon

[1] *Report of the Boundaries Commission*, H.M.S.O., Cmnd. 1899, 1962.

298 Essays in Political Geography

the expressed wishes of the people to 'be associated with the people with whom they felt they had similar customs, language and other affinities'. The end result contained some revolutionary suggestions for re-drawing the administrative map of Kenya into seven Regions and the Nairobi area, each of which are ethnically determined but also display a measure of geographical cohesion, as will be apparent from the description which follows.

(a) The *Coast Region* consists mainly of the former Coast Province and includes the land formerly leased from the Sultan of Zanzibar which formed the 'Protectorate' as distinct from the 'Colony' of Kenya. Prior to independence this area had been integrated fully into the state and this special status had been lost. The region consists mainly of the coastal plain, together with a lowland extension inland along the River Tana, and extends westwards to enclose a portion of the 'nyika' plateau upon which rise the Teita hills. It is populated mainly by various groups of Coastal Bantu peoples and a substantial Arab minority. The initial proposals to include the Somali in this area would have added substantially to the Islamic character of the whole, though there has never been much cultural contact between the Arab and Somali Muslims. The Arabs, and to a lesser extent also the African communities, have in the past supported a variety of political parties, some of which from time to time have advocated secession. Later the Coast formed a major focus of support for K.A.D.U., which has dominated the Regional Assembly, and the parliamentary members have been K.A.D.U. supporters, except for those representing the Teita area. In the Coast Region regional forces are stronger than in most other areas of Kenya.

(b) The *Eastern Region* came into being as a result of the unwillingness of the Kamba to be associated in the same region as either the Kikuyu or the Masai, and also because of the new willingness of the Meru and the Embu, who had previously been grouped with the Kikuyu, to be linked now with the Kamba. As Central Bantu these three groups are all closely related, but Hamitic Boran and lesser groups have been added. These are mainly pagan, and as such are distinct from their ethnic kin, the Somali. The Eastern Region is mainly a dry area, extending northwards into a decidedly arid zone but containing a wetter area on the eastern flanks of Mt Kenya in the Embu and Meru areas. The Boran, who are migratory pastoralists, have very little in common with the agricultural Meru and Embu, though pastoral traditions among the Kamba remain rather stronger. Further problems arise in this region from the lack of an administrative focus and from the lack of communi-

Nationalism, Regionalism and Federalism 299

cations linking its various parts. The pastoral areas have more in common with the Rift Valley Region, with parts of which they had formerly been administered as Northern Province. At the time of the election the Kamba were represented by their own political party, the African People's Party which had broken away from K.A.N.U. but later rejoined it. The Embu and the Meru supported K.A.N.U., but the Boran boycotted the Regional Assembly election and returned an independent with K.A.N.U. sympathies to the House of Representatives.

(*c*) The *Central Region* consists solely of Kikuyu peoples and is therefore the most homogeneous of the regions. The Kikuyu are the most numerous of the tribal groups of Kenya and are concentrated on the lower slopes of Mt Kenya and the Aberdares. Incorporated into this region are many of the former European owned lands, which are being reconstituted as areas for resettlement for Kikuyus from 'squatter' settlements elsewhere, and for the landless peasants from the overcrowded areas of the Kikuyu homeland. From the fertile volcanic soils and the highly reliable rainfall a prosperous farming area, dependent upon coffee, pyrethrum, vegetable and dairy production is developing. Because of their numerical strength, their economic prosperity and from their strategic location dominating the capital, the Kikuyu have emerged as the most powerful political group in Kenya. The role of the Kikuyu in revolt against colonial rule and their early part in the founding of K.A.N.U. have enabled them to consolidate their status in an independent Kenya. At all levels of government the Kikuyu are solid supporters of K.A.N.U.

(*d*) The *Rift Valley Region* is made up mainly of numerous pastoralist tribes of Nilo-Hamitic origin. Many of these, such as the Masai and the Turkana, remain migratory pastoralists living at low densities in arid environments, but are ethnically related to sedentary pastoralists turned cultivators living on the wetter western wall of the Rift Valley, such as the Kipsigi, Nandi and Elgeyo, who now are grouped under the name 'Kalenjin'. The Masai expressed a wish to be separated from the Kamba with whom they had formerly been associated in the Southern Province, and the Kalenjin preferred to be associated with their related Masai. There is no evidence that the Regional Boundaries Commission consulted the Europeans, but most of the European lands not required for resettlement are located in this region, where large scale land units are not abnormal, pressure on the land is not acute, and the registration of land titles is a common practice. There was probably a tacit mutual preference for the European owned lands to be incorporated in this region.

300 *Essays in Political Geography*

It formed one of the main areas for K.A.D.U. support since it was largely from Kalenjin leadership that the party was formed. The Regional Assembly was dominantly but not unanimously K.A.D.U., as were most of the elected members for the central assemblies, but the Masai and the Turkana eventually supported K.A.N.U. for local reasons, and the member for West Pokot changed to K.A.N.U. immediately after election.

(*e*) The *Western Region* is populated predominantly by the Luhya, a Bantu group on the eastern and southern slopes of Mt Elgon, but includes some isolated Nilo-Hamitic groups near the Uganda border. The Western Region came into being from a strongly expressed desire of the Luhya not to be associated with the Luo or the Kalenjins. The Luhya number over a million, and although this is the smallest region much of it is very densely populated. The area has a moderate rainfall and depends upon a relatively low cash return from maize and cotton production. The region lacks an obvious administrative focus since Kitale was allocated to the Rift Valley Region. In the elections to the Regional Assembly, the K.A.D.U., somewhat surprisingly, gained a small majority, but the majority of seats in the House of Representatives was won by K.A.N.U.

(*f*) The *Nyanza Region* is predominantly the area of high density population centering upon the Kavirondo Gulf and the surrounding uplands. The population is mainly of Nilotic Luo origin who number over a million, but includes also isolated groups of Bantu, namely the Kisii and Kuria in the south-eastern hills. The Luo are now mainly agriculturists, growing maize and cotton as cash crops, and have retained cattle and fishing interests, though in places land hunger is acute. A small portion of the western area of the former Masai reserve has been added to relieve the pressure. Nyanza has always been the second major stronghold of K.A.N.U. and the Luo have provided a number of national leaders. Although there has always been the possibility of Luo and Kikuyu factions emerging within K.A.N.U., no differences on these lines have become public.

(*g*) The *North-eastern Region* has come into being out of the demands of the Somali for complete secession, and from their related unwillingness to co-operate with any of the other peoples of Kenya. The population of this area is much less than that of the other regions. As a result of the boycott of elections at all levels the area is administered by a special force under the central government.

(*h*) The *Nairobi area* consists mainly of the built-up area of the capital city together with nearby satellite townships. Its population is

Nationalism, Regionalism and Federalism 301

mixed, but contains large communities of Kikuyu and Asians. Politically its representatives support K.A.N.U. and, although some of its constituencies favour the election of Asians, the elections reveal some examples of inter-racial and non-tribal voting.

This regional account affords the basis for an analysis of party support. After the elections of May 1963 three Regional Assemblies had K.A.D.U. majorities. For the House of Representatives K.A.D.U. had received about half as many votes as K.A.N.U. but had fewer than half as many seats, in spite of a generous allocation of seats to pastoral areas. In the Senate, where K.A.D.U. strength was greater, they were still outnumbered by K.A.N.U.[1] In the months following the election a gradual defection from K.A.D.U. took place.

REGIONALISM IN EAST AFRICA

The effects of regionalism in each East African state can now be compared. In the first place, the constitution of Kenya preserves a regional structure, but gives equal rights to all regions, and not a privileged status to one region as is the case in Uganda. During the course of political evolution in Kenya various proposals had been made to preserve a special regional status for the 'White Highlands',[2] but naturally this was not acceptable to the African community and did not even have the support of the majority of European politicians. Similarly movements have existed for a special status for the 'Coastal Strip', and, although these have been thwarted, murmurings for coastal secession have occasionally been heard. In a sense the Northeastern Region has a special status, though not a privileged one.

Secondly, the forces of regionalism in Uganda and Kenya can be assessed by the nature of control of the local councils. In Uganda the K.Y. movement has dominated the affairs of the Buganda Lukiiko, whereas the D.P. support in each of the other district councils has been reduced until the U.P.C. now predominates in all of them. In Kenya the predominance of K.A.D.U. in two of the Regional Assemblies and a weaker control in a third gave rise to a situation potentially as delicate as that in Uganda. An energetic regional council might have attempted

---

[1] For a fuller analysis of the election see C. Sanger and J. Nottingham, 'The Kenya general election of 1963', *Journal of Modern African Studies*, 2, 1964, pp. 1–40.

[2] See for instance, Lord Altrincham, *Kenya's Opportunity*, London, 1955, and the efforts of the Federal Independence Party.

302 *Essays in Political Geography*

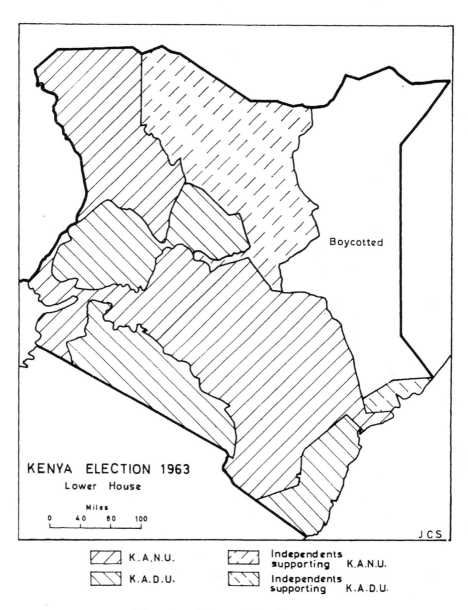

Fig. 16.5. Kenya Elections 1963

Nationalism, Regionalism and Federalism 303

to work on local loyalties at variance with those of the central government. There was a danger that only people of local origin would receive preferment within a particular region, a situation which could have led to administrative difficulties in those areas, especially the Rift Valley Region, where there was a shortage of educated personnel. Likewise there was a danger that central government posts would only be available to persons from the areas supporting K.A.N.U., which in fact, so far as Central and Nyanza Regions were concerned, probably did have a surplus of educated talent. In the event the regions of Kenya have not gained in strength, partly because the central government chose to treat certain constitutional requirements lightly. This in itself reflects a basic difference from Uganda. Kenya has never had political organizations dependent upon kingship, for such paramount chiefs as used to exist were largely the creation of the colonial system. Thus in Kenya the administrative districts and particularly the regions have a degree of political unreality.[1]

In Uganda and Kenya, therefore, there exist varying degrees of regionalism which may potentially operate against the interests of national unity. In Tanganyika such forces, though not entirely absent, are less evident. However, with the union of Tanganyika and Zanzibar as the state of Tanzania, a new situation has arisen. In reality the union exists in little else than its name, and Zanzibar retains complete administrative autonomy which provides a privileged enclave within Tanzania not unlike that of Buganda in Uganda, for here again is a state within a state.[2] If in future Rwanda or Burundi could be re-incorporated into Tanzania, such a development might also give rise to further political differences.

Finally, regional interests manifest themselves even within the organization of the major national parties. These can be looked upon as parochial forces and are stronger in Kenya and Uganda than in Tanganyika. Parochialism can be seen in the virtual necessity for the candidate for a rural constituency to be a member of the local tribe. Exceptions to this are very few, though a less limiting practice may prevail in the towns. Each state has some device for electing otherwise unrepresented elements of society, especially females, for 'specially elected' seats. Further, parochial considerations occur in the allocation of ministerial

[1] With the collapse of the K.A.D.U. the future of the Regional Assemblies is now uncertain. They may become useful organizations for local administration, but the play of politics within them is unlikely to be of national significance.

[2] The union of Tanzania is gradually taking shape, but even by mid-1955 a large measure of administrative independence was still retained by Zanzibar.

304 *Essays in Political Geography*

and sub-ministerial posts. Thus in Uganda, at the time of the U.P.C.–K.Y. alliance, five ministerial posts and five parliamentary secretaries were drawn from Buganda, while every other major district provided at least one minister and the lesser districts at least a parliamentary secretary. In Kenya the allocation of positions of office in the government also represents a careful balancing of local forces. Every region is represented by a minister, though clearly the influence of the main areas of K.A.D.U. support is limited. There is, in addition, a fairly even balancing of influence between the Kikuyu and the Luo, but with the former enjoying a slight preponderance. The union of Zanzibar with Tanganyika in 1964 also presented an occasion for the allocation of official posts between the two.

FEDERALISM IN EAST AFRICA

Although federalism has been eschewed as a form of internal government, plenty of consideration has been given during the past thirty years to the possibility of an interterritorial federation. Indeed, although few detailed statements are available, the formation of a federation had been the agreed policy of each state as recently as June 1963, but what at one time appeared imminent has since been delayed.[1] Few reasons have been made public for hesitation on the part of Uganda or Kenya. Political scientists and economists have expressed views on the advantages to be derived from co-operation, but little explanation has been given as to why the present co-operation is inadequate or what more can be gained from a firm federation.

Some fear exists that without a political structure to support it the present co-operation may cease. Already there is a marked degree of co-operation, mainly, but not solely, through association with the East African Common Services Organization, the successor of the East Africa High Commission and even of the earlier Conferences of Governors. Railways and harbours, posts and telegraphs, airways, meteorological services and much scientific research are all on an East African basis. A modified form of common market and customs union exists, there is a joint currency board and a common income tax policy, and certain legal institutions are joint. Most of these services are legislated for by the Central Legislative Assembly, to which each separate National Assembly elects representatives, but the powers of the C.L.A. are limited by the dependence of these services upon finance derived from the separate

[1] Since July 1964 the prospects of a federation have receded further.

Nationalism, Regionalism and Federalism 305

states. The future of these common services is uncertain but the threat of Tanganyika to withdraw from the organization unless a federation was formed has not been carried into effect.

Geographically East Africa constitutes a convenient unit, distinct from the high Ethiopian plateau to the north, the Congo basin to the west and the savanna lands with pronounced seasonal variations to the south. Nevertheless the limits to an East African geographical region cannot be precisely drawn, and political boundaries only roughly correspond to such geographical divisions as can be distinguished. Within the political area of East Africa the variety of geographical circumstances – the coastal plains, the equatorial plateaus, the lake basins, the rift valleys, the volcanic mountains, and the dry savannas – presents to each territory a diversity of opportunities and problems that can most effectively be studied jointly.

The three states share a common biological environment and possess common ecological problems. Policies concerning such matters as animal conservation, insect control, disease eradication, improvement of grazing lands, cultivation of cash-crops, conservation of forests, management of fishery resources, hydrological control and the like all benefit from a degree of inter-state consultation and research co-operation. A variety of scientific research organizations exists on an East African basis to deal with these common problems, even though it may appear, not always without justification, that the state in which the laboratories and field experiments are located benefit more than the other contributing states.

Economically East Africa is already operating as a unit, and it is obviously desirable that this should continue to be so. As a means of supporting the present industries and of attracting international investment for further industrial expansion the existence of a market comprising twenty-five million people is important. This argument is self-evident so long as the advancement of East Africa as a whole is concerned. However, the advantages in the past have led to the far greater economic advancement of Kenya. A commission has enquired into these discrepancies, and Kenya's benefit is now counteracted by a contribution to E.A.C.S.O. funds.[1] It is questionable whether these monetary compensations are of the right order, and even whether Tanganyika and Uganda would not prefer some other way of redressing the balance. The need for industrial development and the creation of employment opportunities for Tanganyika is great, and for Uganda limitations to industrial

---

[1] *Report of the Economic and Fiscal Commission to East Africa*, H.M.S.O., Cmnd. 1279, 1961 (Raisman Report).

306 *Essays in Political Geography*

development are presented by the 600-mile rail haul from the coast. Given a free choice, industries would continue to develop at Mombasa or Nairobi, where skilled workers are available near to the largest markets and best transport facilities. It is understandable that Tanzania should find the present nature of the common market unsatisfactory and should prefer a strong federation with powers to direct the location of industry.[1] An inter-territorial policy on industrial location might have prevented some of the present anomalies. A cement factory was built in Tanganyika even though the two in Kenya and the one in Uganda were producing far below capacity. An oil refinery is being built at Dar es Salaam, even though the one recently constructed at Mombasa could easily cater for all East African needs. Any policy of industrial planning would place a restraint upon expansion in Kenya. This would lead Kenya to concentrate upon agricultural expansion of sugar, tobacco, coffee, cotton, tea and sisal, in which case it would compete with the other territories on both the internal and external markets, some of which are already subject to international restrictions.[2] Other areas of economic activity in which there is a clear need for inter-state co-operation include tourism, labour mobility and transport. At present a great proportion of the work of East African Airways concerns traffic internal to the area, and the operation of the Lake Victoria steamer service involves the three countries equally. Similarly, so far as the railways are concerned, Uganda is entirely dependent upon the line through Kenya, and a sizeable amount of Kilimanjaro coffee goes out via Mombasa. Although railway expansion in each country has to be financed independently, the case for operating East African railways jointly is strong. Nevertheless, although it is possible to see East Africa as an economic unit, the fact remains that the degree of economic advancement varies between the states. In 1959 Kenya had an average annual income per head of £33 3s., Uganda £23 1s. and Tanganyika £17 6s. Understandably Tanganyika would expect a federation to permit and encourage its economic progress.

The political basis for a consideration of federation has already been prepared. In Kenya and Uganda constitutions designed to preserve the entrenched rights of regions have been created, yet all three countries have a fundamental interest in furthering national solidarity. To some extent these two factors may conflict, and in any case require a delicate balancing to avoid tension. The prospect of a federation introduces a

[1] An agreement between the three countries on the allocation of new industries was worked out late in 1964.

[2] The Kenya *Development Plan 1964–1970* gives a clear lead in this direction.

Nationalism, Regionalism and Federalism 307

third element which could create tension or strain existing compromises. It would not be true to say that Buganda is an obstacle to Uganda's joining a federation, though in the past Buganda has certainly objected to the creation of a federation dominated by Kenya Europeans. More probably opposition to the federation comes from many quarters, and may depend upon national rather than regional attitudes. Dr Nyerere of Tanganyika recognized that if the territories gained their independence separately, national aspirations would lead in different directions; and in order to prevent this he offered to delay independence for Tanganyika until Uganda and Kenya got theirs, if by so doing a federation could be created. In the event, this has not happened, and different courses have in fact been followed in each country. From what were initially different positions in any case, the three states have adopted divergent policies.

Tanganyika is a one-party state with few regional problems, and with political party control over all local governments and trade unions. The government is following a vigorous policy of African socialism, summarized in the spirit of 'Ujamaa' or 'family-hood'. In the effort to build a classless African socialist society without a privileged community, the government has prevented the development of individual land titles, and has attempted to prevent the accumulation of private wealth. The country has an urgent need to increase its industrial development and to overcome problems of internal communications. Normally Tanzania has an overall favourable balance of trade, but it buys goods worth £10,000,000 a year from Kenya compared with Kenya's purchases valued at £3,000,000 from Tanzania, and in addition has a £2,000,000 trade gap with Uganda. These differences are widening, and there is a strong feeling that Tanzania should advance industrially to redress the balance. In the field of international affairs, Tanzania has developed more economic, cultural and even military contacts with communist countries, including China, than has been the case with the other East African states, though the policies of all three are essentially non-aligned.

In Kenya, as has been seen, regional influences have been strong, and national unity is as yet less fully developed than in Tanganyika. Although African socialism has been adopted as the policy of the state, land settlement policies provide for and even encourage the emergence of an African land-owning class. The land settlement policy is involving heavy government expenditure, and temporarily at any rate has resulted in a reduction of agricultural production, while an economic recession

308 *Essays in Political Geography*

is taking place at a time when its neighbours are jealous of Kenya's greater industrial development.

In response, Kenya is focusing attention upon the need to increase cash-crop production and to cater for a population which, at 3 per cent per year, is increasing more rapidly than that of the other states. Kenya is faced with an unemployment problem more acute than elsewhere, and for political reasons this cannot be accommodated by industrial expansion and migration to Uganda may become less easy. Kenya has customarily had a large deficit on international trade, which has only partly been made up by favourable balances with Tanganyika and Uganda, and furthermore has for a long time had a much larger national debt. The financial position of Kenya has also been worsened by the withdrawal of European and Asian capital in recent years. Although Kenya has probably been more fortunate than its neighbours in acquiring international aid and loans, the country may be more adversely affected by the problem of payment of interest.

Uganda has a constitution which entrenches the rights of its regions. It is a two-party state, though with a weak opposition. Uganda has strong social distinctions and an influential community of prosperous entrepreneurs, both African, mainly Ganda, and Asian, many of whom are closely associated with successful schemes for economic expansion. Among the wealthy group are a few large land-owners, but even the moderate prosperity among a large section of the community has engendered a conservative approach to politics. The country's policy embraces African socialism, but this is mainly applied in the field of community development. Uganda has for a very long time had a favourable balance of trade, dependent upon the production mainly of coffee and cotton. The economic and political stability of the country has given rise to a lesser need for external aid. Internationally Uganda has had to deal circumspectly with her immediate neighbours, particularly in respect of refugees from Rwanda, Sudan and the Congo. On a wider front although also officially non-aligned, its affinities with non-Communist countries are close.

It is easy to exaggerate the differences between the three states and to say that they contain elements of incompatibility which would render a federation improbable, but one cannot deny that differences do exist and are in danger of getting greater. Because of the need to take these differences into account a weak federation would be easier to create than a strong one, but Tanganyika's wish has been for a federation with strong central powers. It is evident that in order to divert attention from

Nationalism, Regionalism and Federalism 309

major issues, lesser ones such as the question of the head of state or loss of United Nations representation, have been brought to the fore. Of considerable geographical interest is speculation as to which town should be the capital, and indeed which state should have the capital, were federation to take place. Clearly Nairobi, which on functional grounds would be the most convenient, is politically the least acceptable. However, there are bigger issues at stake. The fear once expressed by Nyerere that 'were they to gain independence at different times, the effect might be to arouse national sentiments which would make negotiation for a federation more difficult', seems to have been justified.

POSTSCRIPT

This essay relates to the political situation as it was in September, 1964, with some minor modifications to take into account developments late in 1964. Subsequent changes have reduced the constitutional significance of regional diversities and in particular the special status for Buganda has been abrogated. On the other hand the amount of inter-state co-operation has also lessened. The rapidity with which the political scene in East Africa changes represents only one of many problems to the political geographer.

17

The Further Partition of the Northwest Territories of Canada:
An Aspect of Decolonization in Northernmost North America
N. L. NICHOLSON

When Canada acquired 'Rupert's Land and the North-Western Territory' in 1870, she also inherited the problem of the creation of administrative units within this vast area of some three million square miles. As the Prime Minister of the day expressed it, the government had one great country before them to do with as they liked.[1] Ultimately this 'unorganized' territory became 'organized' in a number of different ways. Parts of it were added to adjacent Provinces; parts of it were divided into Provinces; other sections were set apart as separate Territories; and still other sections were divided into Districts with limited jurisdiction over their own affairs but under the overall jurisdiction of a neighbouring Province or of the Federal government. The political map of Canada from 1920 to the present day has evolved from a combination of all of these devices. But it appears to have been the over-riding view of the Federal government in recent years that ultimately all of Canada should be organized into Provinces and a good deal of attention has been given to ways and means of accelerating this process in the present Northwest Territories of Canada. In this, consideration has been given to the application of many of the devices used earlier.

ADDITIONS TO EXISTING PROVINCES

In 1953, Hon. Mr Aseltine, speaking in the Senate, said:

> Give the part north of British Columbia . . . to the province of British Columbia. All the travel out of that country is through British Columbia anyway. Give that part north of Alberta to the province of Alberta. That would take in the Mackenzie river valley, all that territory is adjacent to Edmonton, and all the traffic out of that territory is through the northern part of Alberta. Then give the part

[1] *Debates, House of Commons of Canada,* 1883.

L

312 *Essays in Political Geography*

north of Saskatchewan to the province of Saskatchewan, and the part north of Manitoba to the province of Manitoba.[1]

This was developed three years later when, in 1956, the Premier of British Columbia urged that part of the Northwest Territories join British Columbia,[2] and in 1959 he reiterated the suggestion in more detail by defining the part to join his province as the area between 120° N. and the eastern boundary of Yukon Territory, that is the section of the Northwest Territories immediately to the north of British Columbia.[3]

But the general reaction of the Territories to these suggestions appears to have been negative. Senator Aseltine said in the Senate of Canada in 1958, only five years after his original proposal to the contrary, that the Territories 'want to be the eleventh Province of Canada just as soon as they have enough population and get organized for the purpose' and it was reputed that the suggestion of the Premier of British Columbia of 1959 was 'unanimously turned thumbs down' by the Council of the Northwest Territories.[4] The Minister of Northern Affairs and National Resources himself said that 'residents of the Territories resent suggestions that the Provinces take them over'.[5] This was partly borne out by the deliberations of the Northwest Territories Council in 1960, which recognized that 'factors of political advance, communications and administrations suggested a change should be made in the *existing* Northwest Territories.'[6]

A NEW PROVINCE

In the early 1900s, in anticipation of the creation of one or more Provinces out of parts of the then Northwest Territories, it had been suggested that the new Province or Provinces would have no northern boundary other than the North Pole.[7] The Acts by which the Provinces of Alberta and Saskatchewan came into being in 1905, however, clearly indicated that this was not to be so at that time, as their northern boundary was set at 60° N. The Federal government took the view that

[1] *Debates, Senate of Canada*, 1953.
[2] *Vancouver Province*, 27 April 1956.
[3] *Winnipeg Free Press*, 20 July 1959.
[4] *Edmonton Journal*, 18 September 1959.
[5] *Edmonton Journal*, 8 May 1960.
[6] *Votes and Proceedings, Council of the Northwest Territories*, July 1961, p. 68.
[7] N. L. Nicholson, *The Boundaries of Canada, its Provinces and Territories*, Queen's Printer, Ottawa, 1964, p. 108.

Further Partition of the Northwest Territories of Canada 313

the area north of this parallel was 'absolutely unfit for agriculture' and that though it possessed indications of mineral wealth, without agriculture, there could be little hope of 'thick and permanent settlement', and, consequently, stable provincial government.[1] But during 1938 petitions were forwarded to the Federal government from Alberta and British Columbia, advocating the formation of a new Province out of certain of the northernmost parts of these two Provinces and a part of the Northwest Territories – the part that had since 1905 become more easily accessible and more capable of development.[2] It was also the desire of the Alberta government to have the matter placed on the agenda of the 1945 Dominion–Provincial Conference. But nothing came of this and the issue was not actively reopened until 1960.

Even then, it was considered unwise to contemplate a Province the size of the Northwest Territories as 'such a Province probably would not have the financial resources to develop such a large area, thus slowing down development drastically'.[3] Consequently the possible division of the Northwest Territories into two units was discussed and it was clear that two Territories were contemplated – an eastern and a western – with the idea that *each* should eventually be able to advance to provincial status. There was some minor opposition to such a division on the grounds that it would mean the division of the native peoples. In particular it would lead to the separation of most of the Eskimos from the Indians and Metis and this might retard their opportunities for advancement, especially of the Eskimos.[4] But in January 1961, the Council of the Northwest Territories accepted a committee report that 'when the Territories were divided, the western part be called the Territory of Mackenzie and the eastern part possibly the Territory of Franklin'.[5]

Such a division would recognize the very real differences in the geography of the eastern and western parts of the Northwest Territories as well as the fact that, because they are so different, they could not develop at a uniform rate. Some of the present legislation, which now applies to both the eastern and western parts, is inappropriate to one or the other. Furthermore, if the Northwest Territories were divided, their autonomy could be increased by giving the western portion a wholly elected council.[6]

[1] *Ibid.*, p. 82.   [2] *Debates, House of Commons of Canada*, 1938.
[3] *Votes and Proceedings, Council of the Northwest Territories*, July 1961, p. 69.
[4] *Ibid.*, Summer 1963, p. 120.   [5] *Ibid.*, January 1961, p. 7.
[6] *Ibid.*, June 1964, p. 36.

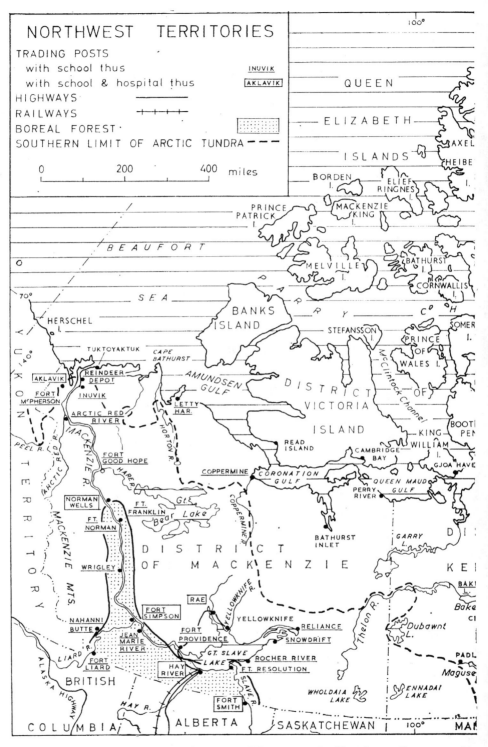

Fig. 17.1. Elements indicative of economic

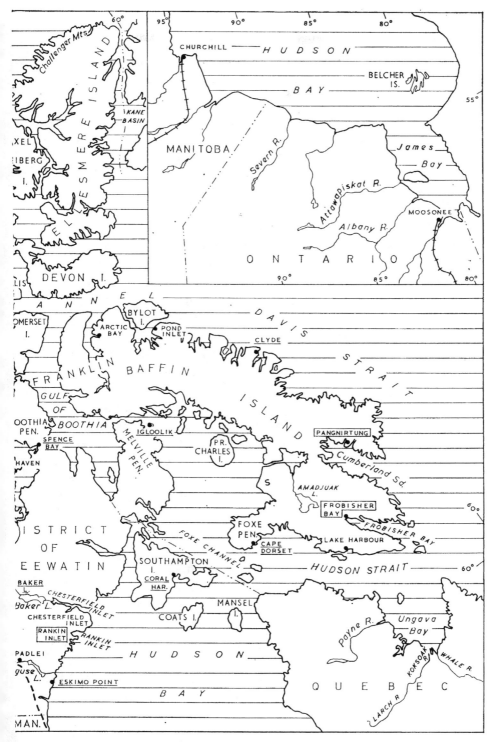

development in the Northwest Territories, 1964

316 *Essays in Political Geography*

NEW TERRITORIES

There was a general agreement that the two new Territories should be efficient and workable political and administrative entities, but attention was focused on the present District of Mackenzie which 'became of its greater population density and economic development, might advance more quickly towards responsible government'.[1] All the arable land in the Northwest Territories (about 2,000,000 acres) is in the Mackenzie area, and good ranching land is available in its south-western portion. It has a better potential for forestry operations than the Yukon Territory and more than half of the total area for fresh-water fisheries in Canada. Its mineral potential was already proven, in part as a result of the discoveries of lead and zinc at Pine Point, the gold mining operations at Yellowknife and the oil field at Norman Wells. There is hydro-electric power in abundance, on the Slave River, where it was estimated that nearly three-quarters of a million kilowatts could be developed.

In suggesting possible boundaries for the proposed Territory of Mackenzie the following principles were initially kept in mind:

1. The existing boundaries of the Northwest Territories as a whole should not be changed. This meant that the western and southern boundaries of the District of Mackenzie would not be changed and that consideration could be confined to the eastern and northern boundaries.

2. The area involved would probably be in excess of 500,000 square miles with a present population of some 15,000. Because of this very large area and the sparse population, government in such a Territory would be costly and complex. Hence the Territory should be created in such a way as to avoid as many extra problems as possible. For example, it should not include any areas where distance and isolation meant that the right to vote could not be made a reality.

3. Any new political unit should exclude areas which could not readily be administered from a centre within the more settled portion of the unit. This meant that King William Island would not be included in Mackenzie because, although water communication with the island is from the west, air communication and administration are provided from the east. The 200 people on the island consider themselves part of the east, particularly since many of their dealings are with Spence Bay, on Boothia Peninsula. Furthermore it was expected that most of the children on the island would go east for their education when the facilities were developed.[2] Similarly it was not administra-

[1] *Votes and Proceedings, Council of the Northwest Territories,* July 1961, p. 111.
[2] *Ibid.,* January 1961, pp. 74–5.

Further Partition of the Northwest Territories of Canada 317

tively feasible to include the Queen Elizabeth Islands in Mackenzie since the lines of communication and transportation run east and south from the Queen Elizabeth Islands to Churchill and Frobisher.[1]

4. Any new political unit should exclude areas with special requirements essentially different from those found in the Mackenzie Basin itself.

5. Any new boundary should be 'visible on the ground' – that is it should follow a river and/or any other easily identifiable physical feature.

Initially it seemed that a major problem in considering the boundaries of Mackenzie Territory would arise because the pattern of economic development is not yet firmly established. Assumptions about transportation routes, mine locations and similar questions may or may not prove to be correct in the future. But the experience in southern Canada has shown that such considerations do not need to play a dominant role in the arguments for any particular new boundary line. There are many places where transportation routes cut across provincial boundaries without causing any insurmountable handicaps. Similarly, mineral deposits lying athwart inter-provincial boundaries have been brought into production without the divided jurisdiction creating any substantial problems. As examples of this one has only to think of the Kirkland Lake–Noranda gold belt of Ontario–Quebec, the Flin Flon base metal deposits which straddle the Saskatchewan–Manitoba border, or the iron ore of the Labrador Trough which extends across the Quebec–Newfoundland boundary. The southern portion of the Alberta–Saskatchewan boundary divided the ranching country when it was established in 1905 and was objected to on these grounds at the time, but it is doubtful whether it has caused any permanent hardship.

Three possible boundary lines were first discussed by the Council of the Northwest Territories. (Fig. 17.1, Lines A, B, C.) *Line A* was defined as

> ... a line drawn generally northeastwards, following the watersheds as much as possible, from a point on the sixtieth parallel somewhere east of the Alberta–Saskatchewan boundary to the point where the present Mackenzie-Keewatin border intersects the Arctic coast; thence through Queen Maud Gulf, McClintock Channel, Viscount Melville Sound and McClure Strait so as to include Banks and Victoria Islands in the New Territory.

[1] *Loc. cit.*, p. 76.

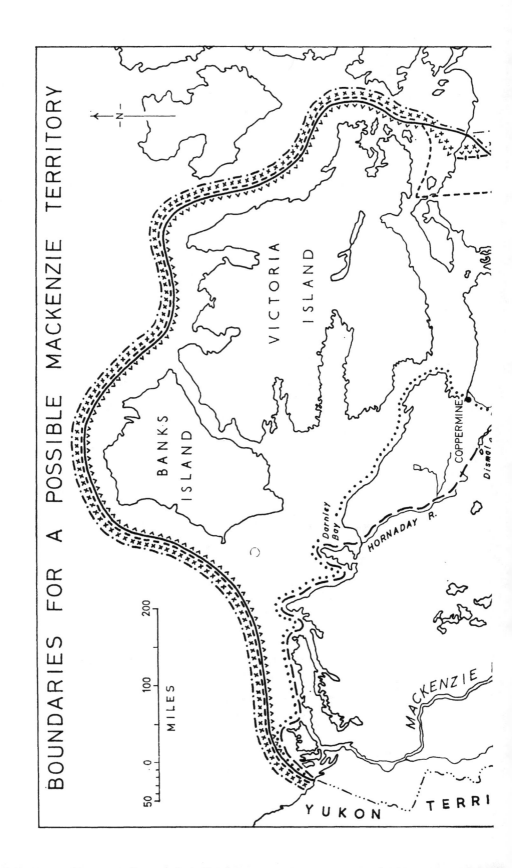

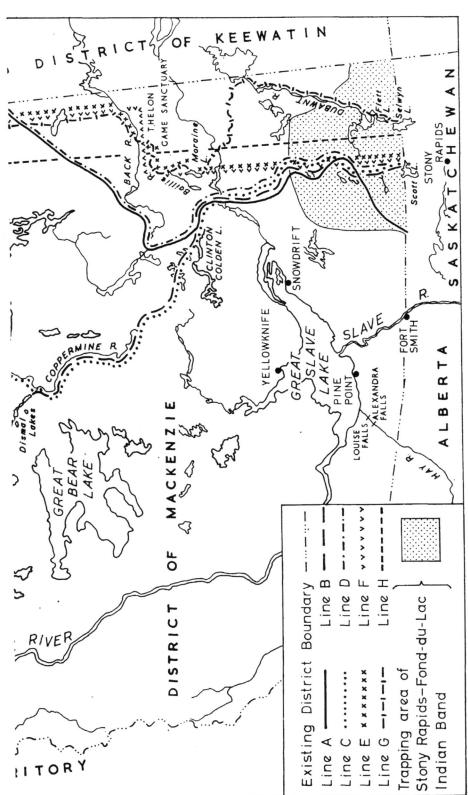

Fig. 17.2. Boundaries for a possible Mackenzie Territory

320 *Essays in Political Geography*

Some members of the council wondered whether a territory with this boundary would be a manageable and efficient unit. As the Mackenzie valley is essentially a treed area, would any useful purpose be served if the new administration became involved in the very different problems of the tundra? Inclusion of the area east of the Mackenzie basin and some of the islands might well tend to delay political development in Mackenzie Territory and would certainly impose a heavy financial burden on its relatively small tax potential.

On the other hand, some favoured the proposed boundary because it included Banks and Victoria Islands and Coppermine in the Territory of the Mackenzie, and the people here were more familiar with the Mackenzie area and were already administered from Fort Smith. In the future, if the area became a Province, it would have the necessary resources to administer these outlying islands.

Some raised objections with regard to the boundary itself, as the heights of land in the tundra are very difficult to determine. No 'slashed line' or boundary vista is possible and, as a result, it would be almost impossible for people on the ground, particularly trappers, prospectors and police to know whether they were inside or outside Mackenzie even if the expensive device of erecting boundary monuments were resorted to. This is a point of practical importance in such an environment.

Line B This proposed boundary followed the mainland coast from the Yukon Territory eastward to the Hornaday River; thence up the river to the Dismal Lakes following the height of land between Great Bear Lake and the Arctic coast; thence up the Coppermine River and the chain of rivers and lakes which now forms the boundary of the Arctic Islands Game Preserve to approximately 107° W. thence south in approximately this longitude following the lake groupings as much as possible and ending at the 60th parallel at Scott Lake, approximately 106° 30′ W.

This line met most of the criteria set forth above. A territory thus defined should be reasonably economical to administer. All the people living west of this boundary look to the Mackenzie settlements as their base of operations, and most of them could have access to polling stations established there. The government of the new Territory would not have to concern itself with the special problems of the tundra and the islands, and their associated costs. The boundary, for most of its length, would be much more determinable on the ground, without survey monuments, than would Line A.

Further Partition of the Northwest Territories of Canada 321

Line C This was, in a sense, a compromise between the other two proposed boundaries. It followed the mainland coast from the Yukon Territory eastward to the mouth of the Coppermine river, thence following the present western boundary of the Arctic Islands Game Preserve southeast to approximately 107°, and thence south on the same course as Line B described above.

Like all compromises, this one had clear advantages and disadvantages. About 800 miles of the Arctic coast would be included in the Mackenzie Territory, despite the fact that much of this coast has a different character from the Mackenzie basin. Revenues to be expected from this area are very limited indeed, and there would clearly be some costs in providing necessary government services there. But this boundary would result in a manageable territory with boundaries which look sensible on the map, and which do not give the impression that they have been adjusted to secure the greatest short-term advantage. The boundary would also be easily identifiable on the ground.

The Existing District Boundary Some members of the Council felt that the existing boundary between the Districts of Mackenzie and Keewatin might suffice as each of the proposed boundaries 'wandered all over the country like a moose'[1] and would be difficult to follow on the ground without very precise survey and demarcation. But the Commissioner for the Territories pointed out that the present line bore no relation to the physical features of the country and was simply a projection of the Saskatchewan–Manitoba boundary. There was no way of following such a line on the ground. Furthermore, if the present Mackenzie–Keewatin boundary were retained as the boundary between the proposed new Territories, it would mean that the easternmost point of the Territory of Mackenzie would be almost impossible to reach from the more settled areas of the Territory.[2] Nevertheless, once the new boundary had been set, Mackenzie Territory would develop a new sense of its areal extent and it would then be difficult to reduce its area. The Territory might be made larger in the future but certainly not smaller.[3]

The Council ultimately decided in favour of a boundary following the combined Lines B and C from Scott Lake to Clinton and running thence along Line A (Fig. 17.1, Line D). However, on referring this to

[1] *Loc. cit.*, July 1961, p. 69.　　　　[2] *Ibid.*, January 1962, p. 36.
[3] The Commissioner undoubtedly had in mind the experience of the Provinces, none of which have been reduced in area since their establishment, but several of which have been enlarged. *Ipso facto* the Territories have been reduced in size on several occasions, as have the Districts within the Territories.

322 *Essays in Political Geography*

the legal surveyors for comment, the Council was advised of the many difficult boundary problems which have resulted from descriptions based on physical features. This view was shared by mining engineers at Yellowknife, who pointed out that 'mining regulations call for detailed locations by meridians and the average traveller, especially prospectors, engineers and geologists use this method exclusively to locate'. Therefore two further proposals were put forward so that approximately the same boundary as Line D could be retained, but the descriptions would be more in terms of latitude and longitude.

Line E Around Banks and Victoria Islands to the point at which the 103rd meridian W. intersects the ordinary high water mark of the Arctic Ocean; south along the 103rd meridian to the point where it intersects the right bank of the Back river; thence following the right banks of the Back and Baillie rivers and the east shore of Moraine Lake to the 106th meridian; thence following the 106th meridian southwards to the 60th parallel.

Line F Around Banks and Victoria Islands to the point at which the 103rd meridian intersects the ordinary high water mark of the Arctic Ocean; southwards along the 103rd meridian to its intersection with the 65th parallel; thence west along this parallel to the 106th meridian; thence south along this meridian to the 60th parallel.

But when these proposals came up for discussion by the Council of the Northwest Territories it was pointed out that the boundary cut across the hunting and trapping grounds of the Stony Rapids Band of Indians. The traditional hunting grounds of this Band are in the Scott Lake–Selwyn Lake area of the Territories. Although the Band spends its summers in the settlement of Stony Rapids in Saskatchewan, it would be inconvenient if its hunting and trapping area was subject to the game laws of several governments.[1] There was also some evidence that some Indians from Snowdrift hunted and trapped east of the proposed boundary. The Director of Indian Affairs therefore suggested another boundary.[2]

Line G From a point on the east shore of Selwyn Lake at 60° N.; thence northerly through Flett Lake to the Dubawnt river thence along the Dubawnt river to the western boundary of the Thelon Game Sanctuary; along this boundary to the Back River; along Back and Perry rivers to the coast; thence around Victoria and Banks Islands to the eastern boundary of Yukon Territory. But ultimately, the Council agreed 'that

[1] *Loc. cit.*   [2] *Ibid.*, Appendix A.

Further Partition of the Northwest Territories of Canada 323

the eastern boundary of Mackenzie should be the 105th meridian from the 60th parallel north to the Arctic Ocean, extended to include Banks and Victoria Islands . . .' (*Line H*).

CONCLUSIONS

The attempts to arrive at a new division of the Northwest Territories which embraces the principles of geographical regionalism and the realities of demarcating a boundary in a tundra environment are an advance on the preliminary considerations which were given to the establishment of Provincial and Territorial boundaries in the past. At the same time the ultimate decision, whether consciously or not, embraces features common to all the major internal political units created within Canada since Confederation. For one thing, an astronomical boundary was selected. A 'natural boundary' appeals most to hunters, trappers, fishermen and those who lead a nomadic existence. It is a feature they can see and recognize and remember easily. But the mining engineer or the forester is more aware of the legal complications that can arise with such boundaries and much prefers to be able to calculate his position accurately with the more sophisticated techniques at his disposal. With an eye to the future, the latter view prevailed. The principle of 'one kind of environment' was also abandoned and if the proposed Territory of Mackenzie ever becomes a Province, it will, like Saskatchewan and Ontario, to choose but two examples, have a 'south' and 'north' which will be markedly different from one another. This may give economic variety, and hence strength, to the Province, but it will also bring its own set of problems as there is almost always a disparity between the economic growth of two such parts.

Less consideration has been given to what will remain of the Northwest Territories after the creation of a 'new' Mackenzie. It is assumed that all that remains will become another Territory (for which the name 'Nunassiaq' has already been approved). The total population in 1961 was a scant 7,045, of whom 75 per cent were Eskimos. More than this, most of the people lived on the west coast of Hudson Bay and Baffin Island, the Island alone supporting about 70 per cent of the total. The Queen Elizabeth Islands and the interior of the present District of Keewatin support very few people. However, it was tentatively predicted that by 1970 the population might be as much as 10,000 which with net immigration could add up to a population at least equal to that of the Yukon Territory.[1]

[1] *Ibid.*, January 1962, p. 44. However, the validity of this argument rests on the

324 Essays in Political Geography

But while access to the area is generally from the east, it is admitted that there is, 'at present stage of development, no natural centre.'[1] Furthermore, Nunassiaq would embrace 772,000 square miles of land – greater than the total area of Ontario and Quebec combined – and would have a north–south extent of more than 2,000 miles – something like the distance from Toronto to Vancouver. But more than this, it would embrace vast areas of water, such as Hudson Bay and James Bay and the many channels and inlets of the far north. Thus it would be essentially a territory of islands. Indonesia, with an area of some 736,470 square miles is the only comparable political entity in this respect. Such a political unit, if it ever became a Province, would be a new experience for Canada.

POSTSCRIPT

In 1965, the Federal Government appointed an Advisory Commission on the Development of Government in the Northwest Territories. It expressed the belief that 'with division there would be a very great risk that the eastern Arctic would become sealed off, would remain dominated by the central (Federal) government and might never acquire anything more than a nominal form of self government'. It would be cut off from 'the most populated and articulate part of the Territories and from an influence from which the Eskimo has much to benefit'. Secondly, a boundary once established is not easily changed and 'not enough is known about the country to determine with informed confidence where the line should run'. Furthermore 'given the likelihood that the governments would enact divergent laws respecting such matters as game control, a line which must inevitably run through land inhabited by an indigenous race would oblige such peoples, as they move in the normal process of hunting, trapping or fishing, to cope with two sets of laws and regulations'. For these, and a number of other, less geographical, reasons, the Commission recommended against division at this time.[2]

---

assumption that the Yukon is a 'viable' Territory with a population of 14,628 (1961). Its population has been as low as 4,157 (1921), which is much less than the present population of Nunassiaq. But its population *when it was created a Territory* in 1898 was 27,000.

[1] *Loc. cit.*, p. 52.

[2] *Report of the Advisory Commission on the Development of Government in the Northwest Territories*, Ottawa, 1966, vol. I, pp. 143–52.

PART III

Aspects of Politico-Geographical Change
in the Old World

18

A Local Perspective on Boundaries and the Frontier Zone:
Two Examples from the European Economic Community
J. W. HOUSE

CONTEXT AND PERSPECTIVE

Many political geographers, who in recent years have felt a need to re-establish the reputation of their discipline after the damage which it has suffered through confusion with an aberrant form of geopolitics, have attempted to substitute a more cautious, empirical approach to specific territorial problems of political organization for the formulation of vast, often untested generalizations characteristic of an earlier period. This reorientation, which preceded that currently in progress throughout other branches of human geography, has taken the form of a focusing of attention upon case studies rather than upon general principles about states and their inter-relationships.

The study of frontiers and boundaries is undergoing particular revaluation at the present, requiring a much wider, more sophisticated perspective than that established by earlier generations of security-conscious soldier-statesmen. In the western world at least, where the tide of aggressive nationalism is temporarily receding, economic and social relations between states are seen to be more complicated, and yet ultimately more fundamental than strategic issues, while absolute sovereignty is being modified in some areas by the emergence of the supranational principle. At the same time the perspectives of both political and general geographers are being directed increasingly to the study of margins of widening diversity, establishing new techniques and seeing the possibilities of integration and intellectual interchange from the study of these perimeters. This has important implications for the study of frontiers and political boundaries, the study of whose principles has been in danger of ossification for some decades.

In physical geography the glaciologist and periglacial morphologist are actively concerned with the ice-margins, as is the biogeographer with the ecological limits of cultivation and the land–sea margin. Economic geographers are tentatively exploring the territorial implications

328 *Essays in Political Geography*

of the concept of marginal utility: for example, the economic profitability of marginal land uses, the limits of the Central Business District or the rural/urban margin. These boundary studies converge with those of the political geographer in the definition and investigation of territorial problem areas within states, where resources may be few, populations declining and where politically-augmented isolation from the economic locus of the state adds a marked deterrent to development. As August Loesch once forecast, the frontier zone often gives rise to a depressed area, the consequences of international policy having underlined an already under-privileged status.

In testing the widening context of boundary study within general and regional geography, it seems particularly appropriate to examine these relationships initially at local level, by topographical-scale investigations into the realities of life among communities within the frontier zone flanking an international boundary. The problems of border communities provide a useful subject for comparative study in differing geographical circumstances, and the limited generalizations which emerge from community level study establish a sound base for a wider interpretation of boundaries and the significance of the frontier zone.

CLASSIFICATION AND CASE STUDY

The study of political boundaries traditionally has progressed in two scarcely related directions, by statement and testing of general principle leading to a reasoned classification, often as a major objective, and, increasingly, by the examination and comparison of individual case studies of entire borderlines. This latter more empirical approach has flourished from the analysis of disputed boundaries, and as the result of work political geographers have achieved in the aftermath of two world wars. The development of case studies has been ill-coordinated, however, as a recent review article convincingly shows,[1] and there has been little relation to the body of formal principles earlier put forward. The methodology of the study of boundaries has lagged behind the fruitful, diverse but ill-related range of individual research investigations, most of them concerned with contested frontiers.

The lack of relation of most case studies to earlier principles and attempted classifications arises partly from the unsatisfactory nature of many generalizations hitherto attempted on the subject of political

---

[1] J. V. Minghi, 'Boundary studies in political geography: a review article', *Annals of the Association of American Geographers*, 53, 1963, pp. 407–28.

Local Perspective on Boundaries and the Frontier Zone 329

boundaries. It is also due both to the inappropriateness of at least some of the latter to the modern world, particularly to most of its peaceable areas, and to the failure to relate many of the principles formulated about boundaries to the field of general and regional geography. Defence, security and readjustment to treaty changes of boundary do not represent the whole of this subject, nor are they particularly appropriate to the present state of world boundaries.

Much orthodox work on principles of boundary study mirrored the merits and defects of contemporary work in general geography. An earlier focus, almost a fixation, on the merits of natural features for the location of political boundaries, for example, had its counterpart in the early twentieth-century hypothesis of the natural region, put forward by A. J. Herbertson and others, but now also out of fashion among most Western geographers. Later classifications of boundaries, in terms of origins, character and extent of success in operation, the last often subjectively determined, were more sophisticated but only gradually was there a widening interpretation of the non-military and non-strategic importance of these characteristic limits of sovereignty. It was as appropriate in the later nineteenth and early twentieth century to have a perspective on the defence of the nation-state and the security of its boundaries, both in Europe and in the areas of expanding colonialism, as it would be inappropriate to think exclusively in these terms today.

An excessive emphasis seems traditionally to have been placed on the classification of boundaries largely as an end in itself, rather than as an intermediate hypothesis for the understanding and comparison of the character and problems of the frontier contact-zones between distinctive sovereignties. That terms must be defined, the range of boundary categories identified, described and their outline effects assessed no one would deny, any more than that grammatical structure, with its irregular verbs, is an essential preliminary to talking meaningfully in a foreign language. Such a tool of analysis, a card index for data, cannot, however, remain an end in itself, any more than the delineation of the boundaries of other types of regions can stand as the prime purpose of study in general geography. 'Peu importe le marge, c'est le coeur qu'il faut avant tout considérer', wrote Febvre, and Richard Hartshorne put this recently into a political context, reminding us that it is the political areas being bounded rather than their boundaries that should be our major focus of attention.

It may reasonably be concluded that the classification of boundary lines has produced valuable, if occasionally misleading, working

330 *Essays in Political Geography*

concepts but that few of these concepts have progressed beyond a very generalized formulation and some are tied to outdated conceptions of geography. Attempts to categorize more sharply and in greater detail have often broken down on the fact that individual cases of similar boundary types occur in such differing geographical contexts that their identity is with the context, and not with the type of boundary related to natural or other features of the landscape. The possibility of universally applicable generalizations about, for example, river-line boundaries or lines of reference is more likely to emerge from the limited generalizations based upon individual case studies, than from those premature categorizations, once beloved by and indeed more appropriate to the military school of boundary-defenders and delineators.

NORMAL BOUNDARIES: THE NEED FOR AN ECONOMIC AND SOCIAL PERSPECTIVE

A survey of world boundaries today confirms that the vast majority are uncontested and mostly have prime economic and social functions, few are controversial and on even fewer is there direct military confrontation or is active revisionism being canvassed. A first group concerns states whose very existence is unacceptable to some neighbouring state which would therefore regard all boundaries of the offending state as equally abhorrent. The situation on the borders of Israel, the conflict between the partitioned states of Korea or Vietnam or the disputed frontier zone of the South Arabian Federation against the Yemen are all of this type. The ill-defined borders of the new state of Somalia and the migratory habit of the border peoples indicate a very old type of transgression but an unusual feature of conflict in the modern world. The most direct confrontations in recent times have been along the Himalayan borderland between India and the Chinese People's Republic or in the short-lived border war between Morocco and Algeria in the north-western Sahara. The Oder–Neisse line remains unacceptable to the German Federal Republic as the eastern boundary to any future German state, and there are unsolved but quiescent boundary problems in Latin America, particularly in the High Andes.

These examples of problem-dominated boundaries are nevertheless surprisingly few in number, and rarely resemble the classical nineteenth century border confrontations between aggressive nationalisms. The defensive qualities of particular types of boundary feature are less applicable to strategic thinking in a nuclear age in any case, while the

Local Perspective on Boundaries and the Frontier Zone 331

growth of supra-national concepts in both the Communist and Western world implies new and ideological bases for revaluation of boundaries and the significance of the frontier zones within which they lie. At the same time the rapid evolution of new post-colonial nation states throughout the tropical world may presage further boundary conflicts once the forces of independent nationalism are directed to the artificial nature of those many frontiers hastily delineated in the late nineteenth-century scramble for colonies.

Minghi[1] has commented on the few studies yet made, and the inadequate attention so far given, to normal boundary contacts between states. Such contacts logically concern economic and social linkages, the nature and extent of trade, the exchange and traffic in goods and services, and the trans-border movements of people, both journey-to-work movement, tourism, or permanent settlement. These contacts must be viewed dynamically since foreign economic policies change, and trade and migrations or price differentials and economic advantage alter at the borderline. The study of such subjects began with the theoretical economists, notably August Loesch,[2] who considered the distortions introduced into circulation fields of goods and services by the interposition of an inhibiting feature such as a political boundary line.

The field opened up by the theoretical economists has been little worked as yet by the political geographer, though its utility and contemporary importance are very great. At all levels in world economic society there is strong consciousness of the great disparities in resources, both natural and human, and in living standards, between one area and another. The relationships between welfare policies, foreign policy and trade are ever closer, not only between power blocs themselves, but also within them and between power blocs and the individual states of the developing world.

In individual states economic imbalance is frequently focused within the frontier zone, as the regional variations in resources, prosperity and economic growth tend to accentuate contrasts in marginal territories, not a few of which are located along or near to the international boundary and far from the developing locus of economic or political power in a state.

Regional policies of governments are notably concerned with the depressed areas of the economy, the areas of slow economic growth or

[1] *Ibid.*
[2] A. Loesch, *The Economics of Location*, New Haven, 1954.

332 *Essays in Political Geography*

stagnation, and also with the need to define and implement networks of economic and administrative regionalization for the better working of internal sovereignty in the state. In the Western world, and particularly in the European Economic Community, agreements by governments on limited devolution of economic sovereignty as the possible precursor to a political union change the perspective on problem areas and revalue the regional character of most frontier zones. The frontier zone tends to display both beneficial and negative aspects of the use of resources, the character of settlement, and population structure, arising from its peripheral location relative to the adjacent state areas. The impact of supra-national policies in the frontier zone may not be the most dramatic of inter-state associations but it can give rise to considerable friction and, where the frontier zone corresponds to an existing economic problem area, can carry important implications for the regional development policies of the participant states.

THE FRONTIER ZONE

While it may be accepted that the frontier is by tradition a zone, whereas the political boundary is a delimited and usually demarcated line within that zone, it is surprising that so little attention seems to have been given to the outer delimitation of the frontier zone within states on either side of an international boundary.

Loesch's work on the financial sphere of El Paso, on the United States–Mexican boundary, implied the definition of hinterlands extending variably from some point facility, in this case the banks in El Paso, variably into the territory of both adjacent states. This is a sophisticated element of service industry but indicative of the very great variety, and complexity of the problem of ascertaining acceptable inner limits of the frontier zone definable often by a multiplicity of criteria. In essence one is initially investigating the zone structure of the diminishing influence of the boundary line, in economic and social terms, as one moves away from it into the area of adjacent states. It may, of course, be argued with some justification that only in a limited sense does movement away from the boundary diminish its significance. The realities of inter-state contact may most severely affect particular industries or communities in any part of the state territory; alternatively, for example, all the farmers throughout a state may be directly affected by some change in economic foreign policy. Nevertheless elements of the frontier zone can be, and traditionally have been, given more precise territorial expression,

Local Perspective on Boundaries and the Frontier Zone   333

because the proximity of the boundary has had a detectable influence on the lives and adjustments in border communities.

In a negative sense economic and social life along militarized frontiers is disrupted, and the use of the land may be limited or indeed totally sterilized, either temporarily or permanently. Such restrictions on access to resources were commonplace throughout inter-war Europe but are less common – though not unknown – today along sections of the Iron Curtain. At its narrowest territorial definition, the problems of life near a political boundary are most sharply expressed in the band of communities (local authorities) immediately flanking the line of sovereignty. These may have become adjusted to the existence of the boundary but the latter nevertheless remains a dominant, and often inhibiting factor in local living conditions. If the frontier zone has poor resources or is inaccessible, the problems may be magnified by the political factor, and issues such as rural depopulation, deterioration of social capital, or inadequacy of infrastructure are more strongly highlighted.

The difficulties of living close to an international boundary line have at various times in the past been recognized by the grant of certain privileges relating to local trading or transborder movement of people within a legally defined frontier zone acceptable to both flanking states.[1] This zone has been variously designated in treaties as the immediately adjacent boundary communes, or quite commonly as a 10-kilometre zone on either side of the boundary, for example in the Franco–Italian Convention of 1951. Occasionally, as in the Italian Peace Treaty of 1947, a demilitarized zone of 20 kilometres was further decreed on the Italian side of the new French boundary. Along the Italo-Yugoslav boundary in recent years a zone of 15 kilometres, later extended to 30 kilometres, was designated a zone of special customs privileges, and in some respects restriction, for border dwellers.

Against the economic disadvantages likely to accrue from living close to an international boundary, certain advantages may occasionally occur, though they are usually much more limited in character and impact. At or near the major crossing-points there is often aggregation of special services at establishments located as close to the boundary as possible in order to take advantage of distinct price differentials between states. Tourist shops, hotels and restaurants are characteristic examples, but in some cases, as on the United States–Canadian boundary through the Great Lakes, or in south-east Limburg between the Netherlands and

[1] J. W. House, 'The France–Italian boundary in the Alpes Maritimes'. *Transactions of the Institute of British Geographers*, 26, 1959, pp. 107–31.

334 *Essays in Political Geography*

West Germany, industrial plants also tend to congregate just within a tariff wall, though they may draw their workers from both sides of it. Alternatively, labour cost differentials between states may themselves attract branch factories to locate within journey-to-work distance of nationals in an adjacent state. The price differentials on consumer goods may also strengthen the growth of an exotic border economy confined to settlements within at most a few miles of a boundary line and not sustained by any sizable hinterland within the domestic territory.

The positive stimulation to the economy of border settlements and the negative inhibiting effects of the boundary line, the latter regrettably hitherto much more common, usually occur simultaneously at different points within the same frontier zone. Loesch drew attention to the frequent coincidence of depressed areas with frontier districts, a state of affairs apparently most common in urbanized industrial countries with their sharp gradient in living standards between the towns and the rural perimeter.

BOUNDARIES AND FRONTIERS WITHIN THE EUROPEAN ECONOMIC COMMUNITY

The long-term implications of implementing the Treaty of Rome may be far-reaching for the internal frontier zones within the European Economic Community. The intention of proceeding by limited stages in devolution of sovereignty, through an initial Customs Union towards closer political association, if not ultimately federal or unitary statehood, is an important prototype for many Common Market systems currently being envisaged elsewhere. Since many of the political boundaries between the European Economic Community countries are of long standing, antedating the major industrial and urban developments of the nineteenth century, some initial dislocation in the frontier zones may be expected and much reorientation of contacts is to be envisaged during the rapid link-up of member states which is now in progress. The great interest for the political geographer here lies in reviewing, almost as a controlled social and economic experiment, the changing significance of political boundaries within the Community during its most formative period in the next decade or so.

The frontier zones and types of boundary feature in the European Economic Community, many of them deeply embodied historically, are remarkably diverse for such a limited area. In the south the Franco–Italian boundary follows the watershed of the western Alps, though

Local Perspective on Boundaries and the Frontier Zone 335

high mountain terrain, whose economy is by tradition sylvo-pastoral, with development of hydro-electric power and some localization of high-energy consuming industries in the valley floors of Savoy and the Val d'Aosta of northern Italy. This boundary[1] has fluctuated during historic times, and at one stage embraced the territories of the Dukedom of Savoy, astride the Alpine watershed. Since the Treaty of Utrecht (1713) it has been in principle a watershed boundary, with a departure in the Maritime Alps, where the frontier lay at intervals along the lower Var, notably from 1815–60. By the Treaty of Turin (1860) the Franco-Italian boundary was moved up to the French glacis of the Alpine watershed, and in 1947 to the watershed line itself. In the 1947 Treaty modifications were made at the principal cols, moving the boundary onto the Italian side of the watershed. Except at the cols the contacts between dwellers on opposite flanks of the mountains have been limited to the high pastures and certain communal woodlands.

The Franco–German boundary in Alsace-Lorraine has had a fluctuating movement over the past century, and indeed throughout the history of the marchland between Teuton and Frank. The successive consolidation of French sovereignty towards the strategic frontier of the Rhine was followed by the 1870 boundary which cut across the iron-ore field of Lorraine and separated the textile industry of the western Vosges from that of Alsace. Restoration to the line of the Rhine in 1919 and 1945 emphasized the economically integrating role of the river basin in its upper course. The Palatinate and Saar boundaries followed the meandering limits of historical divisions, cutting across the Saar–Lorraine coal basin, while further west the Luxemburg–Lorraine boundary cut through the iron-ore field. The run of these boundaries powerfully influenced the settlement and pattern of economic development on either side of the boundary. In the former Saar territory and Luxemburg a fascinating possibility exists for the comparative study of two small areas of sovereignty in a buffer state location.[2]

The northern France–Flanders boundary today cuts through the coalfield and industrial region: at its demarcation, in 1713, only the coal reserves of the Low Countries were known and these were purposely kept within one state. The Ardennes frontier follows an old forest boundary with a similar rural economy on both flanks.

[1] *Ibid.*

[2] H. Overbeck, 'Standortsfragen in der Industriegeographie am Beispiel der Warndtgrenze erläutert', *Festschrift zür Hundertjahrfeier des Vereins für Geographie u. Statistik*, Frankfurt-am-Main, 1936, pp. 279–86; and C. Held, 'The new Saarland', *Geographical Review*, 41, 1951, pp. 590–605.

336 *Essays in Political Geography*

The Low Countries' boundaries date from the Treaties of Paris and Vienna (1815) though the internal boundary, following the partition between the Netherlands and Belgium, dates from the Treaty of London (1839). The latter thus created the appendix of South Limburg, economically a part of the Zollverein until 1867. Only minor boundary modifications have since occurred; Eupen-Malmedy and small tracts passed to Belgium in 1919 and some minor modifications were made to the Dutch–German boundary after 1945.[1]

Though the Ardennes frontier is sparsely settled and has an extensive type of sylvo-pastoral economy, the situation changes sharply immediately to the north, where the Liège–Maastricht–Aachen–Ruhr axis forms the economic and industrial backbone of the entire Economic Community. A total revaluation of political boundaries is imminent around the appendix of southern Dutch Limburg, now at the crossroads of Western Europe, but until recently focused almost entirely on north–south contacts as an isolated frontier province of the Netherlands.

The Dutch–Belgian frontier across the marshes and heaths of the Peel and Brabant passes through marginal land, with the important Campine coal basin and developing industrial zone to the south separated from manufacturing towns such as Eindhoven to the north. The problem of divided sovereignty on the lower Scheldt is paralleled on a grander scale by the Dutch sovereignty over the lower reaches of the Rhine system, a region with an immense potential for development as the economically inhibiting effects of divided sovereignty in the Rhine basin are progressively abated. In the north-eastern Netherlands the heathlands and moors separate the border provinces from those of West Germany. Post-war oilfields have developed on both sides of the boundary, while the Dutch Development Area policy has created a transformation in the borderlands of Drenthe province, for which there is as yet no counterpart on the German side.

The problems of the internal Economic Community boundaries thus fall into two categories. The first consists of areas of poor resources, often with an isolated location and built-in social and economic prob-

---

[1] M. Schwind, *Landschaft und Grenze – Geographische Betrachtungen zur deutsch-niederländischen Grenze*, Bielefeld, 1950; R. S. Platt, 'A geographical study of the Dutch–German border', *Siedlung und Landschaft in Westfalen*, No. 3, 1958; H. Posselt, 'Die Annektion von Dollart, Bourtanger Veen und Nieder Bentheim', *Mitteilungen der Geographischen Gesellschaft zu Wien*, 1948, pp. 145–9; and L. M. Alexander, 'Recent changes in the Benelux–German boundary', *Geographical Review*, 43, 1953, pp. 69–76.

Local Perspective on Boundaries and the Frontier Zone 337

lems of stagnation or decline, necessitating priority aid under government policy, for example the central and southern French Alps and the mountain zone of northern Italy,[1] the Palatinate and the Eifel, both border districts undergoing depopulation with a decaying, outdated rural economy, and the heaths and moors of the north-eastern Netherlands. This category is marginal because of frontier location which has aggravated the basic problems arising from environment and history. It is difficult not to expect further decline in such areas, even though limited inter-government aid may continue to cushion the effects of the developing Economic Community upon such underprivileged areas.

A second category of problems concerns the frontier zone in areas of partitioned natural resources, principally of coal and iron ore, where the boundary produces an impediment to the free flow along the logical routes provided by the river systems or the shortest routes linking major industrial regions. The Saar-Lorraine field, the northern France–Belgium coalfield, the South Limburg–Aachen coal basin, the Lorraine–Luxemburg iron ore deposits and the petroleum and natural gas fields on the German–Dutch border come into this category. In most respects the development of the Common Market will foster a more logical use and interchange of resources and stimulate the cooperative expansion of the partitioned coal, ore and petroleum fields. Yet in other respects governments and private enterprise have followed national investment programmes and there has been duplication of facilities on both sides of the boundary. Rationalization may thus require some closures of plant, while others which were originally located to benefit from the artificial financial advantages of a frontier site will lose their *raison d'être*. Under the Treaty of Rome governments have a moratorium of some years in which to equalize their industrial location policies and reduce aid to those marginal districts, including frontier zones, which cannot be justifiably supported within the wider Common Market.[2]

To focus the issues in the frontier zones of the Economic Community two contrasting case studies will be briefly examined: The Alpes Maritimes (France–Italy), and South Limburg (a contact zone between Netherlands, Belgium and Germany).

[1] J. W. House, 'Western Alpine society in transition: the case for regional planning', *Planning Outlook*, 5, 1961, pp. 17–30.
[2] R. Romus, *Expansion économique régionale et communauté européene*, Leiden, 1958.

338 *Essays in Political Geography*

THE ALPES MARITIMES[1]

The uplands along this boundary have one of the most depressed economies in the Economic Community borderlands. The traditional sylvo-pastoral way of life has been in decay for many decades, a decline accompanied by steady depopulation to the nearby Riviera coast. The gradient in living standards over such a short distance is one of the most remarkable in western Europe. In the immediate hinterland of the Mediterranean coast the peasant economy, traditionally based on the olive, chestnut and the vine has also been declining. The added political ingredient of a boundary change in 1947 further deepened the economic and social problems of this frontier zone.

In the frontier zone along the crestline between the headwaters of the Tinée, Vésubie and the Roya in France and the tributaries of the Po system in Italy there is a similar economy on both flanks of the Alps. The transhumant movements with cattle, and occasionally sheep, have ranged widely, and legal rights of both the individual and the commune are tenaciously held. Wealth is locked up in the communal woodland, the stinted pastures, and the herds and flocks which follow traditional season-by-season transhumance routes. These did not respect the 1859–1860 boundary, though with time they became gradually adjusted to it, nor have they entirely conformed to the crestline of the Alps. The 1947 boundary dislocated the pastoral economy of the communes east of Tende and La Brigue. In 1954, after skilful arbitration by a Swiss pastoral expert, agreement was reached on re-apportionment of woodland and pastures, but structural damage to the rural economy had already taken place. Rural population had been lowered and the density of stock had fallen.

Further south the international boundary cuts across the lower reaches of the Roya valley, with some southward adjustment in 1947 from the strategically important Mt Grazian area formerly in Italy. In this frontier zone of lower altitude the rural densities of population are higher and the farmers are mainly sedentary. The wealth of the communes lies in their olive and chestnut groves and small vineyards. Water is a scarce resource and virtually controls both the size of rural populations that can be maintained and the productivity of the land. The social hinterland of each village is very limited, and life is more self-contained than in the semi-mobile transhumant society further north. The rural economy of these border villages is decaying, a decline

[1] See Fig. 18.1.

Local Perspective on Boundaries and the Frontier Zone 339

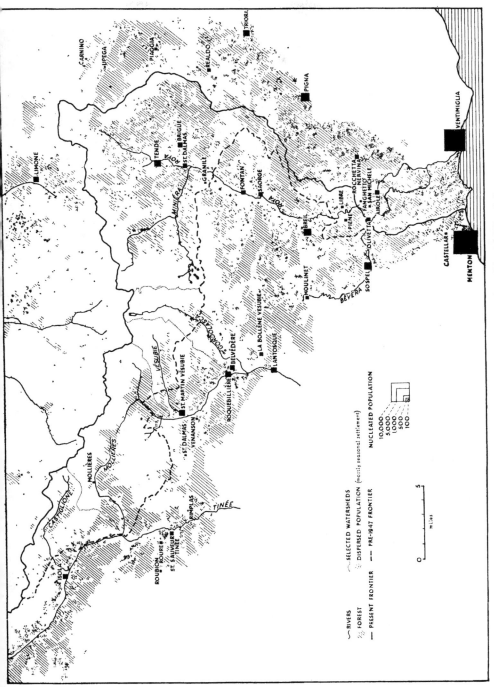

Fig. 18.1. Rural Frontier Zone in the Alpes Maritimes

340 *Essays in Political Geography*

accelerated by the location of some near to the new international boundary. Within France the government has developed a rural support programme for improving the living conditions and the infrastructure of the more isolated settlements.

The Lower Roya was partitioned under the Treaty of 1860; in 1947 France added possession of the headwaters to those of the middle reaches but the lower reaches were retained by Italy. The partitioning of the valley made realization of its hydro-electric power resources a piecemeal affair. More stations were built than were economically desirable; all were of limited potential, and re-apportionment of the upper valley has further complicated the production and export of electric power.

Apart from the heavy tourist traffic along the Riviera coast this frontier zone remains remote from the major circulation currents of the European Economic Community, and the Nice–Cuneo railway, destroyed in the war, has never been restored. The contacts between opposite sides of the boundary remain limited and there is common economic distress in the border communes of both France and Italy. This led in 1951 to a Franco–Italian convention defining a frontier zone 10 kilometres in depth from the boundary, within which movement of persons and products was to be stimulated and protected, in the interests of border dwellers. Latterly both governments have been jointly approached by the local inhabitants of the frontier zone, asking for their problems to be given special recognition.

THE LIMBURG APPENDIX[1]

In almost all respects this region is the antithesis of the Maritime Alps. Its economic structure is partly urban and industrial, with coal mining, in direct contrast to the rural economy of the Alps. Its location, immediately north of the main West–East European axis from northern France and Belgium to the Ruhr, close to where the latter intersects the route from the Randstad cities to southern Belgium and eastern France, is nodal, not peripheral to the economic heart of Europe. Hitherto the advantages of such nodality have been masked by the divided sovereignty of the area, with South Limburg forming an ill-shaped and distant appendage of the Dutch state, remote from the populous urban areas of the lower Rhine and Holland province. Indeed with a rapidly developing population and limited economic resources

[1] See Fig. 18.2.

Local Perspective on Boundaries and the Frontier Zone 341

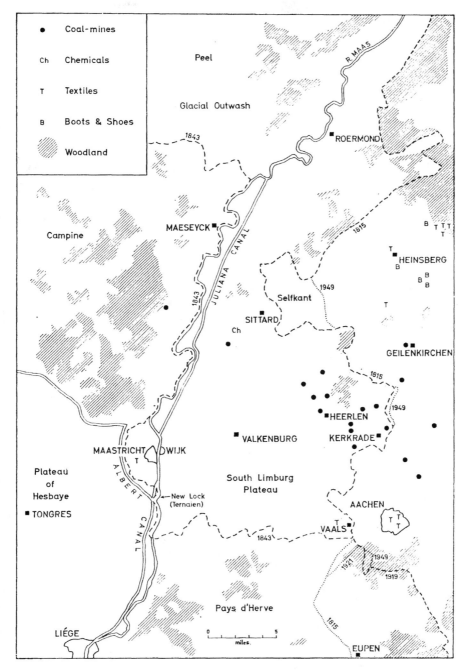

Fig. 18.2. The Limburg Appendix

342 *Essays in Political Geography*

the area has become a Development Area under Dutch economic planning legislation.[1] The traditional trade linkage has been north to south through Limburg, with little consideration for its potential in respect of west–east movement. Even the Benelux agreements after 1945 conferred little direct benefit upon Limburg.

The frontier zone covers the width of the appendix, which at its narrowest is only three miles, and extends into the Campine to the west, the South Limburg loess-covered plateau and Pays d'Herve to the south, and the Aachen coal basin to the east. In contrast to the zone in the Maritime Alps, there is here a lively inter-connection of border traffic passing in both directions across the Dutch frontier. Unemployment in Dutch Limburg is high and labour costs are lower than in either Germany or Belgium. Thus there is a well-developed journey-to-work traffic, into both West Germany and Belgium, including some seasonal and semi-permanent labour migration. Belgian workers cross into the frontier town of Maastricht for daily work, even though direct wages are lower; work is lacking in adjacent areas of Belgium but a compensating system of salary allowances has been introduced.

TABLE 18 : SOUTH LIMBURG :
INTERNATIONAL JOURNEY TO WORK, 1959

Limburg–Belgium	2,600
Limburg–Western Germany	2,100
Belgium–Limburg	3,600
West Germany–Limburg	700
Total	9,000 workers per day

The communications pattern has dominated the development of South Limburg, which for heavy traffic is focused on the Maas waterway. The competition between Antwerp and Rotterdam for the upper Maas hinterland led between the wars to the construction of national canals, namely the Albert Canal, by Belgium, from Liège to Antwerp, and the Juliana Canal, by the Netherlands, from Maastricht to the lower Maas. Both were capable of taking 2,000-ton barges but were not interconnected; the Ternaien lock on the Liège–Maastricht Canal could not take craft of more than 600 tons and until 1936 the limit was only 400

[1] J. Winsemius, *Limbourg Néerlandais: Etudes régionales d'emploi*, C.E.C.A. Haute Autorité, Luxembourg, September, 1957; and H. C. W. Roemen, 'De Technisch-Economische Ontwekkeling van Limburg in de laatse 70 Jaren en het Welvaartsprobleem in de naatste Toekoemst', *De Ingeneiur*, 32, 1952, pp. 1–25.

Local Perspective on Boundaries and the Frontier Zone 343

tons. National interests kept this bottleneck in being until 1963, when a new lock and canal section linked the Albert and Juliana canals, through Ternaien, thus opening inter-connected routeways for 2,000-ton barges from the Rhine–Ruhr to the upper Maas and the lower Scheldt.

The knot of European motorways has focused immediately north of Liège, but the Limburg appendix will soon be more closely in touch with the new feeder network of these roads. Its position is capable of being transformed from that of a remote outer province of the Netherlands to a nodal industrial area astride the major European routes, a transformation which should logically follow the elimination of the divisive political factor of the boundary lines around the appendix.

The effects of the development of the European Economic Community on the frontier zone of Limburg will be more complex than these changes in the communications pattern alone might suggest. In the first place the industrialization policy successfully followed by the Dutch government has already tied the province more closely to other parts of the Netherlands. Fortunately it has been a policy of stimulation rather than subsidized inducement to industrialists, a development based on growth points rather than depressed areas. Reorientation within the wider Common Market economy will thus be facilitated, though it is interesting to note that fifteen years of the Benelux Union surprisingly conferred little benefit on Dutch Limburg.

There have been exotic growths within the frontier zone, inspired by the price differentials in favour of the Netherlands and against her neighbours; foodstuffs, particularly butter and meat, are much cheaper in Dutch Limburg. The frontier town of Vaals, almost a suburb of Aachen in the extreme south-eastern corner, demonstrates this point clearly. The Dutch hinterland of the town is very restricted, but its diversity and number of shops and banks establish the town as an important and thriving service centre. An increasing proportion of its trade is across the border for shoppers from West Germany, who benefit from the lower Dutch prices. Branch plants of the Aachen textile industry have also been set up in the town to utilize more abundant and cheaper Dutch labour and to serve the Dutch market in part from within its national boundaries.

The equalization policies of the Economic Community will diminish the price differentials which at present work in favour of the service settlements within Dutch Limburg and against the German border town of Aachen in particular; likewise there will be less incentive for

M

344 Essays in Political Geography

Dutch workers to go abroad for higher wage-levels. The Limburg farmers should benefit from higher prices in the Community, whose major urban centres are more accessible than those of the Netherlands.

Unlike the Western Alps, Dutch Limburg is poised to take advantage of a revaluation of its European location, freed from the hitherto limiting effects of its national frontiers. At the same time it will need to be more closely linked with the Liège–Aachen axis, already firmly established to the south of formerly neutral Dutch territory.

CONCLUSION

These two examples show almost the extremes within the spectrum of frontier zones in the European Economic Community. Even during the next decade the tempo of economic freedom across political boundaries will sharply reduce their traditionally entrenched nature, and closer contacts, through the greater exchange of commodities and the freer movement of workers, will develop within the equalization policies envisaged by the Treaty of Rome. The revaluation of boundaries will have distinctive effects upon those living within each of the varied frontier zones. Some of these zones have economic and social problems aggravated by the impediments to circulation which political boundaries have by tradition imposed. In others, settlements have been artificially stimulated by the development of land and building use to profit from the inter-state economic differentials at individual crossing points. Both types may exist side by side in the same frontier zone, and both may need a measure of government protection in an interim period of readjustment. Such a policy would be a part of the regional programmes to which most governments in the Western world are now committed. What is worked out for the frontier zones of the European Economic Community in the next decades may later be of interest in other parts of the world as the devolution of absolute sovereignty spreads, and the once barrier-like qualities of political boundaries are progressively reduced in the interests of freer and fuller international trade.

19

The Russian Image of Russia:
An Applied Study in Geopolitical Methodology

LADIS K. D. KRISTOF[1]

Every state has a *raison d'être* – a reason for existing, however defined and justified; this must be fairly intelligible to its citizenry and either specifically expressed in some fundamental statement of purpose, or at least implied in the web of positive law which sanctions the centripetal forces and discourages, or directly outlaws, the centrifugal ones. This quite concrete reason for the existence of the state is usually sustained from below by a *spiritus movens* – a semi-conscious tendency rooted in the collective psychology of national traditions and ambitions – and from above by a state-idea (*Staatsidee*)[2] – a philosophical and moral conception of the state's destiny and mission in terms of universal human teleology.

The state-idea helps the nation to evolve an image of itself: looking through its prism the nation draws strength from a sense of being *pushed* by history and *pulled* by an ideal – from a sense of past fulfilment and a duty to fulfil the future destiny. By linking that which was with that which is to be, the nation develops an image of what it itself is and what it *should become*. Many a nation-in-becoming in today's Africa scans feverishly the records of the past for a hint as to its future identity, and,

---

[1] I wish to express thanks to all the many friends and colleagues, including several I know only by letter, who have spent long hours of their precious time in reading and criticizing the various drafts of this paper and/or giving valuable bibliographical information. Too many have been involved to permit me to make individual acknowledgements, but I would like to mention the names of Professors Richard Hartshorne (University of Wisconsin, Madison) and Nicholas V. Riasanovsky (University of California, Berkeley) who commented in detail on the entire manuscript. Since for technical reasons, or because of differences of opinion, I have not followed up all their suggestions, I wish to emphasize exclusive responsibility for all the views and shortcomings of this study.

[2] The concept of the state-idea (and *raison d'être* of the state) was first introduced into political geography by F. Ratzel in *Politische Geographie*, Munich and Leipzig, 1897. The more recent interest shown by geographers in the concept is due mainly to the discussion of it by R. Hartshorne in 'The functional approach in political geography', *Annals of the Association of American Geographers*, 40, 1950, pp. 95–139, and in 'Political geography', in P. E. James and C. F. Jones, eds., *American Geography: Inventory and Prospect*, Syracuse, 1954, pp. 167–225.

346 *Essays in Political Geography*

conversely, from an ideal of future identity history is selectively re-traced, this or that past appropriated, another rejected.[1] As concepts of state and national identity evolve, there emerges also a feeling of belonging: of identification with a certain world and environment both cultural and geographical. The imperial idea set Britain off from Europe, and identified it with a separate, world-wide and oceanic, cultural-economic community. But as the imperial idea collapsed, the British began to develop a different concept of state and identity; they are now drawing closer to, may even merge with, Western Europe. The Turks of the Ottoman Empire era thought primarily in dynamic Pan-Islamic terms, and sharply contrasted their world with that of Europe. Even the Europeans themselves viewed Turkish Europe as a part of the Near East. But today, on the contrary, the Turks are espousing the Kemalist national-state idea and are strenuously arguing, and trying to prove, that Turkey is an integral part of the West. The cultural-political boundary between Europe and Asia has fluctuated throughout the ages according to the cultural and geopolitical self-identification of the border people.[2]

STATE AND NATIONAL IDEA

The *raison d'être* of the state at its minimum is mainly negative – it is to prevent war from without and from within, that is, to protect life and property. At its maximum it is predominantly positive – it helps and compels the people as individuals and as a collective to achieve certain goals; it guides them toward some 'better' life. The *laissez faire* state's *raison d'être* is primarily negative; the 'organic' ideologic state's *raison d'être* insists on a negative *and* a positive role. In terms of the former, it

[1] African leaders often go through tortuous reasoning trying to define what are 'facts' and what mere 'accidents' in history as well as geography. What the distinction is really based on is whether a fact is judged to be legitimate or not. See the very interesting article by Ali A. Mazrui, 'On the concept of "We are all Africans",' *American Political Science Review*, 57, 1963, pp. 88–97.

[2] So, also has the boundary between Europe and Africa fluctuated. We can only briefly note here that a very instructive parallel can be drawn between Spain and Russia. Both countries were subjected to an outer-European, Islamic occupation and influence; later, in the process of a step-by-step expulsion and pursuit of the enemy, they extended beyond the limits of Europe. Also, both countries went through periods of deliberate, rapid 'Europeanization', yet failed fully to integrate with and remained (though in different degrees) outsiders to Europe, culturally as well as politically. To the best knowledge of this writer, the only author who ever dwelt at some length on this interesting parallel is Gonzalo de Reparaz, *Geofrafia y Politica*, Barcelona, 1929, especially chapters 8 and 9.

The Russian Image of Russia   347

is the nation, more exactly, the multitude of individuals who are the active ingredient. In terms of the latter it is the state and the state-idea which are the dynamic, forward-looking and future-oriented element, while the nation and its idea are the historical factor, the carriers of the heritage of the past.

The *laissez faire* state does not, strictly speaking, have a state-idea, for its scope is too severely circumscribed by the principle 'the government that governs least governs best'. In the 'organic' ideologic state, on the other hand, the state-idea is assertive and claims priority and superiority to the common man's understanding of the *raison d'être* of the state. The state exists for the sake of the idea. In other words, the state is a system, a tool, by means of which a segment of humanity is effectively organized in the image of the idea; the state is the web which 'organically' unites the nation within and with the ideology.

The state-idea does not quite coincide with the national idea. The former is pre-eminently political, goal-oriented and the brain-child of a more or less sophisticated intellectual elite. The latter is less political and more historical and tradition-bound, and pertains rather to the broad masses than to any select group. Still, not even the national idea can be equated with national culture.[1] The cultural heritage, accumulated as it is in various circumstances – on purpose, accidentally, or imposed from without – is a mixed blessing. The national idea abjures some components of this assorted heritage even though they may be firmly woven into the fabric of the national way of life. Who could deny that a conspicuous streak of ethnic, religious and racial prejudice is (or at least was for a long time) deeply ingrained in the mainstream of the American cultural heritage? Yet no-one can say that prejudice has ever been a part of the American idea. The national idea is thus, essentially, an idealized self-image of the nation, the *acceptable* part of the national culture; the heritage, true or imaginary, of which the nation is proud, which is to be emulated. The relationship of the national idea to national culture parallels that of the state-idea to the national idea. It is a relationship of primary dependence loosened through a process of selectivity, intellectualization and innovation, and by the same token gradual politicization.

[1] Some geographers define the state-idea so broadly as to make it practically identical with national culture. This is incorrect. It reduces the usefulness of the concept and tends to blur the issues. The relation of the state-idea to national culture is that of a child to its mother. One mother can give birth to several children who, though related to each other, may exhibit fundamentally different characteristics and vigorously compete with one another.

348 *Essays in Political Geography*

The distinction between the state-idea and the national idea is rooted in the relationship between the *raisons d'être* of the state and nation respectively. The nation need not justify its existence to the same extent as the state, for it simply *is*, and it *is* much more on the basis of certain imponderables and psychological elements than on the basis of a rational set of principles. The national idea – the centripetal sentiments born out of the consciousness of a separate identity – is less an expression of the material state of facts than of a certain state of mind, or, rather, state of heart. Feelings and beliefs, secular as well as religious, are of crucial importance. The cult of a national patron saint, and the place where it is practised, may at times assume major importance. They give the father-land an additional dimension, and sometimes also another capital.[1] They unite the multitude of citizenry on the level of super-natural expectations even at a time when in the natural realm everything seems pulverized in a maze of centrifugal aspirations.

The national idea, the *raison d'être* of a nation, is then rather an internal question of the nation itself – a problem of self-respect, of moral purpose – than a question of external relations. A state often has to justify in the eyes of the outside world its reason of, and right to, existence because its existence depends on the consent, willing or un-willing, of other states. A nation, on the other hand (that is a nation in the cultural and ethnic sense), largely exists regardless of the consent of the political community and law, national or international. In other words, a nation may live irrespective of whether it has any rights, but a state that loses its rights by the same token ceases to exist. The state being in the first place a legal personality, its existence is to a large extent conditional upon substantial conformity to certain uniform standards of behaviour, external and even internal.[2] A nation, on the other hand,

---

[1] *E.g.*, the Mexican *Virgen del Guadalupe*, or the 'Queen of Poland' *Matka Boska Jasnogórska* (in Czestochowa), or the Lithuanian *Vilniaus Ausros Vartu Gailestingumo Dievo Motina* (often referred to in past times as the Queen, or Grand Duchess, of Lithuania). Sometimes the religious and the secular capitals are centres of competing ideas. For instance, in Mongolia, where for centuries religion was national while state power (as well as the state-idea) foreign, the towns are, in their origin, either national-religious centres, *i.e.*, monastery towns, like Ulan-Bator (Urga), or foreign-administrative centres, *i.e.*, centres of power from without, like Jibhalanta (Uliassutai) and Jirgalanta (Khobdo) both of which were founded by the Manchurian conquerors. *Cf.* I. M. Maiskii, *Mongolia nakanune revolutsii*, 2nd edition, Moscow, Izd. vostochnoi literatury, 1959, pp. 96–102.

[2] In the past, the pre-condition for the recognition of a state as a member of the international community (*i.e.*, for the extension to it of the protection of international law) was its accession to a certain minimum standard of acceptable

The Russian Image of Russia 349

survives precisely because of *divergent* behaviour; its *raison d'être* is cultural distinctiveness, a touch of uniqueness.

THE RUSSIAN STATE-IDEA AND NATIONAL IDEA

In practice, the difference between the state and national idea is rather subtle, a matter of shades. In Russia it has, however, been sharpened by a recurring explicit contraposition, an emphasized dichotomy between *narod* and *gosudarstvo* – the aims and ideals of 'the people' and 'the state'. In fact, the official language and terminology has openly acknowledged a certain duality when it sanctioned the distinction between *russkii* and *rossiiskii*, between what pertains to the (Great) Russian people and what to All-the-'Russias'.[1] While the German, French or

---

behaviour in *external* (inter-state) affairs only. More recently, especially under the Charter of the United Nations, there has been an attempt also to set a minimum standard of civilized behaviour in *internal* affairs, that is, to set a minimum standard to which the national law of all member (and possibly also non-member) states should conform. The state that refuses to conform to these minimum standards in either external or internal affairs becomes an outcast; in extreme cases virtually an outlaw, fair game for anyone. In a limited sense, this is the situation in which (mainland) China and South Africa find themselves today for having violated, in the eyes of a segment of the international community, the minimum standard of acceptable behaviour, in external and internal affairs.

[1] Etymologically *rossiiskii* and *Rossiia* are Russified versions of the Latin (or Greek) words for Russian and Russia. They are forms of speech introduced in the sixteenth century when the Muscovite rulers were preoccupied with the adoption of ways, titles and emblems that would emphasize Russia's and its monarch's absolute equality with any European sovereign. (It was then that the two-headed eagle was put on the state seal simply to make sure the Russian tsar was not inferior to the sovereign of the Holy Roman Empire.) Originally, the new forms did not carry a different meaning and were used interchangeably with the old ones. But their introduction having coincided with the creation of a multinational Russian Empire extending far beyond the old Russian (*russkiia*) lands, the connotation imperial Russian became associated with them. The old form *russkii* (and also *Russ*) has been retained for the designation of that which is national (ethnically) Russian. But in certain grammatical formations arbitrariness in the choice between the two forms persists, *e.g.*, the Great Russians are *velikorossy* and the Little Russians are *malorossy*, while the White Russians are *belorussy*; and notwithstanding the form *velikorossy* and *malorossy* when speaking about the respective languages it is *velikorusskaia, malorusskaia* and *belorusskaia mova*. See the articles by P. F. Vinkler, 'Gerb, gerbovedenie', and D. Anuchin, 'Rossiia v etnograficheskom otnoshenii', in *Entsiklopedicheskii Slovar Brokgauz & Efron*, St Petersburg, Vols. 8 (1893) and 27 (1899), pp. 461 and 139 (of second half of the volume), respectively. See also Petr Struve, 'Imperiia i Rossiia', *Rossiia i Slavianstvo*, Paris, No. 202, 8 October 1932, p. 1, and Gustave Alef, 'The adoption of the Muscovite two-headed eagle: a discordant view', paper read at the annual meeting of the Far Western Slavic Conference, Claremont College, 10–11 April 1965. See also below, note 1, p. 372.

350 Essays in Political Geography

Spanish nations had 'their' empires, the Tsarist Empire was officially not 'Russian'; it was not *Russkaia Imperia* but *Rossiiskaia Imperiia*, and the tsar was not *Russkii Imperator* but *Imperator Vserossiiskii*.[1] Some Russian statesmen have favoured the *russkaia* (national) idea, others the *rossiiskaia* (state or, rather, imperial) idea; still others tried to fuse the two. And, of course, there were a variety of nuances of national and state ideas.

The state (*rossiiskaia*) idea as the dominant coalescing force implied that effective integration of All-the-'Russias' was to be by means of 'Rossification' – the development of an unswerving loyalty and direct attachment to the person of the tsar, by God's will the sole power-holder (*samoderzhets*) and head of *the* Church. 'Rossification' was permeation not so much by ways and things specifically Russian as by the spirit of the Orthodox Church. Not unlike the policy of Sovietization of today which applies to minorities the principle 'national in form, socialist in content', 'Rossification' saw the essence in Orthodoxy, not in Russianism. No less an arch-conservative than K. P. Pobedonostsev, the Procurator of the Holy Synod, approved the translation into Tartar of various Orthodox texts to facilitate the 'Rossification' of the Muslim population. He specifically supported the principle 'national in form but Orthodox in content'.[2] The Orthodox idea, not the Russian tongue or civilization, was the *spiritus moven s*of the Tsardom. Russia was first of all Holy, not Russian. Conversely, those who had still not embraced Orthodoxy could not, in the eyes of a Pobedonostsev, be regarded as genuinely integrated, or even wholly worthy of trust, no matter how Russified they might appear. They were not to be trusted except in secondary government positions for they had not internalized that which alone had the power to generate in them a spiritual bond of loyalty and a true understanding of what Russia was and stood for. The

---

[1] Neither is there within the Soviet Union a Russian (*Russkaia*) Federal Republic, only a *Rossiiskaia* Federal Republic; this is apparently in consideration of the various national groups which, though reduced today to the status of small minorities within the Republic, remain conscious of their historical rights which preceded Russian imperial expansion and colonization. Similarly, there is no Russian Communist Party (and not even a *Rossiiskaia* C.P.) although there are Ukrainian, Lithuanian, Armenian, etc., Communist Parties. The highly sensitive distinction between the political connotations associated with *russkii* and *rossiiskii* – nationalistic Russian versus supra-national All-Russian – was the reason why the pre-1917 Russian social democracy also, never called itself *Russkaia* S.-D.R.P. but always *Rossiiskaia* S.-D.R.P.

[2] Robert F. Byrnes, 'Pobedonostsev on government instruments', in *Continuity and Change in Russian and Soviet Thought*, ed. E. J. Simmons, Cambridge, Mass., 1955, p. 126.

The Russian Image of Russia 351

non-Orthodox Russian had merely the capacity to be a *passively* loyal subject – to render to Caesar what was Caesar's – not *actively* to participate in formulating and fulfilling Russia's higher destiny. He could be only in the limited, secular sense a loyal subject of the tsar *qua* sovereign ruler of a multi-racial, multi-national and multi-religious empire. Russia's eighteenth century rulers were time and again criticized precisely on the ground that they used the numerous non-Orthodox diplomats and generals not merely as experts – not exclusively in executive capacity – but abandoned to them also policy-making decisions.

The national (*russkaia*) idea, on the other hand, implied Russification (or at least Slavicization). Slavophilism and Pan-Slavism, the two moulds of the national idea, emphasized the primacy and priority of things and values Russian (or Slav) over and above the imperial state-idea and *raison d'état*. The national idea saw ethnic, not religious, ties as the foundation of loyalty to the fatherland.[1] Hence the geopolitical base of those ties had to be expanded. Lands inhabited by Orthodox Christians, for instance Armenia wrested from the Turks,[2] were also to be opened to Russian colonization. 'The Germans' in the tsar's family and entourage were time and again branded a corrupting, virtually treasonable element, however strict and even fanatic their support of the Orthodox Church and throne. The 'true' Russian ways and ideas were those

[1] The Slavophiles did emphasize religious ideas, but not organized religion. The laymen were seen as guardians of religious truth co-equal with the clergy. In case of conflict, the Slavophiles' sympathies were more likely than not with the dissenters, that is 'the people', who were far less suspect of having become corrupted than the Church hierarchy. In fact, the impression was sometimes created that, ultimately, 'the people' were to be considered the arbiters in matters of religion, for they were the Messiah on earth – the sufferer and redeemer. Hence it was not ties of religion that were binding the people; rather it was the ties spawned by the people that were religious. (Of course, there also was a 'right' Slavophilism, the *kvasnoe slavianofilstvo*, *i.e.* jingoistic Slavophilism, which denied all dichotomy between the state and the nation, the tsar and 'the people', and supported the government and its 'official nationality', including official Orthodoxy. But this Slavophilism would also deny the very existence of our distinction between the state and the national idea.) For an exposition of the views of A. S. Khomiakov, the Slavophile authority on theology, see P. K. Christoff, *An Introduction to Nineteenth-Century Slavophilism*, Vol. I, *A. S. Xomjakov*, The Hague, 1961, especially pp. 157–63.

[2] Barely had the Armenians had time during the First World War to greet the Russian troops as their Christian saviours from sure extermination at the hands of the Turks when they heard about a plan afoot for the sending of Cossack settlers into their country. One should also recall the 1903 confiscation of the treasury of the Armenian Church in Russia which was pushed by the Russifiers in high places.

352 *Essays in Political Geography*

'of the Slavs as of old', and since these were allegedly democratic and dating from pre-Christian times, the question of the relevance and value of autocracy and Orthodoxy for the Russian nation was implicitly, and actually, raised. While the government and Holy Synod equated all dissenters, religious as well as political, with traitors, the Slavophiles elaborated the theory about the natural goodness of 'the people' and intrinsic wickedness of the 'superimposed' state.

The Pan-Slav mould of the national idea tended, in its 'conservative' (imperialistic) variant, to overlap on and off with the state idea. But the Russian Empire could only ally itself with Pan-Slavism; it could use it, but not identify itself with it. A latent tension between the nationalist and the statesman, the national idea and the *raison d'état*, has been a phenomenon recurring everywhere. Bismarck had to face the problem after both Sadova and Sedan. In the enormous Russian Empire, the gap between the national idea and the requirements of the *raison d'état* was particularly acute. In 1897 the ruling Great Russian element constituted only 45 per cent of the tsar's subjects, and the non-Slavs were a majority in extensive areas of the national territory. In terms of the political and geopolitical problems with which the Russian Empire had to grapple, both internally and externally, the national idea was woefully inadequate. It focused exclusively on the Russified off-centre areal core. Worse still, it showed passionate preoccupation with lands and people that were, and have always been, far outside the sovereign realm of the state.[1] At the same time, it was by its very nature incapable of generating an effectively integrating sentiment in much of the Empire's territory.

The Imperial state-idea was in this respect decidedly superior. It had the advantage of operating on two levels. It could either reduce its standard of loyalty to a minimum, that is to purely political matters, or aim at developing a maximum bond of loyalty founded on a religious communion. On the secular level it appealed to the tradition of respect for the established, legitimate, and awe-inspiring might of a great power enhanced by the reassuring image of a benevolent and protective 'father-

---

[1] An interesting case was F. I. Tiutchev, a leading Pan-Slav poet who was at the same time considered the 'de Maistre of the Russian Orthodox Church'. Combining Pan-Slav with Orthodox imperialism, he claimed that the problems of Europe would not be settled until Rome became the residence of an Orthodox pope, subordinated to the tsar residing in Constantinople. Thus Rome was to be the religious and Constantinople the secular centre of 'the great Orthodox Empire, the legitimate Empire of the East'. K. Pigarev, *Zhizn i tvorchestvo Tiutcheva*, Moscow, Akademiia Nauk S.S.S.R., 1962, pp. 125, 130. See also below, note 2, p. 354.

The Russian Image of Russia   353

tsar'. On the spiritual level, on the other hand, it appealed to a super-natural authority and to ideas pan-human in scope. Thus the state-idea could, according to circumstances, cast itself in the mould of a down-to-earth, territorially circumscribed policy, or again emphasize lofty, world-wide aims.

THE ICONOGRAPHY OF THE FATHERLAND

Who would ask an Englishman to die so that other Englishmen might live? It was so that England might live that Englishmen died on the battlefields. 'Who dies if England live?' asked Kipling.[1] The English-men died for an idea of England. With that idea went an image of England, one perhaps quite different from the reality most Englishmen lived in, for, as Kipling again noted,

> If England was what England seems,
>   An' not the England of our dreams,
> But only putty, brass, an' paint,
>   'Ow quick we'd drop 'er! But she ain't![2]

Even a factory hand and native of industrial London 'visualized the England he had fought to save'[3] not as a great city, 'not as his own street but as Epping Forest, the green place he had spent Bank Holidays'.[4] Indeed, the heroism needed to save England in 1914 or 1940 might never have been generated had there been only the *real* England, the one in which the overwhelming majority of Tommies were living, and making a living, and not also the image of a very different, an 'elegant pastoral', 'calm and peaceful, "essentially English" ' England, 'with slow-moving streams and wide expanses of meadow-land studded with fine trees'.[5] It was for that rural, idyllic vision of England that the town-birds of Britain went to their death.

[1] R. Kipling, *For All We Have and Are* (1914).
[2] R. Kipling, *The Return*.
[3] David Lowenthal and Hugh C. Prince, 'English landscape tastes', *Geographical Review*, 55, 1965, p. 187. The article is a thoughtful excursion into a little explored field, in which collaboration between political scientists and geographers (as well as students from other fields, *e.g.*, humanities, litera-ture) might lead to a substantially deeper understanding of countries and peoples. Also useful for comparative purposes are W. Ganzenmüller, *Das Naturgefühl im Mittelalter*, Leipzig and Berlin, 1914, and J. K. Wright, *The Geographical Lore of the Time of the Crusades*, with an Introduction by C. J. Glacken, New York, 1965.
[4] H. V. Morton, *In Search of England* (1927), Harmondsworth, 1960, p. 14. (Quoted in Lowenthal and Prince, *op. cit.*, p. 187.)
[5] Lowenthal and Prince, *op. cit.*, p. 192.

354 Essays in Political Geography

The idea of one's fatherland is abstract; the iconography, the visual image of it, is concrete and alive. 'From the Maas to the Memel [Nemunas], / From the Etsch [Adige] to the Belt' is the German's outline of his homeland.[1] '. . . From Perm to Tauri, / From the cool Finnish rocks to the burning Colchis, / From the disturbed Kremlin to the walls of immovable China' is Pushkin's sketch of Russia.[2] But the intellectual image of one's country is more complex than the mere visualization of the fatherland's boundaries, real or dreamed of. Essentially, it involves three elements: a piece of humanity, a piece of land and a spiritual heritage and aspiration. Between these there may be cleavage, that is, one may find it easy to identify oneself with one or two but not all three of them. One may, for instance, love the people but hate the land, or vice versa.[3] This creates a feeling of disharmony, of alienation which must be overcome, and in order to overcome alienation from reality, one must seek a substitute for reality. That substitute may be

[1] Hoffmann von Fallersleben, *Deutschland Lied* (1841). Originally simply a poem, it became the German national anthem (generally known as *Deutschland, Deutschland über alles*) only on 11 August 1922.

[2] A. S. Pushkin, *Klevetnikam Rossii* (1831). Characteristically, a Pan-Slav poet sketched a much more ambitious 'Geography of Russia', one extending far beyond anything the tsars ever dreamed of ruling: 'From the Nile to the Neva, from the Elbe to China / From the Volga to the Euphrateus, from the Ganges to the Danube . . . / That's the Russian realm . . .', F. I. Tiutchev, *Russkaia geografiia* (1848). See also the poem by a friend of Tiutchev, A. N. Maikov, *The Empress of India* (1877). Whatever title Queen Victoria may assume, says Maikov, she 'cannot be the sovereign of the East', for the peoples of the East instinctively know that 'Close by is now – close is the dawn, / And the kingdom of darkness will yield to light, / To the reign of the white tsar'. Such expansionist (and mainly anti-British) Russian super-patriotism was largely a by-product of Slavophile and Pan-Slav thinking and an outgrowth of the patriotic fervour generated by the Crimean War. However, within two decades after 1856 Russian expansionism was on a collision course with Pan-German ambitions rather than British imperialism. Not satisfied with the boundary outline of von Fallersleben's *Deutschland Lied* (above, note 1 preceding, the Pan-Germans demanded a *Lebensraum* 'from the mouth of the Ems to the mouth of the Danube, from the Memel to Trieste, from Metz to about the [Western] Bug'. Paul de Lagarde, 'über die gegenwärtige Lage des Deutschen Reichs', 1875, *Schriften für das deutsche Volk*, 2 vols., 4th edition, Munich–Berlin, 1940, Vol. I, p. 132. While von Fallersleben and (with reservations) Pushkin were simply patriots voicing sentiments by and large in tune with the spirit of 1848, Tiutchev, Maikov and especially de Lagarde, already belonged to the generation that laid the ground work for the imperialistic ideologies which made a Russo-German (and Slav-Germanic) conflict inevitable.

[3] *E.g.*, persecuted minorities often develop an attachment to the land all the stronger the more they become alienated from the people. A Jewish lady from Poland, settled in Palestine for years, met once by chance a Polish traveller and immediately began to reminisce about her native country, 'that beautiful land' – the pine forests, the lakes, the birch trees, the weeping willows. 'I love

The Russian Image of Russia 355

sought in another, actual or imaginary, reality by shifting on the plane of either time or space, or both. The common *shift in time* is toward an idealized past – towards the 'good' times, the 'pure' past when the fatherland and people were true to themselves. Another quite common shift in time is toward an idealized future – the paradise, the Utopia that is to come to replace that which is. The image of a *future* – land is substituted for the image of the *father's* – land.

The case of a *shift in space*, towards a new geographical location, occurs when we react to a type of alienation which is best described by the French word *dépaysement*. It occurs when we do not feel at home while at home in our own country, and to overcome this alienation we feel obliged to seek another *pays*, another country, a substitute fatherland. The Communist, frustrated by the capitalist regime and bourgeois spirit of his homeland, may feel alienated (*dépaysé*) enough at home to declare the Soviet Union his true fatherland;[1] perhaps he may even migrate there. To many a European of the 1848 generation America became the true home after they could not feel at home in their native land. In Russia, perhaps because of the size of the country, the geographical shifts that followed various kinds of alienation of the *dépaysement* type took place within the bounds of the country. In other words, the shift was merely from one real and/or symbolic centre of the country to another in order to appeal to a different heritage for the sake of a different morrow.[2]

Poland – she conceded with deep conviction, and then, quickly, added – but I hate the Poles'. – The opposite phenomenon – attachment to the people and cultural environment but alienation from the natural environment – is well illustrated by the Englishmen who, having spent years in colonial service in warm lands, simply cannot face the British climate and settle in some place like Tangier only to recreate around themselves a little island of English civilization. See also Ladis K. D. Kristof, 'Political laws in international relations', *Western Political Quarterly*, 11, 1958, pp. 598–606; especially pp. 600–1.

[1] French Communists have in the past often used the slogan 'France is our country, but the Soviet Union is our fatherland'. A Communist deputy, A. Musmeaux, declared in the French National Assembly on 3 March 1950: 'And when you tell us that the Soviet Union is our fatherland we do not consider this an insult. We glorify ourself with it and are proud of it'. On the implications for the political system of such a 'geopolitical schizophrenia' – dichotomy between the geographical and spiritual fatherland – see Ladis K. D. Kristof, 'The nature of frontiers and boundaries', *Annals of the Association of American Geographers*, 49, 1959, pp. 269–82, especially pp. 278–9.

[2] *Cf.* China where the south and the north, with Nanking and Peking as the respective capitals, symbolize two different heritages. Sun Yat-sen chose Nanking as his capital to point out that his movement was linked to the traditions of the South China Ming period. He thus emphasized the national Chinese

356 Essays in Political Geography

Thus the iconography of the fatherland is ever again adjusted to harmonize with the evolving aspirations, with the *anticipated* future. Chronology and chorology – the historical and geographical sequence of events – are manipulated to converge precisely on the spot with which we seek self-identification, and which we call *our* country. For though as men we value human relationships most, we cannot become an integrated piece of humanity in the abstract, only in an environment of time and space in which we feel at home – which we *wish* to be our children's *father*land.

According to which idea and what image of the fatherland is cherished, appeal is made to different cultural and geohistorical heritages, and different ideals and geopolitical identities are seen in the future.

THE IMAGE OF RUSSIA

There have been four *basic images* of Russia – of Russia's people, history and geography – on the background of which concrete ideas of nation and state were projected and construed. Each has mixed reality with idealization, embellished truth and invented myths; each has sought inspiration in a chapter from the past as well as in legend and folklore, and each has visualized a different variant of future civilization, as seen through the prisms of fact and its own imagination. The *first two* of these images are narrower – *strictly* Russian both geographically and historically – and based on a conception of a core area, a cradle of Russia territorial and cultural. The *other two images*, on the contrary, see Russia within a perspective *broader than Russia* itself both in time and space. Consequently they do not concentrate on a cultural-territorial nucleus, a 'heart' from which the country allegedly grew and spread spatially and from which it drew, or at least ought to have drawn, inspiration for further development. Rather, they depict a wide human

---

character of the 1911 revolution as opposed to the foreign heritage represented by the Ch'ing emperor, a descendant of the invaders from the north. The capture, in 1928, of Peking by the Kuo Min-tang, and the renaming of Peking (i.e. Northern Capital) Peiping (i.e., Northern Peace) was not only a military but also a symbolic reassertion of the southern capital's claim to supremacy. Mao Tse-tung's triumph, on the other hand, made Peking once more the capital of China with all the implications that followed. Unable to change the realities, Chiang Kai-shek, as well as his American friends, continue in speeches at least to refer to Peiping, not Peking. See Hugh Tinker, *The City in the Asian Polity*, inaugural lecture, London, School of Oriental and African Studies, 1964, p. 13, and Sen-dou Chang, 'Peking: the growing metropolis of Communist China', *Geographical Review*, 55, 1965, pp. 313–27. See also above, note 1, p. 348.

The Russian Image of Russia 357

and geographical panorama as the background from which Russia emerges as a part of a larger whole. In other words, they are images within images, details of a panoramic picture brought into focus, not individual portraits that may be displayed in the isolation of a wooden frame.

The first image looks back towards medieval Kiev Russ as the spiritual and physical core of Russia. Kiev is the 'mother of Russian towns' and is itself a child of Europe. The 'true' Russia is a democratic and federal Russ within an 'organically' united Christian Europe. A vision of general harmony prevails. Even Russia's geographical environment – the 'true' Russian nature – is seen as harmonious and friendly to man. It is the rich Russian land of the Dnieper, Don and Southern Bug watersheds – not too different from the rolling countryside of Europe to the West – in which summer and winter, spring and fall, evenly divide the year, and water and earth, forest and grass, provide a balanced environment.[1] It is 'the land where everything breathes abundance'.[2] Whoever wants to have 'a live image of Russian nature and nation must see Kiev'.[3] Here is the ancestral home of the agricultural Slavs, not of the nomadic invaders; here is the black-earth steppe, sprinkled with mighty oaks and green like the prairie lands of the Mississippi valley, not the open steppe, burnt by the continental breath and dry like the American Great Plains.[4] There is no need to 'open a window on to Europe'; just turn one's back on 'Mongol-Tartar Russia', on the 'base' mentality of

[1] See, *e.g.*, N. V. Gogol's *Vechera na khutore bliz Dikan'ki* (especially part 2, chapter 3, section 10) where an atmosphere of quiet harmony pervades the country of 'the wonderful Dnieper'.

[2] 'Do you know the land where everything breathes abundance, / Where rivers run purer than silver, / Where the breeze plays with the steppe's feathergrass, / Farmhouses drown in cherry groves, / Bent down are the trees in the orchards / And to the ground dangle their weighty fruits ?' A. K. Tolstoi, *Ty znaesh krai, gde vse obil'em dyshit* . . . (1840s). Tolstoi's model is Goethe's *Mignon*. A. S. Pushkin's *Kto znaet krai, gde nebo bleshchet* (1828) is also modelled after Goethe's *Mignon*. But, in contrast to Tolstoi's poem, the blessed country of Pushkin's vision is not Russia. In another, similar poem, *Kto videl krai, gde roskosh'iu prirody* . . . (1821), Pushkin describes the southern coast of Crimea (Yalta region).

[3] A. N. Pypin, 'Volga i Kiev', *Vestnik Evropy*, 1885, 4, p. 199. Pypin points out (p. 214) that the great historian S. M. Solv'ev never took the trouble to come down from Moscow to see for himself Kiev and southern Russia and that this lack of interest is reflected in the interpretation he gave to Russian history.

[4] Space permits only a brief note here of an obvious parallel and contrast between America and Russia. American historians have pointed out that, in the course of the nineteenth century, there developed on the one hand the vision of America as the Garden of the World – a this-worldly Garden of Eden – which reflected the favourable experience of the settlers in the areas up

358   Essays in Political Geography

Moscow – 'the cursed Moscow, even viler than the Mongols themselves' – and 'return to the original, European channel', to the spirit of Kiev Russ.[1]

This is the image of Russia as cherished by those who, like the poet A. K. Tolstoi,[2] or the politician-publicist V. V. Shulgin,[3] could not see

---

to and especially in the Mississippi Valley, and, on the other, there sprung up the vision of a Great American Desert as soon as the pioneers hit upon the inhospitable Great Plains. In Russia the black earth regions of the Don, Dnieper and Southern Bug watersheds – the 'granary of Europe' – spurred the development of something similar to the Garden of the World vision of the country. But in northern and eastern Russia, *i.e.*, in most of the country's territory, the peasant had to struggle with an environment roughly comparable in harshness to that of the Great Plains. The fact that the proportion of the 'Garden' to the 'Desert' is more or less inverse in America from that in Russia had a considerable effect on the development of the self-image of the two countries. Not surprisingly, it was in America, not in Russia, that the happy image of a 'God-blessed country' prevailed which, incidentally, made more difficult the process of adaptation of American political institutions and laws (*e.g.*, water laws) to the contingencies arising in the not-so-God-blessed regions of the country. – On the American myth of the 'Garden' and 'Desert' see H. Nash Smith, *Virgin Land: The American West as Symbol and Myth*, Cambridge, Mass., 1950; on the problem of adaptation of American political ideas and institutions to the challenges peculiar to arid zones (the 'Deserts') see V. Ostrom, *Water and Policies: A Study of Water Policies and Administration in the Development of Los Angeles*, Los Angeles, 1953, and D. E. Mann, 'Political and social institutions in arid regions', in C. Hodge and P. C. Duisberg (eds.), *Aridity and Man: The Challenge of the Arid Lands in the United States*, Washington, American Association for the Advancement of Science, Publication No. 74, 1963, pp. 397–428.

[1] A. K. Tolstoi, *Sobranie sochinenii*, 4 vols., Moscow, 'Khudozhestvennaia literatura', 1963–64, Vol. 4, pp. 271, 273, 281 (letters to P. B. Markevich of 26 March and 26 April 1869, and speech in the English Club of Odessa, 14 March 1869). Cf. Tolstoi's ballad *Zmei Tugarin* (1867), especially the stanzas 9, 14 and 22. See also note 2 following.

[2] A. K. Tolstoi's dislike for 'Tartar Moscow' pervades his trilogy of historical dramas (*Smert Ioanna Groznogo, Tsar Fedor Ioannovich* and *Tsar Boris*) as well as his historical tale *Kniaz Serebrianyi*; significant, too, in this respect, in his essentially sympathetic treatment of Novgorod in the drama *Posadnik*. The contrast between 'good' Kiev Russ and the Moscow 'stuffed with the ways of the Tartars' is even more sharply drawn in Tolstoi's epics and ballads, *e.g.*, in *Zmei Tugarin* (1867). For these views the poet repeatedly came under fire from both sides of the main nineteenth-century Russian ideological front, that of the Slavophiles versus the Westernizers, although at times one or the other claimed him an ally. Tolstoi's relations with 'official' Russia (i.e., government circles) oscillated, also. Outwardly close to the court he nevertheless repeatedly ran afoul of the literary watchdogs.

[3] V. V. Shulgin was a prominent politician in Tsarist Russia, member of the Duma and owner of the influential daily *Kievlanin*. It should be emphasized that he has been throughout his life a fervent Russian nationalist, not a Ukrainophile. Ultimately, his nationalism even made him come out, in 1960, in support

The Russian Image of Russia 359

any solution in the imitativeness of the Westernizers or the isolationism of the Moscow Slavophiles. It is the image echoed in the historical writings of N. I. Kostomarov,[1] in the ethnographic sketches of A. N. Pypin, in the stories of N. V. Gogol.

The second image of Russia identifies the heart and heartland of the country with the spiritual and physical heritage of Muscovite Russia – the Russia that stood aloof from the Greeks and the Romans and fought for survival against both the barbaric East and the advanced West; the Russia of the Great Russian, the Russ who mingled with the non-Russ, who could not expect kindness from either man or nature and worked hard in the silence of the isolated villages that dotted the forests and marshes of an isolated land.

The backbone of Kiev Russ is the Dnieper-Don to Western Dvina axis which pulls together the Black and Baltic Seas, and with them southern and northern Europe; the backbone of Moscow Russia is the Volga to Northern Dvina axis which has remained for centuries as

---

of the Soviet regime. Like A. K. Tolstoi, Shulgin opposed 'Moscow' precisely because he considered it stood for something not 'truly' Russian. Each of Russia's 'Three capitals' (*Tri stolitsy* is, characteristically, the title of one of his books) symbolizes an epoch and an ideal, and the most genuinely national Russian is that embodied by Kiev. See Shulgin's 'Kiev, mother of Russian towns', *The Slavonic Yearbook* (The Slavonic and East European Review), 19, pp. 62–82, where on p. 71 he gives a succinct summary of A. K. Tolstoi's views on the 'two Russias' (*i.e.*, Moscow and Kiev) and wholeheartedly concurs with them.

[1] N. I. Kostomarov (a Ukrainian federalist Pan-Slavist, not a separatist) was a personal friend of A. K. Tolstoi. His writings influenced and provided a large share of the factual basis for Tolstoi's historical dramas. Of particular interest for our discussion is Kostomarov's essay on the 'two Russian nationalities', *i.e.*, the northern and southern, or Great and Little Russian. In the songs, tales and daily life of the inhabitants of southern Russia, says Kostomarov, one notices a feeling of warm and harmonious interrelationship with nature as well as an appreciation of its beauty. The inhabitants of northern Russia, on the other hand, 'have little liking for nature', even display 'hostility' towards it. This again brings to mind the already mentioned parallel with America. (See above, note 4, p. 357). The American folk songs from the 'Desert' and those from the 'Garden' have two quite different stories to tell. In the former it is nature which is the villain; in the latter it is man (*i.e.*, society and its injustices). – N. I. Kostomarov, 'Dvie russkiia narodnosti' [1861], and 'Ob otnoshenii russkoi istorii k geografii i etnografii', [1863], in *Sobranie sochinenii*, 21 vols. in 7 books, St Petersburg, Literaturnyi fond, 1903–6, Bk. 1, Vol. 1, pp. 33–65 (quoted from p. 67), and Bk. 1, Vol. 3, pp. 719–31. Ideas similar to Kostomarov's were expressed a decade earlier by the historian S. M. Solov'ev, *Istoriia Rossii s drevneishikh vremen*, 29 vols. in 15 bks., Moscow, Izd. sotsial'no ekonomicheskoi literatury, 1959–66, Bk. 1, p. 78. See also Pypin, *op. cit.*, p. 206, A. N. Afanasiev, *Poeticheskiia vozzreniia slavian na prirodu*, 3 vols., Moscow: K. Soldatenko, 1865–69.

360 *Essays in Political Geography*

closed and self-contained as the Arctic and Caspian Seas that knot its ends. 'Volga and Dnieper are symbols',[1] we are told repeatedly. The Russ *byliny* (epics) hail the daring thrusts of the Kievan princes down the Dnieper and beyond to the sea; so do the ballads of the Dnieper Cossacks. The (Great) Russian folk songs remain loyal to Volga and its shores. *Volga Matushka* (Mother Volga) is the symbol of *Matushka Rossiia*; it marks where Europe and Asia meet and merge; it draws together the people of the endless *taiga* with those of the steppe, far as the eye can see; it reunites the people who sought safety in the forests with those who sought freedom in the open spaces.

In the country along the Volga man has been for ages, in the words of a Soviet writer, both 'burnt by the Asiatic sun and chilled to the bone by the Arctic cold'.[2] Here there is no time for spring and nightingales.[3] The visual picture which this country imprints in the memory of the foreign traveller, and which is dear to the native, is that of the winter landscape;[4] an immense canvas painted in white . . . 'an endless wasteland, white and cold; a sea . . . swept by the wind from the Pole to the Black Sea'.[5] Within a panorama of these dimensions the people do not spring to the eye. They remain hidden, huddled somewhere close to mother

---

[1] Shulgin, *op. cit.*, p. 62. *Cf.* S. M. Solov'ev, *op. cit.*, Bk. 1, p. 73.

[2] Leonid Leonov, *Russkii les*, 1953, chapter 7, part 2. See also A. S. Pushkin, *Ia videl Azii bezplodnye predely*, 1820, and N. A. Nekrasov, *Na Volge*, 1860, especially verses 275–8.

[3] In A. K. Tolstoi's epics about Kiev Russ the charm of the Russian spring and the nightingale's song are depicted as exercising a powerful, soothing influence on Russian national heroes, *e.g.*, in *Pesnia o pokhode Vladimira na Korsun* (1869) and in *Svatovstvo* (1871). And in a letter of 26 April 1869 to a friend, B. M. Markevich, Tolstoi wondered whether 'in paradise itself we could feel happier than we are here [in Krasnyi Rog, Chernigov guberniia] in time of spring'. Tolstoi, *Sobranie sochinenii, op. cit.*, Vol. 4, p. 283. See also above, note 2, p. 357.

[4] Perhaps the finest example in literature of such impressions by a foreign traveller is A. Mickiewicz's 'Droga do Rossji' (in his *Dziady*, part 3: *Ustep*). A particular fondness for the beauty of the winter landscape is noticeable in the works of most great Russian poets (A. S. Pushkin, A. A. Fet, N. A. Nekrasov, *etc.*). In sharp contrast to A. K. Tolstoi (above, note 3 preceding), Pushkin says in a poem (*Osen*, 1833): 'I do not like the spring; / I am bored by the thaw; the smell, the dirt – in the spring I am sick'. For a discussion of this contrast see the excellent study by A. Lirondelle, *Le Poète Alexis Tolstoi: L'Homme et l'oeuvre*, Paris, 1912, pp. 496–8.

[5] A. I. Gertsen, *Dnevnik*, 22 January 1843. Gertsen (Herzen) had just read Mickiewicz's 'The Road to Russia' (above, note 4 preceding) and was moved by the vividness of the image it painted: 'O my God! How wonderful is his [Mickiewicz's] picture of the Russian winter road' (*ibid.*). *Cf.* Gertsen [Herzen], *Du Développement de idées révolutionnaires en Russie*, 1850, Introduction. See also A. S. Pushkin's poem *Zimniaia doroga*, 1828.

The Russian Image of Russia 361

earth. Only the government's hand can be seen writing on the white stretches of nature, complained the populists. 'The roads that crisscross the steppe have not been called forth by trade or the people's needs, but traced by order of the tsar'.[1]

The Moscow image of Russia is cherished by those Russians who have seen their fatherland less a part of Europe and more an equal of Europe – who have been proud that their ancestors expanded the little core of a state on the slopes of the Valdai Elevation[2] into an empire larger than Europe. This is the image of Russia of the intense patriots, of the *pochvenniki*[3] literature which speaks of the sacredness and uniqueness of Russia's Mother Earth and its people, and of the nationalist

[1] Gertsen, *Dnevnik, loc. cit.*

[2] The Valdai Elevation (*Valdaiskaia vozvyshennost*), situated halfway between Moscow and Leningrad, and half-way between the ancient cities of (Great) Novgorod and Tver (Kalinin), is a wooded, marshy country of hills sprinkled with patches of cultivable land, in which the Volga, Western Dvina and the rivers of the Lake Il'men basin have their sources. Close by to the south are the sources of the Dnieper, and a little further to the north-east begins the basin of the Northern Dvina. Control of this area meant, in the earlier period of Russian history, control of a strategic portage system, a nodal point of waterways between the north and south and the east and west. At the same time, the area was far enough both north and east to be sheltered from raids by enemies operating from either the steppe or the Baltic region – not once was the Valdai Elevation overrun by an invader – yet not so far removed from the rest of Russia and its agricultural lands as to become politically isolated and economically crippled. Some historians have argued that this area, originally controlled by the Varangians and the epicentre of their commercial-piratical expeditions in the direction of the Black and Caspian Seas, could be viewed as something of a cradle of Russian state power which wise and cunning Moscow princes spread along strategic rivers – Volga above all – until they built a mighty body politic. See N. P. Barsov, *Ocherki russkoi istoricheskoi geografii: Geografiia nachal'noi (Nestorovoi) letopisi*, 2nd edition, Warsaw, K. Kovalevskii, 1888, pp. 16–19, V. O. Kliuchevskii, *Sobranie sochinenii*, 8 vols., Moscow, Gos. izd. politicheskoï literatury, 1956–59, Vol. I, pp. 57, 59 [Kurs russkoi isotorii, Lesson 3], and R. J. Kerner, *The Urge to the Sea: The Course of Russian History: The Role of Rivers, Portages, Ostrogs, Monasteries and Furs*, Berkeley and Los Angeles, 1946, chapter 1.

[3] From *pochva* = soil (more broadly: foundation). The *pochvenniki* were exponents of a 'cult of primitive immediacy', (immanentism) – of an unmediated communion with 'the soil' partly in the literal sense and partly in the sense of those close to the soil, *i.e.*, the peasants (the 'foundation' of the nation). 'The soil' was the bridge which linked together the intelligentsia with the (peasant) masses. Communion with 'the soil' meant reaching into the mystic depths of the national personality, of the meaning of national history; it also meant immersion in (to use C. G. Jung's term) the 'collective subconscious' of the people, its psychic heritage, *i.e.*, the primordial images on which the conscious feeds. The *pochvenniki* were under the influence of F. W. J. Schelling (and undoubtedly also of J. G. Herder). At times they were skirting on pantheism. The *pochvennichestvo* movement emerged in the early 1860s; characteristically it was centred

362 *Essays in Political Geography*

school of history from I. N. Boltin and his environmental justification of Russian nationalism to V. O. Kliuchevskii and his *Course of Russian History* which helps the Great Russian to think of himself as at least a *primus inter pares* within the 'Soviet family of nations'.

The third image, the St Petersburg image of Russia, is symbolized by the outlook of the city itself. Looking through the prism of its own image St Petersburg sees Russia as virtually a part of Europe, more exactly, as a brother, perhaps a younger brother, on the forward path of Western, or, rather, universal history and civilization. Russia may be an independent nation – but neither it nor its people or their destiny can be self-contained or unique. The Russians may, indeed often must, form a closed, solid ring, yet it is only a link in the chain that binds, and guides, all humanity.

The St Petersburg image of Russia has been a latent feature in the thought of all Russian Westernizers, but only twice was it put forward unequivocally, without any reservations. First it was virtually thrust upon the unsuspecting, astonished, and later flattered Russians by the French and German *philosophes*. Having declared that reason knows no boundaries or fatherland, the men of Enlightenment rejoiced when Peter the Great decided, or so they thought, to join their company. Russia, argued Leibnitz, should become the bridge between the only two spots on the globe where reason has become anchored, Western Europe and China, and by the same token, with one geopolitical stroke the triumph of light over darkness would virtually be assured the world over. Hosannas were sung to Peter the Great and then to Catherine the Great, the enlightened despots toward whom Europe was turning hopeful eyes. Voltaire, Mably, Turgot, Condorcet, Diderot and others were indeed for a time convinced that light was coming from the East, or rather, North – *c'est du Nord aujord'hui que nous vient la*

---

in certain journals published in Moscow and had hardly any followers in St Petersburg. Its main exponents were F. M. Dostoevskii, N. N. Strakhov and A. A. Grigorev, and most populist writers (even the realists, *e.g.*, G. I. Uspenskii) were to some extent affected by it. No thorough study of the *pochvenniki* is available, but see V. V. Zenkovsky, *A History of Russian Philosophy*, trans. G. L. Kline, 2 vols., New York, 1953, Vol. I, pp. 400–32; *idem.*, *Russian Thinkers and Europe*, trans. G. S. Bodde, Ann Arbor, 1953, pp. 115–19; and A. Walicki, *W kregu konserwatywnej utopii: Struktura i przemiany rosyjskiego słowianofilstwa*, Warsaw, P. W. N., 1964, chapters 13 and 14. On possible implications of C. G. Jung's concept of 'collective subconscious' for the study of geopolitics, see L. K. D. Kristof, 'The origins and evolution of geopolitics', *Journal of Conflict Resolution*, 4, 1960, p. 19, note. See also below, note 1, p. 366.

The Russian Image of Russia 363

lumière – and might save Europe. And so it continued until the French Revolution when the enlightened despot refused to act in an enlightened way.[1]

The idea of the oneness of Russia with the West – the strenuous denial of any particularities in Russian history – was revived by the Marxists, the heirs to the Age of Reason, but this time it was the Russians who took the initiative in proclaiming it while Westerners, even of the 'left', watched with suspicion. The most consistent in defending this idea were, not surprisingly, the Mensheviks, the most Western among the Russian Marxists.

The fourth image, the Eurasian image of Russia, identifies Russia with that vast stretch of continental land from the Carpathians to the Pacific, which was for centuries controlled by the nomads who roamed the grassy plains between Mongolia and the Pripet marshes. The Eurasiatic steppe, it is said, was the cradle of an imperial state-idea, and the Russians rule an empire which preceded them. There was a 'Russia' (or, rather, a *Rossiia*) prior to the Russian Russia. The Russians have inherited a cultural-political domain and with it a certain teleological impetus conditioned by history and geography. They are the non-nomadic heirs to the nomads; they have rebuilt the Mongol empire from its Western end. In other words, the concept of Russia as Eurasia unites two distinct historical realities and epochs, and it is both logically and historically a two-way street: before there was a European Asia there was an Asiatic Europe.

Indeed [as G. V. Chicherin, the Soviet Commissar for Foreign Affairs, wrote in 1919], the history of Russia and of two-thirds of Asia practically forms one indivisible whole. In the course of historical events two centres of state power emerged alternatively in this part of the world: the centre of Mongol-nomad power, and the centre of Great Russian, agriculture-based power. . . . The Tartar Khans were the immediate predecessors of and . . . to a large extent models for the Moscow tsars. . . . The nineteenth century expansion of Russia into Central Asia was the completion of the process of unification into one state – first under the khans, then under the

[1] W. (V. I.) Guerrier, *Leibnitz in seinen Beziehungen zu Russland und Peter dem Grossen*, St Petersburg, Commissionäre der Kaiserlichen Akademie der Wissenschaften, 1873; D. F. Lach, 'Leibniz and China', *Journal of the History of Ideas*, 6, 1945, pp. 436–55; A. Lortholary, *Les 'Philosophes' du XVIIIᵉ siècle et la Russie: Le Mirage Russe en France au XVIIIᵉ siècle*, Paris, 1951; D. Groh, *Russland und das Selbstverständnis Europas*, Neuwied, 1961.

364 Essays in Political Geography

tsars – of the continuous plain which extends over this part of the world.[1]

The Eurasian image of Russia is not national; rather it is geopolitical. It is the image of a multinational *Rossiia* springing up on the ruins of the Hunnic, Khazar and Tartar empires. While the Moscow image of Russia more often than not identifies itself with Pan-Slav ideas, the Eurasian image rather tends to associate with a variant of the idea of 'Turanianism'.[2]

GENRES DE VIE

The several images of Russia are, to some extent, expressions of what the French geographers call *genres de vie* – specific types of life which are the result of adaptation to the milieu, to the ecology of the place in its historical setting. A *genre de vie* is the art of survival which the genius of the given people develops in terms of a time and place, and by which it modifies the physiognomy of the landscape giving it a characteristic

---

[1] G. V. Chicherin, 'Rossiia i aziatskie narody', *Vestnik N.K.I.D.*, No. 2, 13 August 1919, pp. 1–2. This statement is a succinct summary of the views on Russian history later expounded by the *Evraziistvo* (Eurasian Movement). I quote Chicherin to underscore that this was not, as usually assumed in the West, a point of view invented by, and peculiar to, a group of Russian emigré intellectuals, but well known already before the emergence of the *evraziitsy* (Eurasians) and openly accepted by prominent Communists (even though *Evraziistvo* as such always remained a target of Soviet attacks and ridicule). The most comprehensive account of *Evraziistvo* is O. Böss, *Die Lehre der Eurasier: Ein Beitrag zur russischen Ideengeschichte des 20. Jahrhunderts*, Wiesbaden, 1961. However, Böss' study is not helpful for an understanding of the origins of either the geopolitical or philosophical views of the *evraziitsy*; it does not set them within the broader framework of intellectual and geopolitical developments in Tsarist and Soviet Russia.

[2] The Hungarian concept of Turanianism emphasized the linguistic unity which the Turanian (*i.e.*, Ural-Altaic) peoples have preserved, despite the many centuries of dispersal from the original Turan fatherland (in Central Asia). Political Pan-Turanianism (the Hungarian *Turanismus*) was basically an anti-Slav movement. Its immediate purpose was to check and counter-balance Pan-Slav expansionism in the Balkans by forging an alliance with the Pan-Turkic movement and establishing ties with all the Finno-Ugric peoples of the north from the Baltic to the Urals. Thus the Slaves were to be 'taken from behind' and hemmed in. On the other hand, in Russia an opposite idea took root, namely, one of Slav-Turanian unity born out of Eurasian geo-historical unity. The eastern Slavs, the various Finnish tribes and other Turanian people (even the Scythians have usually been mentioned) have mixed and shared a territory and history for centuries. The Hungarians and the Turks do not fit in, it has been argued, on account of their separate geo-historical developments.

The Russian Image of Russia 365

imprint. It involves a set of techniques, both economic and social. It is associated with certain values, as well as with a certain mood, which find expression in art and folklore.[1]

The Kievan image of Russia can quite obviously be linked to the *genre de vie* characteristic of the Russian agricultural region *par excellence*: the black earth zone of Southern and Central Russia, densely settled and dotted with large estates, where the *barshchina* system of serfdom[2] facilitated a face-to-face, patriarchal lord-peasant relationship that was easily idealized. From the idealized reality it took the imagination only one step to the vision of a rustic Utopia, kingly or Rousseauan according to preference. There were enough external similarities between the black earth Russian villages and the rural landscape and life as depicted in French romantic art and literature to reinforce the assumption that the same 'laws of nature' applied here as there. It followed that the order of things, potential if not actual, of this area was a 'natural order' and consequently ought to be extended to all of Russia, everything to the contrary being 'corrupt', 'unnatural', and 'un-Russian'.

Much of the contrast between the Kievan and the Moscow image of Russia can be understood if we consider that the latter is associated with a quite different *genre de vie* from the former, namely one adapted to the ecology of the podzol zone where agriculture could not quite assure full livelihood and both nobility and peasantry early developed ways and skills to supplement their subsistence with non-agricultural earnings. Consequently, a characteristic of the Moscow podzol zone, and of the *genre de vie* that went with it, was the peculiar *obrok* system of serfdom with its absentee land-ownership and with cash rather than

[1] The concept of *genre de vie* has been the backbone of the French school of human geography. For the original exposition of the concept see P. Vidal de la Blache, 'Les genres de vie dans la géographie humaine', *Annales de géographie*, 20, 1911, pp. 193–212 and 289–304. More recently French geographers have been unsure to what extent the concept is applicable to modern, developed societies. See discussion in M. Derruau, *Précis de géographie humaine*, Paris, 1963, pp. 107–13 (bibliography, p. 551). The Marxist notion of an 'Asiatic mode of production' could be classified as a concept of *genre de vie*. So, to some extent, could W. Eberhard's 'layer theory of society' even though his approach is not ecological. See his *Conquerors and Rulers: Social Forces in Medieval China*, 2nd edition, Leiden, 1965, p. 6 ff.

[2] Under the *barshchina* system the serf was obliged to perform services, *i.e.*, work three or more days each week for the landlord. The latter was thus supplied with an abundant, if not super-abundant, labour force, and encouraged to transform the estate into an elaborately autarkic unit capable of satisfying most consumption demands both economic and cultural. There were manors that had not only craft shops, but also theatres, orchestras, choirs, *etc.*, all staffed by serfs.

366 *Essays in Political Geography*

land constituting the link between lord and serf.[1] Ethnographers have noted that the folklores of the podzol and black earth zones express quite different attitudes towards nature.[2]

It is more difficult to link either the St Petersburg or the Eurasian image of Russia to a specific *genre de vie*. The St Petersburg image had something close to a prototype of a *genre de vie* in the life of St Petersburg itself which was unique on the Russian scene. The contrast between the capital and the rest of the country was by no means simply an urban versus rural, industrial versus agricultural dichotomy. Moscow was larger both as a city and as an industrial centre, and yet it was precisely from Moscow that St Petersburg differed most sharply (and to some extent still does) in ways of life and thinking – from fashion, meal hours, even inflection in speech, to views on art, literature, and, last but not least, politics. The two capitals were symbols both of different ways of life and of different views as to what all of Russia should be like.

A characteristic trait of the Eurasian image of Russia is that it does not look back; it is future-oriented. As such, it strives to mould things to come, not reflect those bygone. It would be meaningless to link it to the nomadic ways the Eurasian peoples may have shared in the distant past. Better perhaps to turn to that part of Russian Eurasia where fate carried people who instead of mirroring the consecrated ways of the past rebelled against them. Specifically, we should turn to Siberia which produced a dynamic, forward-looking society as well as a *genre de vie* which was not only distinct from, but in many ways at odds with the tradi-

---

[1] The *obrok* system of serfdom, prevalent in the north, developed where poor soils and/or climate made intensive agriculture impractical. The landlord here was neither able usefully to occupy his serfs nor tempted to settle all the year round in the countryside. He demanded cash payments instead of services from the peasants, and by the same token encouraged and forced them to seek seasonal, even permanent employment outside the village or to develop a craft industry. Some peasants intensively engaged in trade, especially in forest products abundant in the podzol soils zone. The *obrok* system broke the bond between the serf and the land as well as the personal lord-peasant relationship, and this in turn introduced the practice of the landlord selling his peasants off the estate like cattle. The land, peasant and lord were still related conceptually, but primarily in terms of the overall hierarchical state structure in which everybody and everything had an assigned place and duty. Characteristically, even those among the Muscovite thinkers who (like the *pochvenniki*, above, note, 3 p. 361) spoke of the sacredness of Mother Earth had only an abstract, metaphysical concept of 'the soil' and man's link to it – which was in sharp contrast with, *e.g.*, Lev Tolstoi's much more down-to-earth (even if idealized) notion of a direct man–soil and lord–peasant relationship unmediated by the state.

[2] See above, note 3, p. 359. See also the opinions of Ivan Aksakov cited in Lirondelle, *op. cit.*, p. 86.

The Russian Image of Russia 367

tional pattern of Russian life. One should recall that up to, and even at the beginning of this century, the Urals were much more of a dividing line than their significance as a physical barrier would suggest. The territories East of the Urals were not integrated into the socio-political system characteristic of Tsarist Russia. While in European Russia (and Transcaucasia) the whole outlook of the country was moulded for enturies by a social, political and administrative system based on the division of society into nobility and serfs, in Asiatic Russia, by contrast, no landlords were permitted to establish themselves. Moreover, the peasant commune (*obshchina*), which in most of European Russia played such a crucial role in the lives of the peasants both before and after the emancipation, never took root beyond the Urals. This had a profound effect on the way the Russian society developed in Siberia. The social structure, mores and mentality here were noticeably more democratic, and this was reflected in the temper of the press and political parties, as well as in the men chosen for public offices during the years 1905–1918 when relatively free elections were here possible. Moreover, there developed in Siberia a remarkably well organized cooperative movement, and observers noted that everyone here, including the peasant, was much more open to change, especially technological change, than in European Russia.[1] Last but not least, there emerged in the 1860s a Siberian autonomist (federalist) movement (*sibirskoe oblastnichestvo*).[2] The autonomists emphasized Siberian patriotism and the geographical as well as socio-historical separateness of Siberia from the rest of Russia, and demanded a large measure of self-government, possibly independence. Some even thought in terms of 'United States of Siberia federated with the United States of America'.[3] The Siberians (at the turn of the

[1] *Cf.* D. W. Treadgold, *The Great Siberian Migration*, Princeton, 1957, p. 245, *passim*.

[2] Probably the most important among the founders of the movement was N. M. Iadrintsev, author of a history of Siberia as a colony which remains a classic in its field to this day, namely, *Sibir kak koloniia v geograficheskom, etnograficheskom i istoricheskom otnoshenii*, 2nd edition, St Petersburg, I. M. Sibiriakov, 1892. The only available history of the Siberian autonomist movement is S. G. Svatikov, *Rossiia i Sibir: K istorii sibirskogo oblastnichestva v XIX v.*, Prague, Obshchestvo sibiriakov v Ch.S.R., 1929. Needless to say, the Pan-Slav imperialists, like N. Ia. Danilevskii, both denied the contention that Siberia was a colony (and Russia a colonial power similar to Rome or Great Britain) and strenuously opposed any scheme for autonomy or federal status for the various territories of the Russian Empire. N. Ia. Danilevskii, *Rossiia i Evropa: Vzgliad na kulturnyia i politicheskiia otnosheniia Slavianskago mira k Germano-Romanskomu*, 4th edition, St Petersburg, 1889, p. 531.

[3] P. A. Kropotkin, *Zapiski revoliutsionera*, St Petersburg and Moscow, 'Golos truda', 1920, p. 130. On the various comparisons between Siberia and America

368 *Essays in Political Geography*

century 90 per cent of whom were Great Russians) particularly resented the fact that their land was made into a place of exile for the criminal element which the Russian society West of the Urals was producing in its midst. They complained that their country was treated as a simple colony of Russia – a 'Russian America' – and denied even such limited local self-government as the *zemstva* introduced in European Russia under Alexander II.

The Tsarist government, as behoves an imperial power, heatedly denied that Siberia was a colony and insisted that it was 'one' with Russia. But the colonial status of Siberia was merely emphasized when after the building of the Trans-Siberian railroad a discriminatory clause was inserted in the freight rate calculation system – the so-called 'Cheliabinsk breaking point' (*cheliabinskii perelom*) – to prevent Siberian wheat from competing with wheat grown in European Russia. This amounted to a tariff imposed on a 'foreign' Siberian product for the sake of protecting a 'domestic' Russian product.

Characteristic was the ambiguous attitude towards Siberia of P. A. Stolypin. On the one hand he was the statesman who strove for and finally brought about the gradual abolition, as of 1 (14) August 1911, of the discriminatory freight rate,[1] and who was rather proud that, as he put it, 'Siberia's growth is legendary'. But, on the other hand, he nevertheless felt obliged to warn the tsar that certain measures concerning Siberia were urgently necessary or else 'there will emerge, spontaneously and without regard for any conformity, a huge, coarsely democratic country which will, within a short time, throttle European Russia'.[2] Whether that which Stolypin feared might 'throttle European Russia' could be considered as a way of life roughly fitting the Eurasian image of Russia, need not be resolved here. What matters is that whatever it was that was emerging in Siberia, it did offer an alternative to the ways and images rooted in the traditional centres of European Russia.

---

circulating in nineteenth century Russia as well as the impact of America on political thinking in Siberia see Svatikov, *op. cit.*, especially Chapter 4, and M. M. Laserson, *The American Impact on Russia, Diplomatic and Ideological, 1784–1917*, New York, 1950, especially chapters 10 and 11.

[1] N. Nekrasov (Member of the Imperial Duma for Tomsk), 'The question of the export from Siberia', *Russian Review* (Liverpool), 1, 1912, on pp. 157–8; also L. Kafengauz, 'Novye zheleznodorozhnye tarify', *Russkiia Vedomosti*, 11 August 1911, p. 3.

[2] 'Iz perepiski P. A. Stolypina s Nikolaem Romanovym,' *Krasnyi Arkhiv*, 30, 1928, No. 5, pp. 82–3 (Stolypin's letter to Nicholas II, 10 September 1910).

THE ORIGINS OF THE EURASIAN IMAGE OF RUSSIA

The Eurasian image of Russia is the product of two factors, namely a redirected Russian nationalism that had been rebuffed by Europe, and a growing consciousness of Russia's presence and opportunity in Asia. Its intellectual roots must be sought in the first stirrings of nationalism, perhaps as far back as the eighteenth-century writings of the historian I. N. Boltin. Reacting against the West's contempt for everything Russian, the early nationalists turned their backs on the Europeans without, however, either shutting down the window on European civilization or as yet making overtures toward Asia. But the consciousness of Russia's physical presence in Asia grew rapidly in the course of the post 1850 eastward expansion in the Far East and Central Asia as well as Transcaucasia. Defeat in the Crimean War (1853–6), Europe's threatening utterances during the Polish uprising (1863), then disappointment with the awards of the Berlin Congress (1878), and, last but not least, the contagious example of the world-wide scramble for colonies, these were the factors which contributed to the redirection of Russia's interests and hopes toward Asia. The first official document signalling a reorientation of Russia's policies was a memorandum prepared in 1856 by the Foreign Minister, A. M. Gorchakov. While there is little of consequence that Russia can do in Europe, argued Gorchakov, there is a vast field of activities open to her in Asia; it is there that Russia's future lies. 'I fully agree' was the comment Alexander II wrote on top of the memorandum.[1]

Soon various writers, most notably R. A. Fadeev[2] and N. Ia. Danilevskii,[3] began to reason in a similar vein, but for a time they clung to the idea of the primacy of Russia's Slav mission in Eastern Europe. It

[1] Chicherin, *op. cit.*, p. 1. The idea of such a reorientation of Russia's foreign policy away from Europe and towards Asia, as proposed by Gorchakov in 1856 after Russia suffered defeat, already seems to have been 'in the air' at the very beginning of the Crimean War when the Russian army was still victorious and England and France had not yet joined the Turkish camp. The prominent Slavophile A. S. Khomiakov wrote in 1853 (in a letter to his friend A. N. Popov) that the history of Russia's relations with Khiva, and 'the fear with which Russia inspired all of the Trans-Caspian region, prove our great and centuries' old blindness. While all our attention was constantly turned toward European affairs, our real interests were calling for more energetic actions in the East, which we could very easily have acquired. . . . (Peter the Great's foreign policy) system drew us too far into the European internecine dissensions and suppressed our *natural instinct*. N. P. Barsukov, *Zhizn i trudy M. P. Pogodina*, St. Petersburg: M. M. Stasiulevich, 1888–1906, Vol. 13, p. 16. *Cf.* Pogodin's statement, below, note 1, p. 370.
[2] R. Fadeev, *Mnenie o vostochnom voprose* (St Petersburg, 1870).
[3] N. Ia. Danilevskii, *op. cit.*

370 *Essays in Political Geography*

was only with 'rotten' and 'ungrateful' Europe's stopping of Russia's advance in the Balkans, and the Balkan and Western Slavs themselves proving not too eager to be included in a Pan-Slav Russian Empire, that Dostoevsky exclaimed (in 1881):

> When we turn to Asia, with our new vision of her, in Russia there may occur something akin to what happened in Europe when America was discovered. Since, in truth, to us Asia is like the then undiscovered America. With our aspiration for Asia, our spirit and forces will be regenerated. . . . Our civilizing mission in Asia will bribe our spirit and drive us thither.[1]

Later, in the 1920s–1930s, there emerged within the large post-1917 Russian emigration a formal Eurasian Movement, Eurasianism (*Evraziistvo*),[2] which found expression in stimulating historical, especially geo-historical writings, but rather desultory political thinking. Its spiritual heritage was complex, but it can be traced back mainly to N. Ia. Danilevskii and K. N. Leont'ev, especially the latter.[3] The former, a forerunner of Oswald Spengler, opposed the concept of universal historical development and world civilization with a theory of separate, autonomous cultural-historical types. The Slavs belonged to a distinct civilization which could not and should not merge with the European (that is, Germano-Romance) civilization. In a sense, Danilevskii's point of departure was the familiar Slavophile thesis about the uniqueness of Russia (and the Slavs in general). But the old Slavophile thesis was now bolstered with arguments drawn from history and science. It became in fact, if not in principle, *secularized*. In the deeply religious Slavophile conception Slavdom was unique in the sense that only in its bosom was preserved truth and Christian all-humaneness (*vsechelove-*

---

[1] F. M. Dostoevsky, *The Diary of a Writer*, entry for January 1881, chapter 2, section 4. The historian M. P. Pogodin had expressed virtually the same ideas already in 1854. 'Leaving Europe in peace to itself, in expectation of more favourable circumstances, we ought to turn all our attention to Asia, which we have almost entirely left out of consideration even though it is precisely Asia that is predestined primarily for us; and it is also towards Asia that our enemies – following some instinct, but not with good intentions – want to throw us back! What would the English have accomplished with our local-territorial and other relations with Asia!' 'O Russkoi politike na budushchee vremia', in M. P. Pogodin, *Istoriko-politicheskie pis'ma i zapiski vprodolzhenii Krymskoi Voiny*, Moscow, 1874, p. 242. For a discussion of Pogodin's view of the Russia-Asia relation see N. V. Riasanovsky, 'Russia and Asia: Two Nineteenth-Century Russian Views', *California Slavic Studies*, 1, 1960, pp. 170–81.

[2] See above, note 1, p. 364.

[3] *Cf.* Zenkovskii, *Russian Thinkers and Europe, op. cit.*, pp. 105 and 107.

The Russian Image of Russia 371

chestvo). Insistence on separateness and autonomy was only a temporary protective measure. The treasury of pan-human values had to be preserved from corruption until the day when mankind would merge in a universal brotherhood on the basis of these values. In Danilevskii's 'scientific' world view, on the other hand, uniqueness, autonomy and originality (*samobytnost*) of the Slav civilization were simply certain observable characteristics. Other types of civilization were unique too, and each was to be valued as such and not tampered with. Extension of one civilization into the *Lebensraum* of another, and in general mixing of civilizations, was tantamount to destruction of 'natural', viable cultural entities and led to proliferation of hybrid pseudo-cultures lacking originality. 'An all-human civilization does not and can not exist for it would only be an impossible and wholly undesirable incompleteness. The all-human civilization . . . is an unattainable ideal'.[1]

It was on these grounds that Leont'ev, strongly under the influence of Danilevskii,[2] deplored the 'harmful' influence of the 'civilized but *not cultured*' St Petersburg, the 'window' through which a borrowed, imitative civilization filtered into all of Russia. 'Moscow Russia . . . is more cultured, *i.e.*, original. . . . The faster St Petersburg is transformed into a kind of Baltic Sevastopol or Odessa the better'.[3] Leont'ev's original contribution to Danilevskii's set of ideas was the 'Turanian' or 'Asiatic' argument. If it fell to the Russians to save and protect the other Slavs, it was because they were the most different and unique, that is least European, among all the Slavs.

> Something *spiritually* independent from Europe can be generated only by that Slav nation which from among all of them is the most Eastern, the most, so to say, Asiatic – Turanian. Without this Asiatic influence transmitted through Russia all the other Slavs could at best rapidly turn into the worst Europeans of Europe, and nothing else.[4]

[1] Danilevskii, *op. cit.*, p. 129. For a discussion of the originality of Danilevskii's ideas see K. Pfalzgraf, 'Die politisierung und radikalisierung des Problems Russland und Europe bei N. J. Danilevskij', *Forschungen zur osteuro päischen Geschichte*, Vol. I, Berlin, 1954, pp. 194–202; and R. E. MacMaster, 'The Question of Heinrich Rückert's Influence on Danilevskij', *American Slavic and East European Review*, 14, 1955, pp. 59–66. For a Soviet criticism of Danilevskii's theory of cultural types see E. S. Markarian, *O kontseptsii lokalnykh tsivilizatsii*, Erevan, Izd. A. N. Armianskoi S.S.R., 1962, especially pp. 24–7.

[2] K. Leont'ev, *Vostok, Rossiia i Slavianstvo: Sbornik statei*, 2 vols., Moscow, 1885–6, Vol. I, p. 295, note.

[3] *Ibid.*, pp. 297 and 299.

[4] *Ibid.*, p. 285.

372 Essays in Political Geography

A few years later the ethnographer-geographer V. I. Lamanskii further bolstered Danilevskii's theory by giving it something of a 'geographic foundation'. His point was that between 'Europe properly speaking' and 'Asia properly speaking' there was a 'Middle World', a distinct geographical and anthropo-geographical entity. He also noted that, in contrast to the European World and the Asian World, the 'Middle World' was able (or almost able) to become one political unit. In terms of culture, ethnography and settlement, however, the 'Middle World' was as yet not a homogeneous whole, whatever its potentialities for becoming one; it still remained something rather undefined, 'neither Europe nor Asia properly speaking'.[1] This fitted quite well into Leont'ev's thesis about the imperative task of developing 'our own, original Slav-Asiatic civilization'.[2]

Lamanskii's book was the source from which most of the geopolitical ideas on which Eurasianism relied so heavily were taken, except that greater emphasis was put on economics, especially *autarky*. The Eurasians did, however, add a new argument in support of the 'Middle World' thesis. In the late 1920s, R. O. Iakobson (Jakobson), a scholar now well known in America, came forth with the thesis of linguistic unity within Russia's Eurasian World.[3] Thus, indirectly at least, the

[1] V. I. Lamanskii, *Tri mira aziisko-evropeiskago materika*, St Petersburg, 1892, p. 3, *passim*. It should be noted that, in contrast to Danilevskii, Leont'ev and Dostoevsky, especially the last two, Lamanskii was rather a Westerner, certainly not a doctrinaire anti-European Slavophile. But the idea that culturally Russia was not, and ought not to become, one with Europe was, though on different grounds, not foreign, even to some otherwise staunchly pro-Western and anti-'Asiatic' Russian thinkers. Thus the philosopher V. S. Solov'ev argued that 'Russia became an authentic Empire, and its two-headed eagle a true symbol', only after 'the half-Asiatic Muscovite realm . . . flung wide open a window on West European education refusing at the same time to renounce its own, the fundamental Eastern particularities and traditions'. By avoiding being merely a national state, or one-sidedly either Muscovite or Western, Russia 'reaffirmed its adherence to the Christian truth and recognized, at least in principle, its brotherhood with all nations'. Unmistakably, Solov'ev thinks of an empire in terms of Dante's *Monarchia Christiania* and consequently he considers the post-Petrine supra-national '*state* policy of *Rossiia*' superior to a simply national Russian (*russkaia*) policy. The 'originality' of *Rossiia*, i.e., the originality of its state-idea, is precisely to be 'universal'. See V. S. Solov'ev, *Sobranie sochinenii*, 9 vols., St Petersburg, 'Obshchestvennaia pol'za', 1903, Vol. 8, pp. 698, 697, 699 (from the essay 'Mir Vostoka i Zapada', 1896). *Cf.* above, note 1, p. 349, on the concept of *Rossiia*.

[2] Leont'ev, *op. cit.*, p. 295.

[3] R. O. Iakobson [Jakobson], *K kharakteristike evraziiskogo iazykovogo soiuza*, Paris, Izd. Evraziitsev, 1931; reprinted in R. Jakobson, *Selected Writings*, Vol. I, *Phonological Studies*, The Hague, 1962, pp. 144–201.

The Russian Image of Russia 373

Danilevskii-Leont'ev ideas were now provided with a 'linguistic foundation', too.

The secularization of the Slavophile thesis set in motion by Danilevskii meant not only that the previous relatively mild 'warnings' against 'corruption' coming from the West were now replaced by the concept of 'struggle with the West' for complete independence from Europe. It meant, also, a general politicization and radicalization of the Russia-Europe dichotomy of which the militant Pan-Slavism fathered by Danilevskii was merely the beginning.[1] Ultimately it led from the idea of a symbiotic Slav-Asiatic 'Middle World' independent *from* Europe to the idea of a 'Middle World' allied with 'Asia properly speaking' *against* Europe.

PSYCHOLOGY OF NATIONAL SELF-IDENTIFICATION

The immediate cause for the emergence of the Eurasian Movement was the shock of the Bolshevik Revolution and the realization that Europe was neither able nor willing to offer any solution, be it material or moral, to the Communist challenge, and that the Europeans were so preoccupied with their own affairs and well-being that they were not even interested in either Russia or the Russian emigration seeking a haven in the West. The Russian philosopher, V. V. Zenkovskii, said that

the betrayal of Russia by its former allies, . . . this leaving of Russia politically alone during the years of its fight for itself, has left an

[1] Danilevskii's role in this politicization and radicalization is emphasized by Pfalzgraf, *op. cit.* In Danilevskii's view the counterposition Europe versus Asia, and, even more, the idea of a Europe–Asia struggle, were meaningless, and historically inaccurate, for there was no such thing as a Europe, or an Asia, capable of acting as an entity. There were only certain, rather arbitrary, concepts of Europe and Asia, based on either geographical, or ethnographical, or cultural-historical criteria, each of them changeable and contradicting the other two. Hence Danilevskii's criticism of the historian S. M. Solov'ev's thesis that the 'Eastern Question' was merely 'a phase' in the Europe versus Asia, the good versus the bad conflict – of a conflict between the world under the 'wholesome and lifegiving influence of the ocean' and the world under the 'deadening influence of the steppe'. (Solov'ev considered that all of Russian history was dominated by a forest versus steppe, ploughman versus nomad conflict.) But one wonders whether Danilevskii did not sap the roots of his own argument about the non-existence of a Europe when concluding (even if only in a limited sense) that Russia 'does not belong' to Europe and that 'sooner or later, whether we want it or not, a struggle with Europe (or at least a large part of it) is unavoidable because of the Eastern Question', or when devoting a whole chapter to 'Mimicking the Europeans [*evropeinichanie*] – a sickness of Russian life'. Danilevskii, *op. cit.*, pp. 326–30, 360–2, 474 and chapter 11.

374 *Essays in Political Geography*

indelible trace in the Russian soul. . . . As a reaction against this feeling, there appears a realization in many Russians of Russian strength, of the need to express Russian originality, and finally, an impulse to turn away from those who forsook us in the bitter hour.[1]

The 'betrayal of Russia' was the more bitter in that it was experienced directly, personally, by those most opposed to the new, 'barbarous' and 'Asiatic', power which was bent on destroying precisely what Russia and Europe seemed to share. Having lost Mother Russia they hoped to find a Mother Europe. When Europe proved an alien world, there followed a fundamental re-examination of the self – of what was Russian in a Russian. Old relationships were seen through a new perspective; traditional allegiances were thrown overboard. Some Eurasians went so far as to issue manifestos calling upon 'all the peoples of the world' to free themselves from the influences of European culture.[2] Unlike the Europeans – it was said – the Russians have compassion and affinity for the colonial peoples. The Eurasian Movement was above all an expression of an urge to seek a new identity and new friends. To quote Zenkovskii once more, 'not ideology, but psychology, is essential and influential in Eurasianism'.[3]

Psychology does, indeed, play no less a part than ideology, values or interests in the process of self-identification of a nation – in its creation of an image of itself. The German anthropogeographer, F. Ratzel, said that, essentially, a state is 'a piece of land and a piece of humanity'[4] united by a strong bond. An individual identifies himself with a fatherland by identifying himself with the given piece of land and humanity. But on a world-wide scale nations, also, seek identity with some larger community, that is, in contemporary parlance, with some cultural-political area or block. Like individuals, nations feel a need 'to belong',

---

[1] Zenkovskii, *Russian Thinkers and Europe, op. cit.*, pp. 105–6.

[2] *Evraziiska Khronika*, Prague, Vol. IV, 1927 ?, p. 79, as quoted in Zenkovskii, p. 108.

[3] *Ibid.*, p. 106.

[4] F. Ratzel, *Politische Geographie*, 3rd edition, corrected and supplemented by E. Oberhummer, Munich and Berlin, 1923, pp. 2–3. It may be argued that the Jews have been an exception to Ratzel's generalization. But we should not forget that it was the vision of the 'Promised *Land*' which was the centripetal force holding the dispersed 'Twelve Tribes' together. The controversy within the Jewish Community concerning 'the duty' to settle in the '*Land* of Israel', as well as the related broader question of who is (or can hope to remain) 'legitimately' and/or culturally ethnically a Jew, revolve precisely around the issue of the relationship between 'a piece of humanity' and 'a piece of land'.

The Russian Image of Russia 375

and when lonely feel frustrated and insecure.[1] Rejection and alienation, search for identification and need for belonging, are important psychological factors in the lives of human collectives and affect the attitudes and behaviour of nations. From the psychological point of view, Europe's rejection of Russia – its real or supposed contempt for Russia's civilization and aspirations – necessarily led to an alienation of Russia from the West. Isolation from the West was cultivated as a virtue until in a moment of crisis it evolved into partial identification with the opposite of the West: if Europe does not love us, the Asiatics will; if the Europeans look down upon us, the Asiatics will not. 'In Europe we were hangers-on and slaves, whereas we shall go to Asia as masters' – says Dostoevsky.[2]

The turning towards Asia was, however, at least in the nineteenth century, always a *malgré soi* decision, not a first preference. Those who stressed Russia's separateness and spiritual autonomy still assigned to it a mission in Europe: Russia's isolationism was a precondition for its ability to become a future teacher of the West. It was only when prevented from fulfilling their mission in Europe that the Russians turned to Asia. Frustrated in the West they sought a purpose and self-fulfilment in the East. Neither Danilevskii nor Fadeev were too happy about the prospect of a retreat from Europe. And Dostoevsky expressly said that it should be temporary: 'not forever', only 'for the time being and not altogether . . . We should not abandon Europe completely . . . Europe, even as Russia, is our mother, our second mother. We have taken much from her; we shall again take'.[3] In fact, for Dostoevsky the Asiatic orientation was merely a means to an end, specifically, a means for the renewal of even more intense ties with Europe at some future time: the bold 'new principle' of 'our civilizing mission in Asia' will, on the one

---

[1] 'Nations, like individuals, have three prominent wants: firstly, freedom; secondly, prosperity; thirdly, friends.' So wrote U.S. Secretary of State W. H. Seward on 6 May 1861. He was, incidentally, making the point in the instructions to C. Clay, U.S. Minister in St Petersburg, and went on to say that the U.S. 'early secured the two first objects', *i.e.*, freedom and prosperity, but 'have been slow in winning friends. Russia [however] presents an exceptional case. That power was an early and it has always been a constant friend [of the U.S.]'. Seward urged Clay to cultivate this friendship which he very likely understood in terms of common foreign policy interests rather than of a psychological Russo-American kinship. But anti-Europeanism (based both on fear of Europe and the idea that the Old World was corrupt) was an emotion which Americans and Russians shared in the nineteenth century. *The Works of William H. Seward*, ed. G. E. Baker, new edition, 5 vols., Boston, 1887–90, Vol. 5, p. 246.

[2] Dostoevsky, *loc. cit.*

[3] *Ibid.*

376 Essays in Political Geography

hand, cure the 'piqued, aching *amour propre*' of the 'incapable' Russian and 'resurrect' him 'almost as a genius', and, on the other, puzzle Europe at first but then 'she [Europe] will forthwith begin to respect us'.[1]

Unmistakably, for Dostoevsky the history of the Europe–Russia relationship of the second half of the nineteenth century is a story of an emotional crisis. A bruised ego and rejected affection lead to withdrawal, then to a search for a substitute love; the new love and purpose in life help the Russians to regain self-confidence and independence. This, in turn, makes Europe – the true and never forgotten love – look up to Russia with respect. A happy ending is foreseen.

There is an indicative difference between Dostoevsky's way of speaking about the problem and that of a later generation. He had 'a vision' that Russia *might* 'discover' Asia; the twentieth century Eurasians pointed out that Russia *was* largely in Asia. He spoke of a matter of choice; they of a matter of fact. He yearned for Russians to be recognized as Europeans; they argued that Russians were not Europeans. Dostoevsky wanted to 'turn to Asia' because 'in Europe we were Asiatics, whereas in Asia we, too, are Europeans'.[2] Stalin greeted a statesman from Asia with 'I, too, am an Asiatic', and his successors like to remind us that one-third of Asia's land mass is within the boundaries of the USSR and that 'the Soviet Union has the right' to participate in the Conference of the Afro-Asian Countries (Second Bandung).[3]

THE SPECTRE OF 'AZIATCHINA'

The agonizing soul searching on the question of Europe versus Asia was not a monopoly of Russians under the influence of Slavophile thought. The Westernizers, and among them most prominently the Marxists, also debated and examined their consciences on this issue, but to them the image of Russia as Eurasia brought to mind not so much the Russia present in Asia, or the Russia with a mission in Asia, as the Russia under

---

[1] Dostoevsky, *loc. cit.*

[2] *Ibid.*

[3] Stalin was reported to have said this on 13 April 1941, to Y. Matsuoka, the Japanese Foreign Minister, on the occasion of the signing of the Soviet–Japanese Pact of Neutrality. B. Nikolaevskii, 'Kak Iaponiia prishla k voine', *Novyi Zhurnal*, New York, 11, 1945, p. 328. *Cf.* B. Shub and B. Quint, *Since Stalin: A Photo History of Our Time*, New York and Manila, 1951, p. 93. On the Afro-Asian Conference see E. Primakov, 'Krepit edinstvo stil boriushchikhsia protiv kolonializma: K sozyvu Vtoroi konferentsii stran Azii i Afriki', *Pravda*, 12 June 1965, p. 3.

The Russian Image of Russia 377

the influence of Asia. The problem of the 'Asiatic' heritage – of the *aziatchina* – has, indeed, long been an issue among Russian intellectuals. Some writers, like the historian V. O. Kliuchevskii, have tried to discount Mongol influence in Russia's history. Others, like G. V. Plekhanov, the founder of Russian Marxism, have worried about the possibility of the revival of the 'Asiatic' socio-political system in Russia. In fact, some of the Westernizers probably had their convictions hardened less by a love of, or admiration for, Europe than by a fear of *aziatchina*. They dreaded the thought that what was often considered to be, for better or for worse, typically Russian, might in fact be 'Asiatic'.

To the Russian Marxists the issue had far-reaching implications, both ideological and practical. It was a touchstone dividing those basically committed to the European historical model from those ready to experiment with other, even Asiatic modes. Lenin for one would not be prevented by any spectre of *aziatchina* from becoming alienated from the ways of Western socialists. He and his followers were dismayed to see the fire of national hatreds stirred by the War burn to cinders the whole edifice of European proletarian solidarity. Russia, she alone, raised the standard of revolution and made a last call to the conscience of proletarian Europe. When this failed – when, as Blok expressed it poetically, the 'Old World' refused to 'listen to the barbarian's clarion call to a radiant feast'[1] – the Bolsheviks decided to act as if Russia was Europe: if the Europeans do not make a socialist revolution, we shall make it! The roles are reversed, the leadership has changed hands! What is needed from now on is not a Westernization of Russia but an Easternization of Europe! 'In Western Europe they roared with laughter when we first told them that all civilized countries would follow the path we pointed to first. . . . Now there can be no more doubts about it'.[2]

True, there was an articulate minority among those who helped to bring the Revolution about, who were deeply perturbed by Lenin's 'go it alone' policy. Plekhanov was on record with warnings that that which Lenin would achieve would not be socialism but the restoration of 'our *kitaishchina* [Chinese heritage]', of 'our old half-Asiatic social

---

[1] A. Blok, *Skify*, 30 January 1918. Though far more radical in his 'Asiatic orientation' than Dostoevsky, Blok nevertheless still reflects in *Skify* ('The Scythians') the basic Russian attachment to 'Mother Europe' that Dostoevsky emphasized time and again. Russia, says Blok, 'is a Sphinx' and gazes at Europe 'with hatred, and with love!' On 'Scythianism', see below, note 4, p. 378.

[2] N. I. Bukharin, Bolshevik leader, in a speech on 16 January 1919. *Vtoroi Vserossiiskii S'ezd Professional'nykh Soiuzov, 16–25 ianvaria 1919 goda. Stenograficheskii otchet*, Part I, Moscow, Gosudarstvennoe izd., 1921, p. 5.

378 Essays in Political Geography

order'.[1] And Gorky pleaded with Europe in 1920 not to attempt to 'strangle us [Russians]'.

> I do not believe she [Europe] will be successful in this [strangling of us]. But it is possible that her policy toward Russia might push the Russians on the side of Asia. Don't you foresee in that possible alliance with the peoples of Asia a terrible threat to European culture? For me personally this question becomes a nightmare.[2]

However, the very success of the Revolution in Russia prompted some Bolsheviks to wonder whether the 'Asiatic' element might not in fact be that indispensable spark of youthful revolutionary vigour which the civilized and advanced West so sadly lacked.

> Deeply mistaken were all those who saw in our Bolshevik, communist movement a sign of Russia's backwardness and branded us Asiatic barbarians. The *aziatchina* [of our movement] was the real, living spirit of the revolution; it was Marxism which does not fall on its knees before the state power of capitalism.[3]

Indeed, as Blok's famous poem *The Scythians* shows, the whole Revolution was perceived by many as a breath of youthful barbarism coming from the depths of Asia; as 'Pan-Mongolism' on the loose.[4] The Bolsheviks were not children but stepchildren of Europe. They had, to

---

[1] G. V. Plekhanov, in a speech warning against Lenin's policies, at the 9th session of the Stockholm Party Congress, 1906. *Chetvertyi (Ob'edinitel'nyi) S'ezd R.S.D.R.P: Protokoly*, Moscow, Gos. izd. politicheskoi literatury, 1959, pp. 140–1. The same warning can be found in several of Plekhanov's writings. See discussion of Plekhanov's views on the question of 'oriental despotism' in E. M. Gazganov, 'Istoricheskie vzgliady G. V. Plekhanova', *Istorik Marksist*, 7, 1928, pp. 69–116, N. Valentinov (Volskii), 'Tragediia G. V. Plekhanova', *Novyi Zhurnal*, New York, 20, 1948, pp. 270–93, and S. H. Baron, *Plekhanov: The Father of Russian Marxism*, Stanford, 1963, pp. 299–305, *passim*.

[2] M. Gorky's letter to H. G. Wells, 22 May 1920, *Kommunisticheskii Internatsional*, No. 12/1920, col. 2207–8.

[3] Bukharin, *loc. cit.*

[4] Blok used as an epigraph for his *Skify* (above, note 1, p. 377) two lines from a poem composed by the Russian philosopher V. S. Solov'ev in 1894: 'Pan-Mongolism! Though the name is savage,/Its sound caresses my ear'. (The poem does not seem to have ever been published in full, but see V. S. Solov'ev, *op. cit.*, Vol. 8, pp. 584, 556.) Solov'ev made it clear however that he viewed 'Pan-Mongolism' as nothing less than a 'historical catastrophe'. It was only the younger generation of poets (which matured after the turn of the century) that began to play with 'Scythianism' (*skifstvo*) until it developed the idea of regeneration coming by way of Asia, *i.e.*, the idea of a positive, regenerative 'Pan-Mongolism' a conception which has roots in the old popular belief that the Mongols are God's scourge which punishes the sinful and by the same token cleanses them. This gradual radicalization of 'Scythianism' is particularly

The Russian Image of Russia 379

use Dostoevsky's expression, two mothers: Europe and Russia, and they were not willing to wait till Russia became one with Europe. They were ready to take Russia as it was, half European and half Asiatic; they were ready to forget Europe and consummate the morganatic marriage between Marxism and oriental despotism. 'One cannot build a planned economy the way the Egyptian Pharoahs once erected pyramids', remonstrated a Menshevik to Trotsky in 1920.[1] But that was precisely how Trotsky and then Stalin were determined to solve Russia's problems.

RUSSIA LEAVES EUROPE

The failure of the German revolution and the Allied intervention in Russia were the last drops needed to overfill the cup of bitter relations. By the end of the Soviet–Polish war it was clear that Russia would not follow Europe's cautious rationality nor Europe Russia's adventurous spontaneity. The Western Powers drew the *cordon sanitaire,* and the Bolsheviks convened in Baku the First Congress of the Peoples of the East. At the very moment Europe was shutting the gates tightly on Russia the latter was opening a back-door on Asia.

A quarter of a century later the victory over Germany brought the

---

noticeable when comparing three poems of V. Ia. Briusov—his *Skify* (1900) in which a conjectural meeting with the Scythians, distant ancestors, takes place; his *Griadushchie Gunny* (1904–1905) in which the Huns, coming to destroy, are nevertheless met by the victim like deliverers with 'a welcome hymn'; and his *My – Skify* (1916) in which the merging of 'we' and 'Scythians' is consummated. In the eyes of the Bolsheviks 'Scythianism' was a welcome phenomenon in that it was bringing a youthful stir of an Asia-inspired optimism capable of counteracting both the fear of *aziatchina* and the breath of pessimism blowing from the 'right' (*e.g.,* Leont'ev's reactionary philosophy) as well as the 'left' (*e.g.,* Plekhanov's Marxist analysis of the outlook for the Russian revolution). Of course, the relationship between 'Scythianism' and the Bolsheviks and their Asiatic orientation was surreptitious insofar as Bolshevism *qua* Marxism could not legitimately interbreed with ideas that were much closer to Bakuninism and chiliastic peasantism than to scientific socialism. But Bolshevism of those days was entangled in various misalliances. For one, the Left Socialist Revolutionaries, whom Lenin took into his government in 1918, certainly were very much at home with 'Scythianism' and not at all with orthodox Marxism. For further material relevant to our discussion see chapter 16 in the very well documented E. Sarkisyanz, *Russland und der Messianismus des Orients: Sendungsbewusstsein und politischer Chiliasmus des Ostens,* Tübingen, 1955.

[1] R. A. Abramovich, on 9 April 1920, rebutting Trotsky's arguments for the militarization of the workers and labour unions, *Tretii Vserossiiskii S'ezd Profes-sional'nykh Soiuzov, 6–13 aprelia 1920 goda: Stenograficheskii otchet,* Part I, Moscow, Gosudarstvennoe izd., 1921, p. 96.

380 *Essays in Political Geography*

Soviet might to the Stettin–Trieste line – the line Marx called 'the natural frontier of Russia'.[1] This rekindled in Moscow some European hopes, but no basic Westward reorientation took place, either in policy or in sentiment. The Russians were by now strangers to and in Europe. If the Soviet Union was intervening in the affairs of Europe it was as an outsider, not as a member. It intervened rather out of fear that Europe might hinder it than out of hope that Europe might help or join it. Western Europe, trimmed from world to sub-continental size, became in the eyes of Moscow an atrophied body, merely an appendix of Eurasia. While at one time Russia claimed Western Europe as its head, it saw it now merely as a tail – a tail which, annoyingly enough, grew another head and body further West, on the other shore of the Atlantic. Moreover, the Soviets could not fail to notice that their successes in Europe were primarily military, while in Afro-Asia they were socio-cultural; that in the former they have expanded their zone of influence by *coup d'état*, while in the latter they have done so with the help of popular revolutions. In Europe even the communists have continued to be contemptuous of Soviet civilization; in Afro-Asia many non-communists have been impressed by it. Thus Asia and Africa became the focus of hopes and attention.

And yet, however populous China may be, or however large the emerging Africa, deep in the heart of the Russian Communist there persists the memory of that first mother, the old Europe which has rejected and been rejected but cannot be forgotten. To regain full self-confidence the Russian wants to know that he is looked up to not only by Asia, but that Europe, too, 'begins to respect us'. Africa and Asia can provide the necessary power means for world domination. But they cannot give that final touch to the sense of achievement which a red flag flying over the Eiffel Tower would provide.

BELIEFS AND DEEDS

> You cannot size up Russia with your mind,
> Nor can you measure her with a simple rod:
> Hers is a special stature –
> In Russia you can only believe.

[1] In *New York Tribune*, 12 April 1853, reprinted in K. Marx and F. Engels, *The Russian Menace to Europe*, ed. P. W. Blackstock and B. F. Hoselitz, Glencoe, Ill., 1952, p. 132. Marx was speaking of the 'natural frontier' in the physical geographical sense; the geographical boundary which a powerful Russia was sure to seek.

The Russian Image of Russia 381

So wrote F. I. Tiutchev a century ago.[1] But beliefs about the fatherland do not stand by themselves. There is a close inter-relationship between the objective and subjective elements – the facts as established with the aid of 'a simple rod' and the inspired perception of their 'stature'. Beliefs generate deeds and deeds forge facts. Conversely, facts require deeds which must find a niche in the system of beliefs. The system of beliefs places the nation within a certain value scale, and passes judgment on its deeds. Beliefs *and* deeds, on the other hand, place the fatherland in space and within a specific geographical milieu, physical and human. But the interaction of beliefs, deeds, and facts continuously transforms the geographical environment, both natural and cultural, and by the same token generates a new chain reaction.[2] Thus, virtually all of the human ecumene is not so much in a state of *being* as one of ever *becoming*.

The correlationship or discrepancy between the realities actually emerging within a group's native ecumene (fatherland) and its iconographic expectations is a measure of national success or failure. This is especially true of the tightly-knit and disciplined 'organic' societies where ideology and state-idea provide a framework coordinating all activities. It is even truer of the Communist societies because of the crucial role which the concept of conquest of nature plays in the Marxist world view. The Marxists do not expect to win mankind's freedom in the street battles of the class struggle. The social revolution is merely a pre-revolution. It is a preparatory skirmish for the sake of achieving domestic peace, of creating a united front – a 'popular front' – indispensable for the successful waging of the *real* war: the great assault of man upon nature. Seen from this perspective the revolution is indeed permanent, for the revolt against the irrational forces generated by class society virtually merges with the immediately following intensified revolt against the irrational forces of nature. The realm of freedom can never precede, only follow, man's conquest of his environment, that is, the reshaping of the natural chaos into a cosmos of the artifact.[3]

[1] F. I. Tiutchev, *Umom Rossiiu ne poniat* . . . (1866).

[2] This is why the concept of a 'chain' linking the political idea to the political area developed by S. B. Jones in 'A Unified Theory of Political Geography', *Annals of the Association of American Geographers*, 44, 2, 1954, pp. 111–23, is particularly useful to students of both political geography and geopolitics. See also the 'operational scheme for the study of geopolitics' in Kristof, 'The Origins and Evolution of Geopolitics', *op. cit.*, pp. 35–6.

[3] The Marxist concept of conquest of nature, and, more broadly, of man-nature relationship, is largely taken over from Francis Bacon, and for this reason is not unlike that expounded by the American philosopher William

382 *Essays in Political Geography*

Socialism-in-one-country meant, above all else, the decision to proceed with an assault upon nature within the territory of the Soviet Eurasian subcontinent without waiting until the rest of mankind joins hands. It meant a national as opposed to an international war – a patriotic and romanticized war for the conquest, for the effective occupation of the national territory. The Soviet press reports daily from the 'battlefields' in vivid language. An 'assault' upon Angara is being mounted, an 'engagement' on the Enisei won, Volga 'capitulated', 'our heroes' are 'advancing rapidly'. The elements of nature are personified, the events dramatized.[1]

The Eurasian image of Russia – the image of Russia that builds a Eurasian world of its own – is today the most dynamic for it is in harmony with cherished beliefs as well as emerging facts. The Soviet

---

James. Both Bacon's New Atlantis and Marx's Communist society are, essentially, conceived as scientific (and non-political) constructions made possible through the uncovering of the secrets of nature, *i.e.*, through the establishment of man's effective control over nature. Bacon and Marx do, however, differ fundamentally on the question as to which road leads towards the goal of a rationally ordered society scientifically ruling over nature. Bacon declares the apolitical road to be the shortest; Marx believes the path of political struggle – of conquest of political power – to be the unavoidable first step. The Marxian concept of a two-stage conquest – first conquest of political power (*i.e.*, rationalization of the relations among men), then conquest of nature (*i.e.*, rationalization of the flow of natural processes) – underlies the thinking of Soviet communists. A long article in *Pravda*, 10 October 1962, describing the Soviet Union's road towards success in outer space bears the title 'From the Assault upon the Winter Palace [during the October Revolution] to the Assault upon the Cosmos.' Marx is described by Soviet writers (*e.g.*, in the romanticized biography by G. I. Serebriakova, *Pokhishchenie ognia!*, Moscow, Sovetskii pisatel, 1962), as the Prometheus who 'stole from history the secret of its laws'. He grasped the 'secret' both of the relationship between the two conquests and of the scientific laws of social development leading to the successful completion of the first of these conquests. It is up to the natural scientists to forge ahead towards the second, the final conquest.

[1] A good illustration of such reporting is provided by a series of articles printed in *Pravda* in February and March of 1963 on the erection of the Krasnoiarsk hydroelectric power dam on the Enisei. A special 'field editorial office' was established in Divnogorsk, the very site of the construction, and the paper carried large front-page headlines such as 'Before the Assault on the Enisei', 'Divnogorsk Reports: Ready for the Assault', 'The Assault Has Begun!' 'The Assault upon Enisei Continues', 'Enisei Dammed! He Shall Work for Communism', 'Enisei Subordinated to the Will of the Soviet People', and so on. Towards the end of March 1963, 'in the thick of the battle', virtually every issue of *Pravda* carried on the front and inside pages articles, photographs, as well as reports about telegraphic and telephonic exchanges between Divnogorsk and the then Prime Minister N. S. Khrushchev concerning the progress of the 'battle on the Enisei'.

The Russian Image of Russia 383

creed generates the deeds that grind down the mental and physical distinctions between what is Russia's Europe and what her Asia. Gone are the days when a Russian statesman, hearing about plans for a Trans-Siberian railroad, could exclaim: 'The Neva Avenue [in St Petersburg] alone is worth at least five times as much as all of Siberia'.[1] Gone, too, are the days when the map of Russia's Asia was pocked by 'white spots' of the unknown. Soviet geographers time and again quote Tiutchev only to emphasize with pride that they *did* 'size up' Russia, that they *did* 'measure her'.

One may argue that Imperial Russia was a part of Europe, or hope that the Soviet Union will become a member of a European commonwealth of nations. But to advocate, as General de Gaulle does, a 'Europe stretching to the Urals' is to disregard geopolitical realities. There exists today a continental Eurasia which is an integrated world unto itself. We can imagine this world one day merging with countries to the West into a 'Europe' stretching from the Atlantic to the Pacific; or, conversely, we may even imagine – some of us did a few years ago – a Greater Eurasia rolling from monsoon Asia and across continental Eurasia down to the Stettin–Trieste line, perhaps to the very shores of the Atlantic. But it is extremely difficult today to imagine some line, cultural, political, or even merely economic drawn along the Urals.

THE 'NEW AMERICA' AND THE OLD RUSSIA

In 1913 Blok had a vision of a 'New America' rising beyond the 'water-full river' (Volga). 'Where the steppe's grass bent to earth / . . . / It's dark with factory chimneys / The works' hooters now moan there.'[2] It is

[1] Quoted in A. I. Stepanchenko, *Gordost nasha Sibir*, Irkutsk, Vostochno-Sibirskoe knizhnoe izd., 1964, p. 5.

[2] A. Blok, *Novaia Amerika* (1913). Blok believed that 'the future of Russia lies in its still untouched strength of the popular masses and underground resources'. He hoped for a 'great renewal' through the development of a national industry, especially the mining industry. See annotations to *Novaia Amerika* in A. Blok, *Sobranie sochinenii*, 8 vols., Moscow and Leningrad, Gos. izd. khudozhestvennoi literatury, 1960–3, Vol. I, pp. 596–7. Blok was one of the new, future-oriented romantics who, like the American romantics (at least those of the nineteenth century), turned their backs on Europe and its romanticism which was oriented towards the past. If America was a New Europe, revolutionary Russia was to be a New America. The old, conservative generation of Russian romantics, by contrast, never looked with favour on America; they did not want to borrow anything from it, neither its technology nor its social system. A. K. Tolstoi warned the Russians against 'searching for an ideal in America' for, as he put it, 'America is backward: She is ruled by property and capital'. A. K. Tolstoi, *Son Popova* (1873), 9th stanza. See also, *e.g.*, A. A. Grigor'ev, *Iskustvo i pravda* (1850s), part 3.

384 *Essays in Political Geography*

to this vision, which is now being realized, that we should look for a clue to the real meaning of the Eurasian image of Russia. It does not mean simple switching from expansion in the West to expansion in the (Far) East – from the Muscovite ambition of ruling from Constantinople a Third Rome to the brief St Petersburgian dream of becoming the 'Admiral of the Pacific'.[1] Nor does it mean joining hands with Asia in an aggressive crusade against Europe. What the Eurasian image of Russia really means is turning towards the old dream of 'wakening up' the immense Mother Russia – 'one-sixth of the earth's land surface, larger than the moon', as we are often reminded – and welding her into one, 'organically' united world pulsating with a civilization, superior and, above all, 'our own'. Only a Russia that 'conquers' herself over again can overcome the old dichotomy 'Thou art beggarly, / Yet rich too, / Thou art mighty, / Yet feeble, too, / Mother Russia!'[2]

The Russian Eurasia that emerges today is, however, in one decisive respect far from being what Lamanskii hoped the 'Third World' would be. It is a 'New America' merely in the sense that its skies are becoming as 'dark with factory chimneys' as in Pittsburgh. There is no true Eurasian melting pot of cultures giving birth to a new synthesis, generating a culture as different from that evolved in Moscow as the American is from the English, the Mexican from the Spanish, or the Brazilian from the Portuguese. What takes place is a simple process of expansion and absorption proceeding from the old centre. Sooner or later, with Moscow's blessing, the takeover cannot but be complete, leaving hardly a trace of the cultures of the assimilated 'younger' nations and regions. This is precisely what Lamanskii, the father of the idea of a 'Third World', as well as other critics of Moscow, vigorously opposed. What they hoped for was a mutual enrichment of cultures with preservation of diversity, not a 'oneness' as advocated by M. N. Katkov, and other Moscow-based reactionary Slavophiles, to whom tolerance of national and regional diversity was sin, as A. K. Tolstoi mockingly

---

[1] On the occasion of an official visit to St. Petersburg, August 7–11, 1897, William II was made an Admiral of the Russian fleet. When sailing away on the Baltic he flashed a message to Nicholas II: 'The Admiral of the Atlantic greets the Admiral of the Pacific'. Apparently the message made some impression on the Tsar and thus contributed to the hardening of Russian Far Eastern ambitions and the outbreak of the Russo-Japanese conflict. V. I. Gurko, *Features and Figures from the Past: Government and Opinion in the Reign of Nicholas II*, Stanford, 1939, p. 258.

[2] N. A. Nekrasov, 'Rus' (last poem of Part IV/4 of the epic *Komu na Rusi zhit khorosho*, 1867).

The Russian Image of Russia   385

observed. 'We should press and press / In the Muscovite image all of them.'[1]

Indeed, Moscow 'presses' so hard that it completely stifles not only whatever new and original might have emerged from the free interplay and fusion of the diverse cultural heritages of Eurasia but also the breath of creative renewal which the experience of opening up and coming into contact with new lands and environments normally generates. There is today in the Soviet Union little of that impact the frontier experience had on American life and thought, as well as on the arts. In fact, the regional distinctiveness, originality, and vitality which characterized the Russian settlers in Siberia prior to 1917 is today far less noticeable. The protective cushion of distance between the creative non-conformism of the pioneering country and the bureaucratic orthodoxy of the old centre is rapidly disappearing. What the pioneer country beyond the Volga needs is a rival centre of its own symbolizing and reflecting its youthfulness. Moscow is too steeped in the past – its very appearance evokes and glorifies the old days – ever to become the capital of a land and people that owe everything to the modes and means of the latest age. Peter the Great understood quite well that there is a place-bound inertia which weighs like chains. He knew he would never quite succeed in changing the habits and mentality of his followers unless he uprooted them from a surrounding that breathed only the old.[2] Briefly, what the Eurasian image of Russia needs is a new, forward looking capital closer to the country's heart – a Eurasian Brasilia somewhere between Orenburg[3] and

---

[1] A. K. Tolstoi, *Pesnia o Katkove, o Cherkaskom, o Samarine, o Markeviche i o Arapakh*, 1869.

[2] Peter the Great's successors were of the same opinion. Suffice to read the *Memoirs* of Catherine the Great in which she repeatedly complains about having to come from St Petersburg to Moscow, if only for a few days. The old capital makes on her a depressing impression for everything there, even the buildings, seem to be permeated by the old Muscovite spirit.

[3] The population centre of the Soviet Union is today slightly north-east of Saratov (on the Volga); its area centre is West of Tomsk (on the Ob). Orenburg and Cheliabinsk are at the opposite ends of that pleasant stretch of country which formed the old Orenburg *guberniia*. It straddles the southern tip of the Urals and extends south-west into the agricultural region settled in the past century and the oil and natural gas fields developed only recently. This is an area which lies athwart the major east-west and north-south transportation and power transmission lines. If the scheme for linking the Ob and Volga river systems materializes, the canals are planned to furrow through here. Both Orenburg and Cheliabinsk are within what a geographer, D. J. M. Hooson, has recently suggested is an emerging 'New Soviet Heartland' (the rapidly growing industrial zone between Volga and Lake Baikal). See D. J. M. Hooson, *A New Soviet Heartland?* Princeton, 1964.

386 Essays in Political Geography

Cheliabinsk – built to dare the Russian Cariocas and as new in spirit and outlook as St Petersburg once was.[1]

Whether the Russians will ever build an inland St Petersburg we do not know and may rather doubt. It took the Brazilians one hundred and seventy-six years from the time the revolutionary idea of moving the capital was first put forward to the day Brasilia was inaugurated, and still today the pride, inertia and vested interests of Rio de Janeiro are far from being overcome.[2] There remains, however, the momentous fact that the geography of the country is now being rapidly transformed, the scattered men and lands of Eurasia for the first time pulled together into a national whole. There is, moreover, little doubt in this writer's mind that to the Russian people the conquest of the national territory is the only really meaningful conquest. Another Cuba, Vietnam, Congo and more can hardly make a Russian – non-Party or even Party member – feel as proud or confident about the future as one single new dam, canal or oilfield, built by Russian hands, on Russian soil and for the Russians. The challenge of the Russian natural environment – 'more difficult and

---

[1] The Cariocas (as the proud dwellers of Rio de Janeiro are called) fought tooth and nail against the idea of a new capital and are still not reconciled to the existence of Brasilia. So, undoubtedly, would the Muscovites, along with various vested interests, resist, as in the times of Peter the Great, a challenge to the primacy of Moscow. There is, incidentally, an interesting passage pertinent to this in L. Leonov's *Doroga na Okean* (first published in 1935; available in English as *Road to the Ocean*, New York, 1944), a futuristic novel generally well received by Soviet critics. Leonov describes (chapter 13) the emergence all across Europe and Asia of a 'new world' of 'Soviet republics'. 'The capitals of the young Soviet republics arose far from the former centres. . . . The principal of the four capitals of the new world, we put it near Shanghai . . . Historically and geographically this was the greatest crossroads of the world. We gave this city the name Ocean. . . . But Moscow still lived, pensioned by centuries, a respectable old woman full of museums, the Mecca of scientific socialism, the underground worker of the rebirth of the new world. We surrounded her with a belt of gardens and new city quarters, like old Canton and medieval London. We tenderly loved this city'. (For whatever reason, in the latest, 1961, Soviet edition of the novel the reference to 'the Mecca of scientific socialism' has been left out.)

[2] The transfer of Brazil's capital into the interior was a plank in the revolutionary programme put forward in 1789 by the *Inconfidentes Mineiros*, a rebel political group. After the fall of the monarchy, the Republican Constitution, drafted in 1890–1, included a provision for the moving of the capital inland. But it was only in 1955 that President J. Kubitschek made the final decision as to where exactly the new capital was to be located. L. Costa became the new city's architect and daring planner and, after feverish work and an enormous material effort, Kubitschek inaugurated Brasilia in 1960. The history of the various plans for Brazil's inland capital is reviewed in F. Arnau, *Brasilia: Phantasie und Wirklichkeit*, Munich, 1960.

less benevolent than that with which any other nation has had to contend' says V. O. Kliuchevskii[1] – is enough both to absorb and reward. It draws the Russians inward and is likely to discourage for a long time a reorientation outward.

[1] Kliuchevskii, *op. cit.*, Vol. I, p. 311; see also pp. 46, 71–2, and Vol. 7, p. 139. Practically the same was said by S. M. Solov'ev, *op. cit.*, Bk. 7 (Vol. 13), pp. 8–9; also *idem, Sobranie sochinenii*, St Petersburg, 'Obshchestvennaia pol'za', 1900, col. 762–3 ('Nachala russkoi zemli', Part 1), and 981 ('Publichnyia chteniia o Petre Velikom, 2nd lecture).